MANAGING IN THE POSTMODERN WORLD

❏ America's Revolution Against Exploitation ❏

David M. Boje
Loyola Marymount University

Robert F. Dennehy
Pace University

KENDALL/HUNT PUBLISHING COMPANY
2460 Kerper Boulevard P.O. Box 539 Dubuque, Iowa 52004-0539

❏ CONTENTS ❏

❑ FOREWORD ❑

MANAGING IN THE POSTMODERN WORLD
America's Revolution Against Exploitation

Once in a while any enthusiast experiences the thrill of unexpectedly discovering a rare and special example of the genre that they collect. Occasionally, this has happened to me when I've turned up a rare jazz or blues record on Compact Disc in a specialist shop that I either didn't know existed or had never been able to track down. However, I'm not only a music buff but also an academic: I guess that's why I've been asked to write this foreword. The same pleasure that the discovery of a rare Billie Holiday or John Coltrane disc might cause one paralleled the pleasure of the text found in the volume you are holding now. It is not that this book is one with which one wholeheartedly agrees or which goes where no book has ever gone before—although it comes close to doing that. The pleasure is to be found in a book which is so refreshingly lucid about matters which are so frequently opaque.

The opacity is two-fold: there is an opacity of convention as well as an opacity of criticism.

The opacity of convention is a set of silences, absences, refusals, a general unwillingness, nay, even inability, on the part of mainstream organization and management theorists to engage with the vibrant strand of contemporary social theory represented by the discussion of postmodernism and postmodernity. Irrelevant, awkward, difficult, obscure: these are some of the epithets that one hears hurled against the emergent post-functionalist, post-Marxist, post-Cold War grammar of theorizing being developed in journals such as *Theory, Culture and Society*. In this way another opacity is instituted: the lack of transparency in some of the key texts of postmodernism being sufficient to condemn them to irrelevance.

Yet, the organizations and management fields are not impervious, despite that theoretical engagement between different research and scholarly traditions has only rarely been a feature of an area of work which has been characterized by more than a fair degree of paradigmatic partisanship, postmodernism is trickling into journals like *Organization Studies* and the *Journal of Organizational Change Management* at an increasing rate.

The problems are not just external to the postmodernists but are compounded by differences within the postmodern camp: a key question is whether the postmodern is an era or a style of theorizing, an issue which is central to the argument which this book addresses. It does so with flair and conviviality, engaging the reader in a conversation quite unlike exchanges which one has found represented in other relevant literature. The marketing skills of populism are combined with the theoretical agenda of radicalism to produce a book which no one can deny *a priori* because of its difficulty, impenetrability, etc. It is, simply, a good story, a strong narrative, in which many voices may be engaged, a genuinely pluralist text for postmodern times, one written from within a modernist consciousness which is displayed in the commitment to the story-line. Ultra-postmodernists may not accept this attachment to narrative but it is what gives the book its strength.

The book suggests that these postmodern times may well pass by America, that it will be stymied by the legacies of a post-industrialism in which a form of power/knowledge was institutionalized in corporate embodiments swollen with the bureaucratized complacency that defense-related contracting induced in organizations remote from competitive struggle in a consumer market-place. It is now clear that the post-industrial society was a knowledge-based society shaped by the requirements of the Cold War and the warfare state. It was these which materialized the shift in organizational social relations from an industrial epoch founded on exploitation to one in which value became increasingly fused within the unity of power/knowledge condensed within the global, bureaucratic, corporate frame. America won the Cold War but is clearly in danger of losing the aftermath, not to the old adversaries, but to nations which were not even admitted to the Cold War game as equal players: most noticeably Japan, but also Germany, the powerhouse at the center of the European Community, as well as the Newly-Industrializing Countries of East Asia. Statutorily, of course, the first two were not allowed to play as part of the Cold War settlement at Yalta. Exclusion spawned different strategies premised on structures which were and had always been institutionally distinct.

For as long as the old modernist orthodoxies of management and organization theory held sway the specificity of the differences represented in these overseas cases were hard to see and the institutional frameworks in which they were embedded remained unaccounted. The literature was thoroughgoingly modernist in its assumptions and could only make that kind of sense of the differences which were becoming apparent, too late and too wrong, in the case of Japan, as a *cultural* 'threat' at the dawn of the 1980s. Yet, as this book makes clear, 'It is not the Germans, Japanese and Koreans that are causing America's decline. It is mismanagement of {America's} own human and economic resources.'

What is to be done? Boje and Dennehy are quite clear: first, there has to be a realization that the recipes of modernism were epoch or era specific and may be past their use-by date in some areas of organizational life. Second, that for as long as the lenses through which we focus on organizational life are made to modernist specifications, so that they focus on variables such as formalization, standardization, centralization, etc., as the strategic focus for research and teaching, we will be condemned to doing the 'time-warp' over and over again, stuck in the modernist frame while the spectacle outside turns ever more postmodern. Third, that postmodernism offers an integrative focus which will aid us as teachers, students, researchers and practitioners in overcoming the excessive differentiation which has fragmented our intellectual and praxeological communities. Fourth, that in doing so it will serve to re-vitalize the study of management and organizations by opening it up to the cutting-edge of contemporary social science currents.

It is quite an agenda. Yet it is one which this remarkably lucid, open and engaged contribution advances considerably. Let me conclude this foreword with a pregnant thought from one of the now-neglected grandmasters of modernism, one who hardly figured *in* the modernist consciousness of management and organizations. Even as, by a logic of exclusion codified early in the intellectual career of the field, echoes and traces of Marx's subordinate and ultimately defeated modernist thought delineated the themes that did figure as the victorious current of modernism, this minor European post-Hegelian philosopher and political economist had enough savvy and style to get at least one thing right, and in so doing underwrites the audacity and importance of the project that this book represents, both in its theme and its accessibility:

> People make their own history, but they do not make it just as they please; they do not make it under circumstances chosen by themselves, but under circumstances directly encountered, given and transmitted from the past. The tradition of all the dead generations weighs like a nightmare on the brain of the living. And just when they seem engaged in revolutionizing themselves and things, and creating something that has never yet existed, precisely in such periods of revolutionary crisis they anxiously conjure up the spirits of the past to their service and borrow from them names, battle cries, and costumes in order to present the new scene of world history in this time-honored disguise and this borrowed language. (Marx: *The Eighteenth Brumaire of Louis Bonaparte*)

If the hypotheses and argument that the authors advance are substantially correct, then we stand at one of those moments in history when the urge to resist and understand the limitations of the old slogans is critical. *America's Revolution Against Exploitation: The Story of Postmodern Management* achieves this resistance and this understanding sufficiently to reconfigure our grasp of the modern condition in which we have been while pointing us towards what we may become. One should salute the book as a contribution to one of *the* projects for the future, one which, because of its easy style, deserves to secure postmodernism a good name in management and organization theory circles.

Stewart R. Clegg
July, 1992

Stewart Clegg is the author of a number of books, including *Modern Organizations: Organization Studies in the Postmodern World.* London, Sage 1990, in which some of the ideas of postmodernism were first advanced in the Management and Organizations field.

❏ ACKNOWLEDGEMENTS ❏

Bob: I want to acknowledge my family—Judi, Ann, Kristine, and Neil for their love and encouragement; Father Joseph Sullivan—a priest who walked the village and told stories: his stories of Africa and St. Jerome Parish were inspirational; Jim Noel of GE who observed that introductory management texts bear little resemblance to management in the business world; Arthur Centonze, Frieda Reitman and Don Streever of Pace University, Lubin School of Business for their financial and academic support; the Management students at Pace University who gathered, wrote and presented their stories; Manis Thanawala—my research assistant *par excellence* who can do magical things with a computer; Maureen Furrer—our departmental Secretary who is always pleasant and always willing to help; the members of the Organizational Behavior Teaching Society and especially those who attended our storytelling workshop; our Editor—Joe Wells who was responsive and informative throughout this process; and Dover Press for their library of clip art—you have our credit.

Boj: Hey Margaret, my love, this book is dedicated to you and our kids—Renee, Jason, and Raymond. Thanks for putting up with your rebel! The students of Loyola Marymount University are part of this book. When you read the words *Blue Team,* that is team leader Mike Luken and his mates: Steve Hoffman, Jim Bott, James Leamey, Ed Hsu, Rasa Carneckas, Alnita Blackmon, Danielle Arnerich, and Ross Richardson. The **Blue Team** did the best ever postmod analysis. We put sections of their work in our book. When you read *Gold Team,* we got their permission to use some of their best ever art to illustrate concepts in each chapter. The **Gold Team** has Lisa Humphreys as team leader and her mates are: Shane Bowers, Jeff Keeney, Carolyn Russo, Marc Abenoja, Mark Jambretz, Joe White, and Lloyd Umali. Three student artists did our cover and lots of cartoon work: Rob Trent, Paul Sochiratna, and Rodney Injarusorn. Paula McCarty, our brightest of MBA students, proofed our first draft AND Rosemary Kennedy and Sheila Christof proofed the most recent version. I traveled with an MBA team who took the postmod turn as we traveled to Japan, Korea, Taiwan, Indonesia, and Malaysia. My travel buddies were Elaine Adams (fearless leader), Carrie Greer, Bradley Farnsworth, Luis

Ibarra-Rivera, Michael Koshimizu, Paula McCarty, Kimberly McCullough, Douglas Reed, and Denise Young. These and hundreds of other MBA and undergrad students contributed suggestions and critique that made me reconstruct this book. Though not a self-professed postmod, my mentor: Lou Pondy opened my eyes to stories and discourse. Bill Hetrick started me reading Michel Foucault and Stewart Clegg. Stewart Clegg wrote an awesome foreword and we are in his debt. Jasper Blystone, of our philosophy department let me test some of my ideas in his postmod philosophy class. I have done my best to corrupt Bob Dennehy with postmod ideas. He and Stewart even took a few rides on my Harley Davidson Electroglide. I'm not sure you can be a postmod unless you ride a Harley. Harley riders are American rebels. It's heavy metal thunder, smoke and lighning, and its the best product still manufactured in America. We're all just racing with the wind and me, I'm born to be postmod!

❑ A REBEL'S POSTMOD GLOSSARY ❑

Centering All choice moves through the apex of the pyramid. Centering causes silos (vertical chains for submission of approvals and signatures) that slow down implementation. Monetary systems, production systems, and decision systems can all be centered.

Construction An interpretation that privileges one view over another. Construction can be a term, metaphor, theme, trope or an entire story that casts people in a particular perspective. It can be a plot, dichotomy, dimension, or scenario. In the Vietnam War, "domino theory" was a construction. Common words like "cycle time" can be constructions that coax us to look at efficiency instead of alternative interpretations, such as "slack time" or "break time."

Control Control happens through elite and dominating cadres of executives in back rooms as they chomp on cigars. Besides elite control, there is control by being regulated and institutionalized in what Michel Foucault calls the capillary network of disciplinary and punishment mechanisms that operate from one end and layer of the bureaucratic firm to the other. Foucault makes the point that rather than being controlled by some invisible elite, we are complicit in our own control. We self-observe, self-discipline, and self-control.

Decenter Resources (material, informational, and symbolic) including choice and discretion get channeled through the center. De-centering removes the center position in a network and installs a multiplicity of centers that struggle and compromise to control organizations and the people trapped in them.

Deconstruction A method to analyze and recognize constructions. To deconstruct is to take apart, turn inside out, dismantle, reverse, and distort a construction. In deconstruction, we look for excluded voices, exceptions to rules and prescriptions, and for hidden exploitations left between the lines of a story or other construction. Deconstruction assumes every story has many sides, most of which are understated in a story (See Appendix A).

Difference The postmodern turn is a search for and a celebration of differences. "Vive la difference!" Diversity is an asset, not a cost or something to be controlled or exploited. It is postmod to assume that increasing the heterogeneity of viewpoints, pathways, involvements, relationships, and constructions will free us cogs from the modernist project.

Differential status   Executive officers are at the top, managers and staffs are beneath them. Workers, customers and suppliers litter the bottom of the pyramid. Gender and race can also be categories for differential status.

Discourse   Discourse can be as simple as conversation and as complex as philosophy essays. Even in an essay, the writer is in discourse with the reader. For Bakhtin, the Russian novelist, we speak with a and we listen with a multiplicity of voices. I speak as professor, man, husband, father, rebel, and environmentalist. You listen as student, male or female, rebel, conformist, etc. The discourse therefore is multi-layered and multi-voiced. Organizations are a struggle of pre-mod, mod, and postmod discourse.

Essentialisms   Big words psychologists use to categorize and dehumanize humans. Essentialisms are micro theories that stereotype (even if unintentionally so) classes or groups of people by their essential-personality traits, essential-types, or essential-behavioral patterns. Myers-Briggs, for example says my essential is an "intuitive-thinker" who sometimes acts as a "sensing-thinker," but never as a "sensing-feeler." Postmods do not butt in to other people's categories of who we are. "All labels exploit."

Exploitation   People use other people in ways that bring them power, control, and profit while those being exploited get less and less. Inequity, unfairness, injustice, mixed with some naive or premeditated sleeze is part of exploitation. Exploitation can be sexual, racial, colonial, paternalistic, and bureaucratic. In every social structure, some group of people manage to exploit other groups of people. Many managers practice exploitation while mouthing words like "empowerment" and "human resource management."

Factory-bureaucracy   A combination of Max Weber's bureaucratic rules, positional pyramid, and chain of command with Frederic Taylor's and Henry Ford's factory system. Weber wanted bureaucracy to end the exploitation and inequities of feudal governance. Taylor wanted to end the "systematic soldier" and goldbricking he saw workers doing that exploited owners and managers by dividing the work force into "those who think" and "those who work." Ford sought to regiment labor through mechanized and automated work processes. The combination of factory and bureaucracy is an authoritarian, inflexible, hierarchical division of labor in a mechanistic manufacturing machine. Postmods do not see Japan's so-called "flexible manufacturing system" as much different than traditional factory-bureaucracy.

Marginalizing   Ignoring or discounting other people's reality by constructing and positioning them in ways that undercut their equal participation. Women in traditional paternalistic marriages are denied equal say over their own body, family funds, and shelter. Racial minorities get less play in historical accounts than majority races. There is a saying: "the person with the sword writes the history and makes all the rules." To find the marginals, look for the points of struggle, resistance, and conflict in organizations. Marginals occupy the borders, the shadows, the spaces between and beyond the main and central and dominant discourse. In textbooks, marginal topics like "ethics," "ecology," and "diversity" are put into little boxes, endnotes, or trailing chapters.

Modernism   Also referred to as "Mod." Excluding the stories and voices of the dominated by ignoring anything that does not fit the progress myth which institutionalizes privilege and marginalization.

Narrative: A story or account. People narrate in conversations and in written texts.

Norm   Average. The normative worker is the average worker. The normative manager is the average manager. In either case, the point is to discourage performances that are too weak or too strong, so as to increase standardization and predictable control. Organizations encourage us to be average, not to be deviates, not to rebel, and certainly not to innovate. To norm someone is also to capture them as an average category, something that is predictable and controllable.

Panoptic   Includes in one view, everything that is in sight. A panoptic tower, for example, was frequently used in prisons and concentration camps to keep every prisoner in view. In Victorian workshops, "overseers" sat on high stools to gaze the many rows of workers. Panopticism increases when there is one-way gazing: they can see your every move, but you cannot see them. If you set up control such that workers never know when the boss will stick his head in the door, or look over your workmanship, then the panoptic (gaze) gets internalized. We learn to gaze at ourselves and the panoptic tower and high stools can be removed (a cost saver) and our behavior is just as controlled as before.

Performativity   People are "human resources" to be used by the system in order to maximize system efficiency, production control, capital return, and administrative flexibility. Lyotard (1984) looks at the downside of "maximizing" productivity and treating humans as mere "capital resources." Feminists argue that maximizing efficiency by performativity may increase quality and lower costs, but at the uncalculated and externalized cost of mother earth. Performativity is a narrow and myopic view that discourages diversity, autonomy, flexibility and openness because it interferes with maximizing the bottom line.

Positivism   Treats human experience and people like objects. All knowledge and truth is based on empirical and factual evidence. It is a system of philosophy originated by Auguste Comte in which observable facts are scientific and unobservables are subjective and speculative, and therefore unscientific.

Positivized   When a social scientist or even a bureaucrat converts and captures a person as an array of numbers or a list of categorical terms that can be put into a file. The positivized person has been reduced to a set of normative data points.

Postmodern   Also referred to as postmod. Postmodern is constructing or resurrecting the stories and voices of those excluded, marginalized, and exploited in the modernist project. Postmod can be affirmative in the assumption that exploitation can be countered by more enlightened and empowering administrative and human relations practices. On the other hand, there is skeptical postmodernism, where any formula for fairness and justice can be exploited into a routine of higher performativity, and render any postmod prescription into a modernist command and control tool. This is why postmods avoid solutions.

Pre-modern   Also called pre-mod. Pre-mod is a discourse rooted in the pre-industrial era of America extending back into feudal culture. Fraternities and sororities, as well as Supreme Courts and University Trustees exhibit discursive practices rooted in pre-modern times. The plus side of pre-mod is the sense of craftsmanship and strong sense of community. On the negative side there is slavery, bondage, religious repression, and torture. The modernist project attempted to move beyond pre-mod, but it is our view that much about society in general, and business organizations, specifically, is still quite pre-mod.

Privileging   A construction that benefits one group of people at everyone else's expense. In any social system, some people have more advantage, favor, rights, exceptions, and equities than other groups. Privileged people do not play by the same rules.

Progress Myth   The belief that through technology, training, or education that somehow society is getting better off each year. Skeptics argue that society is not moving forward to perfection. There are many pre-modern practices, such as an appreciation for crafts people and artisans, as well as ways of living that did not consume near as much mother earth resources that deny the progress myth. Proponents of the progress myth point to the many labor saving advantages of technology like computers and fax machines and accuse those who stand in the way of being Luddites. But maybe the Luddites, that group of workers in England (1811–1816) who smashed new labor saving textile machinery to protest their reduced wages and under-employment were right.

Story   A story is a communication between two or more persons during which a past or anticipated experience is referenced, recounted, interpreted, or challenged (Boje, 1991: 111). Stories can be as terse, coded, and abbreviated as when you tell someone else "you know the story" and without unfolding the story, they get the whole story. Or, story can be an entire storyline, complete with plot, characters, dialogue, climax, opener, and a moral point. How coded or how extended the story is depends on the context: do you know the person well enough to assume they can fill in the blanks; do you trust them enough to tell them the whole story; do you have time; do you have the right to tell this story?

Surveillance   Also called "the gaze." Michel Foucault's work focuses our attention on any device, no matter how well-intended, that collects information, observation, and data on our person. With every ounce of gaze, we lose our freedom and our privacy. A simple mechanism like MBO (management by objectives) can collect info on our movements, contacts, and thinking that can be exploited to control and to docilize our behavior. Surveillance gets "internalized" when we are conditioned to gaze at our own thoughts and actions.

Totalism   Writing a total history from one view, usually white-male, while leaving out all "other's" stories. Totalism privilege one particular and usually narrow point of view. The postmod approach is to deconstruct a totalism to include many and often conflicting accounts from many perspectives. Many voices have been left out of history in ways that privilege some and marginalize and even exclude or expunge many others.

Universalisms   Big words sociologists use to dehumanize human beings. A universal is a grand and macro principle or theory. It is a sweeping statement that glosses a whole lot of differences in many local accounts. Universalism is so focused on the whole grand scheme or grand narrative that the diversity of perspectives gets trampled. Postmods deconstruct universals by pointing out exceptions, exclusions, contradictions, and inapplicabilities.

Valorize   To fix or control the value of something or some category by setting it up on a pedestal. Empowerment, for example, is a term that has Mom and Apple Pie connotations, but can be used to cloak more exploitive practices. When we valorize we make something have a sacred or ideal quality and can forget to check it out critically.

Voice When you have a voice you speak and get heard. When you are voiceless, you are mute and silent. Even when you speak, without voice you have no impact. To be voiceless is a deprivation of your ability to speak from your own person. In every social structure, some voices are heard, others speak but are not heard, and some do not speak at all. The exploitation is when your lose your voice and others begin to speak for you or even through you. Can you voice your opinions openly and honestly? When do you speak what the organization prefers you speak? If you are female, do you get to speak as a female or as a male?

White male voices They have traditionally drowned out all "other" voices.

❑ MANAGEMENT IS A STRUGGLE OF PRE, MOD, & POST DISCOURSES ❑

I. What is Planning?

Setting the goals of what to do in the future and specifying the means (strategy & programs) to achieve those goals.

PRE. Craft. Planning and doing are both part of the craftsmen's job.

MOD. Pyramid. Planning and doing get split up as the manager does the brain work and the worker does the hand-work.

POST. Network. Planning head and hand-work is recombined and planning is de-centered to include the needs of customers and suppliers, as well as managers and teams of workers.

II. What is Organizing?

Grouping and assigning people, processes, and resources to accomplish plans people can not do alone while delegating requisite authority and setting the rules by which they interact.

PRE. Crews. Organizing is by skill and seniority in a self-reliant and entrepreneurial brotherhood society of apprentices and skilled journeymen.

MOD. Discipline. Organizing is centralized and impersonal surveillance and penal mechanisms of disciplined time and motion.

POST. Flat. Organizing is *de-centered* with flat, flexible and few layers to distribute autonomous teams focusing on KAIZEN and customers.

III. What is Influencing?

Establishing attitudes and rewards to motivate human behavior over time to enthusiastically achieve planned objectives.

PRE. **Solace.** Influencing is by democratic enforcement of shop rules in a seniority-based, fraternal culture where attitude holds religious significance.

MOD. **Comply.** Influencing conforms and docilizes peole by fear to be cogs in the performativity machine.

POST. **Individual.** Influence is *de-centered* so each person has many voices and selves with unconforming diversity and a celebration of differences.

IV. What is Leading?

Directing and coordinating persons and teams concerning what task activities peole do and how they are to do those tasks to achieve which plans and objectives.

PRE. **Master.** Leading is accomplished by authoritarian, slave-driving, master, tyrants who direct and oversee what and how tasks are achieved in a climate of fear.

MOD. **Panoptic.** Leading is centralized with many layers and divisions of panoptic gazes and penal mechanisms to apply punishments and rewards in ways that sustain power and status differences.

POST. **Servant.** Leading is *de-centered* with an ethic of servanthood as managers serve people who in turn serve customers in a *de-differentiated* network of relationships lead by vision and story.

V. What is Controlling?

Evaluating and measuring performance of persons, teams, and organizations to ensure desired goals are achieved with efficient use of resources and highest quality levels.

PRE. **Slave.** Controlling was according to patrimonial system of class privileges and rights over lower classes of people.

MOD. **Inspect.** Controlling is by impersonal inspection to assure normative compliance and standardized human behavior.

POST. **Choice.** Controlling is *de-differentiated* and *de-centered* so that people make more diverse, individual, and co-responsible setting that balances efficiency with environmental and social audits.

VI. CONCLUSION

Management is an arena of pre-modern, modern, and postmodern discourses.

☐ A REVOLUTIONARY'S NON-INTRODUCTION ☐

☐ LAUNCHING THE REVOLUTION ☐

American management has led our country to ruin. It is time for a management revolution. We have to rebel against the sacred texts, the principles of traditional management that have not changed since the 1950s.

"America's Revolution Against Exploitation" is long overdue. We are a nation founded on rebellion and slavery. With all our prosperity, the gap between the haves and have nots is now a grand canyon. The prescriptions in this book are extreme. It is time to dismantle American "exploitive" management practices that are the same old victimizing games, but written up with more endearing labels. Empowerment is really exploitation. Cycle time is really time and motion study. Access to information is really surveillance. Managers are as exploited as the workers. Managers work in a system of discipline, obedience, surveillance, and prescriptions that keep them from doing much other than exploitation. Both will rise up and rebel against this system of exploitation that is being taught **WITHOUT CRITIQUE** in MBA programs and Colleges of Business Administration (CBA's). In fact MBA is not Master of Business Administration, it is Master of *Bureaucratic* Administration taught in Colleges of *Bureaucratic* Administration. This book is a rebel's guide for post-bureaucratic, post-exploitation, post-racism, post-colonialism, post-sexism, and post-complacency. *"Postmodern Management!"* is our revolutionary battle cry for breaking the shackles of these exploitations.

Postmodern Management is a revolutionary blend of a critique of management traditions with skills to move America to a future without exploitation. We have acquired a new perception and with it new capacities. There are new frontiers of opportunities, risk and challenge. We live in an age of transition from the old "modern" factory-bureaucracy that took us beyond feudal guilds, but is not suited to the diverse workforce and complex world economy of "today," in our "postmodern world". As usual, management guru, Peter Drucker was ahead of his time in 1957 in his book *Landmarks of Tomorrow* when he used the term "postmodern" and went on to say that the postmodern lacks definition, expression, theories and concepts. Between 1957 and 1990, Peter Drucker recognized that we can now specify the "postmodern factory of 1999," but we can not build it yet. This is an important point because there are too many postmodern writers using postmodern language without realizing how resistant the modernist regime is to giving up control over the factory bureaucracy. Exploitation by another name is still exploitation. Postmodernists also exploit when their turgid writing keeps postmodern ideas inaccessible to the general public. An elite group of academics use jargon and prose that Socrates and Einstein could not fathom. Our task is to make postmodern management accessible to the common man. In fact, in this book undergraduate juniors and seniors have done postmodern studies of everyday organizations.

Garfield echoes Drucker in his book *Second to None* where he identifies the era of uncertainty that exists while corporations undergo an extraordinary transformation in attempting to meet challenges. These changes may appear random and chaotic but they are part of a larger pattern whose scope we are just beginning to discern. Garfield calls this new pattern the "new story" of business. We, too, will provide the new story—the postmodern view of organizations.

Vaclav Havel, the President of Czechoslovakia, reflects that the fall of communism is a sign that modern thought—based on the premise that the world is objectively knowable, and that the knowledge so obtained can be absolutely generalized—has come to a final crisis. From an era of systems, institutions, mechanisms and statistical averages, he proposes the task of finding a new, post-modern face. It is not that we should simply seek new and better ways of managing society, the economy and the world. The point is that we should fundamentally change how we behave.

Drucker, Garfield, Havel: three revolutionary voices that call for new stories in today's world. In this book we eagerly take on the challenge.

Pre-modern Management Revolution

Before the industrial revolution, people for many centuries apprenticed in **crafts** and became so skilled that they did not need a lot of other people to tell them how to plan, organize, and control. They knew what to do. On the other hand, slaves, serfs, and indentured servants were exploited to make wealth for masters and kings. Drucker (1992) places the revolutionary transition from the pre-modern era in the 1880s, when America began regulating its unrestricted markets, railroad barons, and in general, wanted to get some control over the emerging industrial revolution.

Modern Management Revolution

Two trends combined in the industrial revolution to become "modern management." First, the industrial revolution model of factory production yielded more products and cheaper costs than the feudal crafts and guild system. Second, bureaucracy was seen as a way to resolve the exploitation of feudal lords and barons by implementing rules, procedures, specialized positions, and layers of administrators. The factory and the bureaucracy fused together in the modernist era to give us the modern factory-bureaucracy. With this machine age, people began to be treated like machines, made to perform very routine, boring, repetitive, and very, very specialized work (like oiling the machine). People did not think for themselves and so they needed great **pyramids** of managers, layer upon layer of managers, to put all the cogs (people) together again.

Postmodern Revolution

This revolution is only beginning. Drucker (1992), for example dates the beginning as 1968–73, when the great "oil shock" and student rebellions across America voiced the pain. Are we are beyond the machine age, beyond the time when people at work had no skill, beyond the time when they are treated like dependent children, and beyond the need for managers at all? In management, will people, once again, be highly skilled? Does working in autonomous teams, in a flat and global **network** of relations make people more empowered, more self-controlled, and less exploitable? Does serving the customer through a lean and flexible service system move us beyond a mass consumption society? Are managers and bean counters going to serve the postmodern network by keeping it configured in ways that meet worker and customer needs? Or, in this postmodern revolution, have the forces of darkness learned to substitute words like "total quality management," "sociotechnical systems," "empowerment," and "flexible manufacturing systems," for the modernist command and control words or even the pre-modern torture and sovereignty words? Are management textbooks keeping their 1950's principles and prescriptions intact, while using more politically correct words like: diversity, multi-cultural, workforce 2000, and substituting minority for white-male photographs? Will the postmodern revolution become a maniacal nightmare where the ills that brought on earlier revolutions pale by comparison. Just because an organization will be flat, speedy, global, and customer-driven does not mean that workers, managers, and customers will be unshackled from exploitation, drudgery, and abuse.

Pre-modern is craft-based management, modern is pyramid-based management, and postmodern is network-based management. But, postmodern is not just a system of managing a flat network form of organization, postmodern is also a method for detecting, and challenging forms of exploitation.

To provide a framework for our book, we provide metaphors of Pre-modern, Modern and Post-modern. The *Pre-modern* represents the crown of the master and also the crown of the skilled artisan. The *Modern* represents the bureaucratic organization chart inside the pyramid with the General Manager at the top with the other managers and employees cascading down to the bottom.

There are several candidate-metaphors for postmodern. One is Peter Drucker's (1990, 1992) image of the modernist firm as the "battleship" and the postmodern image of the "flotilla." Flotillas are small groups of ships that can be reconfigured to cope with changing circumstances. Gareth Morgan, in personal communication has suggested the postmodern image of a termite mound. The idea that each termite is so interrelated with his brother mites to nurture, build, and protect the mound. Lyotard (1984: 17) uses the metaphor of a conversation in contrast to the bureaucratic institution:

> From this point of view, an institution differs from a conversation in that it always requires supplementary constraints for statements to be declared admissible within its bounds. The constraints function to filter discursive potentials, interrupting possible connections in the communication networks: there are things that should not be said. They also privilege certain classes of statements (sometimes only one) whose predominance characterizes the discourse of the particular institution: there are things that should be said, and there are ways of saying them. Thus: orders in the army, prayer in church, denotation in the schools, narration in families, questions in philosophy, performativity in business. Bureaucratization is the outer limit of this tendency.

The conversation is a loosely coupled network where people join in and detach from the dialogue. The rules of the conversation shift as rapidly as the topics and where the conversation will lead is often unpredictable.

Tamara

Our favorite metaphor for postmodern is a mansion with conversations happening simultaneously in many rooms. In the play *Tamara*, instead of one story, one stage, and one plot, told in a linear act by act way to a stationary audience, the stories of multiple characters each unfold as that audience chases actors and actresses from room to room in a reconstruction of an Italian Villa. Tamara is a true story taken from the diary of Aelis Mazoyer and is Los Angeles' longest running play. If we assume that there are a dozen stages and a dozen

The story you follow from room to room.

storytellers, then the number of story lines an audience could trace in their networking as the "wandering audience" chasing a multiplicity of "wandering discourses" is **12!** **or 479,011,600** paths in the Tamara organization. In Tamara, there is no correct, single story, told as one voice as is the case in the modernist organization. Every choice is valid. Every whim or dedication is rewarded in its own way. You choose the play you wish to get. Thus the concept of *Tamara* represents today's diverse, simultaneous, team-based, flexible organization that challenge us to find many new ways to view the world.

Our Voices

One of the freedoms of postmodernism is to own up to your "voice" and stop writing so impersonally that you have no voice. We are Boj and Bob, using our voices, telling our story.

Bob   Dave, besides getting rich and famous, why did we write this book?

Boj   We were at some convention talking with book sellers and started joking around. We have this book idea about telling stories to teach management. You know. Tell the feudal stories of slavery to get at control.

Bob	Textbooks summarize Taylor in two sentences, highlight Gilbreth, condense Fayol, but never tell the whole story—and a really exciting story too.
Boj	I was taught never to write from my own voice. It took me years to use the "I" word in my writing. And, I think we wrote the book to give a voice to other voices not being heard, like the voice of the worker, feminist voices, anti-racist and anti-exploitation voices. In management, as taught in the USA, all you get is one voice . . . bureaucracy.
Bob	I'd like to tell the story of the pre-mod slaves, serfs, craftsmen and artisans. But, I'd also like to tell the story of the bureaucracy, the factory, the mill, the office as well as the story of the postmodern organization with images of Tamara, termites, and the flotilla.
Boj	I think management texts are way behind the times. In fact, I was talking to a textbook salesman. He used the words: "instructor proof." You don't need instructors anymore, except to pick out the multiple choice questions from the test bank that is provided, pick the overheads from the overhead book, and pick the exercise from some manual. The student can read the book, do the pre-test, post-test, read the little inserts and there you have it—fast-food learning.
Bob	What a disappointment. How dull! How boring! Where are the stories? Where's the excitement? We want our book to include the management functions: planning, organizing, influencing, leading, controlling. But we want these topics viewed from the pre-modern, modern, and postmodern perspectives. How can we extract the best from the pre-mod and set the stage for inclusion in the postmodern. We have some exciting possibilities.
Boj	To me the pre, mod, and post are competing conversations. You know, competing discourses that are each in play today, each in struggle with the other. In my life, I am part bureaucrat, part lord of the classroom, and part rebel postmodernist.
Bob	Our task is to rebel against the modern management texts and really provide new life for business education. Stories, history, and competing roles provide the framework for a much more exciting exploration of business today.
Boj	Right, and we have to rebel against the postmodernists too. The stuff is great, but they make it so hard to understand what they are saying. Managers and a lot of students turn off to it after a few sentences.[6]
Bob	That's right, one of our challenges is to make the postmodern message accessible to our students, but we also have to be

circumspect about the postmodernists. The message can easily be diverted into a new form of modernist techniques. We cannot be enamored that postmodernism is nirvana. The message is powerful, but how can we provide some skepticism.

Boj   I just can not teach the old stuff. It is bureaucratic, it does not face the truth. America has a lot of MBA programs and textbook publishers making a lot of money teaching the sacred texts. Even though, Americans know that companies are leaving for other countries, the education system is in shambles, the homeless are everywhere. America is pyramid-bound, pyramid-dependent, and prefers to be blind to the postmodern revolution.

Bob   Students have been conditioned by other textbooks and classroom procedures. Our approach asks them to reconsider their education as we lay out our story and as we ask them to lay out their story. Reevaluate the present state of business in light of contributions from the past. We are asking them to cooperate in this venture to make business come alive.

Boj   Texts are a-historical and even abuse history. Management textbooks do not talk about exploitation, about slavery, about sexism, and racism. There is a mandatory ethics chapter, but basically the books are bland, encyclopedias of scientific-sounding vocabularies. They mask the real message, that the white male pattern of organizing by product, by functions, by aerospace technology that combines functions and project in a matrix of a thousand teams will make it all go away. A matrix organization is just bureaucracy squared. Two bureaucracies instead of one. Some texts change the photos and put in a case about a poly-centered form with a multiplicity of management hierarchies around which the teams get distributed. The same old formula, tweaked here, stretched there, with new rhetoric, but still feudalism and bureaucracy. We have to take a different track.

Bob   Let's take the topic of organizing. We will not use this hackneyed approach in our book. Rather, we will look at the historical development of organizing. Since organizing will be different in the year 2000 than it is being practiced today, we will examine how organizing got to be the way it is, and where can it go from here. In short, instead of looking at organizing as a science of variable relationships, we will look at organizing as a response to the conditions and movements of American society and the global economy. What will it take for America to be competitive in 2001?

Boj   All students are doing is memorizing lists and playing nonsense exercises. Memorizing laundry lists is not teaching students to critique. They are taught to be little docile cogs in the cookie cutter organizational machine. And, we are the cookie cutter monsters.

Bob   The organizational reality of the 21st Century will be too diverse, flexible, dynamic, and turbulent for simple cookie cutter cogs to keep America competitive in the 21st Century.

Boj   I want students to get how stories are a part of the discourse that is pre-mod, part of the discourse that is modernist-bureaucracy, and part of the critical and skeptical discourse that is postmod.

Bob   There is no truth in a story, it is the teller's point of view, based on his or her experience. For the postmodernist, the storyteller's voice is as valid as the voice of any textbook author. Certainly the student's voice is equally valid. Our story and writing are not any more truthful or valid than anyone else's story.

Boj   It is easy, as authors, to hide our own voice and story, by masking our "I-ness" behind sterile rhetoric, encyclopedia lists, and the like. I would like to be bold, and come out from behind the dispassionate, privileged third person. We want to de-privilege the author's voice. Let the student skip around, read the book in the middle, skip to the end, read every third page. Treat their own stories of management as valid and truthful as any they read in our book. We will give our interpretations to these stories, but our interpretation is only our viewpoint. As students, they can generate equally valid viewpoints. Some students may even find their own voice.

Bob   We will define lots of terms, but there are always more than one definition. They can define terms in their own way, based on their own stories. By taking this approach, we are sharing power and ownership with our students. To be empowered, to interpret, and to tell their own stories!

Boj   It's tough, we are asking students to critique traditional principles of management that have been taught as scientifically validated facts. Management principles are history-bound. With each new management revolution, the principles get recreated to fit that time period. Then when the economy, culture, and politics changes, a new set of principles is seized upon as scientific and valid. It's not scientific, it is just more politically expedient to teach people truths instead of historically convenient recipes.

	MODERN	POST-MODERN
Planning	❏ Short term profit goals. ❏ Mass production. ❏ Worker is a cost. ❏ Vertical planning. ❏ Top down focus. ❏ Planning leads to order.	❏ Long term profit goals. ❏ Flexible production. ❏ Worker is an investment. ❏ Horizontal planning. ❏ Internal and external customer focus. ❏ Planning leads to disorder and confusion.
Organizing	❏ One man, one job and de-skilled jobs. ❏ Labor-management confrontation. ❏ Division of departments. ❏ Tall is better. ❏ Homogeneity is strength. ❏ Top has voice & diversity is tolerated. ❏ Efficiency increases with specialization, formalization, routinization, fragmentation, division of labor.	❏ Work teams, multi-skilled workers. ❏ Labor-management cooperation. ❏ Flexible networks with permeable boundaries. ❏ Flat is better. ❏ Diversity is strength. ❏ Many-voices and diversity is an asset. ❏ Efficiency decreases with specialization, formalization, routinization, fragmentation, and division of labor.
Influencing	❏ Authority vested in superior. ❏ Extrinsic rewards and punishments. ❏ Surveillance mechanisms everywhere. ❏ Women paid 68% of men; minorities paid less. ❏ Discourse is white male-based. ❏ Individual incentives.	❏ Authority delegated to leaders by team. ❏ Intrinsic, empowered, ownership over work process. ❏ People are self-disciplined. ❏ Women and minorities equally paid. ❏ Polyvocal/polylogic discourse. ❏ Team incentives.
Leading	❏ Theory X or Y. ❏ Centralized with many layers and rules. ❏ Boss centered. ❏ White male career tracks. ❏ Tell them what to do.	❏ Theory S (Servant Leadership) ❏ Decentralized with few layers and wide spans. ❏ People centered. ❏ Tracks for women and minorities. ❏ Visionary.
Controlling	❏ Centralized control. ❏ End-of-line inspection. ❏ Micro surveillance. ❏ Red tape. ❏ Lots of procedures, rules, MBO and computers for surveillance. ❏ Train top of pyramid. ❏ Measure result criteria. ❏ Hoard information. ❏ Fear-based controls.	❏ Decentralized control. ❏ Quality control is everyone's job. ❏ Two-way surveillance. ❏ Cut red tape. ❏ Dump procedures. ❏ Train people. ❏ Measure process criteria. ❏ Information is given to all. ❏ Self-control.

Table 1: Modern Versus Post-Modern Principles of Management

Bob: We have proof. We can show you that before pyramid, bureaucratic (modernist) management, there were other principles that textbook authors do not talk about anymore. That weakens the modernist's grip on how planning, organizing, influencing, leading, and controlling *should* be done. We can show that by the 21st century, the world will be a very different place than it is today. I think it is reasonable to assume that we will seek out some *principles* that *fit* the postmodern *historical epoch* (our future).

Boj You know what, management principles of Modernist Machine and Service Bureaucracies are the exact opposite of the management principles which our book proposes for Postmodern Management and Organization.

Bob Opinions vary, but what is clear is that the principles of management of modernist-bureaucracy and postmodern self-management are opposite.

Boj The U.S. Department of Labor has conducted a study that makes the search for alternative principles of management an American agenda. Our book plans to address this agenda.

Bob In the next few pages, we can summarize the book by telling the grand stories of the three epochs of management: Premodern, Modern, and Post-modern.

Boj You think that students will get the fact that while we lay them out as historical time periods, all three are very much a part of your life in everyday organizations?

AMERICA'S REPORT CARD

PRODUCTIVITY. Productivity growth (output per hour) in the United States slowed significantly after 1973. Labor productivity actually declined in 1989 and 1990. Some estimate that if current international productivity trends continue, nine countries may exceed the U.S. in output per worker-hour by the year 2020.

EARNINGS AND INCOME. Stagnant productivity has seriously affected workers' earnings. Median family income increased nearly three percent a year between 1947 and 1973, Since 1973, it has scarcely increased at all. Families with heads of households under the age of 34 have watched their real income decline since 1979.

JOBS. Job opportunities in the United States are changing. Twenty years ago, manufacturing accounted for 27 percent of all nonagricultural employment in the U.S.; services and retail trade for 32 pecent. By 1990, manufacturing accounted for only 17 percent of these jobs, while services and retail trade made up 44 percent. In 1990, manufacturing jobs paid an average of $10.84 per hour; while service jobs paid only $9.86 and jobs in retail trade paid only $6.78.

Table 2.

Bob   Yes. We have evidence from past experience with students that they can struggle with different discourses. They can observe the artisan of the pre-mod period, with the assembly line worker of the mod period, and network of workers in the postmod period. Not only do they observe these situations, but they recognize how their own lives reflect these situations. Thus, they become more invested in entering into the struggle. Does that make sense?

Boj   Makes sense to me, Bob.

NOTES

1. Drucker, Peter F. *Landmarks of Tomorrow.* N.Y: Harper, 1957.
2. Drucker, Peter F. "The Emerging Theory of Manufacturing." *Harvard Business Review*, May/June 1990: 94–102. See his 1992 book: *Managing for the Future: The 1990's and Beyond.* New York: Truman Talley Books/ Dutton. Drucker uses the term "post-business society" and lays out an era or paradigm-shift approach to postmodernism (pp. 1–11).
3. Garfield Charles. *Second to None.* Homewood, Il.: Business one Irwin, 1992.
4. Havel, Vaclav. "The End of the Modern Era". *N.Y. Times*, March 1, 1992.
5. Parker, Martin 1992 "Post-Modern Organizations or Postmodern Organization Theory" *Organization Studies.* 13/1: 1–17. Parker makes the distinction between postmodern forms of organization and postmodern methods and critique which he terms "epistemology."
6. See, for example, Rosenau, Pauline Marie's book *Post-modernism and the social sciences: Insights, inroads, and intrusions.* Princeton, NJ: Princeton University Press. 1992: 4. She reviews a lot of the disciplines that are writing textbooks and holding conferences and teaching, but charges economics and psychology as slow learners. Other important books on postmodernism that have influenced my writing are: Clegg, Stewart. *Modern organizations: organization studies in the postmodern world.* Newbury Park, CA: Sage, 1991;
   Harvey, David *The condition of postmodernity: An enquiry into the origins of cultural change.* Oxford: Blackford, 1989;
   Jameson, Fredric 1991. *Postmodernism, or, the cultural logic of Late Capitalism.* Durham, N.C.: Duke University Press;
   Boj: One of the writers on postmodernism who influenced me most was Foucault, Michel, especially his book *Surveiller et punir: naissance de la prison* 1977. I read the English translation by Alan Sheridan, *Discipline and punish* 1977, New York: Pantheon books.
7. Ibid Rosenau, p. xiv.
8. SCANS Report, 1991. "What work requires of schools: A SCAN's report of America 2000." The Secretary's Commission on Achieving Necessary Skills. U.S. Department of Labor (June). ISBN 0–16–035853–1. p. 2.

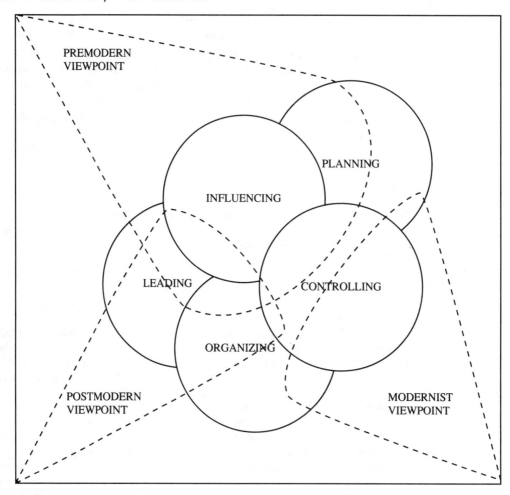

Circles indicate management functions. Centrality indicates dominance in a person's discourse. Size represents relative importance of the function. Top-most position indicates the person's emphasis on a function in their discourse. The point is that a person in their discourse can take in all three viewpoints in the same utterance.

PRE-MODERN, MODERN, POSTMODERN: WHAT IS THE STORY?

In this chapter we will present a capsule description of Pre-modern, Modern, Postmodern approaches to management and organization. Each revolution has two sides to the story. In fact, a multiplicity of sides will be told. We will also show that postmodernism is making inroads in finance, accounting, management, information systems, as well as in management practices.

❑ THE PRE-MODERN STORY ❑

What is Pre-Modern?

Pre-modern is a **discourse** rooted in the pre-industrial era of America. It is rooted in the military, religious orders, and medicine. Fraternities and sororities have much pre-modern discourse because they aim to replicate the Greek discourse. The discourse of each era has the baggage of social relations, prescriptions, ethics, and creeds that shape our behavior today. On the plus side, pre-mod was a period of artisans, craftsmanship, apprenticeship, and pride in the quality of one's workmanship. In fraternities and sororities, rituals of initiation, rites of passage, and a tradition of greek legends, shape the pledges into active members. The skeptical side of the story is that slaves and serfs, used as cheap labor, built the castles, moats, and manors that the feudal lords and ladies inhabited. The have-nots were controlled by torture, bondage, and even feudal religious dogma to be the chattel of the lords and ladies. Women had no voice and with exceptions like Joan of Arc, no history in male dominated relations. Sometimes the hazings of fraternities and sororities go too far. Some religious organizations are cults and people need de-programming to get detached.

Church Story

Parish Priest: I believe in parishioner participation. They always
have the last word: "Yes Father!"

Pre-Modern Stories and Times

In Medieval Times, before capitalism and the industrial revolution of
the 1800s, organizations were sovereign citadels ruled by means of
brute force and torture. The story line was subjugation, degradation of
the working and peasant class by the sovereigns. In the sixteenth and

seventeenth centuries land was taken from peasant families in order to make profit. Instead of farms and forests providing livelihood for a community, it was cut up, sectioned, and sold to provide profit to land owners. Comodification of land led to commodification of labor into larger and larger firms. Centralized monarchies taxed people to raise armies and to build ships for trade. At the same time people had a pride in their individualism, their freedom, and in their knowledge of craft. At one time skilled craftsmen after many years of apprenticeship built cathedrals, stained glass windows, crafted wood objects, the artisan quality of which cannot be duplicated by artisans of today.

Bob: I recall the pride of craftsmanship that my father demonstrated. On one occasion I helped his father install a set of pull-down attic stairs. As the task drew to a close, I suggested that the corner of the enclosure needed a small amount of plastic wood. My father was outraged. "No, my father said: "we will cut a triangular piece of wood to properly finish the job." Pride in his work would allow no compromises.

Other examples of craftsmanship exist today, but the era of the craftsman is identified with an earlier time.

Workers belonged to trade guilds and their allegiance to their trade was greater than their allegiance to management and organization. People worked in large crews and were expected to apprentice to learn their craft. The worker was responsible for the work. The protestant work ethic dominated. People were competitive, innovative, thrifty, hard working, self reliant, and rugged individualists. Only the fittest survived. They were the individualistic entrepreneurs that set America apart from other nations. Unfortunately, we could not keep this work ethic alive.

As industrialization took root, craftsmen were de-skilled. Adam Smith's factory fractionated the craftsmen's work and skills. In premodern times, Indians were dispossessed of their lands, languages and stories. They were herded into camps and reservations by white Europeans. Punishment was a public spectacle. People brought lunches, prisoners performed, and the sovereign gave public lessons on the consequences of insubordination.

Slave auctions were also public rituals performed in the square on Main Street. Nations practiced slavery and serfdom. Abolition of slavery in America is a recent innovation. We can see the struggle between pre-modern slavery and modern capitalism being played out in South Africa. With the coming of the industrial revolution, socialists, unions, and communists sought to control the dysfunctions of factory systems. The working classes were thought to be dehumanized, alienated, and commodicized by capitalism. Pre-industrial critics like Samuel Taylor Coleridge, Thomas Carlyle, Robert Sothey, William Cobbett, Thomas Hood, and Thomas Love Peacock were enemies of the industrial age.[1] They lost the battle and the war. The strong protestant work ethic and the ethics of social darwinism combined to form the survival of the fittest orientation that is the very heart of capitalism. Survival of the fittest was cruel to those who did not survive. Yet, the feudal system was benevolent to its subjects.

❑ THE MODERN STORY ❑

What is Modern?

The modern discourse is one of progress, using technology of the machine and administrative bureaucracy to move man out of slavery, class-based and caste-based social structure into a gentler and more advanced society. The modern organization combines the factory system of Taylorism, as exemplified by Henry Ford's assembly line, with administration by rules and offices of Max Weber's bureaucracy. The fusion of these is the factory bureaucracy. The factory-bureaucracy is performativity, uniformity, surveillance, and control. Most of all it is a style of discourse of how people talk to each other about planning, organizing, influencing, leading, and controlling. The rules and prescriptions of human interaction are carried on the wings of this discourse in ways that are empowering or dis-empowering.

Modern Stories and Times

Brute force was replaced by mechanical force. People became cogs in the machine. The reformers of the pre-modern narrative were Adam Smith, Max Weber, Frederick Taylor and Elton Mayo. Adam Smith told us the story of the pin factory (how to fractionate and specialize labor to produce pins more efficiently). Max Weber told us the story of the bureaucracy (how to attain equality by formalizing, rationalizing, and specializing labor). Frederick Taylor tells the story of Schmidt, the pig iron laborer, who, if he only did his motions and timed his actions with scientific precision, could increase his production. Finally, Elton Mayo, the father of human relations, tells the story of the Hawthorne Experiments. He wanted to critique Taylorism but his social science became one more tool of modern management to make people happy while they were segmented, de-skilled, divided, specialized, and became mechanisms in the grand machine. Scientific organization classifies people into departments, functions, skill groups, levels, layers, and hierarchies. People fit into a system of little boxes, boring and repetitive jobs with no skills, a hierarchy of subordination to the moods and prejudices of superiors (Ferguson, 1984: 108)[2]. The new heroes are putting together organizations that are non-segmented, highly skilled, multiplicative, generalized, and highly flexible, constantly reconfiguring, self-designing networks. Each of the modern storylines became the motif for scientific management, a science that teaches the principles without teaching the founding narratives. It is our task here to reintroduce the original story lines, so we can reveal how the story lines are changing as we move to the postmodern interpretations.

WHAT IS MODERNISM		
  MODERNISM	INSTITUTIONALIZED RACISM INSTITUTIONALIZED SEXISM INSTITUTIONALIZED EUROCENTRISM INSTITUTIONALIZED BUREAUCRACY INSTITUTIONALIZED COLONIALISM	*MOD ACTS OF EXCLUSION* 1. *Positivism* that treats human experience like objects. 2. *White male voices* that drown out all "other" voices 3. *Centering* all choice through the apex of the pyramid. 4. *Differential status* of management and workers. 5. *Universalisms* are big words sociologists use to dehumanize human beings. 6. *Essentialisms* are big words psycholgists use to categorize and dehumanize humans. 7. *Totalism* is writing a total history from one view, usually white-male, while leaving out all **"other's"** stories. 8. *Marginalizing* is ignoring or discounting other people's reality. 9. *Privileging* is a construction that benefits one group of people at everyone else's expense. **DEFINITION: Modernism is excluding the stories and voices of the dominated by ignoring anything that does not fit the progress myth which institutionalizes privilege and marginalization.**

The Modern Service and Product Bureaucracies

In this era, the work ethics of the individual were replaced by collectivism through three opposing forces: Scientific Management, Bureaucracy, and Human Relations. Engineers like Frederick Winslow Taylor developed and evangelized scientific management principles to transform skilled craftsmen in large groups into unskilled workers doing very specialized tasks that are closely supervised by managers. Scientific management created the product bureaucracy. The service bureaucracy was already a reality. In both, the thinking, planning, creating, innovating, quality control aspects of work were taken away from worker responsibility and given over to staff people who did the thinking, planning, and inspecting. The best exemplar of this time period was Henry Ford. His mass production assembly line and the ensuing mass consumption model put American industry on the map. The school systems of America became training grounds to allow people to learn to be cogs in the Ford manufacturing machine as well as dutiful purchasers of Ford Motor cars. The human relations movement, while vehemently opposed to scientific management, performed a more subtle form of modern control. In the name of science, workers were tested, examined, and measured to get them to be what William H. Whyte Jr. called a modern "organization man."[3] An organization man is a bureaucrat, a technocrat, a staff person who chooses the security of the big corporation instead of the life of the innovator.

Education's Role. The education system, consumption system, and the productive system were complementary and synergistic. The education system fabricated workers capable of intense repetition for long intervals under direct supervision. Consider the word "industrious" the type of behavior in school that prepared you for industry. Workers became mass consumers. While the industrial revolution allowed for the establishment and security of the middle class, the sense of adventure and inventiveness of pre-industrial capitalism soon subsided. The factory system and the service bureaucracy flourished. Taylorism, despite human relations and human potential movements became the mainstay of modern organization.

Bureaucracies Isolate. In the name of equality, bureaucracies segment organizational life and isolate people into cells (offices, committees, projects, positions). As isolation takes place, central control is established. Rational administrative rules and procedures apply to all of organizational life. People gave great control to the centralized, bureaucratic machine. As they did so, the cellular structures calcified and adaptability to change and reconfiguration and transformation became problematic.

Pre-mod CRAFT ORGANIZATION " Crews and trades"	Mod MACHINE BUREAUCRACY "Scientific Management"	Mod SERVICE BUREAUCRACY "IRS, Phone Company, etc."
Direct Supervision	Time & Motion control	Standardized skills
Specialize by trade	Specialize by task	Specialize by function/department
Centralized decisions	Centralized planning	Centralized planning
Coordinate by tradition	Coordinate by standard work processes	Coordinate by rules and procedures
Tasks require skilled artisans and craftsmen	Tasks are fractionated, rigidly defined	Tasks based on roles, job descriptions
People plan their own work	Clerks plan all worker's work	Boss plans your work
People loyal to their trade	People loyal to their shift	People loyal to their boss
Boss is autocratic, tough, paternalistic	Boss is rational, instrumental, distant	Boss is administrative, rule-based, political
Communication is informal	Communication is vertical, top-down	Communication is vertical, up and down

Table 1.1 A Comparison of Pre-modern Craft Organization with Two Modern Forms

Bureaucracies Discipline. For Michel Foucault (1979)[4], an organization is a capillary system of discipline, a seamless web of control from the periphery to the center. In fact there is no center, there are many disciplinary nodes: many periphery points of discipline. Deetz (1992) points out how organizations select and produce identities to conduct the discourse of discipline.[5] Managers discipline by suppressing differences, correcting innovation, maintaining the status quo. Differences are blurred, so the voices of diversity do not sound at all unique from one another. Men's voices sound like women's voices. But some groups are privileged in the discourse. Scientific disciplines marginalize lay stories and privilege expert stories. It is natural for men to discipline women, for whites to discipline blacks, for superiors to discipline inferiors. Discipline suppresses conflicting and diverse and alternative voices and fashions the monolithic voice.

Bureaucracies are Paternalistic Patriarchies. Women's voice has been ignored in pre-modern and modern epochs. To be superior is to be man, to be subordinate is to be woman. To be rational and objective is male; to be feeling and subjective is female. In modern times, the narrative rationalized, objectified, and subordinated women. There are many types of feminism: from a fit-in-the-male-system, to liberal feminism to radical feminism (create and empower feminine voices to oppose male-only voices) to ecofeminism (creating discourses that are uniquely feminine).

> Liberal feminism used to be, in Foucault's terms, a voice raised against the dominant discourse; it has now largely become a voice subservient to that discourse (Ferguson, 1984: 193).

Hierarchy and dominance and exploitation are male category systems of control. In the stories of bureaucracy, you hear themes like: women break down and cry, their menstrual cycles will interfere with performance, they distract men. When we include stories that are positive images of women, then this is a political act: it gives women a voice in a male-voiced system. The feminist voice helps us to deconstruct modernist, patriarchal stories and discourse. Some stories are male visions of organizational reality. Other stories are male scripts of how past experience anchors the present. Ecofeminists for example indict "the destruction of rain forests in order to raise cattle for hamburger while diminishing human life by encouraging the consumption of fatty, addictive food . . . abuses animals by placing them in confining factories while using artificial drugs which eventually harm the people who eat them" (Bullis and Glaser, 1992: 19–20).[6] The destructiveness of the organization to the natural world are among the taboo topics of bureaucratic discourse; these are the stories that do not get voiced.

Bureaucratic categories like "workers" and "managers," "blacks" and "whites," "blue" and "white" collar, "women" and "men" define people in ways that pose discourse power advantages for one group over another. Binary categories like these are revealed in story discourse. Even if only one side of the binary is mentioned, the other side, though unstated is still there. At one point in the discourse the worker is a "clumsum," a "grunt," and at other times a "boomer." Competing categorizations can compete and co-exist in the same story. The critical question is, not just the language categories-in-use, but whose interests are being served or marginalized by the use of those particular categories?

Bureaucracy is rigid about categories. For example, if a woman has both Asian and Eskimo parents, is she Asian or Eskimo? If her Asian mother had parents who were Black and Asian, what box does she check on the obligatory race question. There is ambiguity here. How does the organization act, if she puts down Asian, Eskimo, or Black? If we deconstruct diversity, we find many people who do not fit into neat little boxes. There is no "mixed" category on government forms. If your mother was Black and your father is White, then you must choose one category or the other. If you do not have a bureaucratic category for people, you can effectively deny and avoid their very existence.

From the crew based apprentice trades of pre-modern form of management, the modern period popularized the machine and service bureaucracies.

Each epoch answers the Harmony question with its own story of Utopia. After the industrial revolution, man seeks an organizational community in which his autonomy and freedom are valued. Each time period seeks an answer to the puzzle of harmony: how to insure the freedom of the individual in a competitive organization. In crown times harmony was somewhere between benevolence and cruelty. In modern times, Taylorists and Human Relationalists sought harmony that made man a happy cog in the industrial and bureaucratic machines. Unions sought a harmony in which there was strong opposition between workers and capitalists.

❑ THE POSTMODERN STORY ❑

The MAD Story

Boj: When I began teaching at Loyola Marymount University, I began using the I feel healthy. I feel happy. I feel terrific! affirmation in my classes. I even passed out cards with the affirmation done in my own calligraphy. Then, I met a marketing professor, named Bill Hetrick who told me that he was skeptical of affirmations. I invited him to create a skeptical, postmodern affirmation. Bill came back with a card that read: **I feel manipulated. I feel alienated. I feel damaged!** M.A.D. Bill and I are both postmodernists, but I retain a more positive and affirmative approach. Still I like Bill's skepticism. The moral of the story is there are many variations of postmodern between affirmative and total skeptic. In this book our bias is obvious.

To be postmodern is to be against racism, sexism, eurocentricism, bureaucracies, and colonialism. As postmods, we try to construct the stories and voices of those that management and organization texts have excluded, marginalized, and exploited through the modernist project. This we do through the **skeptical act** of deconstruction. Every story is a single "**construction.**" **To deconstruct** means that you take a story and look at whose voice is included in the story, who is centered in the story, what are the status differences, what universal, essentializing, totalizing, marginalizing, and privileging claims are in the story (Refer to Appendix A for student examples of story deconstruction).

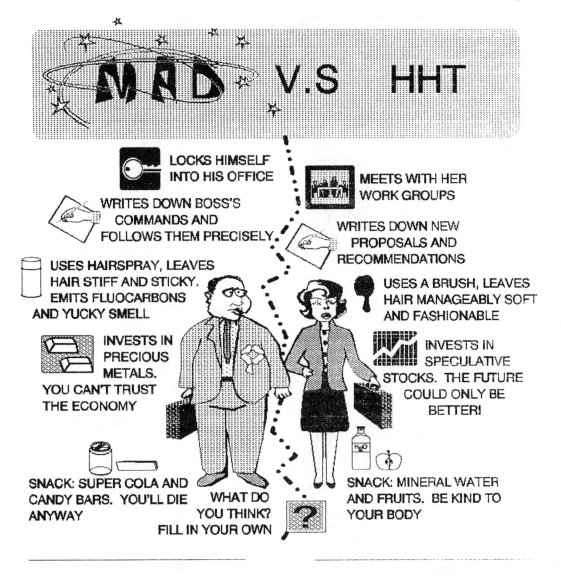

WHAT IS POSTMODERN		
POSTMODERN	AGAINST RACISM	1. Deconstruction Method ❑ Oppositions ❑ Doing the reversal ❑ Questioning the excluded
	AGAINST SEXISM	2. Constructing voices against white male authority
		3. Constructing multi-centers
	AGAINST EUROCENTRIC	4. Less differentiation and status
		5. De-universalizing grand claims
		6. De-essentializing psychological reductions
	AGAINST BUREAUCRATIC	7. De-totalizing simplified histories that exclude
		8. De-marginalizing those left out
	AGAINST COLONIAL	9. De-privileging participation & sharing
		DEFINITION: Postmodern is constructing the stories and voices of those excluded, marginalized, and exploited in the modernist project.

What is Postmodern?

There are as many approaches to postmodern as their are postmodernists.[8] Two approaches to postmodern we will focus on are: the **era approach** (e.g. Drucker, 1990, 1992; Boje & Dennehy, 1992; Clegg, 1990) and the **deconstruction approach** (e.g. Derrida, 1978).[9]

For both era and deconstruction, there are two sides to the story: **affirmative and skeptical.**[10]

SKEPTICAL POSTMODERN I feel manipulated! I feel alienated! I feel damaged![7]	AFFIRMATIVE POSTMODERN I feel healthy! I feel happy! I feel terrific!
1. *Negative World View.* An age of fragmentation, disintegration, malaise, meaninglessness, and societal chaos. Truth is impossible. Man will continue to be alienated, manipulated, and damaged by a cruel and hopeless world.	1. *Positive World View.* Possible to make planning participative, to de-center organizations, to make influence democratic, to let leaders serve (instead of be served), to get to self-control, instead of center-control.
2. *Future.* Overpopulation, genocide, atomic destruction, environmental devastation, explosion of the sun in 4.5 billion years, and the death of the universe through entropy.	2. *Future.* Networks can do better than the central planning, center-organized, hierarchical-led and controlled firms. Old style has not helped counter poverty, starvation, AIDS, drugs, and gang warfare.
3. *Inter-Textualists.* All reality is linguistic convention, arbitrary language practices. "A linguistic habit. Discourse is a disguised power game. Everything is related to everything else in such a tangled way that positing causality is meaningless.	3. *Contextualists.* Organizations are a multiplicity of interpretations, not just one. Why give one plan priority over others? Make plans participative and responsive to customer and environmental needs, not central needs. Stop making diverse people (teams) go through a center. Question authority.
4. *Values.* One value system is as good or bad as another. Ethical choices are just linguistic categories. Give no point of view a special privilege. Rather than a success of Kuhnian paradigms, be done with all paradigms. No view is better than another view.	4. *Values.* Plurality. Some value systems are better than others. Peace is better than war. Environmentalism is better than environmental rape. People valued over corporation. Why privilege male values? Why value profit over mother earth?

Table 1.2

	ERA	**DECONSTRUCT**
AFFIRMATIVE	I. Each era is a paradigm shift that gets progressively better.	III. Deconstructing bureaucratic, racist, sexist discourses will take us beyond exploitation.
SKEPTICAL	II. Each new era gets worse as people are more controlled. Progress is a myth.	IV. Postmodern deconstructions are manipulated to become disguised, modernist discourses of command, control and exploitation.

Table 1.3

I. Affirmative/Era Postmodernism

Postmodernism began in debates in aesthetics, in architecture in the 1960's and moved from there to the humanities in the 1970's. Then the bottom fell out of American industry. Our 1987 merchandise trade deficit was $159 billion and has been increasing each year. Despite prescriptions to get out of manufacturing and enter the service information society, America is losing its competitive edge in the global high-technology markets and our permanently underemployed, increasingly illiterate welfare and homeless populations are growing and growing. What remains a nightmare is that we can not shake our short-term, turn-a-profit-this-quarter mentality. Blaming the worker, while the boss takes yet another fat bonus, is blaming the victim. Are we in an irreversible decline?

Peter Drucker, for example, sees management as going through paradigm shifts from the pre-industrial, industrial, to the postmodern or what he terms "post-business" era. He sees the shift from the "battleship" model of the modernist, factory-bureaucracy: a rigid structure, with every cog fixed in place to do its particular function to the "flotilla" where you have a loosely connected fleet of different types of ships changing formation in response to battle and weather conditions. In the affirmative/era postmodernism, there is a faith in progress through collective action. The industrial revolution may need some regulation of the robber barons such as J.P. Morgan, but the standard of living, the economy, and the nation prosper. For Drucker, as the industrial economy evolved, raw material economy uncoupled from the industrial economy. Manufacturing uncoupled from labor. The location of production and the locale of investment capital in our global economy have uncoupled. The goods and services economy have uncoupled from the money economy. The nation state no longer is the dominant unit of economic life. The postmodern era is the time of the transnational and global enterprise, such as Toyota, out to maximize world market share and destroy enemy companies will to compete.

The Postmodern is a historical movement, just as trade unionism, scientific management, and human relations are historical movements. The postmodern movement recognizes: the liberated role of women and minorities in the workplace; the need to re-skill all workers; the foundation-backbone need for education; the reaffirmation of individualism and entrepreneurial spirit in America; the need to expose subtle bureaucratic control and surveillance mechanisms for what they are and what they do.

The postmodern organizational system is supposed to be the servant of the creative, innovative, and skilled individual, not the dominant and silent elite at the top of the great pyramids taking fat bonuses while laying off millions of American workers made unemployable by years of dependency and de-skilling. Illiteracy is rising each and every year, productivity is falling, earnings are falling, and jobs are getting more scarce. Why should we continue to privilege the voice of industrial leaders and management consultants who have led our nation to ruin?

The promise of postmodern management is to get rid of management. To empower a diversity of people from women, to minorities, to handy-capable, to gays who have been marginalized by center-planned, center-organized, center-led, and center-controlled enterprises. In postmodern management, small is beautiful; temporary coalitions of small groups is power; social problems can be dealt with better by the oppressed than by the bureaucratic oppressors.

Workplace 2000. We are moving from an old modernist or "traditional" model of management and organization into a new era "high performance" era of post-industrialization. For example, the workplace of the year 2,000 will have fully arrived-technology, jobs will be increasingly flexible, and labor-management cooperation will be thematized. A key feature of the workplace will be workforce diversity, including more women in the workforce; more ethnic, cultural and linguistic diversity; and greater variations in educational qualifications and skills of employees.[11]

The Grand Narrative. The critical difference between pre-modern, modern and postmodern is each changes the "grand narrative." In fact, the postmodern is supposed to signal the "death" of the grand narrative, replacing it with a lot of competing narratives. Since postmodern stories are only recently beginning to take shape, postmodern practices exist in a "sea of modernism" (Clegg and Rouleau, 1992).[12] In the modern narrative, scientific management and social science management (human relations) made objects of man. Man was a scientifically controllable and mechanistic instrument. The Weberian project was to rationalize man in a bureaucratic discourse. Big business, like big government must be formalized, standardized, centralized, routinized, and specialized. In the postmodern narrative, man is the victim of a system of so-called scientific categories. He must be set free from his incarceration in the object world. To do this is difficult because man is a willing and unconscious participant in his own incarceration. The postmodern narrative emphasizes the network organization, with flat lines, horizontal coordination, temporary relations between vendors, customers, and workers. In short, hierarchy is discounted. In its place, a very fragmented, temporary, and responsive network obliterates all organizational boundaries. Environmentalism is related to postmodernism in this vein: the modern consumer was a silent partner in the mass consumption process that is destroying the environment. As a backlash, consumers are advocates of recycling product packaging and more environmentally-sensitive consumption.

The Transition to the Postmodern. Increase diversity and celebrate it; ignore the modern machine values; get beyond the cellular life of bureaucracy; freedom from the gaze; change the conversation of Western countries, both its discourse and the subjects of those discourses[13]; to live as a master of one's life rather than a slave to it.[14] For example, after Taylorism spread, it dominated all of bureaucratic discourse. It was assumed that scientific management was enlightened management. Even when the human relations movement challenged this presumption, it made little difference. Planners and executives continued to be the brains, and workers continued to be the hands. Hierarchical supervision and surveillance continued and despite the rhetoric of decentralization, excellence, and empowerment is still centralized. The voice of leadership was privileged and final.

Management is still privileged, workers are marginalized. Training money is spent on management and white collar workers, but not on the people who deliver goods and services. Organizational science, management theory, and organizational behavior are all discourses of control. Turbulent, uncertain, and chaotic forces threaten stability and order, and rational control is the response. "*Managing* is an undisguised code word for (keeping things under) control" (Hawes, 1992: 5). MBO, management strategy and MIS are all about control; all about methods of domination. The primary project of postmodern is emancipation of any oppressed group so they become free agents: free from any form of coercion, especially discursive coercion, knowledge coercion, and normalization (objectification) coercion using social science language and practice.

What is the Postmodern and Post-Fordism? Clegg (1991) argues that modernism characterized the period from Henry Ford to the early 1970s, where mass production and mass consumption dominated society and essentially "worked". Thus the modern was an era in which

"Fordism" or the division and fractionalization of labor was the dominant logic. Mass production, narrow range tasks and jobs, and labor versus management conflict were inherent features of the era. In the Postmodern era, which will be well established by the twenty first century, these bureaucratic management principles will fail. In fact, in this book we have already posed postmodern principles that are the direct opposite of modernist-bureaucratic principles. The inevitable failure of modern principles of management is exemplified in the closing decades of this century by the decline of Western producers and the rise and success of Asian and European producers. Clegg and others argue these Asian organizations use different, i.e. Postmodern organizing principles. In other respects, such as the treatment of women and minorities, dependence on paternalism, Asian organizations are not post-hierarchical at all.

	ERA	DECONSTRUCT
AFFIRMATIVE	I. Each era is a paradigm shift that gets progressively better.	III. Deconstructing bureaucratic, racist, sexist discourses will take us beyond exploitation.
SKEPTICAL	II. Each new era gets worse as people are more controlled. Progress is a myth.	IV. Postmodern deconstructions are manipulated to become disguised, modernist discourses of command, control and exploitation.

Table 1.4

II. Skeptical/Era Postmodernism

The first problem with the era approach, as formulated by Drucker, is that we have not given up our pre-modern roots entirely. The whole progress myth of moving up the social evolutionary chain by injecting larger doses of technology and Japanese management prescriptions is being swallowed, hook, line and sinker by American industry without much challenge, debate, or critique.

Before modernization, could it be that there were management practices that are valuable? Why should we assume that as time marches forward, management has gotten better? Maybe it has gotten worse. Was poverty better before the welfare state, before centralized Housing and Urban Development? Were Americans more entrepreneurial before mass education, mass consumption, and mass production? Why do we privilege modern times?

There is a lot of pre-modern focus on quality, craftsmanship, pride in workmanship, self-reliance, and entrepreneurship that was clobbered by the fusion of Max Weber's functionalist bureaucracy with Taylor's time and motion control and Henry Ford's assembly line. Clearly, Europe kept more of the craftsmanship and craft-guild traditions in its modern work processes than was the case in America. For the Japanese, their pre-modern period was decidedly feudalistic. Their Shogun period of isolationism prevented Japan from living through the pre-industrial growing pains. As a result Japan's approach is a combination of feudalism, industrial bureaucracy, and some concepts such as TQM, JIT, Cycle Time, Empowerment, FMS (Flexible Manufacturing System), etc. that writers such as Stewart Clegg (1990) refer to as a postmodern "form" of organization. The second problem with the era approach is that the pre-modern, modern, and postmodern discourse are all present in today's complex organizations. I am feudalistic, bureaucratic, and postmodern every day. The third problem with the progress era by era model is that history has many voices. Progress for Columbus as Spain colonized South and Central America is one side of the story. The voice of the native South and Central Americans, and subsequently the Mexicans, who were enslaved, tortured, and wiped out in the search for gold is another. Any single-voices statement of history seeks to sustain the benefits and privileges of the majority culture over all other cultures. Skepticism is needed to rewrite history to include the voices of the excluded and oppressed.

The era by era approach is the **"grand narrative"** the single-voiced story that expunges the heroes, stories, and voice of the other: the Native Americans, women, African-Americans, Spanish-Americans, etc. The grand narrative of Marxism has been shattered as the U.S.S.R became the Commonwealth of Independent States. Yeltsin has recently released documents to insure that a greater variety of voices get heard about the age of communism. The grand narrative of Marxism promoted class as the single lens with which to view the struggle of haves and have-nots. Feminists, on the other hand, have argued that it is gender, not class. Culturalist, look at the role of race in the historical transitions and struggles. The point is that history gets sanitized through selective memory and outright exclusion to paint a rather narrow story of society and for our interest the story of corporate America. The problem with the era approach is to determine whose story gets told, that is, whose story is privileged.

Recall our Tamara metaphor. The Mansion with many storytellers telling many accounts with audiences chasing about trying to make sense of it all. In Drucker's approach, the eras are told as a three act play from the point of view of the industrialist. We would like to add other points of view, other stories, other plots, and in the end conclude that much of the history of American management systems is not progressive, it can be regressive. One reason management textbooks, as a rule, leave out the history, is that it is convenient to call management a science, and ignore generations of exploitative behavior. All history is multi-stories, multi-vocal, but only one-voiced when the story is being glossed. Glossing a story toward one point of view privileges one group of tellers, the way the whites in South Africa are privileged, and the Blacks are marginalized. Management is a discursive practice that privileges bureaucratic/modernist discourse over more pluralistic and multi-voiced approaches. Simple formula and programs for administration de-select alternatives and shroud the control and exploitations in the mystic rhetoric of scientific-sounding principles. Deconstruction demystifies the story.

Skeptics argue that Postmodernism is not the same as Third Wave post-industrialism. The post-industrial paradigm was developed in the late 1950's through the early 1970's (Bell, 1973).[15] It was then popularized by Alvin Toffler in *Future Shock* (1970), *The Third Wave* (1980), and *The Powershift* (1990).[16]

> The grand narrative of **Third Wave**—post-industrialism is: give up the mind-numbing, dirty, monotonous work of automated manufacturing in textiles, steel, tire, ship, and auto production, and instead focus on creative, hi-tech jobs in the coming information age of affluence. Factory jobs are boring; we should aspire to service industries and computer-related technologies in the Silicon Valley. The post-industrial story is organized around the theme that prosperity will come from becoming an information age service economy as we work in our "electronic cottages". The information age of the computer will allow new methods of management and new flexible forms (Ad hoc and flex form) to flourish. Following the prescriptions of Third Wave—post-industrialism, America and other advanced capitalist economies began dumping manufacturing industries, in favor of service and high-tech industries. As the electronic industry and recently the computer parts and aerospace industries also started their decline, we were told not to worry, prosperity is around the corner (Winsor, 1992).[17]

Third Wave Burger Flippers. The postmodern skeptical critique of this story asks one important question: if we are a service economy, does this mean we will all be burger flippers, accountants, and insurance saleswomen? At a White house meeting, Alvin Toffler was asked this question by Donald Regan: "So you all think we're going to go around cutting each other's hair and flipping hamburgers! Aren't we going to be a great manufacturing power anymore?" (Toffler, 1990: 67). According to Reich (1983: 207), "one out of every three American workers now depends for his or her livelihood, directly or indirectly, on American industries that are losing rapidly in international competition."[18] And this includes the information industries that were to replace America's manufacturing base.

How do you run giant factories, huge utilities, and Third Wave high tech firms with free self-disciplined people? Obviously, with the breakup of the communist's Soviet Union and the formation of the free market candidate: The Commonwealth of Independent States, the old utopia prescriptions of central planning bureaucracies and ideology and indoctrination, and state surveillance machinery are no longer viable answers.

The Postmodern is the target, but America has been running down the Post-industrial Third Wave path to Obscurity. According to Windsor (1992), and we agree, America is far down the post-industrial path and clawing its way back to the postmodern road.

> It would appear undeniable that we have been on the post-industrial path for some time now, making decisions at both government and industry level that play to the post-industrial scenario . . . On our travel down the path to the post-industrial golden age, we began to notice that the landscape promised to us was not developing according to the itinerary presented by the post-industrial soothsayers (p. 11).

Instead of high-tech jobs, we find foreign investors buying up our entertainment companies, our electronic firms, and have made bids to buy some aerospace firms. We are looking at a post-IBM era, a post-Hughes aircraft era, a post-GM era. If we ever were in an information age race, we are two laps behind the Japanese and Germans. We are eleventh in standard of living ratings and slipping. Some of us want to bring back our product and service leadership by getting back from the post-industrial detour to the postmodern highway.

Like a hearty handshake

Nor, is America likely to build the collective social fabric of a Japan, where government and industry conspire, where consensus structures thrive, and respect for the organization takes on nationalistic fervor. These collective systems do not give people freedom of thought and action that is expected in America. To run big businesses in the future, we have to unleash the individualistic spirit that made America great. We need to radically change our management principles to give a new dignity to the worker.

Americans are less able to cope with today's problems now than at the time of the founding of the 13 colonies. Instead of looking at the causes of our own decline, we are blaming the Japanese for unfair trade practices. It is not the Germans, Japanese, and Koreans that are causing America's decline. It is mismanagement of our own human and economic resources. But, unless we change our educational system, we will continue to slide until we join Great Britain, Spain, and France as "has been" colonialists (You may have your own equally valid and different story).

Skeptics argue that there is nothing sacred about the postmodern era. It is fragmented, disintegrated, alienating, meaningless, vague, devoid of ethical standards, chaotic, and just as controlling and torturous as any era before it. Writers like Baudrillard stress the Nietzchian, dark side of postmodern where happiness is only temporary disruption to chaos and cruelty.[19]

	ERA	DECONSTRUCT
AFFIRMATIVE	I. Each era is a paradigm shift that gets progressively better.	III. Deconstructing bureaucratic, racist, sexist discourses will take us beyond exploitation.
SKEPTICAL	II. Each new era gets worse as people are more controlled. Progress is a myth.	IV. Postmodern deconstructions are manipulated to become disguised, modernist discourses of command, control and exploitation.

Table 1.5

III. Affirmative/Deconstruction

Deconstruction tears a story or discourse apart to reveal hidden assumptions, contradictions, and intent, but typically does not offer an improved, revised version (Rosenau, 1992: xi). However, there are postmodernists who take a more affirmative approach to deconstruction. Feminists, probably have the clearest presentation in deconstructing the white male modernist corporation for its anti-women tendencies in order to suggest an improved discourse between men and women. Joanne Martin (1989)[20], for example, did a postmodern deconstruction of how a CEO of a high tech firm liberated his vice president by encouraging her to have her C-section instead of natural child birth so she could not be away from work as long. He also had the idea of an electronic hookup between the office and her hospital bed.

After the deconstruction, the tearing apart of the story to reveal the hidden traps, the excluded voices, the privileged advantages, then the affirmative postmodernists try to improve on the discourse, revise the dialogue, and strike a new balance of power in the relationships. As we move into the year 2000, with America's diverse workforce, this is a very relevant challenge for us all.

	ERA	DECONSTRUCT
AFFIRMATIVE	I. Each era is a paradigm shift that gets progressively better.	III. Deconstructing bureaucratic, racist, sexist discourses will take us beyond exploitation.
SKEPTICAL	II. Each new era gets worse as people are more controlled. Progress is a myth.	IV. Postmodern deconstructions are manipulated to become disguised, modernist discourses of command, control and exploitation.

Table 1.6

IV. Skeptical/Deconstruction

In skeptical deconstruction, nihilism is the final word. The world is going to hell, and the capitalist, military-industrial complex, despite its rhetoric of progress, is taking us all to hell for the ride. Skeptical deconstructionists are constantly criticized for not going beyond their deconstructive work to propose constructive changes. The rebuttal is that once a change is successful, it becomes a formula which can then be implemented and then transformed into a pattern of exploitation. The utopia becomes a living hell. The voice of the skeptic, while it does not propose solutions, is nevertheless a valid one.

In the 1980's the Excellence discourse of Peters and Waterman (1982) and Deal and Kennedy (1982) became the preferred text of practicing managers.[21] Hugh Wilmott (1992) is skeptical of the excellence literature because "management is urged to become directly and purposefully involved in determining what employees should think, believe or value" (p. 61) by strengthening organizational culture along particular lines.[22] People have to be empowered to think and feel they are autonomous and have control and ownership over their work processes. Improvements in productivity are a result of this empowerment and ownership. As the worker identifies with the company and its products and customers, the individual is also losing the division between personal life, values, and beliefs and the impersonal demands of the organization for greater productivity and quality (p. 63). The skeptics see postmodernism merging with the excellence literature and the Toyota model of flexible production in ways that give the organization more and more dominance and control over the individual's life space. Skeptics conclude that postmodern organizational dimensions such as empowerment and lean production are imprisoning.

What is the Postmodern Critique of the Excellence School? The postmodern critique is (1) Changing managers over to a new language is being used as a way to continue bureaucratic practices, to allow the central and dominant core to control the dependent periphery by changing their language, but not their practices; (2) getting people to give more suggestions and make small win changes to their work life is not really all that empowering or liberating, (3) workaholism is treated as the end all and be all of work life—work faster, shorter cycle times, managers with 100 people reporting to them, round the clock work; (4) the prescriptions and rhetoric are presented without attention to the important historical roots of the practices, such as the fact that Edward Deming brought an important chunk of the quality, zero-defect, measure everything revolution to Japan after World War II at the request of our own government, while we in America spent 40 years ignoring it until there were so many foreign cars, TV's, and VCR's that we had to begin copying the Japanese ways; (5) the post-industrial and postmodern forecasts are an American economy in which 50% of the people will work for small businesses that will network together and sub-contract to remaining large businesses to form a very different economy than painted in the pro-big business practices of the Excellence School; (6) there are Excellence prescriptions that have uncritical and unexplored bureaucratic-machine consequences, such as MBWA (Management By Wandering Around) which can be a surveillance tool of bureaucrats to wander around to gaze at activity of their subordinates. When will the boss wander in? Soon the people are conditioned that the boss is always watching.

The Excellence School is not the same as the Postmodern. Tom Peters has adapted the rhetoric of post-industrialism and Japanese management to push the Excellence approach. Critiques of the first book: *In Search of Excellence* with Bob Waterman, noted that most of the exemplar firms, such as People's Express subsequently failed. Peters' comeback was to suggest that while the organizations had failed, the prescriptions were valid. Most of management academia turned their back on the Excellence project because of this peculiar methodological twist. Tom Peter's reliance on stories to get his points across was also not mainstream quantitative, survey research, laboratory study methodology. Management Academy mainstream did not stop millions of American companies from trying to implement the Excellence approach as a way to survive declining productivity, decreased quality goods and services in our declining economy. Postmodern writers ask for increases in quality, flattening the organizational modern, empowering the people to control their work process, bashing bureaucratic rules that are mindless, going cross-functional, etc.

The Postmodern is not Reducible to Japanese Management! In Japan, communal kinship patterns have been formalized into a net of relationships between paternalistic management who protects worker interests, the boundary of the organization is the whole society (government cooperates with industry; industry cooperates with industry; vendors are partners). Japanese culture is not yet as hegemonic as American culture. Women, for example are very marginalized. The settlement pattern of Japanese transplant assembly plants is away from minority population centers. Clegg (1990) points out that the Japanese patterns of success in business are not easily assimilable into mainstream business management recipes. American principles of management and organization design are quite different. Tom Peters and many others are re-writing the modernist narrative to assimilate the Japanese framework.

It is doubly ironic that America values Japanese management. First, because twenty years ago America thought Japan made cheap, imitative, unreliable products. Second, because Japan imported American quality-control processes and is now teaching Americans a lesson. What Tom Peters and the quality/excellence movement leaves out of the story is the fact that Japan did a wholesale adoption of Taylorism, as recast in the William Deming's teachings, after World War II. General Douglas MacArthur rewrote the feudal, war-lord, narrative in Japan (actually re-wrote the constitution, gave women the vote, introduced land reform, introduced quality control) to transform Japan from a war nation to an economic power. The Japan industrial machine is a modern machine, with a few postmodern parts. More accurately, much of Japan is still agricultural. Only 35% of Japan's employees are part of modern organizations. Most of the small, subcontract companies, the partners to the big Toyotas, Nissans, Hondas, and Sonys are practitioners of more pre-modern practices.

Unions, for example, pride themselves on being skeptical on purpose. While unions are weak in the US and represent less than 11% of the private sector work force, they do have critical voice, even a skeptical voice. Parker and Slaughter (1988), for example, are skeptical of the team approach being advocate as part of the Japanese model of organization that writers such as Clegg (1990) are positioning as postmodern. In the following example, a postmodern rhetoric replaces a modernist rhetoric, while the reality of people's work experience is exactly the same.

MOD DISCOURSE: "the foreman holds a meeting of his group and announces the week's productivity and scrap figures or discusses the latest safety memo. The foreman's "go-fer" takes care of vacation schedules and work gloves" (p. 4).

POSTMOD DISCOURSE: "Hourly workers are organized into teams which meet with their advisor to discuss quality and work procedures. A team leader takes care of vacation scheduling and supplies" (p. 4)

Implications

As postmodern theory makes its inroads into organization theory, it is likely to build a theory of organization that is decidedly affirmative, either in posing a new and more progressive era that has a better socio-technical fit of man and machine or one that looks at changing the discursive rhetoric so that it talks about leaner production, flatter structures, worker empowerment, continuous improvement, and other dimensions identified by postmodernists (Clegg, 1990; Boje and Dennehy, 1992).

The European tradition of postmodern theory, as exemplified in Foucault's reconstruction of the history of discipline and punishment or Derrida's deconstruction method, the postmodern horizon is more skeptical. There are numerous examples, for example in Parker and Slaughter (1988) which show the dysfunctional side of cycle time, continuous improvement, teams, consensus, etc. The contribution of this skepticism is that we are reminded that labeling dimensions of organization as postmodern does not remove the specter of exploitative control of humans by technical, cultural, and administrative fibers. It will be the challenge of American organization theory to not get swept away by mom and apple pie rhetoric as postmodern theory and method makes its presence felt in American organization studies.

Not Just Management, but Finance, Accounting, and Management Information Systems (MIS) are making the transition to teaching postmodern courses, with postmodern textbooks.

Postmodern Finance

Avoiding Irrelevancy in Finance. The following tables are based on conclusions from the Financial Executives Research Foundation.

Postmodernism in Accounting

Objectives of Education for Accountants. According to the Accounting Education change Commission: to become successful professionals, accounting graduates must possess communication skills, intellectual skills, and interpersonal skills . . . Interpersonal skills include the ability to work effectively in groups and to provide leadership when appropriate. . . . They must understand the basic internal workings of organizations and the methods by which organizations change. . . . They should know and understand the ethics of the profession and be able to make value-based judgements . . . Students must be active participants in the learning process, not passive recipients of information. They should identify and solve unstructured problems

---

AVOIDING IRRELEVANCY
Changing Role for Financial Managers.

- ❑ **Global strategy**—for financial systems and services.
- ❑ **Quality and Service.** Financial managers are being asked to accept more responsibility for the achievement of "non-financial" aspects of business performance—such as product quality and customer service.
- ❑ **Customers.** Stream line bureaucratic functions to be more product- and customer-oriented.
- ❑ **Competitive-Team Orientation.** Using financial analysis to enhance the firm's core and strategic competitiveness through customer service, financial leadership, value-added involvement with the management team, and a sophisticated knowledge of the business.
- ❑ **Flexible and Lean.** A trend in corporate America toward leaner, more flexible, and more knowledge-based forms of organization.
- ❑ **New Skill Set for Financial Executives.** Communication and interpersonal skills. These are the skills that business schools are not developing.
- ❑ **Disciplinary Chimneys.** Accounting and finance courses are producing students that emphasize conformity to rules and oversight instead of business problem solving. Students need to "get close to business" by understanding products, markets, competitive strategies, and competitive-team orientation.
- ❑ **Beyond disciplines.** Instead of separate disciplines of accounting, finance, marketing, management, MIS . . . student and faculty must synthesize knowledge.[23]

Table 1.7.

that require use of multiple information sources. Learning by doing should be emphasized. Working in groups should be encouraged . . . Knowledge of historical and contemporary events affecting the profession is essential to effective teaching. It allows teachers to make lessons more relevant and to lend a real-world perspective to their classrooms . . . An attitude of accepting, even thriving on, uncertainty and unstructured situations should be fostered . . . Ability to interact with culturally and intellectually diverse people. . . . Ability to present, discuss, and defend views effectively through formal and informal, written and spoken language (p. 1–7)[24]

Arthur Anderson & Co.
Ernst & Whinney
Arthur Young
Peat Marwick Main & Co.
Coopers & Lybrand
Price Waterhouse
Deloitte Haskins & Sells
Touche Ross

These firms, after also advocating more focused training in interpersonal and communication skills, also recommend these changes in accounting curriculum.

	MODERN Command & Control; Conformance	POSTMODERN "Competitive-Team"
Context: Focal Environment	Corporate/Regulatory	Market
Style of Workplace Organization.	Functional Chain of Command/Fixed routines	Matrix/Integrative
Financial Organization ***Norms:*** Financial Function Mind-set	Oversight/External Accountability	Leadership/Service
Success Criterion	Efficiency/Technical Compliance.	Value-added
Role	Controller/Bookkeeper.	Financial professional/Manager
Source of Status/Legitimacy	Resource steward /Knows the rules /Custodian of the accounts	Business judgement & financial expertise.
Character of Services. Analysis	Internal monitoring downstream/External advocacy	Strategic Upstream, Sophisticated.
Control	Veto power/Arm's length/Technical compliance with External Standards.	Checks & balances maintained collectively by business team.
Accounting	Elaborate, Control laden/Externally driven.	Streamlined/Product oriented.

Table 1.8.

The current textbook-based, rule-intensive, lecture/problem style should *not* survive as a primary means of presentation . . . . Students learn by doing throughout their education much more effectively than they learn from experiencing an isolated course . . . For example, if students are to learn to write well, written assignments must be an important, accepted and natural part of most or all courses. To relegate writing to a single course implies to students that the skill will not be useful throughout their careers and does not require continuing attention . . . Teaching methods must also provide opportunities for students to experience the kinds of work patterns that they will encounter in the public accounting profession. As most practice requires working in groups, the curriculum should encourage the use of a team approach (p. 11–12).[25]

MODERN MIS	POSTMODERN MIS
1. **The Gaze** IS/IT is used to monitor and gaze and thereby control people. Self-gaze occurs as people internalize gaze-possibility. Electronic monitoring of remote work stations.	1. **Gaze-Avoidance** Spatial and temporal diffusion of information to loose & flexible network of semi-autonomous work teams. Opportunity to form flexible networks with electronic mail.
2. **De-skilling.** Rise in #'s of women, temporary workers, non-health plan workers.	2. **Craft Renaissance** With autonomy, people can perfect skills.
3. **Hierarchy Substitute** Managerial hierarchies replaced by IS networks.	3. **Globalization** Traditional organizational boundaries diffused by inter-firm IS nets. Global village of time and space separated work teams working on a project..
4. **Privileged Core.** Periphery is temporary, sub-contractors, and core lives with threat of peripherization.	4. **Freedom for People** Emancipation of less powerful groups from oppressive core. work in indeterminate, flexible networks.

Table 1.9.

Postmodernism in MIS

What M.I.S. has to say about Postmodernism. With the emergence of network organizations in capitalist economies, information technology (IT) and information systems (IS) will change dramatically. The impact of the postmodern on IT will be to make visible previously hidden events, objects and activities (Jones, 1991: 173). IT and IS will be looked at as manifestations of power relations, discipline mechanisms, and surveillance apparatus. IT and IS are not power-neutral. Organizations are decentralizing IT as management hierarchies are replaced by networks with integrated customer and supplier linkages. Some believe IT will further the de-skilling of the worker. Jones suggests a future where at the core of the organization will be a few privileged, stable full time people, while at the periphery, the majority of people will be part-timers, temporary staff, and subcontractors. IS will be crucial to linking this network together. If the periphery is composed of temporary teams and sub-contracting semi-autonomous work units, the traditional bureaucracy will be a thing of the past. IS can facilitate bureaucratic restructuring, reducing hierarchies and distributing information to a wide network of decision-makers. Therefore, the question is: *how centralized and how de-centralized will the network structure be? Will it have a dominant core or be poly-centered?* If the network is centralized, IS can be used to gain more control over a de-skilled work force, customers, and suppliers. Why is it used? What is its historical development and use in a given organization (or inter-organizational, inter-group) network? These are the M.I.S questions to be asking. The next table summarizes the IS/IT differences between modern and postmodern networks and ideas presented by Jones (1991).

❑ THE POSTMODERN BUSINESS EDUCATION ❑

With these changes in management, marketing, finance, accounting, and M.I.S., the need for a postmodern theory of organization and management principles is quite strong in the entire field of Business Administration. The postmodern form is flatter, more diverse, more flexible, more automated, more dispersed, and focuses on narrower niches (customer needs) in the market place. Since the form will be different, the skill set for managers, financiers, MIS specialists, and accountants will be different for planning, organizing, influencing, leading, and controlling.

What are the Trends that are Propelling Us to Postmodern Business Education?

1. Women will comprise over 50% of the work force, but continue to be paid 68% of male wages.

2. Minorities will comprise over 65% of the work force, but continue to be paid less than white males.

3. White males will comprise less than 35% of the work force, but control the majority of high level jobs.

4. 75% of the workers will be dual income families.

5. Illiteracy will continue to grow.

6. Globalization will increase, but America will continue to import more than it exports.

7. America 2000 will become a two class society with 5% upper to upper middle class folks and 95% working class folks; the 21st century will seal the death of the middle class.

8. The computer will make the need for direct supervisors less than ever before and computers will be used to electronically dominate people.

9. With fewer direct supervisors, workers will be expected to self-supervise and therefore do more planning, organizing, influencing, leading, and controlling.

10. Manufacturing will continue to become more flexible, intelligent, and niche oriented, but move to third world nations to save labor and environmental-regulation costs.

11. Over 50% of people work in small businesses.

12. In health care, 26% of the cost is administrative.

13. The administrative and maintenance costs of public housing is so costly that one could take the money spent on public housing projects and house the poor in luxury condominiums in Marina Del Rey, CA.

14. The cold war may be over, but 40 years of a high-tech weapons race spending spree has sucked-dry our education and people-program monies. While US and old-USSR spent $225–250 billion each on war materials annually, the next highest nation spent only $50 billion.

15. The number of people in prisons will double to 900,000 this decade; the two fastest growing professions in America are security and prison guards.

16. 340,000 children are homeless; 30% of two year olds have not been vaccinated; there was a 54% reduction in monies spent on children in the 1980's.

Postmodern in Art and Architecture. One postmodern artist has to be Picasso. In cubism, he represents past, present, and future and multiple perspectives (front, side, back, top views) in one "here and now" canvas. He plays with time and space perspectives. In postmodern architecture you find statements from writers like Baudrillard: Disneyland exists to make LA look normal. Since there is no "real" world, Disneyland is authentic, more authentic that the world around it, that purports to be real. You can see the destructiveness of pyramid architectures such as the "projects" (Housing and Urban Development was an attempt to create modern housing for the poor). Many believe HUD was a way to imprison the poor and separate and segment and bound them away from the non-poor society. The postmodern approach, is exemplified by Jack Kemp who took over a HUD that was riddled with bureaucratic corruption, waste, and practices that imprisoned poor people as a permanent underclass. Kemp's approach to HUD is to empower the poor to control and manage their own housing projects. In order to do this federal HUD is now in a knock down dog fight with local city and state housing authorities. Federal HUD wants the people to control and staff their own services, local Housing

Authority is doing all they can to keep control, keep fat-cat bureaucratic jobs. In HUD and in public as well as private bureaucracies, we are, for example, beginning to think critically about the way bureaucratic discourse "signifies" Women, Blacks, Hispanics, Asians, Indians etc. The language privileges whites, non-women, non-blacks, non-hispanics, non-asians, non-workers, and non-subordinates. Instead of pointing to how one group is categorically different, postmodernists celebrate diversity, plurality, equality, and democracy. It is hegemonic American diversity. To accomplish this celebration it is necessary to point out explicitly how one group is more privileged than another group in the stories and discourse of the modernist organization. In short, postmodern exposes how people are controlled through categorizations in stories and discourse.

❑ SUMMARY ❑

Postmodernism is propelling management education into the 21st century. Pre-modern, modern and postmodern provide the panorama for the adventure. Not just management but finance, accounting and MIS are joining in the postmodern.

The postmodern is not Third Wave post-industrialism. It is not reducible to Japanese management. Neither is the postmodern the same as the Excellence school. The postmodern Project has a different vision. The vision can be skeptical or affirmative. We have opted for the affirmative route. This choice underscores the challenges and advantages of postmodern.

What are the Challenges of Postmodernism? The postmodern future thus appears to include several key features and challenges. First, as managers continue to rely on modern principles, they may be (unwittingly) lowering the performance of employees. Second, the tradition paternalistic, male model or style of organizational management may remain widespread, but it will increasingly be challenged (particularly by women) as the workforce becomes more diverse. Third, the Postmodern will require greater dialogue among diverse subcultures and groups of all types—women, men, Blacks, Asians, Whites, Americans, Japanese, Canadians and others.

What are the advantages of Postmodern Management? First, the postmodern provides an opportunity to enrich management theorizing and practice by embedding management scholarship in broad postmodernist scholarly traditions, particularly European based intellectual traditions such as deconstructionism and semeiotics. This encourages multidisciplinary research and provides a basis for linking management theorizing to general theories of cultural organization. It also encourages the investigation and use of a variety of new and more sophisticated "qualitative methods" for data collection such as story analysis, representation and analysis which can complement present applications of qualitative research on management. Second, postmodern emphasizes cultural knowledge and the national and international context and nature of social organization. Thus, postmodern reshapes the management and organization landscape by moving research away from the organization or individual as a unit of analysis, to consideration of organizations in their societal and cultural context. The Postmodern thus provides an integrative, overarching framework for understanding management and organization. Rather than the specialized, divisionalized pursuit of knowledge, postmodernism argues for integration of the diverse areas composing management scholarship. Third, postmodern views organizations as playing important roles in the crises and critical problems of advanced capitalist society. In adopting a postmodern perspective, one is thus encouraged to address organizationally based social problems which are not often addressed in holistic manner in the management literatures. Fourth, this book extends the current frontiers of management scholarship by incorporating insights from a number of areas outside the core of traditional management research—rhetoric, anthropology, literary criticism, history, and so on. Finally, we argue that an understanding of the postmodernism is essential for the development of theories of the management of social and organizational change which will be needed to "humanize" the social landscape of contemporary and future organizations and overcome or solve the significant problems faced by organizations today.

What are the Emerging Social Issues? The Postmodern as an emerging form of society is of significant general interest to management, since it refers to the social context of management; new and emergent social issues in management including the ongoing management of change, feminist concerns, environmental disasters and corporate crime; alternative and new forms of organizing and managing human resources; the emergence and implications of new technologies; the increasingly global and international nature of business; and the management of an assumedly increasingly diverse work force, to provide a partial list. The Postmodern offers more diverse and pluralistic explanations about the relationship between core and periphery, male and female, majority and minority. There is a strong focus on marginalized social groups resulting from organizational practices that are glossed by modernist theory.

Stories are Political. As America enters a more pluralized and diverse social makeup, the significations, the labels, the categories of social makeup must be challenged to become more equitable, more sensitive, and more accountable. At the same time, if the economic recession, the negative balance of payment, the shrinking middle class, and the other ills continue, there will be great pressure to marginalize more citizens into permanent unemployment categories, like homeless, hard-core, under-employed. In short, in the postmodern era we do not find a utopia. There is a struggle. There are pressures both to privilege the few and to franchise the marginalized. Some significations are more privileged at a given point in history than are others. The study of management stories lets us capture the significations and see how they privilege one group, one practice, one way of thinking over other ways. In this sense, stories are very political: giving one group more language rights than another group. It is necessary to expose the privileged use of categories before we can accomplish meaningful and equal participation of diverse people in the workplace.

Is the Postmodern Management Project Susceptible to these Critiques? Are we, in this book, introducing a new language that will not reform bureaucratic practices, getting managers to give in grudgingly to token participation and token empowerment, getting people to become more fast-paced workaholics, leaving out important pieces of the historical record of management, not attending enough to small business, and worst of all: giving the bureaucrats more tools to stay in power? Probably, but we intend to use stories from pre-modern, modern, and postmodern perspectives to triangulate what are the management practices and principles and show their historical roots.

❑ NOTES ❑

1. Branden, Nathaniel. *Honoring the self: The psychology of confidence and respect*. New York: Bantam Books: 233.
2. Ferguson, Kathy (1984). *The Feminist case against Bureaucracy*. Philadelphia: Temple University Press.
3. Whyte, William H. *The Organization Man*. New York: Simon and Schuster, 1956.
4. Foucault, Michel 1979. *Discipline and Punish: The birth of the prison*. New York: Vintage.
5. Deetz, S. 1992. *Democracy in an age of corporate colonization*. Albany: State University of New York Press.
6. Bullis, Connie and Hollis Glaser. "Bureaucratic discourse and the Goddess: Toward an ecofeminist critique and rearticulation." To appear in 1992 *Journal of Organizational Change Management*.
7. This is what Bill Hetrick always says, whenever I say my affirmations.
8. Rosenau, Pauline *Post-modernism and the social sciences: Insights, inroads and intrusions*. Princeton, N.J.: Princetonn University Press, 1992: 15;
Featherstone, Mike. 1988. "In pursuit of the postmodern: An Introduction. " *Theory, Culture and Society*. 5 (2–3): 195–217.
9. Boje, David M. and Robert F. Dennehy 'Postmodern management principles: Just the opposite of modernist-bureaucratic principles" In Proceedings of International Academy of Business Disciplines, 1992 meetings in Washington D.C.

Drucker, ibid.

Clegg, ibid.

Derrida, Jacques 1978 *Writing and Difference*. London: Routledge and Kegan Paul.

10. Ibid This section is based on Rosenau's categories of affirmative and skeptical, 1992: 109–137. There are, of course other versions of postmodernism.; Agger, Ben 1990 *The Decline of Discourse: Readings, writings, and resistance in postmodern capitalism* New York: Falmer Press; Gitlin, Todd 1989 "Postmodernism: Roots and politics." *Dissent* (Winter): 100–108.; Griffin, David 1988 *Spirituality and society: Postmodern Visions* Albany: State University Press of New York.; Graff, Gerald. 1979 *Literature against itself.* Chicago: University of Chicago Press.; Foster, Hal 1983 "Postmodernism: A Preface." In *The Anti-Aesthetic: Essays on Postmodern Culture*, ed. Hal Foster. Port Townsend, Wash.: Bay Press.

11. Burke, R. 1991. Managing an increasingly diverse workforce: introduction. *Canadian Journal of Administrative Sciences*, 8, 62–63.; Jameson D. and O'Mara. 1991. *Managing Workforce 2000: Gaining the Diversity Advantage.*; Kirchmeyer, K. and J. McLellan. 1991. Capitalizing on ethnic diversity: an approach to managing the diverse work groups of the 1980's. *Canadian Journal of Administrative Sciences*, 8: 72–79.

12. Clegg, Stewart R. and Linda Rouleau. "Postmodernism and postmodernity in organization analysis." To appear in 1992 *Journal of Organizational Change Management.*

13. Flax, Jane 1990. *Thinking Fragments: Psychoanalysis, feminism, and postmodernism in the contemporary west.* Berkeley: University of California Press.

14. Hawes, Leonard C. "Postmodernism & Power/control." To appear in 1992 *Journal of Organizational Change Management.*

15. Bell, Daniel. *The coming of post-industrial society: A venture in social forecasting.* New York: Basic Books, Inc., 1973.

16. Toffler, Alvin. *Future Shock*, 1970; *The Third Wave*, 1980; *Powershift*, 1990. All published—New York: Bantam Books.

17. Winsor, Robert D. "Post-industrial, post-Fordist, or post-prosperity: Talking the post-Fordist talk, doing the post-industrial walk." In review for 1992 issue of *Journal of Organizational Change Management.*

18. Reijch, Robert. *The next American Frontier.* New York: Penguin Books, 1983. See Toffler (1990: 67–80) for his reaction to the burger flipper challenge.

19. Rosenau, ibid.

Baudrillard, J. 1983. *Les strategies fatales.* Paris: Bernard Grasset.

Nietzsche, Fredrich. 1980. *On the Advantage and Disadvantage of History for Life*, trans. Peter Preuss. Indianapolis: Hackett Publishing.

20. Martin, Joanne. 1989. Deconstructing Organizational Taboos: The Supression of Gender Conflict in Organizations. Palo Alto, CA.: Stanford University.

21. Deal, T. and A. Kennedy. 1982. *Corporate Cultures: The Rites and Rituals of Corporate Life.* New York: Addison-Wesley.

Peters, T. J. and R. H. Waterman. 1982. *In Search of Excellence.* London: Harper & Row.

22. Willmott, Hugh. 1992. "Postmodernism and Excellence: The de-differentation of economy and culture," *Journal of Organizational Change Management*, 5 (1) 58–68.

23. Based on Patrick J. Keating and Stephen F. Jablonsky "Changing roles of Financial Management: Getting close to the business."; *Challenge to Management Education: Avoiding Irrelevancy* Published by Financial Executives Research Foundation, Morristown, New Jersey, 1991; See AACSB-sponsored study: "Management education and development: Drift or Thrust into the 21st Century" (McGraw–Hill, Inc., 1988) Lyman W. Porter and Lawrence E. McKibbin; "Objectives of Education for Accountants." Accounting Education Change Commissions: Position Statement No. One. September, 1990.

24. "Objectives of education for accountants." Accounting Education Change Commission. Position Statement No. One. September 1990.

25. "Perspectives on Education: Capabillities for success in the Accounting profession." 1989. New York Arthur Anderson & Co., Arthur Young, Coopers & Lybrand, Deloitte Haskins & sells, Ernst & Whinney, Peat Marwick Main & Co., Price Waterhouse, and Touche Ross.

26. Baudrillard, J. *America* London: Verso.

27. Barely, S. 1983. Semeiotics and the study of occupational and organizational cultures. *Administrative Science Quarterly*, 28: 393–413.

28. Jameson 1991 ibid; Wuthnow, R. W., J. D. Hudson, A. Bergesen, and E. Kurzweil (1984) *Cultural Analysis: The work of Peter L. Berger, Mary Douglas, Michel Foucault and Jürgen Habermas*. London, England: Routledge and Kegan Paul.

POSTMODERN MODEL

	PRE-MOD	MOD	POST
Plan	**CRAFT** Craftsmen Rituals Apprenticeship Fraternal Tales	**PYRAMID** Police Yoke Reports Atomize Monitor Distribute	**NETWORK** Needs Expectations Team 6 W's Organize Responsiveness KISS
Organize	**CREWS** Crews Rough Entrepreneurial Well Knit Community Social	**DISCIPLINE** Discipline Inspection Surveillance Centralization Impersonal Penal Mechanisms Layers Individual Cells Neural Elites	**FLAT** Flat Latticed Autonomous Team-based
Influence	**SOLACE** Solace (fines) Order Lazy Attitude Culture Entrepreneurial	**COMPLY** Conformity Obedience Motivate Performativity Logical Yielding	**INDIVIDUAL** Independent Narcissist De-centered Individual Voices Irrational Diversity Unconforming Affirms the Self Linguistic
Lead	**MASTER** Master Authoritarian Slave Driver Tyrant Elite Ruler	**PANOPTIC** Panoptic Authoritarian Network of Mechanisms Organizational layers Pyramid Inspector Centralist	**SERVANT** Servant Empowers Recounts Stories Visionary Androgenous Networker Team-builder
Control	**SLAVE** Slavery Levels-Classes Arbitrariness Venal Elders	**INSPECT** Impersonal Normative Short-term Goals Pyramid-Surveillance Externally-Driven Conform to Standards Technical Gaze	**CHOICE** Choices Heterogeneity Oppositional Individualism Co-Responsibility Environmental Audit

CHAPTER 2

PLANNING STORIES

WARNING

This material is dangerous to conformity. This chapter does not pull punches or tread lightly. Readers sensitive to the demise of individualism should read carefully.

Road Map

Bob   In the last chapter we gave a broad brush stroke of information of pre-mod, mod, and postmod. Now from that overview, we now want to develop one management function in more detail. We begin with planning and indicate how planning exists in organizations in pre-mod, mod, and postmod configurations. We will provide stories from a variety of time frames: early printing, Harley-Davidson, Taylor and his pig iron, Deming and his work with Japanese planning. But, our voices are not the only voices in this chapter. You will hear from the student voices as well. We think you will be impressed with their presentation and understanding of these concepts.

First, we begin by comparing pre-modernist, modernist and post-modernist definitions of planning. They are contradictory roots that are intertangled in contemporary times.

PLANNING DEFINITIONS

PRE-MODERN PLANNING
Planning is a **Craft**.
C	Craftsmen combined planning, doing, and checking (inspection) into each individual's job.
R	Rituals of work and Rites of passage in the planning of quality work performance.
A	Apprenticeship was a planned progression from "greenie" to apprentice to journeyman artisan in each profession.
F	Fraternal organization of professions dedicated to a steady and gradual improvement of their work quality.
T	Tales telling traditions, customs and beliefs about planning told and retold by storytellers.

MODERN PLANNING
Planning is a **Pyramid**:
P	Police lower level people's time and motions.
Y	Yoke people to their pyramid plan and position.
R	Reports on everyone in the hierarchy so management can gaze their plans and actions.
A	Atomize the pyramid to isolate people into the smallest and most fragmented planning cells.
M	Monitor money, materials, and manpower budgeted for month-end results.
I	Inspect people's MBO's and time schedules for signs of waste and inefficiency.
D	Distribute people, money, material, services, and production into specialized cells to minimize their interaction.

POSTMODERN PLANNING
Planning is a **Network:**
N	Needs of customers get discovered.
E	Expectations of network stakeholders.
T	Team planning among network players.
W	6W's. Who is in the network, where are the resources, what are the goals, wants of each customer, when do customers need their stuff, and wow (is this exciting to customers?)?
O	Organize your network plans.
R	Responsiveness of the network to customers.
K	KISS. Keep It Sweet and Simple: Plan to make customers happy!

Table 2-1.

In this section we here from the student voice. This is how they took the concepts above and implemented them to study Carl's Jr. hamburger chain. Read the brief history to give you some sense of Carl's Jr. They designed in the first table a rating system to assess levels of craftsmanship, rituals, apprenticeship, etc. The higher the number (1–5) the more intense that dimension. Next, the blue team gives us a text of their question and answer sessions with Carl's. The blue team did a content analysis of each discourse to look for combinations of pre-modern, modern, and postmodern discourse. There is a summary table listing their four questions, the three discourses, as well as the team's assessment of how powerful each of the discourse was in the stories and conversation they collected. Note, for example, that in question one, the pre-mod box, there is the word "cr A ft." The capital "A" in "cr A ft" is the Blue team's way of pointing out that the pre-mod discourse centered on "Apprenticeship." If you look at the pre-mod column, the Blue Team believes that 45.3% of the discourse had pre-mod roots. Next, there is a bar chart followed by a pie chart summarizing these overall pre-mod, mod, and post-mod results. The Blue Team illustrates in their analysis the point that in Carl's Jr., as with other corporate discourse, **there are roots of all three discourses.**

❑ HISTORY OF CARL'S JR. ❑

Carl's Jr. have just celebrated their 50th anniversary of doing business. The show all started when Carl and Margaret Karcher purchased a hot dog cart for $326 in 1941. The business continued to prosper and in 1945 the first full–service restaurant, known as "Carl's Drive–in Barbecue" opened in Anaheim.

As they moved into the fifties, they opened the first Carl's Jr. Restaurant in Anaheim and Brea, California. The restaurants were so–named because they were smaller than "Carl's Drive–in Barbecue." With this new restaurant the Carl's Jr. star logo was used for the first time.

By 1960, Carl's Jr. decided to further innovate. Charbroiling was introduced with the opening of the first Carl's Charbroiler in Anaheim. A second Charbroiler was soon opened near Disneyland. By the end of the decade, the company had established 25 restaurants and operation was underway.

In the seventies, the chain began its Northern California expansion with the opening of a restaurant in Santa Clara. The opening of the 100th restaurant was celebrated in 1974. In 1976, the company revenues broke the $100 million mark and the first Carl's Jr. was opened outside of California in Las Vegas, Nevada.

In the eighties, the employee count topped 10,000. In 1984, the Carl's Jr. concept was franchised for the first time. In 1988, an international licensing agreement was signed with Osaka, Japan, and 1989 the first Japanese Carl's Jr. was opened. The company celebrated the opening of its 500th restaurant.

More international agreements were signed in the nineties. They also plan to open restuarants in nine Pacific Rim nations and in the Mexican state of Nuevo Leon. A Carl's "PayPlus System" has been implemented which allows the majority of Californian's ATM cardholders to use their cards at any Carl's Jr. location in the state.

Carl's Jr. is heading into the sixth decade of operations with renewed vigor and commitment to achieving long–term growth for our shareholders.

PLANNING

SCORES	1 2	3 4	5
Craftsmen	There is little inspection of individual's jobs	There is combined planning, doing, and inspection of jobs	The craftsmen are rigid in the combination of planning, doing, and inspection
Rituals	Rituals and rights of passage are dying out of the company	Rights of passage and rituals are well defined for quality planning	Stringent goals for quality are performed before the next step
Apprenticeship	There is an apprenticeship progression, but not followed in depth	Each person follows a progression to knowledge of their job and its standard	Everyone must progress, and does not continue until every level is satisfied fully
Fraternal	Some fraternal ties are evident but limited	Definite fraternal characteristics and starting to decline	A complete, closed fraternal organization with constant quality improvement
Tales	Very few stories shared about the customs and beliefs	Stories are shared amongst the employees	Everyone shares a story in respect to the customs and beliefs
Police	Lower level employees have some restrictions to their time and motions	Employees are set into their roles without their own input	Employees have to report to upper authority to find out what to do and when to do it
Yoke	A flexible pyramid	Each person is joined into the pyramid	People are linked to their specific roles
Reports	Reports flow, but have too little to do with the planning	Reports used in all decisions to some degree	Reports are the main source for planning
Atomize	The pyramid is general and broad	A spectrum of positions for each level in the pyramid	Each person has an exact, isolated position in the pyramid
Monitor	Loose monitoring of materials to influence the planning	Everything is accounted for planning activities	Everyone and everything is budgeted for each month
Inspect	Inspection is limited and minor	Taken seriously to care for all inefficiencies	No waste due to the extreme inspections
Distribute	Interation is limited, distribution of resourses is moderate	Little interaction is allowed to decrease wasted time	No interaction: each person is put into their own cell

PLANNING—*Cont.*

SCORES	1 2	3 4	5
Needs	Aware of customers' needs, but limited	Needs are seen, but at lower ends of the pyramid	The needs are immediately discovered and taken care of
Expectations	Stakeholders are recognized, but their expectations are not	Stakeholders play a role in the planning	Stakeholders' concerns are very important to the existence of the company
Team	Some, but little planning as a whole network of players	Teams are limited to the pyramid	All network players have a role in some team
W 6W's	A few of the W's are a concern in planning	The 6 W's are defined, but need improvement	The 6 W's are an integral part of the planning for the customers
Organize	People are still caught in the pyramid, but try to share their common experiences	Organization of the network share attributes, but not everyone is a part of it	Everyone is organized into flat teams to share experiences and stories
Responsiveness	Customers do not share their stories too much	The customers reshape the company and it responds	The customers carry the company and all planning is responsive to each customer
Kiss	The customer is only satisfied	The customers are happy and serviced accordingly	Customer planning is first and the company sees the purpose of the business is for the customers

	PRE-MOD	MOD	POST-MOD
Q1: What is the training process for your new employees?	The example of the "Mr. Big" video shows a progression through the Company. Each person gains knowledge through each stage. **cr A ft 4** 36%	Through the training process, the employee also see's where he/she fits into the Company. They are joined into this pyramid of positions and shown they move up the ladder of positions. **p Y ramid** 28%	Carl's Jr. is organizing its network players through their training process. They see training as an investment and not as a cost. **netw O rk 4** 36%
Q2: How does an employee progress through the Company?	The board tells every employee what area they have completed. To get a star in an area, a rite of passage must be passed. **cR aft 4** 45%	The managers fill the positions. They are distributing the people into their specialized cells. **pyrami D 3** 33%	The progression comes from both sides working together. The idea is apparent, but the manager has the final word of this team. **ne T work 2** 22%
Q3: What is the chain of command in Carl's Jr.?	Carl's Jr. keeps a family environment from the Karcher family. Carl and Don head the company, and many of the other family members also work in the company. **cra F t 5** 56%	At each level of the pyramid, there are different positions. Each level has fragmented positions to control the responsibilities of each person. **pyr A mid 4** 44%	N/A 0%
Q4: Does Carl's Jr. have a motto or creed that is shared throughout the Company?	Tales like this one are shared amongst the employees to share experiences and to maintain a family environment. **craf T 4** 44%	N/A 0%	The Creed organizes what are the Golden Rules to serve all the stakeholders in the Company. Not only are the customers recognized, but so are the employees and the investors are written down goals which every store k in their back pockets. **net W ork 5** 56%
AVERAGE	45.3%	26.3%	28.5%

netwOrk:
Organize (4) 36%
Carl's Jr. is organizing its network players through their training process. They see training as an investment and not as a cost.

pYramid:
Yoke (3) 28%
Through the training process, the employees also sees where he/she fits into the company. They are being joined into this pyramid of positions and shown they move up the ladder of positions.

crAft:
Apprenticeship (4) 36%
The example of the "Mr. Big" video shows a progression through the company. Each person gains knowledge through each stage.

neTwork:
Team (2) 22%
The progression comes from both sides working together. The idea is apparent, but the manager has the final word for this team.

cRaft:
Rituals (4) 45%
The board tells every employee what are they have completed. To get a star in an area a rite of passage must be passed.

pyramiD:
Distribute (3) 33%
The managers fill the positions. They are distributing the people into their specialized cells.

pyrAmid:
Atomize (4) 44%
At each level of the pyramid, there are different positions (e.g. crew and vice-presidents). Each level has fragmented positions to control the responsibilities of each person.

craFt:
Fraternal (5) 56%
Carl's Jr. keeps a family environment from the Karcher family. Carl and Don head the company, and many of the other family members also work with the company.

Q1: What is the training process for your new employees?

A1: We have a person in each store who is responsible for training our new employees. We are committed to training and it is one of our big areas. Our 'How To' videos are great! There is one where it shows a guy coming into Carl's as a new employee and it shows the stages an employee goes through to get to the different levels, and at the end it shows him sitting at the far end of a long table. At the end of the table there is a name plate with 'Mr. Big' on it then a man in the chair turns. The 'Mr. Big' is actually the employee. This video shows the new employees that they can travel up the ladder to become 'Mr. Big'. That is only one of our videos. We also have case studies and workbooks. We are constantly training on all levels from the counter person to the top. We even have a sixteen week program for people who are hired from outside of the company so they can learn every aspect of the operation.

Q2: How does an employee progress through the company?

A2: It comes from both sides. If the employee wants to move up he can and the manager is there to say like . . . yeah I'll help you get there. In the store is the backroom with a chart with the employee's names on it. Across from the names we put stars to tell which area that employee has done. If you know the cash register and drive-thru stations you would have a star in those sections to say you have done or completed that area. Now if the manager sees that he needs to fill a position . . . let's say assistant manager, then they'll go to the employee and offer it to them. When someone becomes manager, they go through our special training program that deals with different problem analysis or how to deal with the different problems. At each level the person moves up, we have a new training program for them.

Q3: What is the chain of command in Carl's Jr.?

A3: There is first the crew. You know . . . the cooks, register person and so on. Then the shift supervisor has basically has one shift to work with. After the shift supervisor, we have the assistant managers and manager. From the manager we go to the district manager and then the regional director. Finally is the vice-president of operations who is one of seventeen vice-presidents. The other vice-presidents deal with the different resources and so on. Above the vice-presidents are, of course, Don Karcher and Carl Karcher.

netWork:
6 W's (5) 56%
Not only are the customers recognized, but
so are the employees and investors. They are
written down goals which every store keeps
in their back pocket.

crafT:
Tales (4) 44%
Tales like this one are shared amongst the
employees to share experiences and to
maintain a family atmosphere.

Q4: Does Carl's Jr. have a motto or creed that is shared throughout the company?

A4: Yes, here it is (he hands us the card). I've almost got it memorized, and it is what Carl stands by. It says, "Carl Karcher Enterprises will always strive to be regarded as one of the premier organizations in the food service industry. We will earn this regard by consistently exceeding the legitimate and competitive expectations of our guests, our employees, our shareholders, and our franchise owners." You'll find this in every one of our stores probably behind the counter and in the manager's office. You mentioned a creed; I remember when I first joined the company and I went to my first meeting and before it started everyone stood up and said the Pledge of Allegiance and the Prayer of St. Francis of Assissi. It shocked me because I never worked with a company that took a couple minutes out to say the Pledge of Allegiance or a prayer. I felt like I was back in parochial school. At the end of the meeting someone asked if we had any questions and I raised my hand and asked "Do we always start the meetings with a prayer?' and they said "Yes, we do. Do you have a problem with it?" I replied "No.", but I think it's these kinds of things that are different about Carl and how his company is run.

THE CARL'S JR. PLANNING SUGGESTION BOX

AREAS THAT THE NAVY BLUE TEAM LIKED:

❑ Carl's sees training as an investment, not a cost.

❑ Goals are clearly stated posted where everyone can see them.

❑ Customers are recognized as an important factor to the company.

❑ Carl's uses fresh vegetables and high quality meat products.

SUGGESTIONS FROM THE NAVY BLUE TEAM:

❑ Try to implement more teamwork between entry-level and managers.

❑ Some levels of the organization need to be eliminated.

❑ There is evidence of a panoptic gaze, this could lead employees to think that Carl is checking up on them when he visits the restaurants. This should be examined and eliminated where appropriate.

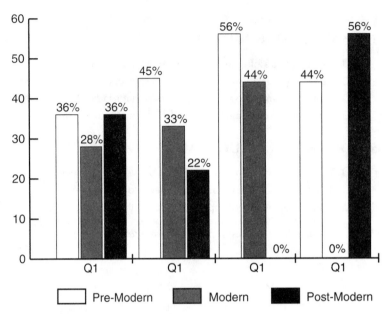

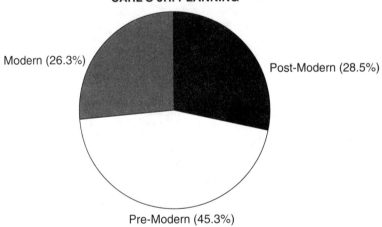

❑   THE HARLEY-DAVIDSON STORY   ❑

Harley Davidson

In this section we want to give you a pre, mod, and postmodern rendition of the history of Harley-Davidson.

The Craftsmen: Pre-modern Roots

In Milwaukee, Wisconsin, William G. Harley, a 21 year old draftsman/toolmaker lived next door to Arthur Davidson, a 20 year old pattern maker. These two neighbors used their mechanical skills to cast an engine, build a carburetor out of a tomato can and complete their first bike in 1902.

Production. By 1906 their yield of 50 motorcycles necessitated a second building measuring 20 by 80 feet. This edifice was financed by a beekeeping uncle. In 1907 Bill and Arthur not only produced 150 machines but also incorporated with all the shares purchased by the 17 employees. By 1910, 3200 cycles were built. Harley-Davidson had arrived.

Quality. From the beginning, Bill and Arthur did not ask: How cheap can we make our motorcycles. Rather they asked: How good can we make them. The price was $200. Skilled motorcycle craftsmen built the bikes—one at a time.

Whatever had to be done was handled by whoever was available with the know-how and time. As Walter Davidson, Bill's brother said, "We worked every day, Sunday included, until at least 10 O'clock at night. I remember it was an event when we quit work on Christmas at 8 o'clock to attend a family reunion."

People. A deep feeling of comraderie existed among the employees. The family-like atmosphere prompted a group of employees to help out a fellow employee who lived in a tarpaper shanty with his wife and two children. Bill Davidson, well known for his kindness and generosity, supplied the materials and the employees built their fellow worker's family a fine two-story house.

The commitment to its employees was also shown in 1933 when sales took a tremendous dip. H-D kept as many employees working as possible, even if they only could work two days a week.

Service. Reduced cycle time is a term that we hear today. Harley-Davidson epitomized this concept in 1916. In March of that year, the War Department requested immediate shipment of a dozen of motorcycles. They arrived in two days ready for use. Later that month a second order was delivered in 33 hours. The motor cycles were equipped with a sidecar gun carriage to serve as a platform for mounting a Colt machine gun. Bill Harley had developed this unique feature.

In 1917, H-D started a service school to teach repair procedures. By the end of the war, H-D was training 1000 riders and mechanics per month.

By the end of the decade, H-D inhabited 400,000 square foot plant with 1,800 employees producing 22,685 motorcycles and 16,095 sidecars.

Dealers. Dealers were received as partners. This relationship was strengthened in 1933 when sales slumped steeply. Industry-wide sales fell to 6,000 units and H-D captured 3,700 of them. Walter Davidson worked closely with dealers to organize rallies, tours, polo tournaments, races, field meets, rodeos, picnics, jamborees, and to start clubs. New riders were attracted and existing enthusiasts remained active and interested. Other services to dealers included:

- ❑ Increased advertising—especially economy of operation, longetivity, and ease of maintenance.
- ❑ Promoted accessory sales- rider jackets, lubricants, parts, luggage racks.
- ❑ Public relations campaign to address negative image of cyclists. H-D also promoted the use of mufflers.
- ❑ "The Enthusiast" magazine was distributed to 500,000 people a month.

Results By 1934 sales moved up to 10,000 units a year and this pace continued into 1940's. During World War II, thousands of military riders were introduced to Harley's. In fact, H-D produced 90,000 military models in various configurations. The production of military cycles also allowed spare parts to be made available to keep the civilian worker alive.

The Corporate Bureaucracy: The Modern Roots

Harley-Davidson came home from World War II. In 1947, H-D resumed full civilian production of motorcycles, parts and accessories. The bikes were updated 1941 models but with hydraulic shocks and added chrome. Accessories included-batteries, leather saddlebags, chrome dress-up, ladies wear, and leather helmet and goggles. But the most noteworthy introduction was the first black leather jacket with chrome zippers and snaps, belted waist and zippered sleeves. Cycles continued to be improved. For example, the 1958 Duo-Glide was unquestionably the most comfortable and beautiful motorcycle on the road.

Pressures. In 1969 the Japanese entered the big bike market. H-D faced a hostile take-over and opted to merge with AMF (American Machine and Foundry). H-D now had to answer to a higher corporate authority.

The fact that Harley-Davidson was no longer worker of its destiny became evident soon after the addition of the AMF corporate logo to all 1971 motorcycle gas tanks. As AMF Harley-Davidson, the loyal enthusiasts were rankled. That summer, AMF flexed its corporate muscle even more by naming a new president. For the first time in 68 years, someone other than Davidson sat in the president's chair.

AMF provided H-D with the necessary funds to modernize new tanks, frames, and fenders. AMF also built a new facility in York, PA. to focus on the production of the V-twin heavyweight models. But despite all of AMF efforts at making the company a more powerful and efficient manufacturing force, many riders and enthusiasts blamed AMF for a number of H-D shortcomings. Relationships between managers and workers were adversarial. Management was at odds with suppliers and dealers were muffled.

Problems surfaced where bikes had either missing parts (one-half the bikes) or in some cases even excess parts. AMF paid $1000 per bike for inspection to check for complete parts. When the bikes produced vibrations or oil leaks, many loyalists would repair the problem. Others, however, bought Japanese bikes. The outcome of the customer dissatisfaction was reflected in the drop in market share of big bikes from 75% in 1973 to 25% in 1983.

The Emerging Postmodern Discourse

To mark the 75th anniversary of Harley-Davidson in 1977, a group of the executives toured the United States following seven different routes and they travelled 37,000 miles to visit 160 H-D dealers. The fact that the people who ran the company were all riders—and that they would take two weeks out of their busy schedule to get on the road and meet their customers—impressed everyone who came in contact with them.

This anniversary ride for customer input was instrumental in stimulating a group of H-D executives to purchase the company from the AMF. In June, 1981, H-D returned to private ownership. The euphoria, however, was shortlived as demand fell by 33,000 units while at the same time Japanese exports soared.

Thus, in September 1982, H-D petitioned the International Trade Commission (ITC) for tariff relief from Japanese manufacturers who were building up inventories of unsold motorcycles. President Reagan put added tariffs on all imported Japanese cycles 700 c.c. or larger for a five year period ending in April 1988. The tariffs began at 45% in 1983 and were scheduled to decline to 10% in 1987, before being phased out.

One of the major factors in the ITC in decsion to recommend tariffs was the fact that Harley-Davidson had started a major revitalization campaign in the late 1970's. The campaign was aimed at improving efficiency and product quality through programs of just-in-time manufacturing, employee involvement and statistical process control. Dealers were also included in the just-in-time inventory management so they could cut their own costs. H-D was particularly concerned about its 120 suppliers since the roster had just been pruned from 320. "We buy 50% of the dollar value of our motorcycles from the suppliers, says Garg E. Kirkham, Harley's manufacturing manager. "So improvements we made (internally) only got us half way".[1]

Under this umbrella of protection its market share soared to 63% in large motorcycles, up from 23% in 1983. The plunge of the dollar after 1985 also helped.

Sales results were reflected in the award of a contract from the California Highway Patrol in 1984, after 10 years of buying from competitors. H-D continued to win contracts in 1985, 1987, 1988 and 1989.

In 1983 H-D not only gained import protection but also formed The Harley Owners Group (HOG) to refocus attention to customer satisfaction after the sale. HOG membership swelled to 90,000 in six years.

The tariffs gave H-D time to complete revitalization which began in late 1970s. The fact that the tariffs were declining acted as a motivator to accelerate the transformation.

Harley-Davidson regained its health so quickly that it asked Washington to eliminate tariffs a year early. The move was unprecedented. No other American company had asked for removal of import protection. The press hailed the request as one of the best public relations moves in history.

In 1991 H-D had 62.3% market share in the big bike category(850 c.c and larger). It had 31% of the street bike market; second-seller Honda had 26%. By way of contrast, in 1985 Honda had nearly 47% of the street-bike market, with Harley a paltry 9.4%.

In 1992 Harley's sales have been constrained by capacity. The company has a new paint facility and two new assembly lines about to open, but for now it cannot make more than 70,000 bikes a year. And

Harley-Davidson Triad

Statstical Operator Control (SOC)

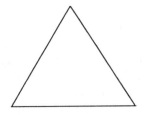

Employee Involvement
EI

Just-in-time
JIT

it exports about 40% of them. Many of the exports are to Japan. Other exports are to Korea where the Korean National Police proudly display their spit-polished Harleys.

Harley-Davidson is America's only surviving motorcycle manufacturer. It pictures itself as soaring like an eagle in touch with customers, workers skilled in process control, and an organization on the path of self control.

"If you can persuade your customers to tattoo your name on their chests they probably will not shift brands". Robert W. Hall said at the Indiana University School of Business, referring to buyers of Harley-Davidson motorcycle.

The next display was contributed by the Gold Team to illustrate the pre-mod roots of discourse.

Craftsmen combined planning, doing and checking into each individual's job.

What methods of inspection do you follow?

Rituals of work and Rites of passage in the planning of quality work performance.

How do the employees' jobs change from day to day?
How is monotony on the job avoided?

Apprenticeship was a planned progression from "greenie" to apprentice to journeyman artisan in each profession.

Do employees start at the lowest level and work their way up?

Fraternal organization of professions dedicated to a steady and gradual improvement of their work quality.

Are all employees working towards a steady goal?

Are they trying to improve the quality of their work?

Tales telling traditions, customs and beliefs about planning told and retold by storytellers.

Our Story!

❑ PRE-MODERN PLANNING ❑

In the pre-modernist period, people planned and inspected their own work. Work was a dignified craft practiced by artisans in fraternal guilds and in the case of Harley-Davidson, tinkering and inventing in the family garage. In feudal times, youth entered work as apprentices and conformed to very strict norms and disciplines of behavior for seven to fourteen years before becoming journeymen. They were expected to practice the protestant ethics of hard work, thrift, and independent-self-reliance. Journeymen could practice thrift and self-reliance to become masters of their own shops and proud members of their fraternity. In the case of the printing industry, they were expected to respect the secrets of their brethren and pass down the secrets of their craft to their devil's apprentices.

Pre-Modern Printing

There is a difference between craft planning and modern business planning. A craftsman, after a decade of apprenticeship became a journeyman. He learned to take the raw materials and plan fine printing. He could plan a job and carry it out from start to finish. Planning was part of his craftsmanship. His own artistic style went into the choice of type faces, the design of each character, their fitting into a line, their layout on a page, the mixtures of inks, and the binding. The stories of the craft era supported a worship of high quality workmanship, an ancient economy of artistic performance, and a noble heritage. Stories gave work practices meaning.

How to Read Stories

When you read stories, look for the pre-, mod, and postmodern roots of concepts that are interwoven in the story. Stories convey not just experience, but whole ways of thinking about management relationships, quality, pride, and planning. People at work tell each other stories all the time, and as you make them your own, you internalize the **voice** of the storyteller. *Voice* is a point of view, a narrator's or storyteller's perspective on reality. The more *voices* in a story, the more points of view and perspectives are brought into the discourse. Each *character* in the story can represent alternative voices. Refer back to our *Tamara* model of many storytellers with many voices telling stories in the storytelling organization. **In each story you read and hear, ask yourself whose voices and which characters get *privileged*, and which voices and characters get *marginalized* (do not get a voice of their own). [Note: Each new term is defined in the glossary at the front of the book.]**

What has this to do with planning?

Have you ever been asked to implement a plan where you had no voice in developing the plan, or then deciding how it would be implemented? If you have, did you feel controlled, unable to alter the parameters of the plan to fit your own unique needs at work, unable to fit the plan to your own uniqueness as an individual. Stories are often plans or visions about the future, about how relationships should be transformed in the future, about a particular scenario that will come into play.

The Gutenberg Bible Story

Gutenberg looked in the mirror one morning and saw a reflection of a hand-scribed bible and said: "Oh that I could but express upon vellum, that which I see in this glass!" He decided then and there to make the best quality bible ever; one so fine it could be passed off as a hand-scribed bible.

"I will work in secret and cast metal type, mix special inks, and hand-peg the type into these chases. Then, I will press the type onto paper using a converted wine press. I could be burned at the stake." He worked secretly for ten years. His production practices were of such high quality that his Mazarine Bible would stand as best and most perfect quality workmanship that could not be improved for the next four hundred years.

Gutenberg was no businessman. "I have a plan. Since the church has a monopoly on Bible scribing, I think they will not take kindly to my inventing a way to do in a few weeks, but takes them many months to do. I will keep the news of this invention secret and get a partner to sell my bibles." Jean Fust and Johanne Gutenberg decided together to pass their printed bibles off on an unsuspecting clergy as original hand-scribed copies. "We will not put a date on them either." Fust and Gutenberg's one apprentice, Peter Schoeffer had all workmen from then on swear an oath of secrecy to never divulge the practices of their Black Art.

Between 1455 and 1457, Fust sold bibles to the clergy for 60 crowns. Scribes charged as much as 500 crowns for their products. The invention of the Black Art soon was suspected. It was not a threat because it could conceivably put clandestine scribes in monastic orders out of work, rather it was thought to be the contraptions and the work of the Devil himself. As the bibles were sold, clergy asked: "How could Fust supply so many bibles so quickly, each copy looking so much like the others, selling for such a low price, and how did he get his ink so brilliantly red? Surely, he has sold his soul to the devil!" They had never seen such a hue of red and never seen scribes produce Bibles that were alike in every minute detail. Surely Satan's blood has been used. The story went that Fust had sold his soul to the devil. This story is one source of the legend of "The Devil and Doctor Faustus."

Jean Fust feared the bible would not sell well and wanting to keep any profit to himself formed an unholy alliance with Gutenberg's apprentice, Peter Schoeffer. Jean Fust's brother, Nicholas, was the judge and gave his brother possession of all the printing inventions, including the racks of set type to produce more bibles. The apprentices of Fust and Schoeffer were from the city of Mentz. They kept their oath of secrecy until their city was sacked in 1462 by Archbishop Adolphuse of Nassau. Fust's printing office was destroyed and during the commotion, apprentices went to Rome, Cologne, Basle, and Strasburg to start their own businesses. They carried the secrets of the Black Art with them and formed a fraternal order of secret apprenticeship practices and a reverence for quality that would last four centuries.

Unfortunately, and as the story goes, like most printers Gutenberg was more of a craftsman than a businessman. He had let Fust take everything and he died poor trying to do some odd printing jobs.[2]

Deconstruction: Affirmative and Skeptical.

1. *Quality is job one.* Gutenberg initiated the quality revolution into printing. Each printer was a skillful artisan who practiced his craft with a sense of aesthetics: an appreciation for taste and beauty in their choice of type faces, margins, inks, paper, and binding. Setting type and printing pages and doing bindery were fine arts more than they were technical productions.

2. *Business and Craft do not mix any better than water and ink.* The story gives credence to the craftsman's attitude that business people will take their skills, tools, and craft away from them. In the modern age, they used the linotype machine and the computerized typesetter and laser scanned press to do just that. But, Gutenberg had used his machine: reusable type and the printing press to put the Scriptoriums out of business.

3. *Do not trust your Devil's Apprentice.* The story demonstrates that an apprentice can swear an oath of secrecy, but take your training and use it to put you out of business. In all trades there are strict periods of highly disciplined and ritualized apprenticeship before a person is admitted as a journeyman into a trade. Drinking, gambling, and hazing were not invented by fraternities, they were sacred practices of the printer's rites of passage.

4. *Printing was a Noble Profession.* For four centuries, printing was a noble occupation. In a time when none but the clergy and the nobility were taught to read and write, you could learn these skills in a print shop as a Devil's apprentice. Benjamin Franklin was apprenticed as a printer and went on to franchise ink and printing companies.

5. *Stories.* Stories convey the aesthetic practices, the hierarchy of apprentice, journeyman, and master printer. A hierarchy that was based on the perfecting of one's own skill; doing quality workmanship.

6. *Stages of Technical Evolution in Printing.* Scriptoriums flourished from 1100 A.D. until Gutenberg's invention. Monks collected tithes and offerings to finance their work (Timperley, 1977)[3] In 1457, Gutenberg brought automation to scribes working in scriptoriums. In the mid-1800's, the hand set type production process would be supplanted by the hot type process of the Linotype machine. Linotype picks up brass slugs and casts lines of lead type for composition. Wooden presses with their loose joints and hand operation were replaced in the industrial revolution by metal presses with motorized parts. The machine was faster, more efficient, less expensive, but it separated man from the aesthetics of his work.

7. *Gender Roles.* By the mid 1950's, computerized typesetting was introduced and a predominately male occupation become gender-balanced. Women were bindery-girls. With the computer age, women who had worked as secretaries took over the computer keyboards. Modernization had done its thing: de-skilled a profession so it could lower wage rates to the bare minimum. Women were paid less than half what the men had been paid.

8. *Sovereign Control of Printing.* Sovereign monarchies had no burning desire to educate the masses. Scriptural critique was heresy and classical works were profane until the Enlightenment. You could be burned at the stake for merely possessing a Wyclif Bible. The masses were more governable when they were illiterate. When William Caxton set up the first press in England in the autumn of 1476, he cautiously and wisely selected a Chapel attached to Westminster Abbey. He located his shop where his customers would be and where he could get symbolic ecclesiastical protection from accusations that he was using a contraption of the devil.[4]

9. *Use of Physical Torture to Discipline Printers.* The infamous "Star Chamber" in England was a punishment court to control who did printing and what was printed. More than one printer was tortured and executed for printing anti-government or blasphemous material.

Pre-Mod Roots of Quality, Individualism, and Pride

Quality did not begin with the Excellence movement of the 1980's. Quality was a very pre-mod outlook. Individualism and pride in one's craftsmanship also has pre-mod roots.

Aesthetic Harmony and Mechanics. First of all you look at the mechanics. The mechanics have to be excellent. Type composition correct, the spacing and that sort of thing exact. No glaring errors and that sort of thing. The press work was to be workman-like and inking even and uniform. After the mechanics are satisfied then you look for the aesthetic detail, the suiting of the typography to the subject, choice of type and size of type, the amount of space between lines. The use of initial letters, display lines and that sort of thing have to harmonize with the subject matter and with the type face being employed. [Boje, 1983, DH-5].

Individualism. It really is true that the compositors carried a stick in their back pocket. They knew that they could get up from wherever they were and strike off down the road. And they could walk in, if they were good at what they were doing and show a guy that they could set type and have a job in five minutes. So they were rather independent. [Boje, 1983. EL-6].

Pride in My Craft. With a craft you take pride in creating something . . . like an artist in effect making something . . . somebody will give you some garbage copy like this. It's just a bunch of hand scratches, some napkin they blew their nose on and when you're through you'll have a nice looking printed piece. It could be a menu, a broadside, it could be a flyer, or a business form or whatever. Look what I've created! . . . I have a printer's eye. I can look at something and tell things, although I'm not a pressman. . . . Some of the printers, just love the work I do because I can take this garbage copy and make it look nice because of the typographic skill I've developed over the years. [Boje, 1983, ER-11, 12].

Deconstruction: Affirmatives

1. *Planning.* In the craft-based work culture, planning was done by journeymen who were spiritually devoted to their craft. They learned to plan in their long years of apprenticeship. They had pride in their ability to plan a job from beginning to end, to do a job with a sense of artisan style and quality. The Chapel was a system for disciplining the work process, including the work planning. Poor planners got solaced (fined).

2. *Aesthetics.* Printers in the craft tradition knew the aesthetics of their work. They planned with a sense of aesthetics.

3. *Pride.* These stories reveal the sense of pride these crafts people took in their work.

The "Tailboard" Planning Sessions*

Sue   "There were once tailboards on the trucks where the crew would meet and the foreman would specify the task for the day. Now they no longer have the tailboards, but the meeting at the beginning of each day is still called tailboard session. We are doing some training to make the meetings more participative."

Mike   "What does participation mean? It actually [is] just a temporary role switch.

Sue   "Yes

Mike   "Participation means let someone else be authoritarian.

Sue   "Yes, in essence.

Don   "You know that's a really interesting dilemma because it doesn't usually mean asking questions. Like let's make sure. What's your opinion? How should we handle this? Got any ideas?

Sue   "Not usually . . .

Doug   "The appraisals will say: "holds good tailboard sessions.

Boj   "Is that right?

Don   "Oh Yeah. There are good and bad tailboard sessions . . .

Deconstruction of Tailboard Planning Story

1. The work crew and the supervisor were responsible for tactical planning.

2. The supervisor while authoritarian, was himself, once a crew member, and therefore respected crew member input, while keeping the final say for himself.

3. *Genders.* The story reveals that crews were a male society. Sue, as a woman, gives several indications of how different the male culture is from her own, and the work she has to do to cross the male boundaries.

*Source: Edison Story Sharing Session, 10–14–1983

Other Pre-modern Examples

It was not just printing that planned around the journeyman system, it included masonry, carpentry, cabinet making, church window making, ship building, mining, and even utility crews.

With the industrial revolution came the modernization of the planning function. People other than the work crew and a supervisor planned the work. Management scientists trained clerks to plan the time and the movements of the workers. Human Relation, social scientists planned the social and group dynamics of the corporation. These two movements: scientific management and human relations, marked an end to the individual work ethic and the dawn of modernist planning.

Modernist planning is blueprinting all the work tasks and administrative procedures to combine workers, machines, and capital to deliver goods and services. Modernist planning combines bureaucratic administration and the mass production factory assembly line into one formula for business success. The industrial revolution model of this combination was Henry Ford's Model T assembly line. Modernist planning is the pyramid atop a factory: layers of management levels, in functional boxes, with workers distributed in cells in the production function doing ever more specialized and mindless tasks, while their heritage of craft and quality atrophied. In the end, the brains plan, and the workers do the hand work.

❑ PART I: FACTORY PLANNING ❑

Part I covers scientific management of factory planning, Part II covers administrative management of the bureaucratic pyramid.

Modern Printing. In modern business planning, with the results of industrial revolution, printers became mechanics, not craftsmen, and these mechanics worked as specialists in a strict pyramid. They are so specialized they can not plan any work at all; they can not recognize quality; they can no longer learn the entire work process from start to finish. The stories of quality and planning were no longer relevant, transmitted, or remembered. In fact, as technology and pyramids combined to make work fractionated, mind-numbing, and routine, workers were no longer trained to plan. In printing, for example, they were trained just enough to feed paper to machines, to oil machines, to pace themselves by the rhythm of the machines.

Quality planning was taken out of the hands of craftsmen and given to financial planners. MBA's were hired to plan; they put all the specialized pieces back together again. As printing went from scriptoriums (hand scribing workshops) to hand set type, to hot type (Linotype

PYRAMID

P
Police
lower
people's
time
and motions

Y
Yoke
people
to their
pyramid plan
and position

R
Reports
on everyone
in the hierarchy
so management
can gaze their
plans and actions

A
Atomize
the pyramid
to isolate people
into the smallest
and most
fragmented
planning cells

M
Monitor
money,
materials
and manpower
budgeted
for month-end
results

I
Inspect
people's MBO's
and time
schedules
for signs of
waste and
inefficiency

D
Distribute
people, money,
material, services,
and production
into specialized
cells to minimize
their interaction

P   How are employees watched over?

Y   Are employees encouraged to step up to the next level?

R   Must all levels of employees report to management on their plans and decisions?

A   Are employees grouped together in small groups to get things done?

M   How is money, people and material allocated each month to meet short term goals?

I   Are people on a daily schedule to make sure no time is wasted?

D   Are workers broken down into groups to do specialized tasks and avoid interaction with one another?

machines invented by Ottmar Merganthaler in 1884 to pick up individual brass slugs and lock them together into a line of type that was cast into lead) to cold type (Late 1950's, computers with font libraries in electronic memory)—the stories changed. Stories are tied directly to technological change.

Why is man managed like a machine? Man began to be molded by the organization machine. He had to fit in, be specialized, and be routinized in order to be a rhythmic cog in the corporate machine.

The Modernization Narrative

The story of modernization is one of prosperity being attained by the application of Adam Smith and Frederick Taylor planning procedures. Man did not need to be a skilled journeyman, if you took his or her work and planned it so each individual did a very minor fraction of the total work process. In printing, modernization began with the introduction of the Linotype machine.

Hand—Hot and Cold Type

Hand Type becomes Hot Type that becomes Cold Type
From Hand set to Hot Metal type

I always ran a machine. I was an operator. I've never been turned on to hand set. There are guys, they think that's the greatest thing in the world. It's classic. It's what Gutenberg invented and they like to hand peg. I was never turned on to it. I can do it. I'm a little slow at it now. I'd have to get my speed up. Yet, Linotype, you know, is a form of automation. You're automating a process by a great degree. I like the Linotype, yet I've never been in love with hand set. I'm not ecstatic by setting type by hand. [Boje, 1983, ER 7, 17].

From Hot to Cold Type Removed Skills

The people who ran Linotype machines were a hundred times as skilled as these people sitting on computer keyboards. The people sitting on computer key boards know how to run that computer. The people that were sitting on a Linotype machine were finished full typographers. They understood type faces, the legibility of open faces, the proper face for certain types of jobs. They knew how to make up a job, to actually make up a page that was legible and attractive. You can teach people to run a typewriter, but its not the same at all [Boje, 1983 EL-3].

From Production to Business Planning

Preparation is the early slogan of the successful business man, and we can not apply that slogan any too soon if we could march with the victorious army of those who lead in their respective lines of business . . . proper *management is a science,* an application of common sense principles, combined with accurate knowledge of one's business . . . [successful printer is a man] "who is willing to specialize," who has "weekly conferences with the foreman of each department," and who is "looking after the training of . . . apprentices."[5]

From Prideful Planning to No Pride at All

There are men working on proof presses who could not set a stick-full of type. There are men on the case who couldn't lock up a four-page form so that it would fold correctly, much less determine the margins. . . . Perhaps this all makes for efficiency, but while this has made it possible for a trade shop to become a profitable business, it has taken something out of the art of printing—there no longer seems to be that pride that accompanies the creation of a well designed job.[6]

From Production Planning to Business Planning

One of the constant discussions is you should know more what the hell happens in the plant. Well, I'm not interested. That's what I hire people for: to make sure the production gets out. . . . Owners rarely, if they're building a plant the size of (3 million plus) get involved the way they did years ago. . . . The printer in the old day was production-oriented, not business-oriented [Boje, 1983, BL-24].

The Sons of Printers are not Printing

I think the business person is running the good shops . . . [New owners] didn't grow up into the business the way you found in the olden days. Father to son, passed on constantly, but I don't think that happens today. Its a rarity that you find that—the son. Now my sons are in the business, but they're working a different way than I worked. . . . My youngest son does research and development . . . his interests are different than mine were at his age. My other son runs [the business]. His interest is in selling . . . in creativity, not what happens in the production [end] of the plant [Boje, 1983, BL #4].

From Hot Type to Cold Type: The Hell Box

I guess the big change came at about 1974, because everybody was getting into phototypesetting and we were doing hot metal. So we bought one machine . . . and so gradually over the next three or four years we were changing over to phototypesetting. So at this point we do maybe 2% of our work—is hot metal and the rest of it is phototypeset. . . . We once had 35 men working with hot metal in two shifts. We've cut that to ten people on one shift with photo-composition . . . I had a lot of interesting experiences in the hot metal, because I . . . ran a Linotype machine . . . I did a lot of hand set, pulled proofs. All those things. In phototype, I haven't really—I learned to run the first machine that we got and since then I haven't really been active in the operation. . . . I'm not that keyed for all the modern equipment and so on. . . . The national (Typography International Association for Employers) had a sort of a retirement sort of thing when a member had been a member for a long time and he retired and this was known as inducting him into the "hell box." Do you know what a hell box is? A hell box is where you throw your broken hand type . . . when it isn't any good anymore . . . Someone would get up and make a little speech about so and so and so and so and so who are now retired into the confines of the "hell box" and they give them a diploma or something. That's about it. [Boje, 1983, BB #25].

From Hot to Cold Machines

I guess it would be heresy to say this today, but I've always considered a computer a very boring instrument and it is not intrinsically user-friendly. There is nothing natural about sitting at a TV screen and watching electrons move across your phosphorescent-coated surface. That's not intrinsically friendly to a human being. That's a basically unnatural, plastic instrument. You can't see an electron move. O.K., you can't pick it up and look at it, hold it, stick it in your pocket or your ear or kiss it or whatever you want. You can't do that. These machines are cold! [Boje, 1983. ER-10]

From Male to Female Work Culture

It's different now with the girls. Back then a job would come in and he was the foreman, you know, and I'd get it from the customer and I'd give it to one of the operators and say "O.K., this is what its going to be, this is what they want." He'd wander off in the back and after a while he'd come back it'd be set and it would be right. He says: "These girls, I've got to mark every single line. They can't create anything. They're good typists. They're fine on manuscripts. They can't do that (pointing to a finely done piece of printing), create things, make it look nice. . . . we had to know and do it and do it right and get it more or less right the first time. "Ah, the girls now a days don't know that. You see they're not printers, we are printers." We were part of a community—I'm a printer—like Benjamin Franklin, he wanted that on his tombstone. First and foremost he is a printer. B. Franklin—Printer. And I'm a printer. . . . But, the girls that are in it now, aren't. They're word processors and key board artists and what not like that, but they're not printers. They never have been and they never will be. . . . Printing classically is a masculine operation, which is one reason I like it. Primarily masculine. There weren't many women in the print shop. There were always bindery girls. But in the print shop there were not that many women. [Boje, 1983. ER-11, 13, 14, 22–23].

From Craftsmen to Modern Technicians

We still use the term craftsman but I'm trying to get them to change that. Because I don't think its true at all. They're not craftsmen anymore. They're "graphic arts technicians" because they're dealing with electronic devices . . . he doesn't go up there and adjust those ink fountains by eye or look at the paper and say no I need a little more ink here. No, he looks at an electronic reading and adjusts it. That's the big change. . . . If we had to do it by hand I doubt if we could. I don't think we have these skills left today. There are a few people but not too many. Its more and more becoming a technical process rather than a craft process. [Boje, 1983. TH-3,8]

Your Identity is your Machine Part

We're all printers. Well a printer has to have ink in his veins. If that's the case then the "typo" has lead in his ass. Cause he likes to sit. Operators, comps, and floor men were all referred to as "typos" because they worked in the composing room and were in a different category from "pressmen" or "bindery men." The "operator" ran the Linotype machine. An "M.O." or "machinist operator" took care of the "machine" in the larger shops. The "comp" or the "floor man" made up the forms from the type he got from the operator. He did this on a "bank," a bench set aside for this purpose. A "combination man" could do both: set type on a Linotype and make up the forms. The "pressman" operated the press and the "bindery man" or "bindery girl" put the printed material together. [Boje, 1983: 14].

From Minor League Technocrats to Techno-phobics

I'll tell you quite honestly my biggest fear was that I still had people that were basically mechanical. You know they were still craftsman. They were to some extent very minor league technocrats. . . . I really thought we would have the technical phobia of this press (a new and ultra-modern web press with computerized consoles and laser scanners) and so I made the determination that I wasn't going to progress any of the people off my existing presses into the press. [Boje, 1983. RG-5].

Deconstruction

1. *Nostalgia.* It is easy to become nostalgic for a work community and a technology that was with us for four centuries in the case of hand set and one century in the case of hot metal. Nevertheless, the skill levels have fallen, the fractionating of jobs into little cells has increased, and the pride and commitment of workers has decreased with each new wave of modernization. In our nostalgia, we should not overlook the fact that we have also ushered in a viable role for women (but not equal pay) and shorter work hours and work weeks.

2. *Stories.* The stories reflect people's concerns with technological change. Some storytellers gave up on progress. They preferred the pace and community of the past. Other storytellers spoke of adopting business as priority and quickly abandoning their production-identity.

3. *Scenarios.* Each story gives its scenario. It explains a transition that is taking place and a forecast.

4. *Decline of Nobility.* The implicit message is that as modernization took place, printers became a less noble, less skilled, less regarded class of people. There are many dualities in these stories. The women are less skillful than the men they replaced; the business types are more noble than the production-oriented types; the more modern printers are more valued than the less modern printers; production printers are more stigmatized as a group, less intelligent, less educated, less successful than the business types; old timers with more skill are more noble than new-comers, mostly females, who have less skill; cold type is better than hot type which is better than hand set type which is better than scribing; artists are better than mechanics.

5. *Machine Language.* With modernization man and woman are defined by their machine position, their machine label, and their machine role. The categories were typo, operator, comps, floor men, machine operator, combination man, bindery man, and bindery girl. Note that women are not women they are girls and they occupy the lowest rung in this classification system.

6. *Progress.* As modernization took place, from hand set to hot type to cold type and finally to laser type, the craftsman did not progress at all. At each juncture, many craftsmen in one technology did not progress to the next wave of modernization. Their skills were out-dated and they were phobic about the newest technology. In the end, the worker is the victim of *planned* obsolescence. Over time an all male culture became a male-female culture. We have assumed that modernization freed man from the boring

work, so that s/he could be more creative. Yet, in pre-modern crafts, there was pride in a skilled and artistic and self-planned performance. The progress toward modernization is a movement away from aesthetic gratification.

Taylorism and Modernist Machine Planning

In the early 1900's, Frederick Winslow Taylor (1856–1915) was the hero of the modernist planning movement. He was the radical revolutionary of his time. Taylor objected strongly and passionately to the impediments to excellence being caused by the "pre-modernist" era. In the pre-modernist phase of industrial history, the trade unions, craft apprenticeship systems, and a managerial class antagonistic to workers and unions dominated capitalist societies. Taylor pointed out the extensive goldbricking or what he termed: "soldiering" going on in the pre-modern firms. His plan was to pay workers more in order to motivate them to increase production. He planned time and motion of each specific work task according to scientific principles. He also wanted leaders to be scientific, rather than individualistic. In 1873, Taylor worked as a supervisor for Midvale Steel Company. His story reveals his theory. We want to analyze the stories told by Frederick Taylor as he set out to evangelize his scientific method of work planning to a country that was already well along the path toward modernization. Taylor is one hero of the Modernist movement.

The Schmidt Pig Iron Story

[Scientific planning increases Bethlehem Steel pig iron production processing from 12 1/2 to 47 1/2 tons (106,400 pounds or 1156 pigs) per man per day (each pig iron weighs 92 pounds)]

"Schmidt, are you a high-priced man?"

"Vell, I don't know vat you mean."

"Oh yes, you do. What I want to know is whether you are a high-priced man or not."

"Vell, I don't know vat you mean."

"Oh, come now, you answer my questions. What I want to find out is whether you are a high-priced man or one of these cheap fellows here. What I want to find out is whether you want to earn $1.85 a day or whether you are satisfied with $1.15, just the same as all those cheap fellows are getting."

"Did I want $1.85 a day? Vas dot a high-priced man? Vell yes, I vas a high-priced man."

"Oh, you're aggravating me. Of course you want $1.85 a day— every one wants it!. You know perfectly well that has very little to do with your being a high-priced man. For goodness' sake answer my questions, and don't waste any more of my time. Now come over here. You see that pile of pig iron?"

"Yes."

"You see that car?"

"Well, if you are a high-priced man, you will load that pig iron on that car to-morrow for $1.85. Now do wake up and answer my question. Tell me whether you are a high-priced man or not."

"Vell—did I got $1.85 for loading dot pig iron on dot car to-morrow?"

"Yes, of course you do, and you get $1.85 for loading a pile like that every day right through the year. That is what a high-priced man does, and you know it just as well as I do."

"Vell, dot's all right. I could load dot pig iron on the car to-morrow for $1.85, and I get if every day, don't I."

"Certainly you do—certainly you do."

"Vell, den, I vas a high-priced man."

"Now, hold on, hold on. You know just as well as I do that a high-priced man has to do exactly as he's told from morning till night. You have seen this man here before, haven't you?"

"No, I never saw him."

"Well, if you are a high-priced man, you will do exactly as this man tells you tomorrow, from morning till night. When he tells you to pick up a pig and walk, you pick it up an you walk, and when he tells you to sit down and rest, you sit down. You do that right straight through the day. And what's more, no back talk. Now a high-priced man does just what he's told to do, and no back talk. Do you understand that? When this man tells you to walk, you walk; when he tells you to sit down, you sit down, and you don't talk back at him. Now you come on to work here tomorrow morning and I'll know before night whether you are really a high-priced man or not."

. . . Schmidt started to work, and all day long, and at regular intervals, was told by the man who stood over him with a watch, "Now pick up a pig and walk. Now sit down and rest. Now walk—now rest, etc. He worked when he was told to work, and rested when he was told to rest, and at half-past five in the afternoon had his 47 1/2 tons loaded on the car. And he practically never failed to work at this pace and do the task that was set him during the three days that the writer was at Bethlehem. . . . He received 60 percent higher wages than were paid to other men who were not working on task work. One man after another was picked out and trained to handle pig iron at the rate of 47 1/2 tons per day until all of the pig iron was handled at this rate, and the men were receiving 60 percent more wages than other workmen around them (Taylor, 1911).[7]

Deconstruction.

1. The workman was carefully selected by Taylor from other work-men to be responsive to the new wage system and to possess the physical skill to do the work. Taylor believed that if you increased a man's pay he would give you more work output if you could remove the man from the peer group influence of his work group.

2. The scientific method was used by having a more educated man assess and then plan all the work tasks for Schmidt. Schmidt no longer plans his own work. After Taylor evangelized his scientific methods to American management, workers were never allowed to plan their own work.

3. There is a science for planning the handling of pig iron that was obtained by observing Schmidt before the new time and motion procedures for pig iron handling were implemented. It was believed that scientific study of a job could uncover the most efficient way to do a job and management types could then impose the patterns on a less skilled worker.

4. The task of the planner is to classify, tabulate, and reduce the knowledge of the worker to a set of rules, laws, and time and motion formula—a science of pig handling that can be used to plan the actions of other men. Science was used to rob the worker of job knowledge by defining that worker as inherently stupid and lazy.

5. The task time and motions are being planned and regulated scientifically. Organizations became very mechanical machines to control people's time and motions—to control their bodies—in the service of production efficiency.

6. *Dualities.* According to Taylor, Schmidt is like an uneducated gorilla who is incapable of understanding the scientific arts of the mechanical sciences underlying each work task Schmidt performs. Therefore, separate out all planning tasks and locate them in the hands of another, more educated college man. The duality here is Schmidt is dumb, scientists are smart. Taylor's characterization of Schmidt as a gorilla is similar to the way defense attorneys portrayed Rodney King.

Taylor's Planning Principles

1. Replace rules of thumb with scientific work planning using time and motion studies, PERT (Program Evaluation and Review Technique) and Gantt charts and time tables.

2. Plan harmony in group actions, rather than discord by keeping workers in very small crews and having managers and clerks plan all work in advance, letting owners profit by savings of scientific work planning.

3. Plan cooperation of human action, rather than chaotic individualism by putting the planning job in the hands of clerks.

4. Plan maximum worker output, rather than peer-restricted output by setting worker quotas by the "best men" standards.

5. Develop all workers to the fullest extent possible for their own and their company's highest prosperity by paying people by their productivity.[8]

Table 2.2.

Midvale Steel Story

"Now, Fred, we're very glad to see that you've been made gang-boss [said one of the workers]. You know the game all right, and we're sure that you're not likely to be a piece work hog. You come along with us, and everything will be all right, but if you try breaking any of these rates you can be mighty sure that we'll throw you over the fence."

The writer told them plainly that he was now working on the side of the management, and that he proposed to do whatever he could to get a fair day's work out of the lathes. This immediately started a war; in most cases a friendly war, because the men who were under him were his personal friends, but none the less a war, which as time went on grew more and more bitter. The writer used every expedient to make them do a fair day's work, such as discharging or lowering the wages of the more stubborn men who refused to make any improvement, and such as lowering the piece-work price, hiring green men, and personally teaching them how to do the work, with the promise from them that when they had learned how, they would then do a fair day's work. While the men constantly brought such pressure to bear (both inside and outside the works) upon all those who started to increase their output that they were finally compelled to do about as the rest did, or else quit. No one who has not had this experience can have an idea of the bitterness which is gradually developed in such a struggle. In a war of this kind the workmen have one expedient which is usually effective. They use their ingenuity to contrive various ways in which the machines which they are running are broken or damaged—apparently by accident, or in the regular course of work—and this they always lay at the door of the foreman, who has forced them to drive the machine so hard that it is overstrained and is being ruined. And there are few foremen indeed who are able to stand up against the combined pressure of all of the men in the shop. . . . The Superintendent accepted the word of the writer when he said that these men were deliberately breaking their machines as part of the piece-work war which was going on, and he also allowed the writer to make the only effective answer to this Vandalism on the part of the men, namely: "There will be no more accidents to the machines in this shop. If any part of a machine is broken the man in charge of it must pay at least a part of the cost of its repair, and the fines collected in this way will all be handed over to the mutual beneficial association to help care for sick workmen." This soon stopped the willful breaking of machines.

. . . Once or twice he was begged by some of his friends among the workmen not to walk home, about two and a half miles along the lonely path by the side of the railway. He was told that if he continued to do this it would be at the risk of his life. In all such cases, however, a display of timidity is apt to increase rather than diminish the risk, so the writer told these men to say to the other men in the shop that he proposed to walk home every night right up that railway track; that he never carried and never would carry any weapon of any kind, and that they shoot and be d———.

After about three years of this kind of struggling, the output of the machines had been materially increased, in many cases doubled, and as a result the writer had been promoted from one gang-boss-ship to another until he became foreman of the shop. For any right-minded man, however, this success is in no sense a recompense for the bitter relations which he is forced to maintain with all of those around him. Life which is one continuous struggle with other men is hardly worth living. His workman friends came to him continually and asked him, in a personal, friendly way, whether he would advise them, for their own best interest, to turn out more work. And, as a truthful man, he had to tell them that if he were in their place he would fight against turning out any more work, just as they were doing, because under the piece-work system they would be allowed to earn no more wages than they had been earning, and yet they would be made to work harder (Taylor, p. 50–2).

Deconstruction

1. In the pre-modernist system of trade unions, there was no differential pay for performance. Taylor's modern revolution was to pay people according to their work output, not by their trade.

2. In the pre-modernist period, 20 to 30 trades subdivided labor into distinct specialties. Men were more committed to their craft brothers than to demands for management to work faster. Taylor wanted to modernize the work place by giving management more control over the work tasks, the scheduling of tasks, and the scheduling of workers to a given task.

3. In the pre-modernist system, workers retained control over the knowledge of their craft, the timing of their work, the motions of their body, and the tools of their trade. They were craftsmen. The modernization of the work place resulted in the deskilling of the worker to a few tasks on the assembly line.

4. In the pre-modern work systems, the workmen got together to plan just how fast each job should be done and how much production was allotted to each machine throughout the shop. In this way, they opposed the efforts of any manager to speed up production because increases in production did not mean increases in wages and their experience was that when output increased, members of their brotherhood got fired. Workers who rate-busted were penalized by other workers. The modernization of the workplace labeled this goldbricking or what Taylor called "soldiering" (putting the needs of the brotherhood ahead of economic output).

What does Taylor contribute to Machine Bureaucracy? Taylor is not only the "father of scientific management," he is also the "father of modern times." Charlie Chaplain is his "son" in the movie "Modern Times." Taylor's formula for success transformed the workplace into a systematic, rational, deliberate, scientific, and planned—modern machine. In the machine the worker is as good as their cycle time (time to complete a task of work) and a leader does not need to be bold or charismatic or tough: they are just cogs in the modern machine: called by the machine to deal with system-exceptions. Taylorists replaced the pre-modern apprentice system of craft-based unions with the scientific training of time and motion engineering.

How was Schmidt's Work Planned? For example, Schmidt, the Bethlehem Steel pig iron worker, was studied at length, along with the other pig iron laborers.

If Schmidt had been allowed to attack the pile of 47 tons of pig iron without the guidance or direction of a man who understood the art, or science, of handling pig iron, in his desire to earn his high wages he would probably have tired himself out by 11 or 12 o'clock in the day. He would have kept so steadily at work that his muscles would not have had the proper periods of rest absolutely needed for recuperation, and he would have been completely exhausted early in the day. By having a man, however, who understood this law, stand over him and direct his work, day after day, until he acquired the habit of resting at proper intervals, he was able to work at an even gait all day long without unduly tiring himself.

Now one of the very first requirements for a man who is fit to handle pig iron as a regular occupation is that he shall be so stupid and so phlegmatic that he more nearly resembles in his mental make-up the ox than any other type. The man who is mentally alert and intelligent is for this very reason entirely unsuited to what would, for him, be the grinding monotony of work of this character. Therefore the workman who is best suited to handling pig iron is unable to understand the real science of doing this class of work. He is so stupid that the word "percentage" has no meaning to him, and he must consequently be trained by a man more intelligent than himself into the habit of working in accordance with the laws of this science before he can be successful. (Taylor, p. 59).

What was Taylor's Formula for Management and Worker Harmony? Taylor's prescription for workers and employer to split the gains from increased worker productivity is the same prescription that the Japanese have brought to the marketplace since World War II. Both recommend investments in training and development to increase the pace of work (the Japanese call it "cycle time") and double the output of each man and each machine.

Why was Taylor Controversial? Frederick Winslow Taylor advocated the maximization of **time and motion** productivity through the application of scientific principles. Taylor believed management and worker interests were in harmony because "the principal object of management should be to secure the maximum prosperity for the employer, coupled with the maximum prosperity for each employee" (p. 9). Taylor wanted to pay men better than they were getting in exchange for increasing the productive efficiency of each worker. The planner did the thinking and the worker did the labor.

Was Taylor a Revolutionary? Taylor, the revolutionary, appeared before congressional hearings to explain why his methods would not rob employers of their judgment and discretion; why unions would not be toppled; why workers would not be laid off in mass when productivity doubled. Taylor is the hero of modern scientific management: what we are calling the "modernist" movement.

Three major challenges to planned work principles were presented to Taylor when he appeared in front of Congressional hearings or did public presentations:

1. Increasing output per worker would put people out of work. Working at full pace would harm the brotherhood of workers by throwing brothers out of work. It is better to curtail output.

   Taylor's response: Increasing output, reduces cost, which in turn increases consumption. Increases in mechanization have put more and more people to work.

   Taylor's story: "It evidently becomes for each man's interest, then, to see that no job is done faster than it has been in the past. The younger and less experienced men are taught this by their elders, and all possible persuasion and social pressure is brought to bear upon the greedy and selfish men to keep them from making new records which result in temporarily increasing their wages, while all those who come after them are made to work harder for the same old pay" (p. 22).

2. It is in the interests of managers for workers to need close supervision in order to protect manager's jobs.

   Taylor's response: Workers work at a slow, easy gait, even though it is against their own best interests because management pays the energetic and the lazy man the same wage. They will restrict machine output to keep the production targets from increasing.

   Taylor's story summarized: Managers are ignorant of science and have surrendered the workplace to the workers. They let workers decide the best way to do a given job. The worker has the final responsibility to do each job as he sees fit. Managers could, in fact, train workers in the sciences of how to do their jobs better and workers are indeed not capable of understanding those sciences. Managers were letting workers select people for their own crews. The job of the manager is to develop the science of how to do work and help the worker assume responsibility for work results. Now, management tries to get workers to produce, but does not train them in the sciences and does not pay them any more for their increased output. This is why pre-scientific management is characterized by warfare between workers and management.

3. Rule-of-thumb methods practiced by workers are protected by trade unions to insure union survival even though they are inefficient.

    Taylor's response. Educated men of science are better able than ignorant workers to set up the procedures, movements, and schedule for a job. The rule of thumb procedures are controlled by work crews that value the brotherhood of workers over increased productivity.

Story of Shoveler Planning

At Bethlehem Steel there were about 600 shovelers. A scientific study was conducted to design shovels for different types of materials and tasks.

In order that each workman should be given his proper implement and his proper instructions for doing each new job, it was necessary to establish a detailed system for directing men in their work, in place of the old plan of handling them in large groups, or gangs, under a few yard foremen. As each workman came into the works in the morning, he took out of his own special pigeonhole, with his number on the outside, two pieces of paper, one of which stated just what implements he was to get from the tool room and where he was to start to work, and the second which gave the history of his previous day's work; that is, a statement of the work which he had done, how much he had earned the day before, etc. . . . yellow paper showed the man that he had failed to do his full task the day before, and informed him that he had not earned as much as $1.85 a day, and that none but high-priced men would be allowed to stay permanently with this gang. . . . So that whenever the men received white slips they knew that everything was all right, and whenever they received yellow slips they realized that they must do better or they would be shifted to some other class of work.
Bob: I recall a shovelling experience where the straw boss said, "Fill your shovel or fill your jacket." Partial *load* means you file out the *door*.

The Modernist Planning Unit. Dealing with every workman as a separate individual in this way involved the building of a labor office for the superintendent and clerks who were in charge of this section of the work. In this office every laborer's work was planned out well in advance, and the workmen were all moved from place to place by the clerks with elaborate diagrams or maps of the yard before them, very much as chessmen are moved on a chess-board, a telephone and messenger system having been installed for this purpose. In this way a large amount of the time lost through having too many men in one place and too few in another, and through waiting between jobs, was entirely eliminated. Under the old [pre-modern] system the workmen were kept day after day in comparatively large gangs, each under a single foreman, and the gang was apt to remain of pretty nearly the same size whether there was much or little for the particular kind of work on hand which this foreman had under his charge, since each gang had to be kept large enough to handle whatever work in its special line was likely to come along. (Taylor, p. 68–9)

Critique of Taylorism

The problem is Taylor gave all the managers the head work of planning, organizing, influencing, leading, and controlling. Workers got to do all the boring, repetitive, rhythms of the machine. Engineers trained inspectors and clerks to control quality, rather than training workers in the sciences of quality control. Workers became machines who could be adjusted, incentivized, trained and selected to work at a faster tempo. Taylor's planning squeezed the maximum productivity out of every second and out of every space on the human chess board, but made the worker park her brain at the door.

What the Japanese flexible production system is teaching us is that the worker who participates in the planning, organizing, influencing, leading, and controlling produces more with higher quality and lower costs (less waste). The work is not planned for uneducated Schmidt's, it is planned for intelligent workers.

Taylor saw that in the craft age of pre-modernist, the man was first and the system was second. In the scientific modernization of corporate life, the system became more important than both craftsman and leader. In the postmodern movement, the system is returned to its subordinate place with respect to man.

"The best management is a true science, resting upon clearly defined laws, rules, and principles, as a foundation" (p. 7).

The difference between modernist and postmodernist planning is in who the planning is for. In the pre-modern apprentice organization, bosses plan for the workers, but workers were responsible for the quality of their work. In Modern times, if workers do plan, they only plan to meet the needs of bosses, the clockwork direction of the planning clerks, to meet the quotas and standards of the system. The system plans and the worker acts. In the postmodern organization, everyone at every job, no matter what level, thinks, plans, and works hard to make the customer happy.

Summary

What are the two elements of Modernist Planning? Answer: Time and Space. By planning, we allocate resources: people, money, services, production, and social auditing in time and space.

Time. After Taylor initiated modernism, planners continued to pre-plan tasks into parallel time intervals, evenly spacing workers, supervised in smaller groups, and all controlled by time-tables. At the end of each time interval clerks inspected the results and workers who were slower were paid less and sent back to slower work gangs, services that were botched got paid less, and so it went. The time table was inflexible, like the machines and shovels that were more important than the humans that were governed by their rhythmic movements.

Space. Planners move the shovelers about like men on a chessboard, using elaborate diagrams or maps of the yard space. Planners put people into their spaces at precisely the right times. We are standing in the space of a modernist enterprise. Space is also divided between shovelers and superintendents. High spaces go to bigger supervisors. Parking spaces are reserved for high status executives. Employees who serve customers walk farther from their parking spaces, eat in distant cafeterias, work in windowless office cubicles, and stand in line to receive their shovels.

Taylorism, is but one side of the mechanization of man. Taylor is the father of machine bureaucracy. There is a second, more ubiquitous form: **service bureaucracy,** which we will examine in the chapter on influence.

❑ PART II: THE MODERNIST SERVICE BUREAUCRACY ❑

Modernist planning is rooted, not only in the factory model, but in the service bureaucracy (usually government) as well. Bureaucracy is part of both service and product organizations. Bureaucracy and scientific management were compatible allies in the de-skilling of pre-modern men and women. Every organization has some bureaucratic discourse.

Henri Fayol (1841–1925)

In 1916 he published *Administration Industrielle et Generale.*[9] He is the father of **Administrative Principles of Management.**

FAYOL'S 14 PRINCIPLES
1. **Division of Labor.** This is the classic division of labor prescribed by Adam Smith. Division of labor reduces the number of tasks performed by a job unit to as few as possible. This improves efficiency and effectiveness because it allows for the simple but rapid repetition of specialized effort.
2. **Authority and Responsibility.** Authority is the right to give orders and the power to exact obedience. Responsibility accrues to those who have position authority. If you have responsibility, you must also have commensurate authority.
3. **Discipline.** There must be obedience and respect between a firm an its employees. Discipline is based on respect rather than fear. Poor discipline results from poor leadership. Good discipline results from good leadership. Management and labor must agree. Management must judiciously use sanctions to ensure discipline.
4. **Unity of Command.** A person should have only one manager and receive orders from only one manager.
5. **Unity of Direction.** The organization, or any subunit thereof that has a single objective or purpose, should be unified by one plan and one leader.
6. **Subordination of individual interest to the general interest.** The interests of the organization as a whole should take priority over the interest of any individual or group of individuals within the organization.
7. **Remuneration of Personnel.** Workers should be motivated by proper remuneration. Remuneration levels are the function of many variables, including supply of labor, condition of the economy, and so on.
8. **Centralization.** Centralization means that the manager makes the decisions. Decentralization means that the subordinates help make the decisions. The degree of centralization or decentralization depends on the organization's circumstances.
9. **Scalar Chain.** Managers in hierarchical organizations are part of a chain of superiors ranging from the highest authority to the lowest. Communication flows up and down the chain, but Fayol also allowed for a communication "bridge" between persons not on various dimensions of the scalar chain. The "bridge" would allow subordinates in different divisions to communicate with each other—although formally they were supposed to communicate through their bosses and through the chain of command.
10. **Order.** There is a place for everything, and everything [everyone] must be in its place—people, materials, cleanliness. All factors of production must be in an appropriate structure.
11. **Equity.** Equity results from kindliness and justice and is a principle to guide employee relations.
12. **Stability of tenure for Personnel.** Retaining personnel, orderly personnel planning, and timely recruitment and selection are critical to success.
13. **Initiative.** Thinking our and executing a plan. Individuals should display zeal and energy in all their efforts. Management should encourage initiative.[10]
14. **Esprit de Corps.** "In union there is strength." Union builds harmony and unity within the firm. This harmony or high morale will be more productive than discord, which would weaken it.[10]

Table 2.3.

Henry L. Gantt (1861–1919)

A disciple of Taylor, Gantt joined Taylor ad Midvale Steel Company in 1887. He invented the "Gantt chart" as a way to schedule work crews across a series of tasks. The chart breaks time into time-events (milestones) which are then related to the production sequence of deliverable projects. Gantt wanted to pay workers a bonus if they completed their milestones on time. Supervisors would get bonuses based on how many of their people completed work by deadline.[11]

TASKS	WEEKS											
	1	2	3	4	5	6	7	8	9	10	11	12
Read Text	x											
Pick 4 Firms to Study	x	x										
Design questions	x	x	x									
Divide up interviews			x									
Schedule interviews			x	x								
Conduct interviews				x	x	x	x	x	x			
Write up results						x	x	x	x	x		
Edit report								x	x	x	x	
Submit final draft												x

Table 2.3. Gantt Chart for a Course Project.

PERT (Program Evaluation and Review Technique). PERT was developed by the Special Projects Office of the US NAVY, with help from Lockheed and the Booz, Allen & Hamilton consultants for work done in 1958 on the Polaris Weapon System. The tool has been computerized and is used to this day throughout the Aerospace industry. PERT is a network tool for flow charting the production process to display what people, materials, and tasks will be networked and how long each task will take to complete. Notice the similarity to the Gantt chart.

1. Brainstorm a list of all tasks to be completed.

2. Determine how long (time elapsed) each task will take to complete.

3. Identify who will complete each task.

4. Specify which tasks must logically be done before a subsequent task can be started and which tasks can be done simultaneous with other tasks.

5. Draw a flowchart with circles and arrows between circles with time estimates written on each arrow.

6. Critical Paths are the longest time-to-complete paths in the time-event network.

7. Estimate the "optimistic" and "pessimistic" time to complete the total project.

Activity	Description	Prior Activities	Optimistic Time	Pessimistic Time
A	A-Read Text.	None	5	10
B	B-Choose Industry.	A	1	4
C	C-Design Questions.	A,B	3	7
D	D-Schedule Interviews.	B	2	7
E	E-Do Interviews.	A,B,C,D	6	12
F	F-Write up Interviews.	E	2	5
G	G-Organize Chapter.	C	1	4
H	H-Draft Chapter.	F	3	7
I	I-Edit.	H	2	4
J	J-Final Report.	I	2	6

Table 2.4. PERT Chart of a Team Project.

AUTO MANUFACTURER'S PERT CHART

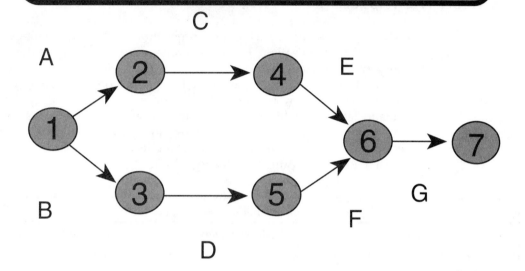

A computerized PERT chart can tabulate thousands of events and pathways. PERT forces management to plan how all the pieces of a task will fit together. Each person can see what he or she is doing in the total plan. As a network, people who screw up will create downstream problems for other people's tasks. Managers work to keep the total network on schedule.

PERT Critique. The problem with PERT works when you can foresee all the contingencies and relationships in advance. Schedules are guesses. In repetitive events, such as in mass production, PERT is not necessary because the sequence of events and time management issues are worked out once and there is no need to keep working them out again and again. PERT puts planning into the hands of the engineers and programmers who work out all the guesses and time-event inter-relationships. In complex projects, without computerization it is difficult to keep re-modifying a PERT chart in order to keep pace with the delays and false starts in thousands of event arrows.

Max Weber (1864–1920)

Weber saw bureaucracy as a way to get beyond the shortcomings of pre-modern organization. His conclusions were based on studies of long-term organizations like the Catholic Church, the Egyptian empire, and the Prussian army. These shortcomings included nepotism, inequity in how people were selected and managed, and inefficiency. Charismatic leaders, in his view, were less reliable in these areas than more rational, legal leaders guided by rules, laws, and policies. He vested control of the bureaucratic machine in the particular offices by which a service bureaucracy was organized.

Principles of Weber's Bureaucracy
1. *Division of Labor.* Divide labor into specialized expertise areas throughout the organization.
2. *Chain of Command.* Pyramid position defined by a hierarchy of authority and an explicit chain of command.
3. *Rules and Regulations.* Formal rules governing decisions and actions of everyone. Allows continuity in event of personnel changes.
4. *Impersonality.* Be detached with employees so that sentiments do not distort objective judgment.
5. *Selection.* Select workers by their technical utility. Friendship or fraternal favoritism is ruled out. Advancement is by seniority and achievement. Pay them with salaries.
6. *Documentation.* Keep records to document, monitor, and evaluate.
7. *Centralization.* Centralize all decisions at the top.[12]

Table 2.5.

Weber Critique. The ideal model of bureaucracy does not specify the role of informal organization. Technical expertise is put at the bottom of the pyramid, while authority and control is put at the top. Impersonal hierarchy makes people docile and discourages individual entrepreneurship and initiative. People stick by the rules and resist change.

Summary

The pyramid is a combination of Taylor's scientific management, Weber's bureaucracy, and Fayol's administrative bureaucracy. Despite the adaptations Elton Mayo and hundreds of other human relations advocates, the modernist form of organization is the dominant American form of organization in the private and public sector, in both product and service organizations. Each of the classical pioneers were revolutionaries in their zeal to displace pre-modern organization with modern organization. As we transition to postmodern planning, keep in mind that most large organizations contain strands of pre-modern craft-based planning, modernist brains and hands planning, and postmodern planning. Just because America and the USSR's centralized bureaucratic planning models collapsed—do not for a moment think that modernist organization has lost its steel grip on the capitalist economies of the world.

POSTMODERN PLANNING

Getting Started

There are three questions in the minds of people who become interested in postmodern management principles.

First, how do the principles of postmodern management differ essentially from those of ordinary modern management? Before Schmidt and before Human Relations, the worker planned his own time, and retained control over the knowledge of his own work. Schmidt grew up in the pre-modern age of union crafts and had worked as an apprentice pig iron worker. With the application of engineering and social science, the modern age began. Management planners observed workers to extract detailed knowledge of the worker's crafts. These scientific observations were converted to time and motion rules, laws and time-tables, and norms of group functioning. Managers became systematic recorders, indexers, and scientific data gathers.

Second, why are better results attained under postmodern management than under the older types? After the 1970s (jump in trade deficit, gas wars, rise in Japanese flexible production), the planning function began to be re-integrated with the worker's job. Workers are now trained to plan more of their own work and to participate more fully in the planning of the enterprise. The over-specialization of work tasks under modernism is being re-integrated under postmodernism. The results are better, because the new methods of work planning allow more decentralized and flexible production systems to adapt more quickly to customer needs and to attain higher levels of quality when people are skilled enough to inspect their own work.

Third, doesn't it all depend on the type of people you have, how old your technology is, the stability of the customers you serve, the country you are in? Doesn't it all depend on contingencies? No. The postmodern approach looks at the historical interface of management style and industrialization from one generation to the next. Contingency theory, on the other hand, is an a-historical stop gap theory. Contingency theory was one more attempt to make management into an a-historical science of terms, concepts, and measurements: a list of terms, conditions, and variables without stories and without history. It seeks to explain anomalies in the transition from the modernist to postmodernist period of production. It falls short.

❑ N-E-T-W-O-R-K ❑

NETWORK PLANNING: Postmodern planning is network because many *voices:* suppliers, customers, workers, communities, etc. get heard and networked into the planning process.

N   *Needs of customers get discovered.*

The purpose of business according to Peter Drucker is to **"create and maintain a customer."**

Plan around customer needs. There are two types of customers: the external one that buys the goods and services, and the internal customer that receives the results of the work you do. Postmodern planning is network planning. In a network of small and large producers, suppliers, movers and shakers, there are a lot of internal customers. Talk to the internal and external customers to find out their needs.

Plan for the niche needs. Service, quality, and uniqueness define the customer niche of any organization. Once upon a time Henry Ford could make any car as long as the Model was a T and the color was black. Now the preferences of each customer are communicated through dealerships to the choices of models and colors planned to come off the assembly line in the Toyota flexible production system. The planners make more short runs. A black car followed by a red sedan, and three blue convertibles. The worker has to think about which interior, which steering wheel, which doors, and a hundred other elements. Instead of massive inventories between each process, suppliers are told through computer terminals, triggered by assembly counts, when to bring the "Just In Time" inventory to the factory, to be fork lifted to the necessary location "Just In Time." [Refer back to the Harley-Davidson section for more JIT].

Space is allocated to customer need fulfillment in the postmodern concern. If we define the environment and mother earth as a customer,

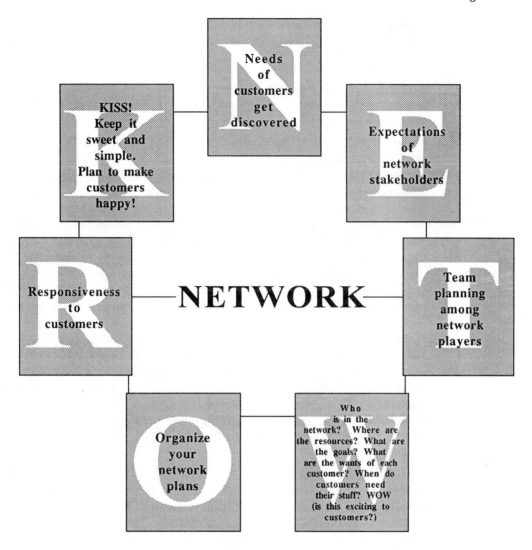

N   How do the needs of customers get discovered?

E   How are employees' needs met?

T   How do all the employees work together?

W   The six W's.

O   How are long and short term plans put together?

R   How does an employee respond to the need of a customer?

K   What programs are set up to make customers happy?

then plan some space to give to social and environmental causes, like food and education for the homeless.

E   *Expectations of network stakeholders.*

What is a stakeholder? Anyone (individual, group, business, community organization, agency) who has a stake (expectation) in the product/service network.[13]

What is network planning? Network planning is taking into account all the various stakeholders that constitute the delivery network for products and services, the community has a stake in the activities of that network as does the environment and even good old mother earth. Rather than a planned network, the network adapts and flexes and contracts and reconfigures to develop and deliver quality goods and services. Planning in a postmodern network is planning how to bring the ad hoc stakeholders together to shape, bend, and untwist the network relationships. The postmodern networks are not only cross-organizational, they are global. Products are composed of parts and services from several nations, composed in yet another nation, and sold in another.

How can you plan your time schedule and your movements so that you create and maintain internal and external network customers? First, get up and go visit internal and external customers. Plan to move where they move, and spend time where they spend time. Plan to tune into their reality. Ask the value-added question: How does what I do add value to the person or persons who receives the results of my work? Spending quality time with customers is the first priority of value-added planning.

Internal and External Customers Expect Quality. Plan for quality. Customers define what is and is not quality products and services. Do not lie to the customer and promise quality that is not there. The American automobile companies did this in the 1970s and customers left in the millions. Do not expand on the truth or stretch the truth. When the CEO's of Hewlett Packard address their employees at their annual meetings they are beginning to tell the truth about quality. Xerox corporation distributes customer dissatisfaction letters and posts summaries and excerpts of customer complaints on their corporate walls.

The Community is a stakeholder with Expectations. Companies like Control Data Corporation plan to give to their community, even when their community investments are not as profitable as alternative investments. CDC conducts high tech training aimed at unemployed and under-employed minorities. They recruit drop outs and gang members and fabric good citizens.

Mother Earth is a Stakeholder with Expectations. If we do not change the patterns of consumption and production in America and in particular, in third world countries, our planet is going to die. Our planning parameters are avoidance-oriented. We avoid pollution laws by building plants in countries with weaker laws. While we do negative-earth planning, global warming increases, the Amazon Rain Forests are cut down, and toxic waste levels build up in our oceans, streams, and underground water sources. There are a few organizations, like Ben and Jerry's ice creams, that have environmental and social consequence auditing built into their plans and disclosed in their annual reports.

T   *Team planning among network players.*

How do you plan the creation, modification, or reformation of networks? Bring together teams of people throughout the network that do not normally get to interact on a face to face basis. Let the customer for calculators meet the person who works on the circuit boards. Teams can meet to define the needs of the network. Networking depends on the continual negotiation of collective needs and expectations as participants try to discover and negotiate common issues. To create a network, you have to bring the potential participants together to talk out their issues. To modify a network you bring people to the table who have not met before so they can form new pathways in the net-. work. To reform a network, you break network boundaries and broaden the participation.

Ram Charan vividly demonstrates the effectiveness of networks at Conrail, Royal Bank of Canada, Dun and Bradstreet Europe. He concludes that by forging a strong set of relationships and values, networks reinforce managers' best instincts—and unleash emotional energy and joy of work.[14]

Postmodern Storytelling Teams. In the postmodern era, planning teams are comprised of social auditors, employees, managers, customers, vendors, and stockholders. Each has a stake in the planning process. The stories of each are told and retold, until the teams emerge with a story of a plan that will guide the firm into the 21st century. As the organization plans to make customers and mother earth happy, it is rewarded with long term survival.

W   *6 W's. (Who, where, what, wants, when, and wow).*

Who is in the network? A network is a pattern of information and resource exchanges recurring and enduring over time. The exchanges occur all the way from resource supplier, to producers, service providers, and all the way to end users.

Where are the resources? Information, people, money, and materials (even borrowed ones) are resources.

What are the goals? The goal is to survive as a network by keeping customers happy with their services and products.

Wants of each customer? Customers are internal and external. Anyone with a stake in the network. The wants of customers vary and need to be identified and responded to.

When do customers need their stuff? Customers want their goods and services now. Networks that provide quick response time, short cycle times, are going to be more competitive.

Wow (is this exciting to customers?)? Anything worth doing is worth doing with a sense of enthusiasm and excitement.

O   *Organize your network plans.*

Planning the organization of a network. Networks have a core of participants who are more dominant than more peripheral actors in a given network. They are more central to the information, decision, and resource pathways of the network. Do you organize to give that core greater control over the peripheral stakeholders? Do you mobilize stakeholders that can oppose the grip of the core? Do you break up a hierarchy of prestige and privilege to form a new pattern of resource allocations? Pecking orders in networks are just as entrenched as Weber's bureaucracy. The postmodern project is to give more marginal and peripheral stakeholders more voice in the organizing of the network.

In Ram Charan's network study, membership criteria are simple but subtle: What select group of managers, by virtue of their business skills and judgements, personal motivations and drive, control of resources, and positions at the juncture of critical information flows are uniquely qualified to shape and deliver on the corporate strategy.[15]

How to induce networking? People network out of self-interest and out of an understanding of shared fate. Shared fate means what I do affects your outcomes and what you do affects my outcomes, even though we do not directly interact. For example, homelessness lowers everyone's standards of living, even though you may never meet a homeless person. To induce networking, get people to define common needs, common outcomes, common enemies, and shared fate. What are the inducements to participation and what are the contributions you can expect from each participant? Get people to share their stories about the past.[16] Get them to share their stories about future scenarios. Exchanging stories is a primary basis for network formation and reformation.

R   *Responsiveness of the network to customers.*

How do you deconstruct and then reconstruct networks to be responsive to customers? Define the needs and expectations of customers. Organize story exchanges between customers (both internal and external) and different groups of network players. The customer's story has to be championed and broadcast to all network participants. What is the customer's story? What are the stories of how different players in the network have or have not been responsive to customers? Storytelling is political. Stories bring new definitions of customers, new customer needs, new customer expectations, and new customer solutions to the table. The stories are scenarios of how to behave in ways that do or do not promote customer responsiveness. To deconstruct a network, buy off its resources. Dumping more money into public bureaucracies, for example, did not make them any more responsive to customers. Most of the money that is taxed on the middle class to be redistributed to the poor reaches the pockets of professional bureaucrats in entrenched bureaucratic networks that resist any and all attempts to make the bureaucracy accountable to the customer (defined as tax payers and recipients of aid). Grass roots lobbying, demonstrations, strikes, boycotts, and other rebellions (from vantage point of the elite center) are necessary to reshape bureaucratic networks. Jack Kemp, for example, at HUD, is setting up oppositional networks called "Economic Empowerment": where the customers of the housing projects, the tenants, run the housing, the way that free citizens run the services of a private condominium. Kemp wants to see people get financing to buy their own units, contract their own services, and manage their own affairs.

Loosen or tighten the network. Loosely coupled networks are adaptive. Tightly coupled networks, with empires and central dominance, are typically rigid and unresponsive to customers. To make a network more responsive, the network has to be loosened up so that new patterns of relationship can form with the customer as the center of attention and responsiveness. This can be done by cutting off resources, inviting new players to the network, getting peripheral members to coalesce in order to take power away from the core, setting up a competing network to serve customers, and non-violent protest.[17]

Stories. Stores can be told that highlight victories over enemies, identify customer needs, promote positive network actions, and shape network futures. There is a history to how the network got started, a scenario of dramas about how it evolved, stories of its important leaders, dramas about the pathways it has incorporated and deconstructed from the network. Networks can be transformed by stories of network possibilities for being customer-responsive. Stories can motivate stakeholder participation. Stories convey the language metaphors that define customers: serfs and slaves versus customers as kings and rulers. To reshape a network, reshape the language, the common stories, their sense of common history, and their common vision of the future.

Ram Charan confirms the story message when he points out that the network must share openly and simultaneously each member's experiences, successes, and problems, soft information that cannot be captured in databases and spreadsheets and that remain hidden for as long as possible in most traditional organizations.[18]

K   *KISS. Keep It Sweet and Simple: Plan to make customers happy!*

KISS is Happy Customer Planning. Making and keeping customers happy is the purpose of business. All planning must start from this premise. The network must service the needs, expectations, wants, quality definitions, and responsiveness dictates of customers.

❑ THE ROLE OF STORYTELLING IN POSTMODERN PLANNING ❑

Collect planning stories to show parallels and differences with the stories of Frederick Taylor. Gather stories from unhappy and happy customers. Keep modifying plans until customer stories report higher levels of satisfaction with service, quality and uniqueness.

What is the story line of your time and motions? Are you an individual or are your time and motions carefully programmed for you?

Stories of Customer-Driven Plans of Time and Space

Instead of just mass production, Converse shoes is making shoes one at a time. Customers, with money, can pay to have customized shoes. Larry Bird can go to the high tech design room to plan shape, color, and style. Larry is then taken to the Bio Room to get the shoes shaped by making a custom cast of his feet. The cutting room takes over and custom moldings are formed and the rubber and other fabrics are vulcanized in ovens until they cure. Larry gets control of both the time and spaces of the Converse production process as they just do it one at a time.

Planning is a story about the future. But, the lessons of the past are instructive. A manager who tells the first story makes one point, a manager who tells the second story makes a different point. To plan the future, find out the stories your customers are telling about your services and products now. This is where you find the needs. You could employ experts to define multiple choice questions and endless statements followed by seven point scales, but do the experts know your customers? How can they be expected to ask the right questions?

Why not do some story listening? This is done quite efficiently by inviting customers to focus groups.

At the Stew Leonard's organization there is a focus group every week. Every week, Stew Jr. and his other family members sit and listen while customers tell them stories about services and products. This is the best planning data there is. Stew Leonard's is the biggest dairy store in the world, selling more per square foot than any store in its class. Everyone at Stew's is an innovator. Each day customers stuff a suggestion box with hundreds of ideas which are typed by 10 A.M. and distributed to each work team. Work teams meet weekly to implement new ideas. Tactical planning for happier customers has been decentralized.

I think managers who do planning without doing customer listening are risking the success of their enterprise needlessly. But to do listening means the manager must be humble enough to listen to the customer. There are many firms who have stopped hiring MBA's. "The MBA is not humble, he will not listen to experienced executives and it is beneath him to listen to customers." Is it any wonder that the MBA's of the 1970's and 1980's have led the United States down the path to financial ruin.

The Story of W. Edward Deming and Japan

"William Edward Deming was born October 14, 1900 in Wyoming. He attended University of Wyoming and got his Ph.D. in physics from Yale University. It is interesting that he worked in the Hawthorne plant of Western Electric. He also worked for the U.S. Department of Agriculture.

"Dr. Deming worked for the department of Agriculture and developed sampling techniques used in the 1940 census. In 1947, U.S. General Douglas MacArthur hired Dr. Deming to consult with 21 top business leaders in Japan. He introduced them to statistical quality control. In 1951, the Japanese honored him by establishing the Deming Award.

Right after World War II, the Japanese economy was in ruins. General Douglas MacArthur was asked by Harry Truman to rebuild the Japanese economy. MacArthur began with the communications industry. He wanted the Japanese people to be able to hear his voice. MacArthur recruited the best American talent to advise the Japanese on how to build viable industries and the Japanese listened. MacArthur gave women the vote, introduced land reform, and set Japan on a course for economic revitalization. One of the key people MacArthur brought to Japan was William Deming. William Deming set up a new way of organizing. Walter A. Shewart of Bell Laboratories did work in the 1930s that Deming followed. In the early 1950s, Joseph Juran published an influential book on quality control and did key seminars in Japan. Armand Feigenbaum of General Electric and a Japanese citizen, Dr. Genichi Taguchi published key pieces and did teaching that had a strong effect on Japanese production methods.

In the United States, those who did not know the secret transfer of postmodern organization to the Japanese, wrote management books proclaiming that there were unique differences in the Japanese culture that made flexible production and continuous improvement possible for the Japanese, but impossible for the Americans. Yet, William Deming and his followers could not get a speaking engagement in the United States and no American textbook to this day gives Deming more that a page or two of definitions to memorize. We would like to propose a different approach. It is Deming who inspired the Japanese to get on the path to continuous quality improvements. As we have already stated, in the previous chapter, the Japanese took Deming's ideas and improved upon them. They got beyond the strict division of labor notion of dividing functions between people so that managers and their cadre of clerks did the quality inspecting, and workers treated as brainless did the actions. Instead, the Japanese recombined the divisions of Plan-Do-Check-Action back into each individual's job. The Japanese still maintain a strict chain of command, but balance that with an informal fraternal (pre-modern) system where recruits are treated as entering fraternal classes who get socialized and bonded together, such that they stay in contact throughout their entire career. The point is that America sent the basic technology and recipes for total quality organization to the Japanese at the end of World War II, but at home stayed on the modernist, post-industrial (let's all be burger flippers) path. The postmodern metaphor for organization is the circle network.

Deming Chain Reaction. Improve quality and your costs go down because of less rework, fewer mistakes, fewer delays, fewer snags, and better use of machine time and materials. Once costs decrease, productivity improves, allowing the firm to capture market share by providing higher quality products at a lower overall price. This keeps the organization in business and provides more jobs for people.

To increase quality, it is necessary to increase the quality of incoming materials from suppliers. Instead of awarding contracts on lowest possible price, seek suppliers who can form a long term relationship with your firm to improve product quality. Deming taught the Japanese how to test incoming materials, machines, and assembly methods for quality.

Customer Focus. Do your homework to Deming meant getting to know your customers and building your products and services around their preferences.[19]

William Deming's 7 Deadly Sins
1. **Lack of Constancy of Purpose.** Without constancy of purpose, impending doom looms on the horizon. Management must look beyond the quarterly dividend and develop long term plans. One way to accomplish this is to make a commitment to training and the constant upgrade of machinery.
2. **Emphasis on short-term profits.** The organizations of today are run by financial wizards and lawyers who are subservient to the stockholders. Organizations must grow away from this trend and allow those who are committed to both the quality of products and long-term growth, run the organization.
3. **Evaluation of performance, merit rating or annual review.** Such performance ratings encourage (1) short-term performance at the expense of long-term planning (2) discourage risk-taking, pit people against one another for the same rewards, promote fear, and undermine teamwork.
4. **Mobility of top management.** How can managers be committed to long-term change when they are constantly building their resumes? The way to build a top management team is to move them through the ranks in a progression that takes decades to reach the top.
5. **Running a company on visible figures alone "counting the money.** As Lloyd S. Nelson stated: "visible figures are important, but it is the figures that are unknown and unknowable, that are much more important."
6. **Excessive medical costs.**
7. **Excessive costs of warranty, fueled by lawyers who work on contingency fees.**

Table 2.6.

Deming's 14 Points

1. **Create constancy of purpose for the improvement of product and service.** Management has two sets of problems: those of today and those of tomorrow. The problems of today reflect concerns with profits, forecasting, employment, service, budget, how to maintain quality, and how to match output to sales. If you focus on these today problems, then there will be no tomorrow. "When employees are working for a company that is investing for the future, they will feel more secure and less likely to look for jobs in companies that appear more promising." **Constancy of Purpose.**
    A. *Innovation.* This is more than improving a product.
       What materials will be required, at what cost?
       What will be the method of production?
       What new people will have to be hired?
       What changes in equipment will be required?
       What new skills will be required, and for how many people?
       How will current employees be trained in these new skills?
       How will supervisors be trained?
       What will be the cost of production; cost of marketing; cost of methods of service?
       How will the product or service be used by the customers?
       How will the company know if the customer is satisfied?
    B. *Resources.* Put resources into research and education: "To prepare for the future, a company must invest today. There can be no innovation without research, and no research without properly educated employees."
    C. *Continuous Improvement of product and service.*
    D. *Maintenance.* Invest in the maintenance of equipment, furniture and fixtures, and in new aids to production in the office and in the plant.

Table 2.7.

2. **Adopt the New Philosophy.** Quality must become the new religion! Organizations can no longer afford to live with the ill wind of mistakes, poor training, and bad materials.

3. **Cease dependence on Mass Inspection.** Quality comes not from inspection but from improvement of the process. The old way: inspect bad quality out. The new way: build good quality in. Build statistical methods of sampling into the production system.

4. **End the practice of awarding business on price tag alone.** Choose the suppliers, not on price tag along, which seems to be the American way of doing business, but look for quality and that long term commitment.

5. **Improve constantly and forever the system of production and service.** Improvement is a never ending task, it is not a one time effort. Every department, as well as individual, must adhere to the basic philosophy of "continual improvement."

6. **Institute training and retraining.** Do not allow employees to learn their jobs from other employees. Train individuals in conducive environments, and use statistical control with various charts to measure an employee's progress. Use this information for feedback purposes.

7. **Institute Leadership.** Remove the barriers that prevent people from taking pride in their jobs, such barriers as poor tools, too much time spent on rework, a deaf ear to their suggestions, turning out the product quickly rather than correctly, and an emphasis on numbers. Managers need to "take charge."

8. **Drive out Fear.** "The economic loss from fear is appalling!" People are afraid to point out problems for fear that they will start an argument, or worse, be blamed for the problem itself. To remove this fear, managers must break down the "great wall" that exists at all levels within the organization.

9. **Break down barriers between staff areas.** Each department within an organization has its own goals. If there is a lack of goal congruence within the organization and its respective departments, diverse staff goals can be devastating. Team work is the way to go.

10. **Eliminate slogans, exhortations, and targets for the workforce.** Rid the organization of company-produced slogans such as "Don't skate on an oil slick, Zero Defects and Do it right the first time!" Sometimes such slogans are offensive to employees, treating them in a dependent manner. Allow the employees to make up their own slogans.

11. **Eliminate numerical quotas.** Quotas or other work standards such as, measured day work, or rates impede quality more than any single working condition. When management sets rates too high, it demoralizes the people. If rates are set too low, once quotas are met, people stop working and just linger until their shift is over.

12. **Remove barriers to Pride of Workmanship.** Listen to the employees and their complaints. Field their questions and take action.

13. **Institute a vigorous program of education and retraining.** It is not enough to hire good people. They must continually acquire new knowledge and new skills to deal with new materials, new methods of production. Invest in training and retraining the people for the long haul.

14. **Take action to accomplish the Transformation.** Plan, Do, Check, and Act.
    First Step. The first step is to study the process, decide what needs to be changed to improve it, develop a team to answer questions like: What dates are necessary?; Does the data already exist?; Is it necessary to carry out a change and observe it?; Are tests necessary? Do not proceed without a plan.
    Second Step. Organize to carry out the tests, make the change. Start on a small scale.
    Third Step. Observe the effects.
    Fourth Step. Ask: What did we learn? Repeat the test if necessary, perhaps in a different environment. Look for side effects.[20]

Table 2.7.—Cont.

Skeptical of Deming

The Japanese began with the Deming cycle, but quickly noticed that they could simplify it as PDCA (Plan, Do, Check, & Action). They also found the Deming concept relied too much on a Bureaucratic "Division of Labor" principle: a division of labor between supervisors (planners), inspectors (checkers), and workers (doers). Just as in America, inspectors were checking workers' results and worker-action only happened to correct mistakes, rather than to continuously improve. In the Japanese reconstruction of the Deming Cycle, PDCA took on new meanings. The idea was to continuously improve quality by having each worker responsible for PDC and A. *This reintegrated planning back into doing, something consistent with postmodernism and pre-modernism but hateful to modernism planning logic.*[21]

Kaizen

Kaizen means continuous improvement involving everyone. It also means "continuing improvement in personal life, home life, social life, and work life."[22] The PDCA wheel is at the very heart of Kaizen. While America practices result-oriented, division of labor—planning, the Japanese have been working on continuous improvement planning for 40 years. The American version of PDCA is PDCF: engineers plan, workers do, supervisors check, and if it does not go well, the manager comes around and fires the workers to get a quick fix solution they call "fire fighting."[23] In Japan the worker is taught the planning tools, the Doing practices, the Checking of their own work, and they are expected to take Action to improve their work process again and again and again.

> The KAIZEN concept means that everyone, no matter what his title or position, must openly admit any mistakes he has made or any failings that exist in his job, and try to do a better job the next time. Progress is impossible without the ability to admit mistakes.[24]

Result-Oriented Management

The American emphasis is on controls, performance, results (usually financial), or the denial of rewards and even penalties. R-Criteria, or P-Criteria, are easily quantifiable and short term. American management emphasizes R Criteria almost exclusively.

Process-Oriented Management

The Japanese emphasis is on KAIZEN. P-Oriented managers support and stimulate efforts to improve the way employees do their jobs. It is a long-term outlook. Attitude factors are rewarded including: discipline, time management, skill development, participation and involvement, morale, and communication.[25]

R-Criteria	P-Criteria
❑ Number of successful sales calls.	❑ Amount of time spent calling on new customers.
❑ Amount of money saved.	❑ Time spent generating solutions to problems.
❑ Increments to this quarter's profits.	❑ Time spent improving the work process.
❑ Discipline. Getting fired for talking back.	❑ Discipline. Coming to work on time each day.
❑ Got customers to increase orders by 10%.	❑ Improved customer order handling by 10%.
❑ Met quarterly profit goals.	❑ Improved the quality of the work environment.

Table 2.8.

Modernist Wisdom The American Way	Postmodern Wisdom The Japanese Way
Higher quality leads to higher costs.	Higher quality leads to lower costs.
Larger inventory lots lead to lower costs.	Smaller inventory lots lead to lower costs.
Workers do not need to be taken into account.	A thinking worker is a productive worker.
Experts, not workers generate new ideas.	Workers ideas improve work process, increase quality, and build customer satisfaction.
The manager is the judge of quality.	The customer is the judge of quality.[26]

Table 2.9.

		Japan's Application of the Deming PDCA Wheel
P	Plan.	Everyone plans improvements in present practices using statistical measurement tools, such as Pareto diagrams, cause-and-effect diagrams, histograms, control charts, scatter diagrams, graphs, and checksheets.
D	Do.	Doing the plan—making, or working on—the product or service that was planned.
C	Check.	People doing the work Check to insure that the plan satisfies customer needs and expectations.
A	Action.	In case a complaint is filed, or a mistake is made, or a better way is discovered—it has to be incorporated into the planning phase, and positive steps (action) taken for the next round of efforts. Action here refers to action for implementing continuous quality improvement.

Table 2.10.

1. *Pareto diagrams.* A diagram that classifies problems according to reasons why something is not high quality. Quality and service snags are diagrammed by priority using a bar-graph format. For example if a customer has to wait, what are all the reasons?

   ❑ Not enough help.
   ❑ Staff is at lunch.
   ❑ Staff does not know answers to questions.
   ❑ Staff does not know location of merchandise.
   ❑ Staff has to wait for manager's signature.
   ❑ Customer is asking for wrong item.
   ❑ Staff engaged in lengthy conversation.
   ❑ Staff does not understand customer request.

   To do a Pareto diagram, someone must systematically record how often a given glitch is observed to occur. Then the chart is made up, analyzed, and problem solved. The PDCA is set in motion.

2. *Cause-and-effect diagrams.* Use to analyze a process according to factors such as men, materials, methods, machines as branches on a tree or bones in a fishbone or "Godzilla-bone graphs." The problems within each element are listed as sub-branches or connecting bones on each main branch.

❑ Deconstructing Postmodern Planning ❑

1. *Japanese Management is not the same thing as Postmodern Management?* Japanese production systems began with the biggest wholesale adoption of Taylor's scientific management in combination with Japanese human relations consensus engineering that the world had ever fabricated. Thousands of workers began to apply Taylor-principles as part of a collective machine. However, Japan began to bend and improve and adapt the Taylor machine methods to their own culture. Instead of strict division of labor and the separation of planning and doing, the Japanese did not strictly divide labor or separate planning and doing, brains and hands. Each worker became an entrepreneur producing quality and dedicated to customer satisfaction.

   Since the Japanese system is the most well known and researched role model, we can make observations about postmodernism using the Japanese system as a case study. In addition, Japan marginalizes women. Many of the Japanese life time employment benefits go to men, not to women. Women are on the periphery doing more of the temporary work.

   The Japanese have a saying *deru kugi wa utareru* "the nail that sticks up, gets pounded down." It is no less true in America.

There is often no place in the corporation for individuals. People who plan their time and motion around doing something unique, something high quality, something innovative and sticking with it until it takes hold in their corporation.

2. *Cycle Time.* With cycle time the definition of every step of every work process and every individual's job is more and more specified and increasingly the worker is controlled by the process. The postmodern rhetoric says that the worker is getting increased control over the line and can even shut down the line to make sure that quality levels are achieved. However, the skeptical counter is that as cycle time is implemented, individual discretion and pace decreases. Loyotard (1984) brings up the concept of *"performativity."* Rosenau (1992) defines performativity as "modern criteria by which judgment is made on the basis of pragmatic performance or outcome ("capacity, efficiency, control,") . . . Postmodernists argue that performativity discourages diversity and autonomy, flexibility and openness. Performativity through cycle time removes discretion and control over the pace of work from the worker. Workers can not schedule breaks, speed up or slow down their pace in response to fatigue cycles, and as a result become more and more an extension of their machines.

Bob I saw an ad that said robots do not need breaks, do not go to the bathroom, do not eat lunch, or come to work late.

Harley-Davidson Triad

Statstical Operator Control (SOC)

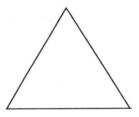

Employee Involvement   Just-in-time
EI   JIT

3. *The Productivity Triad.* Planning is all about improving productivity. At Harley-Davidson, for example, their **productivity triad** consists of employee involvement (EI), statistical operator control (SOC), and just in time (JIT) (see Reid, 1990).[27] There is EI in the planning process, which from a postmod perspective gives the worker increased control over their own work. However, a skeptical

analysis would point out that with EI there is less need for supervisors and staff positions, which in the modernist firm, did all the planning **work** for the workers. The workers were the hands and the staff was the brains. People are now expected to think on the job and the thinking and actions they now take on, allows management to save money by reducing its overall staff investment. One of the grand revelations, as management of Harley-Davidson executives visited the Marysville, Ohio Honda plant, was that there were no computers and no legions of staff planners running around. Productivity was higher with fewer people. How is it that fewer people do more productive work than many more people? The usual story is that when workers think for themselves, are trained in planning their own work, and as systems are streamlined by, for example, getting rid of overly complex computer scheduling of the line as well as giving the worker local discretion over planning their work—then these facets lead to improved productivity with fewer people. Nevertheless, the skeptic must ask if these workers, working faster cycle times, and thinking as they work, and working at much more rapid assembly line speeds are over-worked. Are they in fact getting more discretion or are they more tightly coupled, than even Frederic Taylor and Henry Ford imagined, to their production function?

Statistical Operator Control (SOC). In the 70s and 80s the U.S. experimented with quality circles. Workers were trained in brainstorming and problem solving techniques by legions of consultants. They made tons of suggestions, which management labeled griping and complaining. Management just was not prepared to implement quality circle productivity and planning suggestions. This is the usual story for quality circle failures. However, there is a more fundamental reason for the failure of quality circles. W. Edward Deming and Joseph Juran, when they were brought to post-World War II Japan by General Douglas MacArthur, taught the Japanese workers and managers the arts of SOC. The workers now had the means to chart their own productivity variances and show management bar charts and histograms of the impact of weakly designed parts from suppliers, inconsistent machine settings, etc. The charts showed clear paths to increasing productivity and management was quick to implement the results. With more SOC training and more SOC implementation, continuous improvement (KAIZEN) became reality. Now what is the skeptical analysis here? For one thing, isn't SOC just time and motion study done with stop watches and gauges the way Frederic Taylor did it? The crucial difference is instead of a staff of people going around inspecting the worker's routines, the workers now do time and motion studies on their own work process. Foucault would term this internalizing the gaze. As surveillance tasks are taken on by the worker, then you no longer need staffers to do the gaze. Therefore foremen can be released, time and motion people can be released, preventative maintenance people can be released. The worker self-supervises, does the work and the maintenance, and does her own time and motion studies. The worker is every bit as controlled in this postmodern dimension as she was in the modernist period of Taylorism.

Just In Time JIT. With JIT, management can plan to lower its inventory levels. It is a pull system instead of a push system. Pull means that computer algorithms track the parts, predict how many parts are needed when, and transmit orders and reorders to suppliers. In JIT, it is a pull system of planning. As workers on the line need more parts, their bins get empty. This is obvious to people who keep the bins full and the supplier is informed more parts are needed on the line. At Harley-Davidson the results were quite dramatic. In the 70s and early 80s, massive rube-goldberg overhead conveyors carried parts all around the plant. And there were massive levels of available inventories spun about on these conveyors. The problem is that the parts did not fit, were rusted, or could not be found. As JIT was implemented, first in a few sectors of the plant, then spreading throughout the manufacturing centers, a marvelous result occurred. If a part did not fit, the worker now armed with SOC and EI notified the supplier to fix it immediately. This lowered the waste, improved the quality, and brought up the productivity. Instead of huge hospital bays with hundreds of new Harleys needing to be repaired, be fitted with parts that could not be found, or shipped to dealers with a bag of parts yet to be installed, the Harley's were coming off the line with high quality. Costs were lowered, the rumbling, noisy, cumbersome overhead parts conveyor was dismantled.

What is the skeptical analysis of JIT? How about the fact that lowering the assembly plants inventories, raises inventories at the supplier's plants. The cost of inventory can be shifted from manufacturer to supplier. In an ideal world, the supplier would also use JIT, produce smaller lot sizes while getting up-to-date feedback from assemblers that parts fit. JIT, like cycle time, takes more slack out of the work process and thereby adds more stress to the worker. According to Parker and Slaughter (1988) at the NUMMI (New United Motors Manufacturing Incorporated) plant in Fremont, California, the supposedly postmodern system of flexible manufacturing (cycle time, continuous improvement, JIT, etc.) has led to increased worker stress, increased health problems, etc.

4. *Greed and Letting Investment Bankers do Planning.* One primary cause for the ruination of the US economy is greed. Greed is the penchant and obsession with quarterly returns. Make a quick score, get promoted, make another quick score, and move on before the roof caves in. Many finance MBA's do precisely this. And it is not the MBA who is to blame. The blame must lie with the MBA degree factories, those bastions of wisdom, populated by people who, for the most part, never worked as an executive or a manager, or a shop keeper. The so-called "professional" educator who never worked. Their advice was short term profit, with the share holders as the only relevant customers. Well guess what happened? A whole lot of foreign customers, in cooperation with their governments, began to engage in long term investments in people training, better work processes, more flexible production systems, and innovative research. These new "postmodern" producers are teaching the U.S. a lesson we shall never forget. The problem is the MBA mills are still turning out financial geniuses who are obsessed with short term gains, short term financial markets, and to hell with long term customers, long term employees, and long term growth. Dismantle, sell off, acquire, merge, and absorb. Collect businesses in unrelated industries to hedge your bet that any one will fail. Planning has become akin to gambling. And the loan sharks are winning.

   Here is a worst case scenario story.

   America is a bunch of burger flippers, insurance salesmen, and importers. We are working in companies owned by off shore interests, managed by long distance, and employing millions of temporary workers, who do not receive medical benefits, and can be laid off without notice.

   Here is the best case scenario story.

   America begins to invest in long term growth planning, customer listening takes precedence over stock speculating, and our government begins to facilitate competition that meets the challenge of the world economy. We are working in companies that invest in long term training, provide excellent benefits, and if someone must be laid off they spend their off time in training.

5. *Planning for Social Audits.* What if profit is not the only thing important to organizational success. In the postmodern organization, success is also defined by meeting customer needs, meeting societal needs, and by meeting the needs of mother earth. What good is a company whose profits suck the marrow from mother earth; rape her environment, and leave her discarded as a pile of deserted waste? Plans that focus on short term gain at the expense of a long term balance of mother earth interests are short

sighted. Ben and Jerry's is an ice cream company. It is also a company that invests 5% of its earnings into the environment. At the end of each year, an external firm audits their environmental performance. They look at pollutants, packaging and other factors that waste mother earth's resources. Maybe if we care more about mother earth resources we will care to about human resources too. It is colonization at its worst to build factories in Mexico and in third world countries so we can avoid pollution standards, employ child labor, and pay them poverty wages. This demeans us all.

Perrow observes that as you squeeze more and more cycle time and JIT out of the planning of your production function, the speed of the line goes up, the cost of the products goes up, the number of workers goes down, and profits improve. The problem that Charles Perrow notes is that the narrow focus on productive efficiency, generates costs such as unemployment, declining health, and worker stress. These are *externalities,* social costs of activity that are not included in the price of goods or services, but absorbed by non-owners. These costs have to be paid by the American public. Perrow is quite skeptical. He goes so far as to claim that with rises in efficiency, companies have littered the American Dream with unemployable adults, undereducated and underskilled citizens, and more homeless citizens.[28]

Perrow's sentiments are echoed by Ben Hamper in his book *Rivethead.*[29] A fourth generation auto worker, Hamper spent 11 years as a riveter at General Motors Corp.'s Truck and Bus Div. plant in Flint, Michigan. A nervous breakdown in 1988 compelled him to give up his cherished nightmare of someday winning a 30-year pin at GM. Angry yet comical, *Rivethead* is about people who sweat for their pay. These folks, Hamper says, still toil in unsafe factories for companies that often treat them like children.

❑ RADICAL POSTMODERN PLANNING PRESCRIPTIONS ❑

First. We need to cut down the amount of time that workers and managers spend in planning teams, quality committees, and brainstorming groups. American management is obsessed with spending all its productive time in group meetings. Meetings give the modern organization more inertia, not less. Cutting out meetings would help individuals regain control of the bureaucracy.

Second. People need to be more career centered than organization centered. This prescription flies in the face of the Japanese system, which is more organization-centered than career-centered. Face it, America is a mobile society with very temporary attachments, even to family groups. The thing that will stimulate individualism is educating the individual to be well rounded. Now, we train people to fit into the organization, not to bring education to the corporation that bends the corporation. And, this is more likely liberal arts and fine arts education than science, engineering, law, and management education. The educated generalist is more curious than the specialized company man. Education needs to stimulate individualism and stop making people take standardized tests, and move through a standardized time table of classes, sitting in egg carton classrooms, learning to imitate an instructor. Students need to be taught to follow their bliss, not fit into the corporate staff, and rise rung by rung up the corporate ladder.

Third. Topple the corporate ladder. The postmodern form of organization is more a flat network of relationships (many of them temporary) than a tall hierarchical system of supervision. People climb a ladder of supervision rather than perfect themselves as individuals to build better products, services, and life styles.

Fourth. Fight the organization planners. In particular, fight bureaucratic planning systems like management by objectives and bottom up planning, and corporate vision retreats. They do feel good, you do get exhausted, you do produce a whole lot of paper, but no one reads the paper, and the plans never get implemented.

Fifth. Capitalize on diversity. If there is one American virtue it is diversity. By the year 2001, the white male dominated corporation will cease to be viable. In its place, we will see a work place with 50 percent women, over 70% minorities, and a wider range of ages and disabilities. Unfortunately, the middle class will have trouble coping.

❑ SUMMARY ❑

The modern organization plays checkers with man using Taylor's principles of scientific management and human relations social science principles of group harmony. In the process, the entrepreneurial spirit of the Americans has been tamed and confined to work in a bureaucratic corporate machine that values conformity and docility above all else. It is man's destiny to be controlled by the modern organization and he is a willing collaborator in his own mechanization. In the authoritarian system of scientific management it was easier for man to see his own imprisonment. In the human relations movement, the plans to control man in the group machine are often too subtle to be noticed. It is like the story of frog in the pot of water. The frog does not notice that the water is gradually heated to a boil until it is far too late for the frog to jump out of the pan. In the authoritarian system, man had a clear target; in the human relations system, there is only a steamy fog to resist. In both modern systems, man is a planned and captured being, without independence, and without an innovative spirit.

The hero's journey. For Taylorism, the hero is the engineer who plans the time and motions of everyone in the firm. For Mayo and the human relationalists, the hero is the group facilitator who establishes harmony among the workers and bureaucratic administrators. For the Postmodernist, the hero is the individual who resists the modern organization and does the work of the entrepreneur. He makes the organization secondary to individual performance. He does not surrender to benevolence. He steps off the bureaucratic treadmill and spends time with customers. He knows there can never be harmony between his entrepreneurial spirit and the administrator. The hero of postmodernism is the rebel with a cause. Through the struggle with organization, he rekindles the American innovative spirit of capitalism.

So What Happened? Management researchers in the 1950s and 60s began to notice a decline in entrepreneurship, creativity, and individualism in the bog of corporate systems. By the 1970s there were severe drops in product and service quality. The rhetoric of the time was "oh well, forget these hard industries, we will become an information society of softer technologies and service industries." Through the 1980s America has gotten out of the manufacturing business. In the 1990s management has the challenge of teaching people to be creative entrepreneurs inside of big corporations.

With books like *In Search of Excellence* by Peters and Waterman, although the social science research was marginal and many of the firms they studied did in fact fade out of existence, it was clear that a new movement was happening. The management science and human relations movements were being pushed aside by the excellence and total quality management movements. Toyota of Japan was the exemplar of flexible production, high innovation, high quality, and high customer service. Leaders were supposed to topple bureaucratic corporate industrial administrators and do things like "create a vision" and "make everyone in the company an individual entrepreneur" who "added value to customers." But, by this time the scientifically-based modern organization was the very fabric of the American capitalist economy. The inertia of the status quo is deeply entrenched not only in industry, but especially in business education. We will look at the pioneering work of William Whyte, Jr. who in the 1950s was among the first to spot the modernist organization man.

In the postmodern era, people are more important than time. The earth resources are more important than the time table of any plan. The needs of customers are more important than the time intervals.

❑ Notes ❑

1. Business Week 1/27/92 p. 59. See also 27

2. Adapted from *Notes adn Queries* issues: Vol II, 1868: 386–7; Vol XI, 1861: 23. See Boje, David. "The passing of the ancient printer and his folklore." (December) 1983. UCLA working paper 83–27.

3. 1977 *Encyclopedia of Literary and Typographical Anecdote*, Volume One, New York: Garland Publishing, Inc. (Original Printing, 1839).

4. Deacon, Richard 1976. *A Biography of William Caxton: The first English editor, merchant and translator.* Chatham: W. and J. Mackay Limited. p. 110.

5. From *The Inland Printer*, October, 1917. vol. 60, No. 1: p. 97.

6. A. Raymond Hopper in *Print*, 1945, p. 48.

7. Taylor, Frederick Winslow. *The Principles of Scientific Management.* New York W. W. Norton & Co. Inc. The material was copyrighted in 1911 and first published by Norton in 1967 after being published in many other place. pp. 44–7.

8. Based on Taylor's works: *Shop Management* (originally published in 1903); *Principles of Scientific Management* (originally published in 1911), and Testimony before the Special House Committed (1912) reported in *Scientific Management* (New York: Harper and Row, 1947).

9. English translation. *General and Industrial Administration.* London: Sir Isaac Pitman & Sons, ltd, 1949.

10. Adapted from Daniel A. Wren, *The Evolution of Management Thought* (New York: Wiley, 1979): 218–221; Koontz, Harold, Cyril O'Donnell, and Heinz Weihrich. *Management.* 7th Edition. New York: McGraw-Hill, 1980: 45–47; Taylor's writings, Ibid.

11. Gantt, Henry L. "A bonus system of rewarding labor," ASME Transactions 23 (1901), 342–72; *Work, Wages, and Profits* (New York: Engineering Magazine Company, 1910.; *Organizing for Work.* New York: Harcourt, Brace, and Howe, 1919.

12. Durkheim, Emile *De la Division du travial social.* Paris: F. Alcan, 1893; Gerth, H. H. and C. Wright Mills, (trans.) *Max Weber: Essays in Sociology.* New York: Oxford University Press, 1946.; Parsons, Talcott (trans.) *Max Weber: The Theory of Social and Economic Organization.* New York: Free Press, 1947.; For critique see: Selznick, Philip, "Foundations of the Theory of Organization," *American Sociological Review* Vo. 13 1948: 25–35; Gouldner, Alvin W. *Patterns of Industrial Bureaucracy* Glencoe, Ill: Free Press, 1954; Merton, Robert K. *Social Theory and Social Structure* Glencoe, Ill.: Free Press, 1957, 2nd Ed.; Simon, Herbert *Administrative Behavior* New York: The Macmillan Company, 1945; Wren, Daniel A. *The Evolution of Management Thought* New York: John Wiley and Sons, 2nd Ed., 1979.

13. Mason, Richard O. "A Dialectical Approach to Strategic Planning." *Management Science* 15 (1969), B403–B414.; Manson, Richard O. "Management by Multiple Advocacy." Unpublished working paper, UCLA, 1978.; Mason, Richard O., Ian Mitroff, and James Emshoff "Strategic Assumption Making: Arriving at Policy through Dialectics.: Unpublished paper, UCLA, 1978.; Boje, David and Terance J. Wolfe "Transorganizational Development: Contributions to Theory and Practice" In Leavitt, Pondy, and Boje (Eds). *Readings in Managerial Psychology*, 4th Ed, 1989: 733–754.

14. Charan, Ram. 1991. "How Networks Reshape Organizations—For Results." *Harvard Business Review*. Sept–Oct, pp. 104–115.

15. ibid Charan, Ram. 1991.

16. Boje, David M., Don Fedor, and Kendrith Rowland. "Myth-making: A qualitative step in OD interventions." *Journal of Applied Behaviorial Science*, 18 (1982): 17–28. Boje and Wolfe, 1989, Ibid. p. 747.

17. Simon, Herbert "The architecture of complexity." *Proceedings of the American Philosophical Society* 106 (December, 1962): 467–82.; Weick, Karl E. "Educational organizations as loosely coupled systems." *Administrative Science Quarterly*, 21 no. 1 (1976) 1–18.; Pfeffer, Jeffrey and Gerald R. Salancik. *The External Control of Organization: A resource dependence perspective*. New York: Harper and Row, 1978; Aldrich, Howard *Organizations and Environments*. Englewood Cliffs: NJ: Prentice-Hall, 1979; Boje, David and David A. Whetten. "Effects of organizational strategies and contextual constraints on centrality and attributions of influence in interorganizational networks." *Administrative Science Quarterly*, 26 (1981): 378–95.; Boje and Wolfe, 1989, Ibid.

18. ibid Charan, Ram. 1991.

19. Deming, W. Edward *Statistical Adjustment of Data* New York: Dover Publications. 1964; *Quality, Productivity, and Competitive Position* Boston: MIT Press. 1982; Walton, Mary. *The Deming Management Method* New York: Dodd, Mead & Company. 1986; Gitlow, Howard S. *the Deming Guide to Quality and Competitive Position*. New Jersey: Prentice Hall, Inc. 1987.

20. We would like to thank LMU MBA student and now graduate John Bennett for his research assistance in reviewing the W. Edward Deming philosophy.

21. Imai, Masaaki *Kaizen: The key to Japan's Competitive Success*. 1986 New York: McGraw-Hill. p. 60–65.

22. Ibid. Imai p. xx.

23. Ibid Imai, p. 61–2.

24. Ibid Imai p. 64.

25. Ibid. Imai based on p. xxii, xxiv, 16–21.

26. Ibid. Adapted from Imai p. 205–9.

27. Reid, Peter C. 1990. *Well made in America: Lessons from Harley-Davidson on being the best*. New York: McGraw-Hill Publishing Company.

28. Perrow, Charles. 1991. "A Society of Organizations". *Theory and Society* 20: pp 763–794.

29. Hamper, Ben. 1992. *Rivethead: Tales from the Assembly Line*. N.Y.: Warner.

ORGANIZING STORIES

Pre-modern, modern, and postmodern will be presented as historical epochs in organization theory, but please do not be fooled. As you can see in the Blue Team's presentation of Carl's Jr.'s organizational discourse, the three perspectives are very much a part of every contemporary organization.

ORGANIZING DEFINITIONS

PRE-MODERN ORGANIZING
Organizing in **Crews.**

C   *Crews.* Organizations are fraternal societies of apprentices and journeymen, organized into work crews, with rank determinied by a castesystem of skilled workers.

R   *Rough.* Managers are rough, tough, macho-types with an adversarial stance toward workers.

E   *Entrepreneurial.* Strrong sence of innovation and personal self-reliance.

W   *Well knit Community.* Organizing around the community of crafts and artisans.

S   *Social.* People worked eith their wives, brothers, uncles in the same trades.

MODERNIST ORGANIZING
Organizing in **Discipline.**

D   *Discipline.* Discipline time and motion.

I   *Inspection.* Do not let people inspect their own work. Keep them engaged in brain-dead tasks.

S   *Surveillance.* The gaze is everywhere.

C   *Centralization.* Centralize decisions, policies and objectives.

I   *Impersonal.* Bureaucratic offices, rules, and departments. No connection between people and customers.

P   *Penal Mechanisms.*

L   *Layers.* Organized into pyramid layers.

I   *Individual Cells.* Division of labor into military units.

N   *Neural.* Control physical bodies of people.

E   *Elites.* Elites have status trappings.

POSTMODERN ORGANIZING
Organizing is **Flat.**

F   *Flat.* Flat and flexible with few layers of management. Forever serving customers.

L   *Latticed.* A *Circle* network of relationships between autonomous teams without going through a center pyramid. Circle includes suppliers and customers. Many centers or no centers at all.

A   *Autonomous.* Postmodern man is the self-disciplined entrepreneur who balances leisure with temporary commitment to formal organizations. Diverse individuals make-up the teams.

T   *Team-based.* Teams of equals are skilled to do their own planning, organizing, and controlling. Teams sub-contract work across organizational and global boundaries. Team focus in on **KAIZEN**—continuous improvement involving everyone.

Table 3.1.

ORGANIZING					
SCORES	**1**	**2**	**3**	**4**	**5**
Crews	Few fraternal socieites—rank occasionally based on a caste system		Some fraternal societies—rank partially based on a caste system		Fraternal services—rank given out in a caste system of skilled workers
Rough	Managers listen to employees' suggestions but are rarely receptive to their needs.		Managers are somewhat abrasive to employees' suggestions and needs		Managers are rough with an adversarial stance towards workers
Entrepreneur	A little creativity and a heavy reliance on managers		Some creativity and personal confidence		Strong sense of innovationn and personal self-reliance
Well knit Community	More organized around the individual—little sense of common experiences or accomplishments		Beginning to show signs of being organized into a community of workers		Clear organization around the community of workers
Social	People share only a few outside relationships with co-workers		Employees have loosely connected relationships outside of work		People work with family members in the same trades
Discipline	Little control over time and motion		Moderate control over time and motion		Exact discipline of time and motion
Inspection	People oversee their own work		Little connection between employees and qualify of final work		No one inspects their own work
Surveillance	Unstructured plan of surveillance		Loosely formalized plan of surveillance		The gaze is everywhere
Centralization	Input on final decision is highly limited		Decisions are frequently made only by one or two individuals		Centralize decisions, policies, and objectives
Impersonal	Slight connections between people and customers		Weak connection between people and customers		No connection between people and customers
Penal Mechanisms	Subtle use of disciplinary powers. Employees forced to respect managers.		Occasional public use of disciplinary power. Employees' respect stems from fear.		Use of disciplinary powers in subtle, discrete, and omnipresent ways
Layers	Moderate boundaries between levels of management		Distinct separation between layers of management		Organized and structured into pyramid layers

ORGANIZING—*Continued*				
SCORES	1 2	3 4		5
Individual Cell	More unity of labor/similar objectives/Cells are not strictly militarized	Clear sense of division of labor and the beginning of militarized orders from managers		Complete division of labor military units
Neural	More variety of direction and purpose/Employees have possibility of changing positions	Employees are often stuck in their own position—unable to change teams		Control physical bodies of people
Elites	More variety of command/managers are more likely to share benefits	Managers are seen as elites—they control many of the privileges		Elites have status trappings
Flat	Some layers of management. Customers are secondary concern	Few layers of management		Few layers of management. Forever serving the customers
Latticed	Little communication between teams/Team structure is very dependent on other resources	Communication between teams is fair		Circle network of relationships between autonomous teams
Autonomous	Most individuals are ordinary. Teams are used to repetition and routine.	Unique individuals have most control of the team		Diverse individuals make up the teams
Team-based	Team members are not all equal. Only a few are concerned with improvement.	Teams work with other teams and occasionally improve their own performance		Team focus on continuous improvement involving everyone

	PRE-MOD	MOD	POST-MOD
Q1: How do you monitor the work force for efficiency?	Promotions are given out once workers master specific skills like in a caste system. C rews 5 50%	Discipline of time and motion is used to control customer flow and monitor efficiency. D iscipline 5 50%	N/A 0%
Q2: What kind of environment is set for the employees in the work area?	Employees are encouraged to function as well knit communities or "families". cre W s 3 30%	Advancement is encouraged, but only through gradually ascending the layers of management. discip L ine 3 30%	Managers focus on continuous improvement by giving employees freedom to implement ideas. fla T 4 40%
Q3: How do you implement employee suggestions?	An attitude of strong innovation and self-reliance is acknowledged and commended through a rewards program. cr E ws 2 33%	N/A 0%	A circle network exists between management and employees so ideas are implemented quickly and needs are addressed properly. f L at 4 67%
Q4: How do you implement a new company venture?	N/A 0%	Needs are addressed and projects are established through a centralized decision making process. dis C ipline 5 71%	Once the project has been designed, skilled individuals are brought together to function as a team. fla T 2 29%
AVERAGE	28.3%	38.8%	34%

Discipline:
Discipline (5) 50%
Discipline of time and motion is used to control customer flow and monitor efficiency.

Crews:
Crews (5) 50%
Promotions are given out once workers master specific skills like in a caste system

cre**W**s:
Well knit Community (3) 30%
Employees are encouraged to function as well knit communities or "families".

fla**T**:
Team-based (4) 40%
Managers focus on continuous improvement by giving employees freedom to implement ideas.

discip**L**ine:
Layers (3) 30%
Advancement is encouraged, but only through gradually ascending the layers of management.

cr**E**ws:
Entrepreneurial (2) 33%
An attitude of strong innovation and self-reliance is acknowledged and commended through a rewards program.

f**L**at:
Latticed (4) 67%
A circle network exists between management and employees so ideas are implemented quickly and needs are addressed properly.

Q1: How do you monitor the work force for efficiency?

A1: Besides the electronic clock at the drive-thru, or the three to five second service at the register that I told you about (in the control section), we monitor the work force by implementing a system of performance reviews. The manager of each store keeps a chart in his office with each section name and the name of each employee. Once an employee has successfully mastered all the skills needed in that section he receives a star on the chart showing that he passed. For example, the employee may be stationed in the dining room evaluation he must keep the tables clean, know how to change the trash bags, and properly deliver food to the customers. At the end of a three month period we go through an individual employee review and base all raises and promotions on the chart.

Q2: What kind of environment is set for the employees in the work areas?

A2: We stress a family oriented environment and encourage employees to express their feelings about how things are being done. We train our managers to be receptive and open minded when it comes to implementing these suggestions. The employees tell the managers what they want to do and the managers let them learn from their mistakes and accomplishments. This puts tremendous cultural support to grow within the company. If you want the opportunity to advance, we provide it. This is something we tell our employees right away making it a major part of their training. We show them videos on how they can go from a counter person to 'Mr. Big'. This is all just a part of the attitude we want our employees to develop. We want them to stay with the company for as long as possible.

Q3: How do you implement employee suggestions?

A3: We have a suggestion box program in which we give financial rewards on all levels from corporate employees to counterpersons if we use their suggestion in the company. We also have a 1–800 number called "FYI to training". Operators direct suggestions from the field to the appropriate manager or department. Improvements come from field observation and implementation of new ideas. All suggestions are quickly responded to.

disCipline:
Centralization (5) 71%
Needs are addressed and projects are established through a centralized decision making process.

flaT:
Team-based (2) 29%
Once the project has been designed, skilled individuals are brought together to function as a team.

Q4: How do you implement a new company venture?

A4: Two things happen in an organization: you have process and you have project. Process makes the whole thing go: issue pay role checks, do this, do that . . . but that's just the engine that runs the whole thing. When you are going to institute something new or make any kind of change, that's a project. In the project area you may need to pull people from different parts of the company to make things go. This is where we truly function as a team-based company. We have a certification process that the leader of the team must go through so he knows what the needs and why the project is being developed. The certified manager then comes up with a preliminary concept. He then goes through an operation test and a market test to try out his possible solution. After that, notices are sent out to the departments that will be effected by the project and a team is developed to work on the project and implement it into the process.

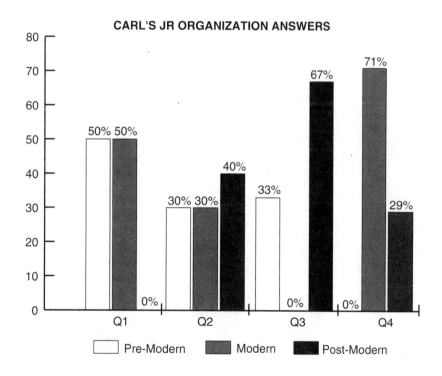

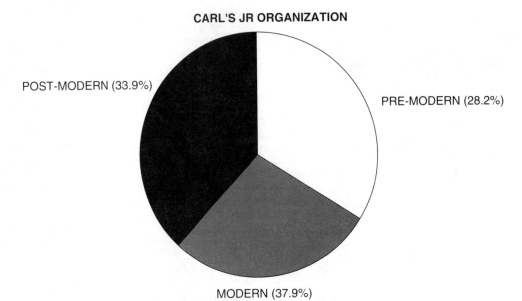

CARL'S JR ORGANIZATION

THE CARL'S JR. ORGANIZING SUGGESTION BOX

AREAS THAT THE NAVY BLUE TEAM LIKED:

- ❑ The suggestions from employees are responded to quickly.
- ❑ Always looking to promote employees (i.e. by using the "STAR CHART").
- ❑ The 1–800 number for suggestions, complaints, etc.
- ❑ The financial rewards given for outstanding performances.

SUGGESTIONS FROM THE NAVY BLUE TEAM:

- ❑ Break down the decision making process for the managers.
- ❑ Create a more positive atmosphere by forming a more customer-oriented, team-based philosophy.
- ❑ Concentrate more on the attitude of the employee in the training programs and videos.

Crews
Organizations are fraternal societies of apprentices and journeymen, organized into work crews, with rank given out in a caste system of skilled workers

Rough
Managers are rough, tough macho types with an adversarial stance toward workers.

Entrepreneurial
Strong sense of innovation and personal self reliance.

Well-Knit Community
Organizing around the community of crafts and artisans.

Social
People worked with their wives, brothers, and uncles in the same trade.

C How are employees cast into a system where rank is relevant?

R Does a flexible relationship exist with upper management?

E Is innovation and upward mobility present in the working atmosphere?

W How is the office filled with employees capable of doing their job?

S Is there a family type atmosphere present within the company?

❑ PRE-MODERN ORGANIZING ❑

Introduction.

From the late 1700s to the early 1900s, pre-industrial workers were herded about in large 30 to 100 person work gangs or crews. People were organized into their trades and served seven to ten year apprenticeships to become journeymen in a given trade. Once you mastered a trade, such a printing, carpentry, stained glass, or silver smithing, you could become the entrepreneur, open your own shop, and train your own apprentices. Management in the big firms of the early 1900s such as railroads, water and power, mining, and automobile manufacturing maintained and preferred an antagonistic and adversarial attitude towards trade unions and workers. In short, there was competitive struggle in the small and the large business.

After the Civil War, the ideas of Charles Darwin's *Origin of the Species* also took root in the American attitudes. "The total social good is enhanced by an unregulated process of struggle which will ensure the "survival of the fittest." "[1]

> "In every store and factory there is a constant weeding-out process going on. No matter how good times are, this sorting continues . . . out, and forever out, the incompetent and unworthy go. It is the survival of the fittest".[2]

Should Chrysler be Saved Next Time?

The pre-modern philosophy was: if organizations and individuals fail the natural struggle, they should fail to survive. The weak are not supposed to survive. Those who are rich are destined to be so; those who are poor are undeserving. Intervening in the social Darwin process is considered by many to be socialism or communism. Because of the heritage of Social Darwinism attitudes, there are those to this modern day who believe the government should in no way intervene to save a Chrysler Motor Car company or help a group of US computer chip manufacturers compete more effectively with the Japanese partnerships of industry and government.

> Nevertheless, it is easy to see that this self-fulfilling theory provides a solid base for viewing workers and employees as simply parts in a machine with no particular merit or rights—except the right to join in the struggle for survival. . . . Riches, incidentally, were often considered a measure of virtue and heavenly reward. Thus, the fittest were also the most virtuous.[3]

If the rich got richer, it was because God meant them to be rich. If the poor were exploited, it was their destiny on earth to be so. In the pre-modern craft-based organization, there were tough bosses, a caste system of apprenticeship, rites of passage into the organization and into one's rank.

The following stories were collected from a utility company, we shall call "Edison."[4] As you read the stories, please deconstruct them using the guidelines in the Appendix on story deconstruction.

Pre-Modern Stories of Clumsums and Shovelers

Tim "I don't know who was telling me. There was a foreman out in San Bernadino who used to physically beat up his people. Just a brute of a person. I don't know who was telling me that. An intimidator and so on. And if you didn't do what he said: "I'll knock your block off type stuff." And he always wanted em to do everything and knew exactly how to do stuff. Well he was on an emergency assignment to a different crew and in a different area of the town and he climbed the pole. Or he told people to climb the pole and the pole switched. And they said: "Don't do that, because that's going to take out a whole section of a town unnecessarily. That's the wrong thing to do." "Don't bother me. I'll beat your butt into the ground if you don't get up there and clear that pole. And they said: "we told you not to do it." And he went up there and he pulled the switch and out went part of the (pause). And they fired him because they now had something to get rid of him. And his people said: "Hey, we're just doing what he told us to do.""

Doug "There's the old term where they see they'll be a group referred to or former linemen, they're now former linemen who are now foremen as *"clumsums."*

Boj "Clumsums?"

Doug "Yes, because the old story is that when you were going to hire a lineman and you're the boss. Well you say: "have you clum?" "Well, yeah, I've clumsum, haven't you?" He's a clumsum.

Mike "I never heard it referred to as a noun. I've heard it as a [interrupted]

Doug "He's an old clumsum. You've never heard that in customer service? . . ."

Sue "No, are they going to beat me up?"

Doug "When you go back out just for—and I'd be interested in what happens. Ask somebody if they know who some of the clumsums are around here. And, I'd be delighted to hear what the response is."

Sue	"Am I coming back in with two black eyes?"
Doug	"No, no, no. What it means is—and then the word *"boomer"* you see. And they'll refer to old boomer."
Don	"What's a boomer?"
Doug	"Well a boomer, of course was a lineman that went and traveled with the weather almost. In the midwest, when the poles got freezing and they'd have ice on the pole. It was awfully difficult to climb up. So you came to California because of the weather. Then you moved around. You boomed. You were a boomer. And you had to be very careful. I know when I was an employment interviewer, we had to be very careful that we didn't hire boomers, because not only did they not last, but many times they were not really journeymen, quote, linemen. So we had an old superintendent in the distribution area that was a manager. And as the final passing grade after we got through interviewing them and we made telephone checks to find out that they hadn't been in the slammer for too long. You know, cause that's pretty hard living, hard drinking group. And if all things look pretty good, we'd send the lineman, so-called lineman. He'd say he was a journeyman—down to have this superintendent interview him and he would say: "how much cluming have you done?" (pause) And then he would determine whether they were a boomer or not."
Sue	" . . . I have a story regarding when I had to do some training with the linemen splicers. . . . I went out and road with the crews for two days. So first they cleaned up their language and whatever. And when I did the training program several of them who didn't know that I had ridden with the crews . . . said "how do you know so much about us?" And the passage of you're OK is if you get invited to their bar after work. If you're invited to the Copper Door, you are in. If you don't get any invitations, you know they can be polite to you in the program, but if you really want to know if you are in, it's if they tell you, you can come into their bar.
Boj	"It, interesting, it's sort of a rite of acceptance. . . ."
Mike	" . . . I can tell you a story about my two year career in the steel business [laughs of recognition for this story from the group]. I was hired to work in a steel mill in Cleveland. I was a teenager, young adult, and times were tough. It was in the late 50's. It bore the first of the modern recessions and I got caught up in. And I reported for work and I was hired as a laborer and my job was to shovel out the coal cups because there were seven or eight of these things and one of them were always cold because that was the one they were repairing and

they would run the other six blast furnaces. And I got assigned to a crew, a brick laying crew is was called, because these things are lined with fire brick. And the guy said: "OK, follow me. What we are going to do." And he says: "follow me." We walked over to a wooden box and put three sticks of dynamite in his hip pocked [laughter from group]. Follow him? Well OK, and he starts going up the outside of this thing on a ladder, a steel ladder. You know? And that bugger's a 100 feet tall. Follow him—bugger. And after about 40 feet, I'm getting scared. "Wait a minute, what's going on here?" Not a word, just: "follow me." OK. So he goes up to the top and throws his leg over that blast furnace and takes some of this dynamite and lights it and boom. [more group laughter]. [pause] It goes all the way down the stack. And so OK, now we go back down and then of course, our job is to shovel this out. And there's a space. Now why they couldn't build it six feet tall instead of four feet tall. But the space underneath is four feet tall. So you have to shovel this stuff bent over into a little cart and then push it up an incline and then someone else takes it away. And that was my job. I lasted two hours.

Sue "They fired you?"

Mike "I walked off. I didn't even collect my money. [more laughs]

Boj "A chance for a real "quality of work" line? [lots of laughs and cross talk] . . ."

Don "Oh, I know of a crew they assigned to go out and dig a hole out in Pullman. Do you know where Pullman is? [No, says the group] Its down by Riverside. The ground is hard. Real hard. In between rock and granite, somewhere like that, and they sent these two guys down there to dig this hole. You know and they really pumped em up for it. And they got out there and they started digging. And they got down about that far (motions six inches). And they put the boom and the auger on and it wouldn't go anywhere so they probably got down about this far (displays about nine inches) an they probably figured well, we'll fill it full of water. It's Friday and we'll come back Monday and finish. They came back Monday and the water had gone down about half an inch. And they just kept razzing these guys and hassling them about [it]. "Get those holes dug. We gotta put. We gotta do some work." And they'll use that hole digging as punishment or *discipline* or starting a new crew guy out. "You grab a shovel and dig me a hole for a pole."

Doug "That's a grunt. A groundman is called a grunt. Now surely you've heard the term grunt? (Sue nods acknowledgement).

And those grunts are the ones that used to dig the holes. Of course now they have more sophisticated equipment. But the grunt used to literally "grunt" when he was digging the hole.

Sue "Another thing there's a caste system. Like with our line crews, you start out with the groundman and then you have the apprentice lineman and linemen splicers. There's before work. They all have a table and you do not go over to the other table. There's a groundman table. there's a lineman splicer table and you don't go over unless you're invited. Otherwise, you are really hazed. At least, that was the custom of this one district. I don't know—has anyone seen that for other districts. . . .

Don "Well I spent a day with a transmission crew and they had a backhoe working. And the foreman was very explicit about that. When I have a new guy around, well I'll have him dig a hole. But today we've been really working hard and everything else, so I'll have the guy on the backhoe dig the hole. And, he'd just swish, swish, swish, and there's this hole. And it's all dug and everything else. But, he won't use him, if he's got something he wants to teach somebody, right in there and shovel that hole.

Doug " . . . we had a Christmas party and Christmas dance at the Ontario American Legion club. And now it was on Friday night and bear in mind that all of the crews have worked all that day climbing poles. And they came in the evening with their wives. Came at it and hit the bar and went at it with both hands and then as dinner was announced they ordered more drinks and took the drinks . . . and then the band came and they were dancing and so all the women took their shoes off and the men. And they were out there and they played this stomping music. And so then the band was through about 12 and they antied up [passed] around the hat to pay more to the band and so they danced till 2. Now mind you, they've clum poles all day they dance till at least 2 or 2:30 and now they decided now we're all going to go bowling [lots of group laughter]. And they all went bowling and they all had breakfast about 7 o'clock in the morning. And you tell me where the average dude can handle that? And that's the life. They still do it today.

Don "Those are very strong, very strong norms."

Boj "I think those stories are very important. At least I'm able to learn very quickly some of the norms and which ones not to violate. . . ."

ASPECTS OF THE PRE-MODERN WORKPLACE	

Tough Bosses:
     Beat up his people
     Brut of a person
     An intimidator
     Knock your block off type
     "I'll beat your butt into the ground
 	
 Rites of Passage:
     Getting accepted is getting invited to their bar
     ❑ Hole digging
         —to haze the new grunt
         —is discipline
         —to teach them something.
	Clumsums:
	     ❑ Climbs power poles.
	     ❑ Have you clumb sum?
	     ❑ He's a clum sum.
	 Boomers:
	     ❑ Old boomer
	     ❑ Moved around—You boomed
	     ❑ Came to California for the weather.
	     ❑ Don't hire boomers.
	 Caste System:
	     ❑ Grunts—Grunt when the dig. Groundsmen.
	     ❑ Grunts are apprentices.
	     ❑ Groundsman's table
	     ❑ Lineman Splicer's table
	     ❑ Journeymen haze new grunts.

Table 3.2. Pre-Modern Story Discourse Summary Box

Mike   "I would like to share with you one sentence that I heard that made such an impact upon me that I remember it verbatim. A middle manager with 22 years experience with the company was commenting on the things that I think we are talking about. And he said and I quote: 'The ABC's of getting ahead in this and he mentioned the department. The ABC's of getting ahead here are that you have to be Authoritarian, Belligerent, and Cruel." And that was a spontaneous kind of thing. Now he was not advocating that. He had 22 years with the company and he was making a sad observation."

Deconstruction Points.

1. In many ways the pre-modern organization, with its crews, apprentices, and hazing rituals, does resemble the organization of a fraternity or sorority. There are parallels in the language and practices between the greek system and the pre-modern crews.

2. The organization is culturally anchored in its past. A past that is communicated and sustains through storytelling. Stories are passed from journeymen to apprentice and from these executives to their managers and trainers. The pre-modern organization is a rank and caste system.

Discipline

Discipline time and motion.
If something goes wrong, how are employees punished?

Inspection

Do not let people inspect their own work. Keep them engaged in brain-dead tasks.
Are there supervisors who regulate and inspect employees work and actions?

Surveillance

The gaze is everywhere.
Is someone constantly looking over the employees' shoulders or is a lot of freedom given on the job?

Centralization

Centralize decisions, policies and objectives.
Is there a board of directors who make decisions and run the company?

Impersonal

Bureaucratic offices, rules, and departments. No connections between people and customers.
How are the different departments connected?

Penal Mechanisms

In what ways are employees punished for their wrongful acts?

Layers

Organized into pyramid layers.
Is there a defined top layer of employees and a distinct lower layer?

Individual Cells

Division of layers into military units.
Do employees only take care of one responsibility at a time or do they find themselves in charge of many things at one time?

Neural

Control physical bodies of people.
How does management understand the physical and mental parts of your job?

Elites

Elites have status trappings.
Does status play a large role in everyday activities?

3. Pre-modern patterns of organization are present to this day in an organization, like Edison Utility Company, that is quite modern. In any organization you can look for strands of pre-modern (crews, castes, rituals), modern (ranks, divisions, watches), and postmodern (flexibility, participation, diversity). In short, it is not the age of the organization or the time period being studied, it is the historical origins of each facet of the organization. The norms are established and rooted historically, but each of the three facets of the organization is changing at its own pace, some more pre-modern, many modern facets, and others more postmodern.

4. The organization is a mechanism of discipline; disciplining people to move from rank of apprentice to journeyman; disciplining the scheduling of the day; journeymen haze apprentices; disciplining the movements of people during the day; disciplining the norms of behavior at any given moment by every single person. In the pre-modern facet, the discipline comes from the peer pressure of the crew system.

❑ MODERNIST ORGANIZING ❑

INTRODUCTION.

Groups of people are mechanically and hierarchically constructed and coordinated to seek common and many specialized goals in a strict division of labor. Modernist organizations resemble one huge machine with specialized human and machine parts. U.S. education fabricates human cogs for this machine.

The Story of the Ingenious Modern Educational Machine

In stagnant societies, the past crept forward into the present and repeated itself in the future. . . . The key to the system, however, was its absolute devotion to yesterday. The curriculum of the present was the past.

The mechanical age smashed all this, for industrialism required a new kind of man. It demanded skills which neither family nor church could, by themselves, provide. . . . Above all, it required that man develop a new sense of time.

Mass education was the ingenious machine constructed by industrialism to produce the kind of adult it needed. The problem was inordinately complex. How to pre-adapt children for a new kind of world—a world of repetitive indoor toil, smoke, noise, machines, crowded living conditions, collective discipline, a world in which time was to be regulated not by the cycle of sun and moon, but by the factory whistle and the clock.

The solution was an educational system which, in its very structure simulated this new world. . . . Yet the whole idea of assembling masses of students (raw materials) to be processed by teachers (workers) in a centrally located school (factory) was a stroke of industrial genius. The whole administrative hierarchy of education, as it grew, followed the model of industrial bureaucracy. The very organization of knowledge into permanent disciplines was grounded on industrial assumptions . . . regimentation, lack of individualization, the rigid systems of seating, grouping, grading and marking, the authoritarian role of the teacher . . . (Alvin Toffler).[5]

Deconstruction Points

1. Mass education served the interests of a mass production and mass consumption society by pre-adapting children to the machine-paced discipline of mass production.

2. As modern organization deskilled jobs, specialized workers into individual tasks, made jobs very boring, the worker did not require or benefit from intellectual education, basic skills were adequate.

3. Since industry did not demand high education standards, workers with illiterate skills satisfied industry, providing the workers were used to being paced by a regulated and disciplined education machine.

4. To this day the mechanisms of student regulation (time and motion movement) receive more attention than the content of their education.

5. There are parallels between the industrial organization and the education organization:
   a. Both are regimented.
   b. Both have many discipline mechanisms.
   c. Both resist reform.

6. The schools instilled a new time-bias, away from the past and onto the present. What is needed now is a future-oriented education system that helps students deal with change and instability.

In the modernist epoch, Taylor's scientific management and Henry Ford's assembly line combined to produce an organizational machine to temper the human body to the machine. The problem, however, was how to prepare workers from childhood to maturity who were disciplined early in life to work in the organizational machine. The American education system became the instrument of calibrating

MOD MODEL	POSTMOD MODEL
STRATEGY ❑ mass production ❑ long production runs ❑ centralized control	❑ flexible production ❑ customized production ❑ decentralized control
PRODUCTION ❑ fixed automation ❑ end-of-line quality control ❑ fragmentation of tasks ❑ authority vested in supervisor	❑ flexible automation ❑ on-line quality control ❑ work teams, multiskilled workers ❑ authority delegated to workers
HUMAN RESOURCES ❑ labor-management confrontation ❑ minimal qualifications accepted ❑ workers as a cost	❑ labor-management cooperation ❑ screening for basic skills abilities ❑ workforce as an investment
JOB LADDERS ❑ internal labor market ❑ advancement by seniority	❑ limited internal labor market ❑ advancement by certified skills
TRAINING ❑ minimal for production workers ❑ specialized for craft workers	❑ training sessions for everyone ❑ broader skills sought

SOURCE: Adapted from Scans Report, 1991.[6]

Table 3.3. Characteristics of Modernist and Postmodernist Workplace.

youth to be machineable cogs that with minor lubrication fit precisely into the modern industrial machine.

The U.S. Department of Labor has released a recent report that calls for a revolutionary reformation of the educational system because it is out of touch with the need of industry in the year 2000. While we are reassured because the report points out the differences between the modern and postmodern forms of organization, what is depressing to us is that the report does not address the role of education. Is the only role of education to produce students who will fit into a less modern, and a more postmodern industrial machine?

America 2000. In order to engage in World Class Competition, American Education will need to train for the Postmodern workplace. The ethics of America 2000 are "commitment to excellence, product quality, and customer satisfaction." America 2000 workers will have to manage themselves because there will be fewer supervisors to plan and organize their work. The will need these competencies:

NEW WORKER COMPETENCIES
RESOURCES   Workers schedule time, budget money, materials, space, and assign staff;   **INTERPERSONAL SKILLS**   Working on teams, teaching others, serving customers, leading negotiating, and working well with people from culturally diverse backgrounds to solve problems; they responsibly challenge existing procedures and policies;   **INFORMATION**   Workers are expected to identify, assimilate, and integrate information from diverse sources; they prepare, maintain and interpret quantitative and qualitative records; they convert information from one form to another and are comfortable conveying information, orally and in writing, as the need arises;   **SYSTEMS**   Workers should understand their own work in the context of the work of those around them; they understand how parts of systems are connected, anticipate consequences, and monitor and correct their own performance; they can identify trends and anomalies in system performance, integrate multiple displays of data, and link symbols (e.g., displays on a computer screen) with real phenomena (e.g., machine performance).   **TECHNOLOGY**   High levels of competence in selecting and using appropriate technology, visualizing operations, using technology to monitor tasks, and maintaining and trouble-shooting complex equipment; ensuring the cogs and gears of the entire firm operate as a harmonious system.
FOUNDATION FOR COMPETENCIES
BASIC SKILLS   Reading, writing, arithmetic and mathematics, speaking, and listening;   **THINKING SKILLS**   Thinking creatively, making decisions, solving problems, seeing things in the mind's eye, knowing how to learn, and reasoning;   **PERSONAL QUALITY**   Individual responsibility, self-esteem, sociability, self-management, and integrity.

SOURCE: Adapted from SCANS report, 1991.

Table 3.4

Education in Crisis

Schools are not able to graduate literate citizens, let alone educate them for the ideals of our changing work place. Instead of a world class workforce, business are dumb-ifying their work procedures, systems, and supervision approaches to deal with a work force that is not as well skilled as the Japanese and German workers. Postmodern workers need to come out of high school with creative thinking skills, technical skills in spreadsheet programs, statistical process control, and an ability to work in teams, with the entrepreneurial attitude to challenge systems to continuously improve.

A well-developed mind, a passion to learn, and the ability to put knowledge to work are the new keys to the future of our young people, the success of our businesses, and the economic well-being of the nation (SCANS, p. 1).

Postmodern organizations will differ from the Modernist, in the same way that Henry Ford's assembly line differed from hand made horse drawn carriages. The routinized, repetitive, hierarchically supervised workplace will give way to one that is a network with flexible, customized, non-routine, organization of goods and service production; an organization that is customer and quality driven.

> Like the dinosaur with its limited intelligence, doomed to extinction at the hands of smaller but craftier animals, the traditional model cannot survive the competition from high-performance organizations that depend on the intelligence and ingenuity of their managers and employees. High-performance organizations are relentlessly committed to excellence, to product quality, and to customer service (SCANS, p. 4).

In order to get beyond bureaucratic product and service organizations, we must confront the major obstacle that is holding back that transition: the subtle bureaucratic discipline machine. It is so entrenched that merely changing the practices, people, or even the education system will not loosen its grip on the American organization.

❏ THE MODERN DISCIPLINE MACHINE ❏

> *Disciplining the Modern Dinosaur.* The goal of modernist organizing is to discipline people, keep them docile, and to keep them submissive, stupid, and correct. Modern organization is a network of disciplinary mechanisms that runs the length of the production and service delivery process. In this way the individual becomes part of organized behavior. But, if the individual is disciplined by the dinosaur, he can no longer be self-disciplined, self-managed, or self-directed the way he was in the pre-modernist epoch when self-reliance and individualism were king.

The Purdue Recruiting Machine Story

> I have never been able to erase from my mind the memory of an ordinary day at Purdue's placement center. It is probably the largest and most effective placement operation in the country, yet, much as in a well-run group clinic, there seemed hardly any activity. In the main room some students were quietly studying company literature arranged on the tables for them; others were checking the interview timetables to find what recruiter they would see and to which cubicle he was assigned; at the central filing desk college employees were sorting the hundreds of names of men who had registered for placement. Except for a murmur from the row of cubicles there was little to indi-

cate that scores of young men were, every hour on the half hour, making the decisions that would determine their whole future life (William H. Whyte, Jr.).[7]

The Human Machine. What was upsetting to William Whyte Jr. in 1956 and is still upsetting to us today is that the students were not repelled and are still not repelled by this social machinery. The Taylorists, Weberians, Fayols, and as we shall assert even the Human Relationalists have contributed their sciences to the bureaucratization, standardization, formalization, centralization, and mechanization of the organizational machine. Students sign up to become part of the status quo, to be part of collective group work, to be conservative. Despite the fact that over 50% of Americans are employed by small business and Alvin Toffler (1990) predicts an even higher percentage by the year 2000, the lines of entrepreneurship are very short in the placement office.[8] Students are not in revolt against the bureaucratic machines they are normalizing (trying to be average) themselves to fit into it.

The Executive Ladder Story

"You get into a certain position," one forty-year-old executive explains, "and you start getting scared that somebody else might want the job you have. You can't tell who he might be, so you take on the protective coloring so you won't look as if you are ambitious and have the others move in on you." The best defense against being surpassed, executives well know, is to surpass somebody else, but since every other executive knows this also and knows that the others know it too, no one can ever feel really secure. Check vacation records, and you will find that the higher up the man is, the more likely is the vacation to be broken up into a week here and a week there and, furthermore, to be rescheduled and postponed to suit the company rather than the family. "I like to take my vacation in two or three stretches instead of three or four weeks," one executive confesses. "I don't do it for my health. If you go away for three weeks, when you come back you find that they have rearranged your entire job. Someone has to carry on while you are gone and they are in your files, and when you get back the people will ask you questions about your job on account of what others did while you were away. I don't blame them, mind you; I would do exactly the same thing."[9]

Panoptic Discipline

As the modernist period of industrial science progressed, the organization became a machine of discipline. Organizing combines scripts and discourse with architectures, scientific rationality, programs of disciplinary correction with production processes. Michel Foucault (1977) calls this the "**Panoptic**" machine.[10] It is a different view of organizations. By contrast, the organization in American textbooks is described as a hierarchy of objectives; each unit has its objective and objectives of one level in the hierarchy are means for the objective ends of higher levels. While this is one way to look at organizing, the "panoptic" interpretation is that each level practices surveillance or what Foucault calls the "**gaze**." With the gaze hierarchy, managers, staff, and workers become more docile performers than they would be as individuals. It takes a great deal of docility to behave correctly in the machine.[11]

Discipline practices. The administrative management principles of Henri Fayol considered discipline one of the key principles of management. Workers must be disciplined to willfully obey the rules of the organization by exercising leadership, clearly communicated work policies, and fairly applied penalties. Discipline in the modern organization was also the cornerstone of the military organization. Yet, since the 1970's, military training at West Point and other military institutions has sought a more postmodern path to discipline. Rather than demanding unquestioned obedience and discipline, the new military leader helps the troops establish self-reliance and self-discipline: to make sense of their situation, utilize their resources, and coordinate among themselves using teamwork to meet a challenge. In this way, the military discipline becomes less a vertical dictatorship and more a horizontal network of intelligent interaction. It is curious that modernist management textbooks have almost nothing to say about discipline, yet that what is central to all organizational structures.

What are people disciplined for? The organization enforces violations of time (lateness, absence, interruption); activity violations (negligence in attention, lack of zeal; behavior violations (impoliteness, disobedience, disrespect, insubordination); speech violations (idle chatter, insolence, racial slurs, phone use); body violations (incorrect attitudes, irregular gestures, lack of cleanliness; physical and sexual abuse); sexuality violations (impurity, indecency, abuse, dating).

How are people disciplined and corrected in organizations?

Light physical punishments (work reparations, repetitions of unacceptable procedures and processes); deprivations (removal from office, reduction in rank, failing an examination); petty humiliations (dressing down in front of others, relentless questions, standing before a panel, wearing badges of dishonor); coldness and indifference (stares, extinctions (ignoring something); non-responsiveness, stern replies, body language).

What are the multiple and pervasive organizational apparatus of discipline that comprise organization?

1. *Gaze Mechanisms.* Organizations coerce discipline by observation. The eyes are everywhere in a continuous and encompassing network of surveillance that runs the length of the production technology. The gaze is a multiple, automatic, continuous, hierarchized, and anonymous power functioning in a network of relations from top to bottom, from bottom to tip, and laterally to hold the whole organization together, functioning like an ingenious piece of fine machinery (Foucault, 1977: 175–80). Spatially, offices, cubicles, and desks are arrayed along long corridors like a series of small cubicles with supervisory offices located at regular and strategic intervals. People leave their doors open to voluntarily subject themselves to the gaze. Because management can not see into all the cells of the organization simultaneously, the gaze is sub-divided and networked in hierarchical relations at key relay points and the monitoring is collated and tabulated at key levels.

    The symbol of the gaze mechanism and its ideal case is the "**panoptic**" tower in the center of a circle of workshop cells and offices. The tower has one way mirrors so the boss can look in at what you do, but you can not tell if she is observing you at this instance or not. As a worker or supervisor your work cell is exposed to the gaze. The only entrances and windows are toward the tower, not towards the outside. The tower and the circle of stacked cells is the ideal image. More popular is the long corridor of work cells.

    Through the gaze mechanism, the worker is conscious of the potential for visibility that surrounds her every movement. Since the worker never quite knows if the gaze is in effect, s/he internalizes the gaze. You do not need anyone standing behind the tower's one way windows, the workers behave as if they are being continuously gazed. The gaze is internalized. Foucault refers to this as Bertham's Principle: power should be visible and unverifiable. The worker has become the principle of his/her own subordination.

    The panoptic machinery is no longer architectural. Bosses no longer sit atop tall stools on elevated platforms to micro-supervise by direct observation the people doing work at long tables arranged in neat rows and corridors. Although, there are some special collection sections of libraries that operate precisely such a gaze mechanism.

The central inspection hall is the pivot of the system; without a central point of inspection, the gaze ceases to be guaranteed . . . the more accurate and easy the surveillance, the less need will there be to seek in the strength of the buildings guarantees against attempted escape and communication between the inmates (Foucault, p. 250).

The gaze has taken on more subtle forms: recording, examination, normalization, etc. With modern computers, the time and motion behaviors of each work can be gazed without a person at the gaze terminal. In telephone answering operations, such as at a customer service number, operators have their calls monitored for how long they are on the phone with each customer; and supervisors will even cut in to monitor the conversation of a call and rate that conversation on seven-point scales. There are delicate issues of privacy here. At some banks, the supervisor is required to beep the customer service operator to let them know that they are being gazed. Instead of putting workers in cells, they are put into star shaped cubicles with other operators. A supervisor walks the floor, roving between cubicles. A battery of clerks monitor the computer reports on hundreds of operators. The operator is controlled by the computerized gaze. Police departments are already confining people to their homes instead of in over-crowded jails by hooking them up to electronic monitors that dial the police station if an individual walks more than 100 feet away from his/her home. More and more people are carrying electronic beepers and others carry scanners to log and report their every movement. For those of us who are not electronically monitored, we just leave our doors open and type up and then submit endless forms and attend endless debriefing committee meetings.

Bob: I recall my supervisor, at a major computer company, spent an inordinate amount of time re-writing my reports under the guise of "word-smithing"

MBWA. Even Management By Wandering Around (Peters and Waterman)[12] is a form of gaze. Managers do not just wander the halls to empower workers, they exercise power over the workers by showing up at random times and at random spaces to gaze the workers performance efficiency. People begin to self-monitor, in case the boss shows up.

2. *Recording Mechanisms.* Staffs of clerks, foremen, supervisors, assistants, and secretaries are watchers of time, recorders of movements, allocators of space, and observers of waste and inefficiency.

Organizations maintain vast files and computer records on each individual.

3. *Penal Mechanisms.* A penal mechanism is an adaptation of the judge and jury. It can be as minor as a search committee reviewing applicants, interviewing candidates, and then deciding its recommendation. The organization is a network of minor penal mechanisms to effect disciplinary power in subtle, discrete, and omnipresent ways. The espoused objectives of these penal mechanisms are to control stealing, cheating, abuse, inefficiency, or to give an unbiased, equitable and fair decision—but at another level these mechanisms control and docilize people. Workers and managers are caught in an array of punishment and penalty mechanisms.

4. *Examinations.* Managers judge. With modernization, the examination of everyone in every way by every foreman, supervisor, superintendent, director, and executive has been increasing at an increasing rate. People are classified, categorized, segmented, and deselected through employment examinations. Accountants wanting to be CPA's are given examinations. People are examined for promotion, reassignment, and skill development. Each worker is classified, fixed, transcribed, averaged, and normed into a cumulative record keeping system, called: the case file. Some case files are physical, others are converted to computer disks. In this way the exam combines an observing and examining hierarchy with normalizing (make man into string of numbers) judgements. Exams can discipline, punish, classify, select, and exclude.

   In the question and answer process of the examination, each worker is diagnosed, the examiners deliberate and a judgement is rendered. Just as exams marked the end of course-work, the business exams mark the end of periods of training, apprenticeship, and rank. Exams hierarchized good and bad workers, managers, administrators, and staff in relation to one another. Exams distribute people by aptitude, conduct, skill. In sum, the exam is a constantly applied ritual of power; dominance and subordination, authenticating the distribution of people into ranks, levels, and cells, and marking their movement from one part of the organization to another.

5. *Scientific Normalization Mechanisms.* Social science divides man into categories, partitions people, and dimensionalizes human conduct. People are indexed and known by their scores. People too far above or too far below the norms are sanctioned. Norm scores are used to decide and distribute rank and privilege. Clerks maintain computer scores and documents with norm scores. Performance reviews are done at intervals to derive norm scores. Workers

with low norms are penalized. Social science constructs the valid and reliable dimensions of performance reviews.

Social science has constructed GMAT norms used to admit or deny admission to MBA programs. The person's life to date is summarized and transformed into numerical scores. The gaze in the GMAT-based admission process works this way. You do not need to look upon the person or to interview them at all. The person never sees the faces of the admission committee who reviews the scores. In most MBA programs, a computer performs a calculation of grade point and GMAT norms and automatically admits students. Marginal cases are reviewed in committee. MBA programs advertise their norms; what GMAT and grade norms does the average student possess. Normalization and examination are both measurement without end and the gaze without end.

6. *Gratification-punishment mechanisms.* The greater your rank in an organization, the more you are treated as an individual. Popular managers dispense more rewards than penalties. The manager enforces a micro-accountancy of privileges and impositions for each person. Those with greater positive balances get more rights and privileges in the organization.

Summary of Modernist Principles for Applying Discipline

Principle One: Isolation. Isolate workers and managers from the external world and monitor their movements. Isolate workers and managers from one another and let them combine only in ritual and under hierarchical surveillance. Isolate people into homogeneous departmental groups and gaze the isolated work in a strict hierarchial framework. Discourage and punish non-isolated behavior patterns. Rank the person by their willing participation in the hierarchy of surveillance.

Principle Two: Regulation on the Treadmill. Do not let the worker or manager be idle. Let people do their work in strict time intervals and regulate away all possibilities for idle contact. Bend the person to rhythmic, repetitive time movements. Make man the slave of his machine. The longer and more repetitive the period of regulation endured, the more docile the worker becomes. The worker becomes hypnotized by the time machinery of the work discipline machine. Treadmill work does not contribute at all to "value-added" actions. Most treadmill time is not value-added, but it keeps people busy and docile. The movements of the cogs in the organizational machine are predictable.

Principle Three: Transform the Person over Time. Over time, the person becomes disciplined to the routines of the organization. Promotion tracks are made for those who subscribe to correct behaviors. Promotion tracks perform a transformative progression and socialization on those following the track. Promotion is a reward for corrective behavior and it is a disciplinary mechanisms for incorrect behavior. Pay raises and merit raises and bonus payments perform disciplinary functions. Management molds the human resource and reforms his character through disciplinary transformations. Rank is a trap. The higher the rank, the more freedom you have to be radical, but the more programmed you are *not* to be radical. The lower the rank of a manager, the more radical she can be, the more the hierarchy of surveillance will discipline attempts to deviate from organizationally-correct behavior.

Principle Four: Co-op the People through Cycles of Reform. Organizational renewal, transformation, development and reform programs reproduce exactly the same organization of panoptic discipline mechanisms. The labels differ, the players rotate, and the language changes, but the game is exactly the same as before. In each type of reform, many documents are generated, there are endless meetings, new slogans are put on the walls, but the system is the same system as before. If anything, during the process of reform, the hierarchy accomplishes more concentrated and pervasive surveillance of its people than during time intervals of non-reform. It is the same hierarchical surveillance mechanisms that dominated the system needing reform. Inertia is strong.

Results of the Modernist Panoptic Mechanisms

The organization practices a physiology and a psychology of discipline. The organization orders time and space rhythms on a grand scale. The instruments of discipline are the gaze, endless recording, and subtle penal mechanisms distributed in a network of discipline devices throughout the productive corridor of the organizational machine. Each penal mechanism is sanitized, gentile, rational, and civilized. The problem with the discipline machine is that it lacks the flexibility and innovative renewal potential required for competition in the global economy.

Foucault's Panopticon gives us a framework for assessing the results of the disciplinary organization.

1. *People are disciplined for norm and rule violations.* Conformity is preferred; anomalies are not tolerated. Surveillance and penal mechanisms are networked to form a continuous and hierarchical gaze of correct behavior. The surveillances are polite and the coercions are gentle, the penalties are mild, but the total effect is severe conformity. Punish the slightest indiscipline, conduct the

gaze regularly, and maintain a technology, some of it computerized for reporting, monitoring, ranking, and normalizing the individual.

2. *The Discipline machine recruits, fabricates and consumes its own delinquents.* The modernist service and production bureaucracies recruit people made docile by the school system. People who can not conform are deselected, demoted, and expelled. The 90–10 rule applies. 90% of the disciplinary structure is designed to control the 10% who resist and rebel against conformity. The greater the discipline, the more the system fabricates people who are rebellious, resistant, covert aggressive—in short delinquents. This means there is a tug of war between those made docile and those made delinquent. Delinquents, therefore, are a continuous birth and death object of the discipline machine. The system is insistent on surveillance and penal penalty, even though many resist such devices.

3. *The Discipline Machine makes the power to punish and penalize natural and legitimate.* In feudal times, corporal punishment was the tool of choice in schools, homes, and even workshop apprenticeship. If an apprentice messed up and left his candle burning, the journeymen could either solace (fine) him or throw him across a wooden table give him "what for". Now the physical torture of the body has been transformed into the technical and quasi-scientific, and pseudo-scientific tortures of being rhythmically coupled to the machine and in more recent times to the computer. Organizations are continuing to lower the threshold of tolerance to penalty mechanisms. Management renders justice to the workers. Management is the judge, the prosecutor, and the jury. While most of management discipline is taken-for-granted and widely accepted, the power of the manager is still very sovereign and her disciplinary mechanisms are sanctioned by scientific rationality. The manager does not personally punish, the examination does in a more anonymous, detached, and distant way. Managers do not have to bully people in verbal and confrontative spectacles, their preferred use of power is to put a letter in your personnel file, a letter you are not privileged to see.

4. *The Discipline Machine coopts social science to normalize people and make powerful judges out of managers.* Judges assess, diagnose, classify normal and abnormal, recommend correction, utilize experts, and decide human affairs. The manager is a judge with access to a system of inspection, a system of examination, a system of distribution, a system of surveillance, and in the end these things normalize the individual. MBA programs produce administrators who administer the technologies of this discipline.

5. *The body of the worker has been captured in the perpetual gaze, the knowledge accumulation system, and the panoptic cage.* Organizations are obsessed and voracious consumers of methods to fix, decide, classify, record, examine and ultimately objectify behavior. Social science legitimated the examination for discipline and the use of scientific instrumentation to make man conform to organization. These is a prevalent and seemingly uncritical application of scientific analysis to effect man's domination. There is also pseudo science. Handwriting experts divine placement decisions based on handwriting samples subjects do not know they have provided. People are placed on the basis of personality inventory scores. GMAT's decide entrance into business school. The bureaucrats and technocrats and plain clerks accumulate an amazingly complete and encompassing dossier of information on all aspects of the body human. The human being has been caged, not by the Rube Goldberg machine of discipline devices, but by the hard drives of the computer, and stored politely as so many bubbles of binary memory.

6. *The Discipline Machine meets any force to reform with great inertia.* The organization can be defined as a relay network of discipline mechanisms and surveillance systems. Many of these systems are being computerized. In these ways the individual through measurement becomes a case, an object of power, an object of knowledge, an element of the hierarchical gaze, and a mere normalized judgement. The reduction of people to their norm scores is a disciplinary mechanism to classify and distribute people in the modern business machine.

Under What Conditions Will the Discipline Machine Loosen Its Grip on the Human Body?

1. *When the utility of disciplinary surveillance operations ceases to be an effective way to docilize the workforce.* With the ubiquitousness of the computer and its efficiency as an information processor, a single executive with an extensive computer reporting network can review the time and motions of hundreds of people. This is one reason that once tall, multi-level organizations are becoming flatter. Middle managers are being laid off or put on temporary contract. The span of control (# of people reporting to a given manager) has been widening. The Tom Peters camp recommends that the span of control be widened even further. In one supermarket chain the store manager complained about their meddling regional manager. Top management responded by assigning additional stores to the regional manager. The widened span of control reduced the meddling. With wide spans of control,

the computer becomes the most efficient discipline instrument. People can input their goals, motions, time expenditures, and the computer can analyze this data and call the executive's attention to any discrepancy, any people who are significantly above or below a set of a priori norms.

In short, direct surveillance loosens its grip, when indirect surveillance mechanisms accomplish the same result at lower costs. The computer is replacing the panoptic tower as the ideal an perfect cage for human discipline. Like the panoptic tower, the human does not know what information is being gazed, who is seeing it, and when the computer monitor has been engaged. The gaze is asymmetric because the worker can not see the gazer.

2. *The proliferation of experts lessens the need for direct and hierarchical surveillance.* Expert disciplines in science, psychology, psychiatry, educational psychology, managerial psychology, engineering, organizational sociology, accounting, management information systems, and the like assume more of the supervisory and judging roles in the discipline machine. With more experts who administer the diagnosis, classification, and sentencing, there is less need for an extensive supervision hierarchy. If we train people to be expert inspectors, we do not need to employ inspectors as a separate discipline. If we teach workers to do the scheduling, recruiting, and performance review tasks of the foreman, then we do not need to hire foreman as an occupational category. As standardized tests proliferate and as these tests can be administered at a computer terminal which analyzes the results, there is less need for a testing person.

The Center of the Discipline Machine is a Machine not a Boss or a Dominant Coalition of People. At the center of the organization, was once a cigar smoking, cursing boss who dogmatically balanced the organizational disciplinary apparatus. Now, the organization has no one center. There are many centers. It is poly-centered. If anything, at the heart of the disciplinary machine, there is no dominant boss, no arrogant sovereign, no psychology expert, and no computer whiz kid. Rather at the center is a network of computers that monitors norms of organizational behavior and call in a given expert, strategists, or negotiator when abnormal behavior is measured. In this next section, we examine the forms of organizing that the modernist business is based upon.

Upon what other forms of organization is a business organization based? If we take an historical approach to organizations, we find that business organizations have borrowed organizing practices from nonbusiness forms of organization. The business firm has practices derived from: the family (a family of brother, sister, and elder workers in a team); the army (commanded by a head and divided into divisions and squads, with people assigned to ranks); a workshop (with supervisors, foremen who regulate work schedules and movements); the judicial form (justice is dispatch each day to discipline minor and major offenses); a monastic order (where the path to enlightenment is through discipline, cellular life, and hard work); sciences (technologies for measurement and normalizing personality, behavior, and skill); and the prisons (a system of penal disciplinary systems, time regimentation, cellular occupations, and dormitory housing). Business has also exported practices to these varied non-business forms.

The Story of Modern Edison Organization Being Adopted from the Navy Form of Organization

Mike   " . . . You know bureaucracies are set up to be, you know, the outlets to the military. We do have remnants of a military type of things here. You know, in the language. Like in power supply, for example, they go on a 24 hour clock basis. Ummm they don't have shifts, they have watches. And they have station chiefs and watch engineers.

Don   "That's right!

Mike   "And another bit of—a little story that has developed there that I've heard. Uhhh . . . the story goes that well I think that in power supply, it's customary to start work at 7 o'clock in the morning and work till 4:45 like everyone else. I understand the way that got started was that these chief whatever they ares, there first thing—what they wanted to find at 8 o'clock in the morning was find out what is wrong on the other two shifts.

Doug   "Read the morning report?

Mike   "Read the morning report at 8 o'clock. . . . Yeah OK. So if you're sharp then that's got to be ready. So the people that get the information for the guy had to come in at seven in order to get ready for him. And that just kind of happened. So now its a *norm*.

Bill   "That's the old concept of a half day is working from seven to seven.

Ted   "Yeah, that's right—power of the plant! [lots of group laughter].

Don   "When we first started here in a sense. When I say we, I mean the three years ago or so when a kind of a major set of changes were going on here in the division. One of the questions which came up was our time scheduling at work.

Should you be here on time? What's our flexibility in going places and that kind of thing. [*Note: the transition of Modern to Postmodern Planning and Organizing*] And our boss at that time at department level was a former power supply guy and I remember him saying to me: "Hey, you know I've got no problem, we've got flex time. We've got flex time just like we had in power supply. There's core hours, that's six to six. You can come in before that anytime you want. You can go home after that anytime you want." [Lots of group laughter and cross talk] . . . And it was straight and he was very comfortable with it and very proud of it. Twenty eight years before I got to this job. Twenty eight years and I never went anywhere without a beeper and I was on call seven days a week.

Boj "That's interesting.

Doug "Well, you see the watch engineer thing has some history to it. You see we started out with steam plants. And the only place you got people who know about steam plants was from the Navy. And our chairman of the board was the head of the steam division. In fact, he had been out in the field as a steam plant operator. And the one I told you about that was a Navy chief, well then, he was head of that organization in the operating department too. And so they went by the Navy time and the watch engineer bit. And there's pictures around. I think Peter has a picture cause that's where he came up. And all the guys from steam crew, they're all standing there with their arms around each other with their little white suits on cause that's what [they] used to wear.

Don "White suits, is that a fact?

Boj "Like the Navy?

Doug "Yeah and they all came from that type of environment. As much as we have nuclear engineers today. Now the guys that are starting to make it in the company now are—the vice presidents have their Navy Academy. Naval Academy graduates with Nuclear Rickover background. And they seem to like—topside seems to like the Rickover influence. So that's, that's a new—I watched that one come down the steam now. And there'll be a new one next week and we just had a couple more just a little while back. . . .

Mike " . . . I think we've given up the dream of someday being able to work with top management of this company and they would recognize all the great things we can do and the wisdom and everything and Yeah, they want us to consult with them. And I think our strategy whether we articulate it that way or not is to focus on those middle people that are influenceable but not as powerful, but are candidates four, five, or ten years who may be in those top chairs. Then, its right off to conference.

Don " . . . if a manager in one area of this company wanted to do something different, he'd start getting heat from other places. "Why are you doing this? You are breaking the unspoken agreement that we all stay the same!"

Mike " . . . And there is a balance too. You know? I value the heritage. I value 57 miles of road in 90 days and Big Creek and you know a lot of these old cowboys. You [know] some of these people are my friends.

Doug ". . . that's reality. They'll bitch, but then problem. When there's a panic or a crisis. There's a power supply. They pride themselves on the fact that when you flip that switch boy the lights go on. And they are going to do anything come hell or high water to make sure that those lights are reliable service that those lights are going to be on for you.

NAVY DISCOURSE
Top Side (CEO's and VP's)
Navy Time (24 hour clock)
Watches and Watch engineers
Station Chiefs
Morning Reports
The Rickover influence
Navy Academy
Nuclear Rickover
Dressed in their Whites
On call
Military discipline

STORY: Modern Organization was Adopted from the Family Model.

Bill "One of the things that surprised me when I came to this company was the average in terms of number of years that employees stay with the company. Its not like three or four, its ten, fifteen. An awful lot of the people stay a very long time and families work, husband and wife, husband and wife and child. Third generation families.

Mike "There's nepotism here and its valued.

Bill "It blew me away when I first got here that husbands and wives and families worked together. In other organizations that I have worked with it's absolutely forbidden and here it's rewarded.

Tim "Yeah it's valued and rewarded, but you do have some constraints. You can't report to the same boss and relatives can not report to each other. But, there are Edison families, 2nd and 3rd generation.

Don "Well, look at our own group. He's got Lois and her husband, is in power supply.

Tim "Elaine's got cousins and nieces working here.

Bill "Karen: her sister, her mom, her brother, your brother.

Ram "My ex-wife and step father, and brother in law.

Boj "This really is an Edison family, isn't it?

Bill "They pride themselves in the use of that term: family. You hear that from the day you walk in the door.

Sue "I got that in my interview in 73. That was made real clear . . . you are going to [be] working for a family, the Edison family. I got that from the interviewer and I got that from the boss . . .

Doug "You'll hear some of the old timers lament that its not the old Edison family that it used to be. My answer is that "well no how the hell could it be with 16,000 people over 70 million miles or whatever it is."

Tim "Another thing too, there's been some informal research done about how people get their jobs here. And, its most people get their jobs by being referred by someone who already works here. . . .

And this guy now I can hear him talk. "I can improve productivity. I know how to do this. Every time I make a suggestion they don't listen so, what's the use." So all this creativity is going down the tubes. This guy has got something because he's doing it on the outside and there are other people. Everybody has got something going and a lot of people have something going on the side and I'm still very curious. Is this Edison company specific? Is this typical in the industry because they are not as entrepreneurial as other places, or is Southern California the only [place]?

EDISON FAMILY DISCOURSE

Edison Family
Husband, wife, child, brother, sister, cousin
In-laws, step father
Second and Third Generations
Nepotism
"Should be grateful to be a part of the Edison family"
"They haven't forgiven the Edison Family for acquiring them" (in merger)
Edison Family Picnics

Deconstruction Points

1. *Innovation.* In the mechanistic organization, the classic military model, and the administrative bureaucracy, change is not an asset. Innovation is upsetting to the status quo. The dilemma for the postmodern organization, is that with the minimalist attachment of Dustin Hoffman to the organization, he will not innovate any more than the modernist navy man or the pre-modernist John Wayne. John Wayne and Dustin Hoffman are more the individualists than the modern, organizational man. However, John Wayne's square dealing, hard working ethic is not the more leisurely ethic of Dustin Hoffman.

2. *Harmony.* An organization is a connector between people and technology; between people's technology and the environment of customers, vendors, and global competition. Pre-modern harmony was based on a paternalistic contract which said that the crews would work hard, but in return, be treated squarely by management. In the modern organization, the harmony contract states that if you are a good old boy, the family takes care of its own. In the postmodern organization, the harmony contract says: if I work for you, I expect to go home at 5 P.M., be off most weekends, and I won't kill myself to make an organization that successful, when I know I will work somewhere else in a few years. My postmodern contract is one of temporary employment.

3. *A Variety of Forms.* The modernist organization is an overly of a variety of organizational forms: church, family, military, school, and prison.

Redefining the Modern Organization Principles

In the following table below, we present a reformulation of Henri Fayol's classic Administrative principles of organization. The column on the left present almost opposite, postmodern, viewpoints on the 14 modernist principles.

POSTMODERN PRINCIPLES	FAYOL'S 14 PRINCIPLES
1. *Multiplication of Labor.* Increase the number of tasks performed by a worker to as many as possible. This improves efficiency and effectiveness because it allows for complex and flexible production systems.	1. *Division of Labor.* Classic division of labor to reduce the number of tasks performed by a worker to as few as possible. This improves efficiency and effectiveness because it allows for the simple but rapid repetition of effort.
2. *Delegation and Empowerment.* Authority is delegated to the person closest to the action. People are empowered to take corrective action to systems and processes that need adjusting and changing.	2. *Authority and Responsibility.* Authority is the right to give orders and the power to exact obedience. Responsibility accrues to those who have authority. If you have responsibility, you must also have commensurate authority.
3. *Self-Discipline.* There is self-discipline instead of hierarchical and punitive discipline. Sanctions which remove self-discipline are removed. People are selected and trained to be self-starters, self-motivators, and self-discipliners.	3. *Discipline.* There must be obedience and respect between a firm and its employees. Discipline is based on respect rather than fear. Poor discipline results from poor leadership. Good discipline results from good leadership. Management and labor must agree. Management must judiciously use sanctions to ensure discipline.
4. *Variety of Command.* A person should have many managers who supply resources and expertise to remove barriers to performance.	4. *Unity of Command.* A person should have only one manager and receive orders from only one manager.
5. *Variety of Direction.* Plans unfold and get modified quickly to allow the organization to adjust to shifting environments. The individual is frequently reassigned from one team to another, as needed.	5. *Unity of Direction.* The organization, or any subunit thereof that has a single objective or purpose, should be unified by one plan and one leader.
6. *Subordination of general interest to individual interests.* The interests of the individual are temporary and end when the project ends. Individual is part of a continuously redesigning whole. Allegiances are more sideways than vertical.	6. *Subordination of individual interest to the general interest.* The interests of the organization as a whole should take priority over the interest of any individual or group of individuals within the organization.
7. *Intrinsic Remunerations.* People are motivated by the work they get to do and the relationships they get to form. People will work in many organizations during their lifetime.	7. *Remuneration of Personnel.* Workers should be motivated by proper remuneration. Remuneration levels are the function of many variables, including supply of labor, condition of the economy, and so on.

Table 3.5 Comparison of Postmodern and Modern Principles.

POSTMODERN PRINCIPLES	FAYOL'S 14 PRINCIPLES
8. **Decentralization.** Decentralization means the managers help people make decisions. If there is centralization, it is only temporary.	8. **Centralization.** Centralization means that the manager makes the decisions. Decentralization means that the subordinates help make the decisions. The degree of centralization or decentralization depends on the organization's circumstances.
9. **Cycles not Chains.** There are no sign offs and bottle necks. Each person is expected to take action to remedy a problem and keep the process quality high and the customer happy. Scalar chains slow down response time to adapt the organization to its environment. The silos slow down cycle time and cycle time is the key to competitive success.	9. **Scalar Chain.** Managers in hierarchical organizations are part of a chain of superiors ranging from the highest authority to the lowest. Communication flows up and down the chain, but Fayol also allowed for a communication "bridge" between persons onto various dimensions of the scalar chain. The "bridge" would allow subordinates in different divisions to communicate with each other—although formally they were supposed to communicate through their bosses and through the chain of command.
10. **Diversity.** Man-in-a-slot is outmoded bureaucratic tradition. The slots change too fast and reconfigure too often to become orderly. The variety of people do not classify into stable categories.	10. **Order.** There is a place for everything, and everything must be in its place—people, materials, cleanliness. All factors of production must be in an appropriate structure.
11. **System Integrity.** Quality results from continuously confronting a system to improve service and quality performance. Integrity is a system delivering what it says it will deliver when it says it will.	11. **Equity.** Equity results from kindliness and justice and is a principle to guide employee relations.
12. **Transient Personnel.** Organizations are increasingly temporary networks of associates who work on a few aspects of a project for several organizations.	12. **Stability of tenure for Personnel.** Retaining personnel, orderly personnel planning, and timely recruitment and selection are critical to success.
13. **Entrepreneur.** The real problem is entrepreneurship in the face of rapid change.	13. **Initiative.** Individuals should display zeal and energy in all their efforts. Management should encourage initiative.
14. **Rebellion.** Harmony can be forced cooperation which suppresses conflict. Conflict is the other side of the harmony coin.	14. **Esprit de Corps.** Builds harmony and unity within the firm. This harmony or high morale will be more productive than discord, which would weaken it.[13]

Table 3.5 Continued

❑ POSTMODERN ORGANIZING ❑

INTRODUCTION.

Our metaphor of the postmodern organization is flat. Flatter organizations produce more at lower costs by flat with fewer layers, latticed networking among teams, more autonomy for the individual, while being part of KAIZEN teams. Peter Drucker has suggested the flotilla, a small group of ships that can reconfigure in response to changing battle conditions as a better metaphor of organization than the modern metaphor of the battleship. If an organization is a battleship, it tries to do everything itself, and is not flexible like the flotilla. What about the metaphor of Terminator II. McKinsey's Smith in *Fortune* (May 18, 1992: 98) says the flat and flexible organization will be a powerful competitor.

Terminator II, the movie where Arnold Schwarzenegger faces a metal monster that liquefies, then hardens again in a new shape—now a man, now a machine, now a knife. Says Smith: "I call it the Terminator II company." How'd you like to have to compete with one of those?

Boj: You know I ride a Harley that looks a lot like the black, rolling thunder Harley-Davidson Schwarzenegger rides in Terminator II. They did a sketch with me in my Harley-boots taking apart some executives office who had been abusing his workers with modernist principles.

Flat and flexible organizations lower costs. Part of the lower costs comes from having fewer inspectors, quality checkers, supervisors, and middle managers. Fewer salaried people save money. In fact, *Fortune Magazine* had a recent article titled: **"The Search for the Organization of Tomorrow."**[14] American organizations are restructuring for the 21st century. Flexible Manufacturing System (FMS) with its **flat,** lean, Total Quality Management (TQM), empowered, cycle time focus is supposed to replace the tall hierarchical, modern organization. Workers with statistical quality control charts and information technology will speed up their work. Drucker says the battleship organization form will give way to the flotilla of lesser organizations that combine and recombine the way a fleet of battleships redeploys. The Pharaoh's pyramid is dead and giving way to *"post-hierarchical, flat and horizontal organization design principles"*.

1. *Create a High Employee Involvement Workplace.* Self-managing teams of empowered employees participating in productivity, quality and more job satisfaction. A discovery of the Tavistock Insititute of Human Relations in London, some 43 years ago at a coal mine. Self-managed teams deliver more output. Teams at Toyota are 4 to 6 in size, teams in American companies are 10 or more.

F L A T

FLAT	LATTICED	AUTONOMOUS	TEAM-BASED
▪ ▪ ▪ ▪ ▪ ▪ ▪	▪ ▪ ▪ ▪ ▪ ▪ ▪	▪ ▪ ▪ ▪ ▪ ▪ ▪	▪ ▪ ▪ ▪ ▪ ▪ ▪
Flat and Flexible with a few layers of management	A circle network of relationships between autonomous teams without going through a center ground	Post-Modern man is the self-disciplined entrepreneur who balances leisure with temporary commitment to formal organizations	Teams of equals are skilled to do their own planning, organizing and controlling

F How is the hierarchy of management set up within your organization?

L How do managers interact with the customers along with the employees?

A How much freedom do you have as a manager? Are you able to treat situations as you see fit?

T Does your organization work on team based ideas or does the work process end up more individualized?

Teams with members that can do multiple tasks can be reduced in size. Some teams have members from up and down stream operations. In some plants workers can rotate through different work areas every six months so that workers understand up and down stream operations. People get incentive pay for each rotation, perfect attendance, productivity, and for completing training. Cross-functional self-directed teams cut new-product development time. A network of work teams linked together in a circle instead of a pyramid. Organizations are flexible networks of semi-autonomous teams, with poly-centers of coordination, diverse and educated social make up, designed to achieve a diverse goals through processes of continuous quality improvement involving everyone in the organization including cooperative networks with customers and vendors. The mode of discipline is self-discipline. People are vigilant to resist the gaze.

2. *Organize around Processes instead of Functions.* Dissolve functions into the flow. Instead of a box of employees break out a part of a process map. Companies were set up by product type or by job function are not being arranged by process.

   Basic Processes: new-product development, flow of materials, order-delivery billing cycle. Disperse functional expertise along the process where it is needed.

   The vertical, functional pyramid organization is giving way to the serving customers and making products organization. Organizing around processes allows companies to dismiss unneeded supervisory hierarchies.

   a. Process uses external and system-wide objectives such as inventory turns or end-of-process tallies (customer satisfaction, on-time delivery) instead of unit costs.
   b. Process groups/locates workers with different skills to accomplish a piece of work.
   c. Info moves to where it is needed, instead of up and down the hierarchy. You deal with up and downstream problems instead of going to a boss. Who talks to their boss?
   d. Process is based on flow charting the entire process then organizing around that process.

3. *Use Information Technology to Make Information Accessible to Everyone in the Organization.* Knowledge, accountability and results info distributed rapidly anywhere in the flotilla. Fine fibers of communication, decision, and coordination traverse the flat, horizontal organization in a pattern of inter-team relationships that self-adapts to constantly changing environment (political, economic, governmental, community, mother earth, etc.).

4. *JIT*. JIT allows a sharp job in inventory. At GE appliances, a $5.4 billion-a-year business, the drop was $200 million in average inventory by implementing JIT. It is all about raising productivity while cutting costs in inventory and in personnel. Redesign is done to get improved performance and cost measures of performativity.

All of these principles are supposed to replace command and control with empowerment, self-management, and self-control. The command and control hierarchy topples in favor of the perpetual-learning machine. It is self-management when the workers run the plant, as with the Gaines pet food plant in Topeka, Kansas which Fortune reports has been self-managed for 20 years and has higher productivity than comparable command and control pet food plants.

Drawing the Circle Network

To get a picture of the postmodern organization, draw a series of small circles to represent autonomous work teams and connect these with a larger circle.[15] Kilinski and Wofford (1973) advocated non-pyramid form of organization, a network of teams where the basic element was the small work team of 12 to 20 persons. Each team was responsible for its own work functions and communication was to be face-to-face. The network organization was to have the bare minimum of layers and the leaders job's was to make the network function effectively. The more layers you have, the longer it takes for communication to go up then back down the layers, and the more distorted that communication process becomes. As people are conditioned to wait up their hierarchy for approval, they stop taking individual initiative for process improvement. With the circle network, teams can easily be re-configured to respond to changes in the environment. The idea is to minimize all the bureaucratic formality and emphasize the workings of the informal system. It is the job of each individual to plan, organize, innovate, influence, lead, and control. The divisions of labor into these functions are reconstituted back into the individual. The circle network is not without a rudder. The circle connecting the teams is the coordination mechanism. The steering of the organization is a shared responsibility. Cutting out organizational layers means getting rid of middle management, lots of bureaucratic staff positions, and foremen. Each team handles its own management. Instead of staff people doing the interviews, representatives from relevant teams are trained to do the interviewing themselves. If there are key decisions to be made, belts to be tightened, opportunities to consider, then representatives from all the teams do the thinking. The ideas for change come from those closest to the work processes and those closest to the customers, instead of those farthest away. The circle network has an agenda:

de-bureaucratize the firm. Cut the layers and recombine the functions, re-integrate the work place.

The Circle Network. The circle network gets away from the chain of command, the artificial division of labor, traditional spans of management, status-oriented job titles and job-trappings, and centralized control.

As Alvin Toffler says "Each age produces a form of organization appropriate to its own tempo" (1970: 143). The tempo of postmodernism is flexibility, co-equality instead of subordination, and temporary attachment, instead of long term security and confinement. Executives coordinate among diverse work teams composed of diverse, multi-skilled associates. The Executive is the servant to the functioning of this flexible and diverse and redesigning organization.

Post-Modern Circle of Teams

CompuAdd, a Postmodern Organization. According to Browning et. al (1992), CompuAdd is a postmodern organization.[16] It emphasizes leanness, speed, and power and it is nomadic. It is more flexible and powered than IBM or Texas Instruments. It has many diverse, heterogeneous elements that combine in different ways. Polyvocal code— varying situations and relationship in a fabric of supple segmentation. Work by temporary, cross-functional, diverse teams that are disassembled when the task is done. People are in flux networks where people are interchangeable, and defined only by their state at a given moment. "We teach everybody to go out and ask the customers "How are we doing? What are your requirements?"

Human relations helps people get into effective group harmony and confrontation quickly, but is not a means of human control. People no longer have the time to form permanent and impactful group relations. People who work in network organizations are not climbing the corporate ladder because it is not there anymore. There is a professional staircase, but one not tied to a single organization, it is tied to becoming better at your individualistic career. The conditioning of rewards and punishments does not work well on postmodern man. He is the free lance entrepreneur, the rebel out to reform, the inventor who seeks novelty and adventure. He is self-disciplined, not organizationally-disciplined. Well, not yet, but we can hope for the best.

What are the components of the circle network? The elements are teams, innovation, and self-discipline.

Teams

1. The team is the basic unit of PDCA (Plan-Do-Check-Act developed in previous chapter). The team plans its own work, is trained to do the work, is trained to check and inspect its own work, and is trained to take actions that re-define, re-shape, re-configure, and continuously improve the work processes.

2. Within each team there is mutual influence and mutual discipline.

3. The team is responsible for hiring and firing its own people. The team can ask for new types of expertise. The team takes responsibility for getting the job done in the best possible, most self-improving, continuously improving manner.

4. One member of the team serves on a coordinating team that links together other teams in the work place. This overlapping team membership insures team coordination.

5. The role of leadership is to make sure teams get the training they need to PDCA. The leader, as we shall explore in the leadership chapter, is a servant to the teams. Cypress Semiconductor has a

management system which tracks corporate, departmental, and individual performance so regularly and in such detail that no manager can possibly claim to be in the dark about critical problems. T.J.Rodgers, CEO, recognizes that people are going to have goals they don't achieve on time. When managers do have a problem, Rodgers usually intervenes with a short note: "Your delinquency rate is running 35%, what can I do to *help?*"[17]

6. The organization has no layers. Everyone is equal. Everyone uses the same bathrooms, eats in the same dining facilities. There are no reserved parking places for anyone. As much as possible all status trapping that de-mark and separate and subordinate one person to another are eliminated. That means freedom in dress styles. It means not hiding rank in a special badge or jacket or button.

Innovation Versus Kaizen.

KAIZEN: Continuous improvement involving everyone. As Masaaki Imai in the book *Kaizen* defines it: it means continuing improvement in personal life, home life, social life, and working life . . .—managers and workers alike" (p. xx). American's prefer result-oriented thinking to process-oriented thinking. Americans expect to leap frog the Japanese by engaging in big innovations, big changes in the organization, big changes in the production mechanisms. They hire, fire, dismantle, layoff, re-hire, re-fire, and reconfigure, but the bureaucratic machine is still the same. In Japan, the improvements are continuous, a series of *small steps* that everyone takes in order to keep the organization constantly changing and improving every day.

American industry is scrambling to try to get up to speed on continuous improvement organizing based on small step Kaizen rather than expert-driven, big step technology leaps that wipe out employment. If you haven't noticed, America does not have a booming, fast-growth economy. The technologies and work processes are deteriorating. America, unless willing to make radical changes in organizational form, is on the decline. One-shot, quick fix, high-tech rhetoric solutions are not cutting it. The Air Force, this past decade, has mandated continuous improvement and total quality management programs for all its military-industrial-complex sub-contractors. By all storied accounts, the Aerospace and other high-tech contractors can not wean themselves away from big bureaucratic machine organization. They call it matrix management and personal empowerment, and team-building, but it is just bureaucracy with new language. People are not giving up their small step Kaizen suggestions, and the brass at the top is still "Big John Wayne" calling all the shots.

	KAIZEN	INNOVATION
1. Effect	Long-term and long lasting but undramatic	Short-term but dramatic
2. Pace	Small steps	Big Steps
3. Time-frame	Continuous and incremental	Intermittent and non-incremental
4. Change	Gradual and constant	Abrupt and volatile
5. Involvement	Everybody	Select few "champions"
6. Approach	Collectivism, group efforts, systems approach	Rugged individualism, individual ideas and efforts
7. Mode	Maintenance and improvement	Scrap and rebuild
8. Spark	Conventional know-how and state of the art	Technological break-throughs, new inventions, new theories
9. Practical requirements	Requires little investment but great effort to maintain it	Requires large investment but little effort to maintain it
10. Effort orientation	People	Technology
11. Evaluation criteria	Process and efforts for better results	Results for profits
12. Advantage	Works well in slow-growth economy	Better suited to fast-growth economy[18]

Table 3.6. Comparison of Kaizen and Innovation.

Suggestion Systems

At Toyota Motor Company workers submit 1.5 million suggestions a year and 95% of them are implemented in a practical way. Did you know that the U.S. Air Force along with an outfit called TWI (Training Within Industries) exported suggestion systems to Japan in the postwar years of Deming and Juran, but at home American management stayed on the modernist path and refused and scoffed at suggestion systems? Oh yes, there was a brief flirtation by Americans in the 1970's and early 80's with quality circle teams and incentive-based suggestion programs with prizes and trips and other price-is-right hoopla, but in the main American workers saw that management was not implementing any of their ideas and they continued to do what they always did: put their gum and cigarette wrappers into the suggestion boxes. Did you know that 30 years ago, the Japanese had this very same problem with suggestion systems?

It was the U.S. Air Force and TWI (Training Within Industries) brought suggestion systems to Japan. The American system gave economic rewards for suggestions, but did not implement any of them.

Workers in America typically put gum wrappers and used kleenex in company suggestion boxes. In Japan, they actually implemented suggestions that improved one's own work, saved energy, improved the work environment, removed drudgery from work, improved processes, improved quality, and improved customer service. The Matsushita Company of Japan has over 6 million suggestions. One individual submitted 16,821 suggestions in one year. Companies in Japan pride themselves on who can collect and implement the most employee suggestions. In the 1950's Japan and United States each only had a handful of suggestions per year. The U.S. still has a handful, Japan has hundreds and thousands of ideas a year from each worker. What is the difference? How did Japan pull this off? The answer is (1) Japan implements the ideas, (2) Japan treats individual ideas as an opportunity for the person to stretch, grow, and improve.[19] With this program, the Aisin-Warner company that manufactures transmissions had 127 suggestions per worker in 1982. That is a company-wide total of 223,986 suggestions and they implemented 99%. At Canon Corporation, employees submitted 390,000 suggestions worth $84 million dollars in 1983. $1.08 million was paid out in rewards ranging between $200 and $2. Team suggestions get substantially larger rewards. And, it is management's responsibility to help get all the ideas reviewed, discussed, and implemented. Aisin-Warner and Canon, like most other big Japanese firms use computer systems to process this volume of suggestions. Suggestions are reviewed and given award payments.[20]

The Story of Enemies at Nippon Steel

Thirty years ago, Karoru Ishikawa encountered this problem head-on while employed as a consultant to Nippon Steel. In one instance, Ishikawa was investigating some surface scratches found on certain steel sheets. When he suggested to the engineer in charge of that particular process that his team review the problems together with the engineers in the following process, the engineer replied, "Do you mean to tell us that we should go examine the problems with our **enemies?**" To this Ishikawa replied, "You must not think of them as your enemies. You must think of the next process as your customer. You should visit your customer every day to make sure he is satisfied with the product." However, the engineer insisted, "How could I do such a thing? If I show up in their workshop, they'll think I've come to spy on them!"[21]

Deconstruction

1. Ishikawa is given credit for defining the term "**internal customer.**" The person or group that is in the next process from where you are is your internal customer.

2. Open communication. In order for the internal customer concept to take hold, workers and managers had to be willing to be frank about their problems and mistakes. They had to quit blaming the system and begin to work together to change and improve the system. The system is you.

3. Suggestions. The reason suggestion systems, 30 years ago, were as bad then as American suggestion systems are now, is that managers thought suggestions was none of the worker's business. The worker was the enemy and the manager had all the suggestions. "Park your brains at the door, do the job, even if it is wrong, and keep your trap shut!"

4. Engineers Myopia. In Japan as in America, the engineers stayed away from the shop floor. The engineer designed the work systems. After all, Frederick Taylor's scientific management principles and Fayol's Administrative management principles prescribed a separation between functions, a strict division of labor, and the inferiority of the worker. "Why bother listening to an inferior, less educated being?"

5. Customer Voice. The moral of the story is that to increase the quality and service to the external customer, the voice of the customer must be heard in the deeds of the internal customers.

JAPANESE SUGGESTION SYSTEMS

1. Improvements in one's own work.
2. Savings in energy, material, and other resources.
3. Improvements in the working environment.
4. Improvements in machines and processes.
5. Improvements in jigs and tools.
6. Improvements in office work.
7. Improvements in product quality.
8. Ideas for new products.
9. Customer services and customer relations.

Results

In the 1950's the average number of suggestions per year per employee was five.

By the 1980's:
- Matsushita Company generated 6 million suggestions in 1985.
- One individual gave out 16,821 suggestions.
- Hitachi Company generated 4.6 million suggestions in 1985.
- Companies like Aisin-Warner generate 223,986 suggestions and implement 99% of them.
- Cannon, in 1983, generated 390,000 suggestions worth $84 million and paid out $1.08 million in payback.[22]

Table 3.7.

How it works. The job of management is to read all these suggestions, rate them, get the practical ones implemented, celebrate the ideas and their implementations with ceremonies, awards and money. That is a whole lot of very disciplined work that most American managers are not willing to invest in their organizations. In addition, people need to be given time away from task to think up their ideas, write up their ideas, and implement their ideas.

The suggestion system is an absolutely critical element of Kaizen. It has to be well organized, careful administered, and the ideas have to be strategically implemented. Management has to respond to the ideas and manage the feedback and reward system. The more successful systems are based more on the idea of each individual being a real part of the organization, contributing to its success, which contributes to their own growth and employment—rather than just a meaningless game of incentives and hoop jumping.

Autonomy and Self-Discipline

Postmodern man is self-disciplined. Even his allegiances to his profession and expertise, which while over-shadowing his organizational loyalties, are not too confining because the boundaries between specialized disciplines are coming down. Problems are multi-faceted and not contained by professional boundaries. The specialist knows a given field well for only a short while. Self-discipline means continuous education, continuous improvement of the quality of one's knowledge. Discipline is the ability to perform well in a temporary, ad hoc network.

How do you effect discipline without inducing docility? The result of over-discipline is rebellion, retaliation, and complacency. With modern discipline the education system fabricates people who respond favorably to routine, repetition, and regimentation. The problem is these secure, stable, unchanging dinosaurs are rapidly becoming extinct. Once the America 2000 project to transform the curriculum and educational experience of schools has been implemented, we will fabricate a very different type of adult for organizational consumption.

Self-discipline will replace machine discipline. The results of a positive discipline environment is people work in a system of performance that is customer-focused and quality-driven. The needs of our industrial global economy are for increasingly flexible organizations able to adapt quickly and efficiently to a wider variation of market niches. To work in a network organization, a network of customers, workers, and vendors—requires each actor in the system to be more educated, trained, and accountable to make their individual behavior make total system behavior work better. The needs of each individual are necessarily subordinate to the total system.

Business Educates Because Schools are Failing. With the decline in the ability of the American education system to produce literate citizens, larger corporations are investing in on-site remedial schools to train workers to read and calculate. Motorola has one of the most extensive programs at its Motorola University.[23] The postmodern form of organization is heavily dependent upon an educated workforce to function. Educated people are necessary because they need to deal with computers and assume responsibility for their own supervision. There are fewer bosses and foremen around to tell people what to do, how to do it, and when to do it. Organizing the work will, as in the pre-modern era, become more the prerogative of the workers.

Postmodern organization through storytelling. People are buried in a mind numbing avalanche of information. People are more culturally diverse than ever before and therefore, except for television and pop culture, do not share a common and shared cultural experience. Our mass media culture makes information bits, rather than integrated knowledge found in stories. Stories are the conduit of experience. The news media, textbooks, newspapers, annual reports overloads us with information, but we are not learning the stories, at least not any noteworthy stories. In management textbooks, we get a lot of encyclopedic information, a veritable dictionary of terms and dimensions, but the textbooks do not tell the stories undergirding their jargon. In this way the information age isolates the individual in a sea of seemingly-scientific information, alienates the individual from the story roots, and rationalizes management as a social science instead of historically anchored performance art.

Through stories, people learn the epic side of management practice, the wisdom of experience is imparted in the stories. The stories told to children at bedtime by their mothers have shaped more ethics than all the ethics textbooks combined. If storytelling is ignored, then the community-processing of experience decreases.

The Storytelling Organization

The postmodern organization is an information network: a set of exchanges among internal and external stakeholders. Stakeholders are customers, vendors, communities, schools and they are employees, managers, clerks, and janitors. Each has a stake in the activities of the organization. As an information processing network, stories serve the collective memory, the processing of past experiences into information about policy, decision, and precedent. A mass of detail buries meaningful experience. Increasing the effectiveness of storytelling increases meaningful communication and increases organizational memory effectiveness. The role of the manager is the role of all people in the organization, hear many sides to each story, processes the stories of past and future organizational experience, and make the best choices. Stories make experience meaningful; stories connect us to one another; stories make the characters come alive; stories provide an opportunity for a renewed sense of organizational community.

If we normalize, dimensionalize, and do the discourse of scientific management—the result is a manipulative language with manipulated meanings that befuddle interpersonal relations. Without story, information is oversimplified in the name of science. Watch the news and you see the infantilization of the American culture; the manipulation of information bits to produce the broadest mass appeal, the highest of common denominators, the minimal transmission of experience from newscasters to the mass audience. Mass information destroys collective experience. Storytelling builds collective understanding, collective appreciation, collective imagination, and collective memory.

Storytellers apprehend experiences and communicate those experiences to story listeners. The story listener does not just receive the teller's story, the listener is a co-processor, a co-producer, a listener mingles their own experience with the experiences of the teller. As such, story listening is not a passive event. Story listeners leaven the experiences they have received. People see the characters dance in their imagination, capture the interacting characters in their mind's eye, and fill in the blanks the storyteller leaves in the story.

Skeptical Assessment of Postmodern Organizing.

1. *TEAM Concept* The postmodern building blocks of the "new" organization is the team. Parker and Slaughter (1988) have challenged the team concept as being as alluring as Mom and apple pie. In fact, so alluring that we are not asking some basic questions. If we organize teams so that every person is multi-skilled and can do everyone else's job, then have we lost the advantages of specialization in the football or basketball team. Can the outfielders pitch, catch, and play shortstop? Is this approach to teams realistic? Can one person be gifted in all these areas? Isn't the whole thing about a team to have the specialized crafts come together with some synergy?

   In fact, the main place in our language where "team" implies interchangeable members is where it refers to a team of horses—beasts of burden of equal capabilities, yoked together to pull for a common end (determined by the person holding the whip) (Parker & Slaughter, 1988: 4).

2. *Same walk, different talk.* A postmodern discourse can replace a modernist discourse, by substituting a few well-sounding words and catch phrases for the old modernist principles. But, even though the wards vary, the reality of people's work experience is exactly the same.

MOD DISCOURSE: "the foreman holds a meeting of his group and announces the week's productivity and scrap figures or discusses the latest safety memo. The foreman's "go-fer" takes care of vacation schedules and work gloves" (p. 4).

POSTMOD DISCOURSE: "Hourly workers are organized into teams which meet with their advisor to discuss quality and work procedures. A team leader takes care of vacation scheduling and supplies" (p. 4).

What does changing the rhetoric do? We are lulled into a state of docility, as we suspend our critical judgement.

3. *Nordstrom's Approach to Job Enlargement.* The affirmative rationale is that in order to serve the customers, the service representative should not pass the customer from one person to another. The skeptical observation is that the salesperson is now the delivery person, who must deliver packages on their lunch hour and be so highly motivated that they do not dare to ask for compensation.

4. *Suggestions Systems.* Getting knowledge of the worker's work processes and the worker's knowledge of the work being done and turning it into management control data. Parker and Slaughter (1988) point out how giving away knowledge is often done without implementation, recognition, or compensation. "But once the suggestion is made the knowledge becomes part of management's power to control every work on the line" (p. 19).

5. *KAIZEN.* Under Kaizen, there is continuous improvement involving everyone. This is supposed to empower the workers to get more and more control over their work process. Coupled with statistical process control training, the workers are able to become their own time and motion self-observers. The workers are doing what Michel Foucault calls "internalizing the gaze." The workers gaze their own time and motions, then suggest Kaizen ways of improving their fit into the production process. Workers may well be loosing flexibility, autonomy, and control by increasing their coupling to the machine, volunteering surveillance information, and even displacing the time and motion monitors by doing self-surveillance.

Conclusions

With all the positive press about lean production, flatter hierarchies, and getting America to pull itself up by the bootstraps of Kaizen and cycle time, we have not listened to the voices of workers and unions. Are workers losing discretion, being asked to do more work for the same pay, being asked to take on the functions of inspector and supervisor, doing the multi-tasking while a co-worker is laid off, etc. only to find out that management is getting all the empowerment and the corporate owners are saving all the bucks? If this is true, then is not the postmodern organization just another solution to scientific management?

Computer innovations have made the application of quantitative decision and problem solving and the scientific measurement of each person's performance more a reality now than in the early 1900's.

Scientific management has been too easily dismissed by management texts as essentially irrelevant once the management theorists envisioned an organization responding to an environment and once more organic, and less mechanistic theories of organization had been concocted. But, concocting an organic theory of organization, does not mean that organizations have become less mechanistic, less modernist. Most of us work in a system of mechanized surveillance.

The fundamental aspect of all organizations is discipline. Discipline the people to discipline the delivery of goods and service. The pre-modern discipline was quite physical. Modern discipline is machine oriented. Postmodern discipline is the computerization of man.

Organizations are combinations of the strands of pre-modern crew-based apprentice societies, modernist military machines, and postmodern flexible networks with temporary attachments. John Wayne still climbs poles and drinks with both hands. The Navy brass still prefer half days that are 12 hours long. Dustin Hoffman still prefers to leave work at five and head for the RV. While all three strands of organization are there to this day in every large corporation, the Dustin Hoffmans are beginning to take over.

NOTES

1. Ibid. Albanese, p. 226.
2. Quotation from Elbert Hubbard, A Message to Garcia, ed. R. W. G. Vail (New York: New York Public Library, 1930), p. 14 in Reinhard Bendix, Work and Authority in Industry (New York: John Wiley & Sons, Inc., 1956), p. 265.
3. Ibid. Albanese, p. 227.
4. All the Edison, John Wayne stories come from: Boje, David M. "Edison Story Sharing Session" October, 1983; Boje, David M. "Organizational Mythologies in Conflict in a Utility Company: John Wayne Versus Dustin Hoffman." UCLA-GSM Working Paper 83-77. (November, 1983).

5. Alvin Toffler. 1970, *Future Shock*, New York: Random House p. 399–400.
6. "Competing in the New International Economy." Washington: Office of Technology Assessment, 1990. Also in "What Work Requires of Schools: A SCANS report for America 2000", Secretary's Commission on Achieving Necessary Skills, U.S. Department of Labor, (June, 1991): 3.
7. Whyte, William H. *The Organization Man* Garden City, NY: Doubleday Anchor Books, 1956: 70.
8. Toffler, Alvin. *Powershift: Knowledge, wealth, and violence at the edge of the 21st Century.* New York: Bantam Books.
9. Ibid. From *In Blandings' Way* by Eric Hodgins, quoted in William Whyte Jr. p. 177–8.
10. Foucault, Michel. *Discipline and Punish: The birth of the prison.* Translated by Alan Sheridan, New York: Pantheon Books.
11. This section on Panopicism comes from: Boje, David M. 'The University is a Panoptic Cage: The Disciplining of the Student and Faculty Bodies." (December) 1991. LMU Working paper.
12. *In Search of Excellence*, ibid.
13. Adapted from Daniel A. Wren, *The Evolution of Management Thought* (New York: Wiley, 1979): 218–221 summary of Henri Fayol principles; Alvin Toffler's "Organizations: The Coming Ad-hocracy" in *Future Shock*, 1970 (New York: Random House): 124–151.
14. *Fortune*, May 18, 1992: 92–98.
15. Credit for the circle network goes to Kilinski, Kenneth K. and Jerry C. Wofford *Organization and Leadership in the Local Church.* Grand Rapids, MI: Zondervan Publishing House, 1973: 142–151.
16. Browning, Larry David, James J. Ziaja and Debra R. France. "A postmodern organization goes for a modern prize: A brief ethnography of CompuAdd's application for the Malcolm Baldrige National Quality Award." *Journal of Organizational Change Management*, 5 (1): 69–78.
17. Rodgers, T.J. "No Excuses Management"; *Harvard Business Review* July/August 1990 pp. 84–98.
18. Ibid From Imai, p. 24.
19. Imai, Masaaki Kaizen: The Key to Japan's Competitive Success. New York: McGraw-Hill, 1986: 112–113.
20. Ibid. Imai p. 115–120.
21. Ibid. Imai, p. 51.
22. Ibid. Adapted from Imai, p. 111–124.
23. Wiggenhorn, William. 1990. "Motorola U.: When Training Becomes an Education." *Harvard Business Review*, July–August, p. 71.

CHAPTER

4

INFLUENCE STORIES

INFLUENCE DEFINITIONS

PRE-MODERN INFLUENCE
Influence is **Solace.**

S   *Solace:* Journeymen could call a democratic meeting to vote in a fine (solace) to enforce a shop rule.

O   *Order:* There is a divinely-inspired pre-destined order to the universe. Social Darwinism: man is destined to be poor or rich. Do not interfere with God's "survival of the fittest" order.

L   *Lazy:* Man fought the temptation to be lazy, sinful and prideful by meditating on virtues.

A   *Attitude:* Attracted or repelled success or failure. PMA (Positive Mental Attitude). Use PMA-Affirmations like: "**I feel healthy! I feel happy! I feel terrific!**" Attitudes had religious significance.

C   *Culture:* The craft-based, fraternal culture influenced behavior.

E   *Entrepreneurial:* Self-reliant entrepreneurs could graduate their apprenticeship and be master of their own enterprise.

MODERN INFLUENCE
Influence is **Comply.**

C   Conformity. Correct and docilize. Use human relations approaches to peer group influence.

O   *Obedience:* There must be obedience and respect by employees for their firm. Discipline is based on fear, surveillance, and the internalized gaze.

M   *Motivate:* Use rewards and punishments (carrot and stick). Pay them to comply and keep an eye on them.

P   *Performativity:* People are human resources to be used by the system to maximize its performance.

L   *Logical:* Man seeks equity and integration, reacts rationally to rational circumstances.

Y   *Yielding:* Man yields to the pace of the machine, to the layers of authority over him.

POSTMODERN INFLUENCE
Influence is **Individual.**

I   *Independent:* Avoid domination, be private, seek freedom from collective influences.

N   *Narcissist:* In search of a self-image, self-will.

D   *De-centered:* Person is a multiplicity of selves, practices many logics, dis-unified, not-centered.

I   *Individual:* Spontaneous (not planned or rehearsed), unique in thought and action.

V   *Voices:* Each person has many voices in them. Some have less influence, some have more.

I   *Irrational:* Fragmented, willing to participate in contrary causes and multiple realities.

D   *Diversity.* Discord and variety are balances to unity, conformity, and community.

U   *Unconforming:* Self-disciplined rather than other-disciplined; rebel against authority; defy totalitarianism.

A   *Affirming the Self:* Self-affirmatives like: "**I feel healthy! I feel happy! I feel terrific!**" to gain personal control over mind (avoid outside influence and coercion), to promote the self, and retain freedom to choose feelings and actions.

L   *Linguistic:* Individuals influence by language, by categories, by storied personifications.

Table 4.1.

INFLUENCE

SCORES	1 2	3 4	5
Solace	There would be no voting to enforce any rules	A presence of voting, but you still did what you were told to do	Democratic meetings called to vote to enforce shop rules
Order	Everybody is living in a confused world	Some kind of order is starting to form	A definite divine-inspired predestined order to the universe
Lazy	Activities are not being done because of laziness	People start to realize they cannot be lazy and do quality work	There is no temptation to be lazy, people want to do quality work
Attitude	Definitely a bad attitude about their work	Not sure if they like their work or not, a mixed attitude	"I feel healthy! I feel happy! I feel terrific!"
Culture	Culture is pretty primitive	Culture is starting to develop, but still pretty basic	Definite craft-based, fraternal culture influenced behavior
Entrepreneur	Not enough knowledge to be on their own yet	Learning how to be a self-reliant entrepreneurial	Master of their own enterprise
Conformity	Use of some human relations approaches to peer influences	Employees corrected and docilized by human relations approaches	Human relations approaches are used to correct and docilize all employees
Obedience	Employees have no respect for their firm	Definite means of obedience and respect to the firm	Discipline based on fear, surveillance, and the internalized gaze
Motivate	No motivation is present to get people working	Leaders are trying to use verbal skills to motivate	Established rewards and punishments
Performativity	Efficiency is less important than human condition	Person treated as human resource to production function	People exploited to maximize production
Logical	There is little logical approach to a task	People start to analyze the situation better	Man seeks equity and integration, and reacts rationally
Yielding	Everybody looks at themselves as the best	Man starts to yield to the pace of the machine	Man yields to the layers of authority

INFLUENCE

SCORES	1 2	3 4	5
Independence	People dominated by others and they want to be public	Man starting to avoid domination	Definite signs of being private, avoiding freedom from collective influences
Narcissist	Man living under the image of others	People starting to realize that they have to find own self-will	Self-image and self-will finally found
De-centered	Logic is not being practiced, people unified	Still centered and unified	Definite multiplicity of selves practice many logics and not centered
Individual	Not very unique, coming straight from the book	Definite signs of beginning to be spontaneous	Very spontaneous and unique in thought and action
Voices	Each person has one voice in them	People starting to speak out more	Many voices. Some have less influence, and some have more
Irrational	Unwilling to participate	Beginning to be fragmented	Willing to participate in contrary causes and multiple realities
Diversity	Variety is not a balance to the community	Signs of being more balanced	Discord and variety are balances to unity, conformity, and community
Unconforming	Supporting totalitarianism and no rebelling activities	Still other-disciplined rather than self-disciplined	Rebel against authority, totalitarianism, and self-disciplined
Affirming	No personal control over mind or freedom to choose feelings or actions	Starting to promote the self	"I feel healthy! I feel happy! I feel terrific!"
Linguistic	Individuals are not influenced by anything	Influence is starting to take control of people	Language, categories, and story personifications influence

	PRE-MOD	MOD	POST-MOD
Q1: How do customers managers and employees voice their opinions?	Carl's votes upon whether or not the suggestions should be used and how much the person who made the suggestion should receive. **S olace 4** 31%	Carl's rewards in implemented suggestions with cash. They have established a reward. **co M ply** 38%	Each person has many voices in them that need to be heard. Carl's asks to hear their voices through their suggestion box system. **indi V idual 4** 31%
Q2: How independent are the individual stores?	Carl's evaluates every suggestion and then votes upon if it should be implemented. Their presence of voting, but they still do what they are told. **S olace 4** 44%	Carl's does not let individuality of their restaurants to exist. Each individual restaurant must yield to the layers of authority over them. **compl Y 5** 56%	**N/A** 0%
Q3: How is the work force motivated?	Carl's motivates its employees by providing a family atmosphere. This fraternal culture influences behavior. **sole C e 5** 38%	Carl's rewards its employees with medical and dental benefits. Rewards have been established. **co M ply 5** 38%	The employees in Carl's have the opportunity to move up if they desire. Employees must develop a self-will in order to survive. **i N dividual 3** 24%
Q4: What is the target market?	Carl' new commercials show Happy always being negative about the future, it could be considered a satire on what Carl's Jr. truly believes. **sol A ce 4** 36%	Carl's is logical about their target market. They know that to target an older market would be profitable. **comp L y 4** 36%	Carl's uses cariety of their target market to balance the conformity within the industry. **indivi D ual 3** 28%
AVERAGE	37.3%	42%	20.8%

solaCe:
Culture (5) 38%
Carl's motivates its employees by providing a family atmosphere. This fraternal culture influences behavior.

coMply:
Motivate (5) 38%
Carl's rewards its employees with medical and dental benefits. Rewards have been established.

iNdividual:
Narcissist (3) 24%
The employees in Carl's have the opportunity to move up if they desire. Employees must develop a self-will in order to survive.

complY:
Yielding (5) 56%
Carl's does not let individuality of their restaurants to exist. Each individual restaurant must yield to the layers of authority over them.

Solace:
Solace (4) 44%
Carl's evaluates every suggestion and then votes upon if it should be implemented. There is a presence of voting, but they still do what they are told.

Q1: How is the work force motivated?

A1: Well, our greatest motivational factor would be our family atmosphere. It makes the employee feel like an important part of Carl's, not a just cog in the wheel. We also have the standard benefits such as medical and dental . . . Let's see. . . Also, the opportunity for promotion is made readily available for the employees to use. That way the employee does not feel as if he or she is stuck in one position for a long amount of time.

Q2: How independent are your individual restaurants?

A2: Well, too much independence for the franchises can creates problems and is not practical. Much of our evaluation is done by sales levels, with a lot of independence you are asking for a competition that may not be healthy for Carl's as a whole. Like if the manager of one store comes up with a great idea to bring more customers in, he may keep it to himself so that only his restaurant will benefit. This is why we encourage employees to use the suggestion box system, great ideas can be presented to the main office for evaluation, if they like it, it will be implemented throughout all of the stores, and if they don't, it can be rejected. We have a reputation to hold up and people expect a consistent experience with each Carl's that they come into.

IndiviDual:
Diversity (3) 28%
Carl's uses variety of their target market to balance the conformity within this industry.

compLy:
Logical (4) 36%
Carl's is logical about their target market. They know that to target a older market would be profitable.

solAce:
Attitude (4) 36%
Carl's new commercials show Happy always being negative about the future, it could be considered a satire on what Carl's Jr. truly believes.

IndiVidual:
Voices (4) 31%
Each person has many voices in them that need to be heard. Carl's asks to hear their voice through their suggestion box system.

Solace:
Solace (4) 31%
Carl's votes upon whether or not the suggestions should be used and how much the person who made the suggestion should receive.

coMply:
Motivate (5) 38%
Carl's rewards the implemented suggestions with cash. They have established a reward.

Q3: What is your target market?

A3: Carl's Jr.'s target market are persons from the ages of 18 to 40. . . . We make no discrimination between male or female. Since we give the impression of being an "up scale" fast food restaurant with better quality food and relatively higher prices, we are more apt to bring in an older, more educated customer than our competition. With our latest commercials, if you listen to what "Happy" (the star) has to say, its humor is not something that a younger person would understand. I like it, I think they're funny. These new commercials will hopefully extend our market to even an older, more educated crowd.

Q4: How do customers, managers, and employees voice their opinions?

A4: Well, I'm not sure what exactly you are looking for. . . . There is what we call a suggestion box system that is used. The way it works is that any one person can make a suggestion on another division that might improve it in some way. We do that so if, for instance, a truck driver whose job includes finding quicker routes for delivery, cannot suggest how to have quicker routes and then expect a cash bonus. It is part of his job. But if he were to suggest how packing could make a more efficient package design his suggestion could be submitted for review. If his suggestion is implemented, the employee would receive a cash bonus, the amount determined for each suggestion implemented is completely up to upper managements discretion. Usually it is based on how much money the suggestion has saved the Carl's. I've heard of $50 bonuses and I've heard of $5000 bonuses. There isn't a customer suggestion box, we've had a few customers notify us of ideas that would save us lots of money, but they want the money up front before they give it to us. We never got back to them.

THE CARL'S JR. INFLUENCE SUGGESTION BOX

AREAS THAT THE NAVY BLUE TEAM LIKED:

- ❑ Carl's listens to the voice of the employee through the suggestion box system.
- ❑ The family atmosphere that Carl's provides for its employees.
- ❑ The opportunity for promotion through training.
- ❑ The diversity of Carl's target market.
- ❑ The humor in the television commercials.

SUGGESTIONS FROM THE NAVY BLUE TEAM:

- ❑ There needs to be a suggestion box system for the customers.
- ❑ More individuality for each store could improve the family atmosphere.
- ❑ More motivational factors such as social gatherings for employees.

CARL'S JR. INFLUENCE ANSWERS

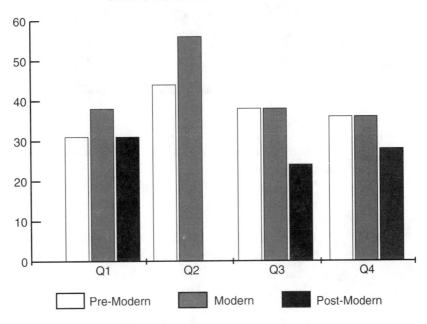

CARL'S JR. INFLUENCE

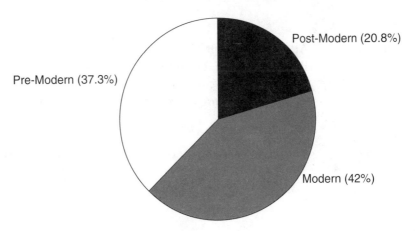

S O L A C E

Solace   **Journeymen could call a democratic meeting to vote in a fine to enforce a shop rule.**
How do you decide how to enforce a rule?

Order   **There is a divinely-inspired pre-destined order to the universe.**
What do you to inspire your employees to work up to their potential?

Lazy   **Man fought the temptation to be lazy, sinful, and prideful by meditating on virtues.**
Do you expect your employees to do things that they don't want to do because they don't think it is morally correct to do?

Attitude   **Attracted or repelled success or failure.**
Positive Mental Attitude.
If an employee comes into work not happy or enthused to be there, do you do anything to get them to have a positive mental attitude?

Culture   **The craft-based, fraternal culture influenced behavior.**
How do you influence the way your employees behave toward the customers?

Entrepreneurial   **Self-reliant entrepreneurs could graduate their apprenticeship and be master of their own enterprise.**
Is there a point in time when an employee would feel that they are pretty much in charge of what they do?

❑ PRE-MODERN INFLUENCE ❑

Introduction

Pre-modern influence featured a fraternal culture with peer influence. Religion affected attitude. Individuals fought laziness and sought to develop an entrepreneurial spirit. Feudal people had deference to authority and their masters did not to consider influence beyond the whip and rack. Modern influence utilizes scientific management, behavioral science and human relations to achieve compliance. Yield, obey, conform are the watch words. Postmodern influence focuses on the individual with self affirmation and self discipline. But the self is not isolated. Sensitivity to a variety of voices is stressed. In multiple networks we find participation, fragmentation and diversity which avoids categories. Woven throughout this approach is a value for feelings and emotions. One of the critical questions here is are people more or less empowered with postmodern influence?

Pre-modern influence is solace. Solace, order, lazy, attitude, culture, entrepreneurial. In pre-modern stories, influence was accomplished by the craft culture where journeymen could vote in fines ("Solaces"). God was more alive before modern technology. Sin, virtue, and attitude told the story of a man's influence. Despite the influence of guild and religion, people retained a more entrepreneurial and self-reliant spirit.

Pre-modern influence is ubiquitous in American society. Fraternities and sororities, for example, influence actives (full fledged members) to initiate pledges with rituals acts of influence, such as interviews, fetching and carrying for the actives, reciting Greek texts, and instilling that special Greek character through all manner of influence that has been passed from upper to lower classman since the origin of fraternities in the late 1700's. Phi Beta Kappa, was the first Greek-letter fraternity with secret handshakes, mottos, and rituals. On December 5, 1776, the College of William and Mary started a system that has spread its secret influences around the world. The National Interfraternity Conference in Indianapolis, represents 400,000 mean in 5,300 chapters on 800 campuses in the United States and Canada. Pledges are always influenced more by what they see rather than the stories they are told. Brothers and sisters have a duty to "get to know" pledges and to develop the pledges sense of brotherhood or sisterhood. Pledges are reviewed, evaluated, and voted upon from the beginning to the end of the pledge process.

Brothers and sisters are influenced to be enthusiastic members and righteous representatives of a chapter. Pledges are initiated and grilled to keep the secrets of the chapter and show proper respect to the chapter and its initiated members. Through constant supervision and coaching, the pledge is influence to smooth off the rough edges and develop character worthy of chapter initiation.

Fraternities and sororities are also bureaucratic in their influence, with executive committees, steering committees, chapter advisors and moderators, and extensive charters with rules and policies to influence all facets of the pledges and actives life space. Fraternities and sororities are influenced by the interfraternal council as well as their faculty moderators and advisors.

Boj: Bob, I could tell you about the secret rituals of initiation in my fraternity, but then I'd have to shoot you.

Pre-modern influence is found to this day in churches, universities, military organizations (especially boot camp), Toastmasters, Alcoholics Anonymous, courts, and even the Congress of the United States. Each has a sense of more senior people bringing along the new comers to be influenced to become upstanding members of their organization. These are strong cultures with numerous rituals, ceremonies, and historical traditions to influence their members.

Here are our stories.

Printing Apprenticeship Stories

The Compositors Wore Swords

They were fond of impressing the newly entered apprentices with the advantage they held over mere tradesmen and artisans in belonging to so ancient and honorable a calling as that of printing: telling them that "in olden time, when none but the privileged classes were permitted to go armed, the compositors wore swords by their sides" (being gentlemen by virtue of their art, and because the first comtor was a knight) and sat at case, to mark the distinction between themselves and ordinary mechanics, who stand to their work.[1]

The Father of the Chapel

The chappelonians walk three times round the room, their right arms being put thro' the lappets of their coats; the boy who is to be made a Cuz carrying a wooden sword before them. Then the Boy kneels, and the Father of the Chapel [the oldest freeman], after exhorting him to be observant of his business, and not to betray the secrets of the Workmen, squeezes a sponge of strong beer over his head, and gives him a title, . . . Whilst the boy is upon his knees, all the Chappelonians . . . walk round him, saying the Cuz's anthem, which is done by adding all the vowels to the consonants.[2]

Instruments of the Chapel Ceremony

The Chapel was a system of discipline, initiation, and drinking that the journeymen and apprentice maintained from the 1600's to the early 1900's. "The Chapel cannot err . . . for the good of the Chapel" (Avis, 1971: 27; Boje, 1983: 10). Chapels collected fines for incorrect behavior, birthdays, weddings, and spent the money on drink and to support brethren who were out of work. Unemployed brethren were entitled to food and lodging, if they could verify Chapel membership in another town.[3] Those who failed their apprenticeship in a Chapel could be excommunicated. In the 1800's Germany abolished the Chapel by law, since it encouraged drinking and its initiations were considered bizarre. The 1600's rite of passage to journeyman included the apprentice, two godfathers, and a priest for the ceremony (often the master/owner of the shop). In this ceremony, there was an axe, plane, saw, compass, grape stripper, tooth extractor, fox tail and bells. Other ceremonies included soaking the journeyman in baptismal fashion. "Every printer defends himself, but is proud when the ceremony is over and is duty bound to buy a drink for each of the brethren." In the "Kissing the Bookbinder's Daughter" ceremony of the 1800's, the apprentice's face, neck, and head were massaged with glue by means of brushes and a plentiful supply of white shavings, after a gob of paste had been applied to his mouth. He was then held upside down in a bin of white wastepaper to complete the ritual.[4]

Ben Franklin Visited by Ralph, the Ghost

A "solace" is a rule voted in by the journeymen, such as "no swearing" or "do not leave the candle burning." Ben Franklin refused to pay his solace bill to the Chapel and was visited by "Ralph," a unfriendly ghost. Ralph pi-ed (mixed up or dropped) Ben's type.[5]

Deconstruction of the Chapel Ceremony Stories

1. *Adaptations of Religious Categories.* Each ceremony is a stylized adaptation of a medieval age church ceremony to people's role in the technology of their craft. Words like Chapel, Priest, Baptismal, Altar are examples of the adaptation of Church language to business. There is also an adaptation of the technology: words like chase, cuz, bookbinder, paper-board, pi-ed. . .

2. *Discipline.* Any journeyman could call a Chapel meeting to vote in a new fine called a "solace." A solace was imposed to enforce a shop rule such as no swearing, no fighting, do not leave your candle burning.[6] Remember the craftsmen, as bizarre as these initiations and punishments may seem, were in fact exercising

self-discipline. You were disciplined by your peers when you practiced poor work quality. The Chapel discipline mirrored school discipline where master teachers taught their lessons to obedient students. Anyone refusing to pay, could be taken by force and laid on his belly across the correcting-stone, while his brethren applied a paper-board to his buttocks.[7]

3. *Community of Influence.* The printer was influenced by the community in which s/he apprenticed to become a journeyman and master. The rituals of the Chapel was the center of their informal influence.

Ben had PMA! Perhaps no one sought more to discipline his thinking and PMA than Benjamin Franklin. According to his autobiography, Franklin wanted to control his habits by focusing his mind on the best possible virtues. Franklin was following the advice of Pythagoras in his Golden Verses, which advocated a daily examination of one's virtues.

The Ben Franklin Story Pre-Modern Man

Franklin made up a book to record his meditations.

"I ruled each page with red ink, so as to have seven columns, one for each day of the week, marking each column with a letter for the day. I crossed these columns with thirteen red lines, marking the beginning of each line with the first letter of one of the virtues, on which line, and in its proper column, I might mark, by a little black spot, every fault I found upon examination to have been committed respecting that virtue up on that day" (Hill and Stone, p. 125).

Since there are 13 virtues and 13 times 4 = 52, Franklin could also dwell on one virtue for an entire week, and be able to cycle through his list four times a year. Each week he could look at ways to build that virtue. In this way Benjamin Franklin worked in a very self-disciplined way to modify his own attitudes. Here is a list of his virtues and the chart he used to keep his mind focused on PMA.

BEN FRANKLIN'S 13 ATTITUDES
1. *Temperance:* Eat not to dullness; drink not to elevation.
2. *Silence:* Speak not but what may benefit others or yourself; avoid trifling conversation.
3. *Order:* Let all your things have their places; let each part of your business have its time.
4. *Resolution:* Resolve to perform what you ought; perform without fail what you resolve.
5. *Frugality:* Make no expense but to do good to others or yourself, that is, waste nothing.
6. *Industry:* Lose no time; be always employed in something useful; cut off all unnecessary actions.
7. *Sincerity:* Use no hurtful deceit; think innocently and justly, and, if you speak, speak accordingly.
8. *Justice:* Wrong none by doing injuries, or omitting the benefits that are your duty.
9. *Moderation:* Avoid extremes; forebear resenting injuries so much as you think they deserve.
10. *Cleanliness:* Tolerate no uncleanliness in body, clothes, or habitation.
11. *Tranquility:* Be not disturbed at trifles, or at accidents, common or unavoidable.
12. *Chastity:* Rarely use venery but for health or offspring, never to dullness, weakness, or the injury of your own or another's peace or reputation.
13. *Humility:* Imitate Jesus and Socrates.[8]

Table 4.2.

VIRTUE TO FOCUS ON THIS WEEK: *Temperance* "Eat not to dullness; drink not to elevation"							
Daily Inventory:	Sun	Mon	Tues	Wed	Thur	Fri	Sat
1. Temperance							
2. Silence							
3. Order							
4. Resolution							
5. Frugality							
6. Industry							
7. Sincerity							
8. Justice							
9. Moderation							
10. Cleanliness							
11. Tranquility							
12. Chastity							

Table 4.3.

Self-Influence & Discipline. Success for the pre-modernist begins with **Positive Mental Attitude (PMA).** Norman Vincent Peale, in his book: *The Power of Positive Thinking* (1952) reflects the pre-modern influence when he recommends people memorize these quotations to establish more PMA mind conditioning:

POSITIVE MENTAL ATTITUDES

- ❑ As he thinketh in his heart, so is he.
- ❑ If thou canst believe, all things are possible to him that believeth.
- ❑ Lord, I believe; help Thou mine unbelief!
- ❑ I can do all things through Christ which strengtheneth me.
- ❑ If ye have faith . . . nothing shall be impossible unto you.
- ❑ According to your faith be it unto you.
- ❑ Faith without works is dead.
- ❑ What things soever ye desire, when ye pray, believe that ye receive them, and ye shall have them.
- ❑ If God be for us, who can be against us?
- ❑ Ask and it shall be given you; seek and ye shall find; knock, and it shall be opened unto you.

Can people think their way to success? Pre-modern man made it a habit to pray and seek the happiness that flows from PMA. "If your thinking is wrong, it is wrong and not right and can never be right so long as it is wrong" (p. 210). You are what you think.

Direct Your Thoughts with PMA

to Control Your Emotions

and to

Ordain Your Destiny

Source: Napoleon Hill & W. Clement Stone[9]

If you focus your mind on the goals you want to achieve and write those goals down, you are more likely to achieve those goals. If you focus your mind on your fears and worries, then what you fear will come to pass. In short, pre-modern belief is the mind attracts or repels your success and failures. To discipline your mind, discipline your thoughts. Use self-talk and self affirmations to program your mind for success.

❑   Do it Now!

❑   Please God help me write!

❑   I am Enthusiastic!

❑   They want to hear what I have to say.

❑   To be enthusiastic, act Enthusiastic!

❑   That which you Share with Others will Multiply!

❑   Whatever the Mind of Man can Conceive and Believe, it can Achieve through PMA!

❑   I can do this!

❑   **Sow a thought, reap an action.**
     Sow an action, reap a habit.
     Sow a habit, reap a character.
     Sow a character, reap a destiny![10]

How can you be enthusiastic? To be enthusiastic, ACT enthusiastic! "Nothing great was ever achieved without enthusiasm" (Abraham Lincoln).

HOW TO ACT ENTHUSIASTICALLY!

1. *Talk loudly!* This is particularly necessary if you are emotionally upset, if you are shaking inside when you stand before an audience, if you have "butterflies in your stomach."

2. *Talk rapidly!* Your mind functions more quickly when you do. You can read two books with greater understanding in the time you now read one if you concentrate and read with rapidity.

3. *Emphasize!* Emphasize important words, words that are important to you or your listening audience—a word like **you,** for example.

4. *Hesitate!* When you talk rapidly, hesitate where there would be a period, comma, or other punctuation in the written word. Thus you employ the dramatic effect of silence. The mind of the person who is listening catches up with the thoughts you have expressed. Hesitation after a word which you wish to emphasize accentuates the emphasis.

5. *Keep a smile in your voice!* Thus in talking loudly you eliminate gruffness. You can put a smile in your voice by putting a smile on your face, a smile in your eyes.

6. *Modulate!* This is important if you are speaking for a long period. Remember, you can modulate both pitch and volume. You can speak loudly and intermittently change to a conversational tone and a lower pitch if you wish.

7. *Butterflies.* When the butterflies stop flying around in your stomach, you can then speak in an enthusiastic, conversational tone of voice.[11]

Table 4.4.

The Healthy, Happy, Terrific Story

Jerry Asam has PMA. And Jerry Asam loves his work. He finds satisfaction in his job.

Who is Jerry Asam? What does he do?

Jerry is a descendant of the Hawaiian kings. The job he loves so much is that of sales manager for the Hawaiian office of a large organization.

Jerry loves his work because he knows his work well and is very proficient in it. Thus, he is doing what comes naturally. But even so, Jerry had days when things could be a little rosier. In sales work, days like this can be disturbing—if one does not study, think and plan to correct difficulties and to maintain a positive mental attitude. So Jerry reads inspirational, self-help action books.

Jerry had read such inspirational books and learned three very important lessons:

1. You can control your mental attitude by the use of self-motivators.

2. If you set a goal, you are more apt to recognize things that will help you achieve it than if you don't set a goal. And the higher you set your goal, the greater will be your achievement if you have PMA.

3. To succeed in anything, it is necessary to know the rules and understand how to apply them. It is necessary to engage in constructive thinking, study, learning and planning time with regularity.

Jerry believed these lessons. He got into action. He tried them out himself. He studied his company's sales manuals, and practices what he learned in actual selling. He set his goals—high goals—and achieved them. And each morning he said to himself: "I feel healthy! I feel happy! I feel terrific!" And he did feel healthy, happy, and terrific. And his sales results were terrific too!

When Jerry was sure he himself was proficient in his sales work, he gathered about himself a group of salesmen and taught them the lessons he had learned. He trained the men in the latest and best selling methods as set forth in his company's training manuals. He took them out personally and demonstrated how easy it is to sell if one uses the right methods, has a plan, and approaches each day with a positive mental attitude. He taught them to set high sales goals and to achieve them with PMA.

Every morning Jerry's group meets and recites enthusiastically, in unison: "I feel healthy! I feel happy! I feel terrific!" They laugh together, slap one another on the back for good luck, and each one goes his way to sell his quota for the day. . . They know that what the mind of man can conceive and believe, the mind of man can achieve with PMA. . .

"I feel healthy! I feel happy! I feel terrific!" Another young salesman in the same organization on the mainland learned to control his mental attitude through the use of Jerry Asam's self-motivator. He was an eighteen-year-old college student who was working during his summer vacation selling insurance on a cold-canvas basis in stores and offices. Some of the things he had learned. . . . In your moment of need, use self motivators such as **I feel healthy! I feel happy! I feel terrific** to motivate yourself to positive action in the desired direction. . . .

By Friday night of that week, he had succeeded in making eighty sales—twenty short of his target. The young salesman was determined that nothing would stop him from achieving his objective. . . . Although the other salesmen in his group closed their week's work on Friday night, he was back on the job early Saturday morning.

By three o'clock in the afternoon, he hadn't made a sale. He had been taught that sales are contingent upon the attitude of the salesman—not the prospect.

He remembered the Jerry Asam self-motivator and repeated it five times with enthusiasm. **I feel healthy! I feel happy! I feel terrific!** About eleven o'clock that night he was tired, but he was happy! He had made his twentieth sale for the day! He had hit his target! He had won the award and learned that failure can be turned into success by—keeping on trying.[12]

Boj's Story. I was taught the **I feel healthy! I feel happy! I feel terrific!** self-motivator by Richard Chavez, of the Chavez Training Institute in Los Angeles. Richard is a polio victim who lives his life in a wheel chair during the day and in an iron lung at night. He is not physically healthy; he is mentally healthy. After learning this self-motivation and teaching it to people in my business, our personnel agency sales tripled within two months. I have been teaching the self-motivators to others ever since then. My contribution is explain what the three phases mean.

Deconstructing: I Feel Healthy, I Feel Happy, I Feel Terrific.

The H.H.T. story has themes, motives, values, purposes, motifs, dichotomies, dualism, relationships, scripts, scenarios, and recipes that we can interpret, deconstruct, and expose. Here are a few. You generate your own deconstructions.

1. *The Power of Positive Thinking.* Positive thinking (PMA) is a theme in the stories that contains a dualism and a recipe. If you think positive, you get more success than if you think negative. Therefore, underneath the story, man is struggling with the opposing

forces of negative and positive, bad and good, devil and God, sinful and rightful thinking. For Jerry, he was able to negative his negative thoughts. Jerry's day could be rosier, there were difficulties, but instead of surrender, he set out to correct the difficulties, maintain his PMA in the midst of negativity and he did this by using self-motivators. The power of PMA is the power to deconstruct and reconstruct mental experience and to rescue a positive voice that is usually subdued.

2. *The Magnetic Attraction of H.H.T.* If I think healthy affirmations, make the happiness choice, and set a terrific challenge for myself, then what? The story recipe is that if you use self-motivators, set a goal, and learn the rules of the game, then you are more apt to attract, recognize, focus on, and send out magnetic signals to attract positive results. If I think negative affirmations, decide to be unhappy, and do not seek challenge, then I am subject to manipulation, alienation and damage.

3. *The Power of Negative Thinking.* What is the other side of the coin? If I think negative, then I am entering the dialectic, the negation of the positive. I assume that what I think is going on, what I hear people saying, is indeed not what is going on and not what they are doing. There are bad people and they do bad things. For every plus there is a minus. For every unity, there is diversity. I attack the Pollyana surface to expose its negative underbelly. But, I also negate the negatives, the NMA (Negative Mental Attitude) around me, in order to affirm the positive. PMA is a negation of the negatives. Only by negation, does the individual break out of other people's chains and into freedom.

4. *Mind Control.* I am opposed to mind control, but I am in favor of self-reflection. Marcuse writes: "Thought "corresponds" to reality only as it transforms reality by comprehending its contradictory structure . . . to comprehend what things really are, and this in turns means rejecting their mere factuality. Rejection is the process of thought as well as of action. . . . Reason is the negation of the negative."[13] Mind discipline is intelligence, but mind control is domination of men and women by an oppressive instead of liberating thought process. If instead of limiting thought to positives, we see thought as a struggle of good and evil, of positive and negative, then instead of mind control, we have the freedom to choose and to change.

5. *The Affirmation of Freedom.* I do not have to surrender to a negative environment, to negative circumstance, or play someone else's game, or perform a role in someone else's scenario. I can create my own environment, change the circumstances, re-define the game rules, and fashion my own unique role in my own

story. The message of the story is to rebel against other people's negative expectations by setting a positive mood. Self-talk using self-affirmation is reasoned self-discipline and self-control. Man can use thought to change his affirmations and to then go out and change the world. Emancipation and freedom are choices.

6. *Self-Influence.* In the story, Jerry and his 18 year old apprentice were able to ignore their environment and engage in self-influence. They reacted to the world on their own individualistic terms. They intervene in the natural taken-for-granted order and did the entrepreneurial walk. Jerry's actions was based on a re-definition of his situation. He constructed a creative meaning and he deconstructed a negative (status quo) meaning. Jerry experienced the tension between accepting the meaning others were handing to him and creating his own interpretation.

7. *Words have Power.* There are words that motivate and make us more creative and bring us more freedom. There are words that depress us and make us afraid to create and take away our freedom. The negative imprisons us, denies our options, and robs our potential to be unique. PMA can be domination too. The H.H.T. people can oppress and dominate the NMA (negative mental attitude) people. The domination is linguistic. The PMA community has a language that gives them their identity and sets, up an optional enemy: the NMA language community. But, inside each person is that battle between the NMA voices and the PMA voices, between the self-negatives and the self-positives, between the inhibitor words and the liberator words. Self-help tapes, books, and seminars are popular with sales people and executives. They seek to sustain PMA in a world full of NMA.

8. *Feelings are Choices.* Feelings are a combination of my response to the environment and my response to myself. I intend to be H.H.T. by affirmation. I intervene in how I internalize and externalize my feelings. I am critical of how I naturally feel about myself in the world. I become a spectator of my own feelings and my experience of the world. If I can choose how I feel, then I can choose how I act.

I feel HEALTHY. PMA is a choice. You can program your mind to be more positive. In this way you seek out positiveness in the world and since you are positive, you attract more positive opportunities to you. Joseph Campbell says the hero follows his/her bliss. To be the hero of your own journey, you need to think healthy thoughts. Your story has two expectations. First, you have to affirm that you can do something. "I can give this class." Second, you have to affirm that you will get rewarded by the taking the journey you are starting. If I eat less, I will loose weight, and that will allow me to buy the clothes I want to wear.

I FEEL HEALTHY

I FEEL HAPPY

I FEEL TERRIFIC ⋗·G

I feel HAPPY. Happiness is a state of being, not doing and not waiting for some outcome. If your happiness, depends on results and contingencies, you are controllable by the modernist machine—others control your happiness. Being happy means finding those moments each day that are energizing. I like to ask the question: "which of these things I have to do will I remember 20 years from now?" Often that is skipping the big meeting and going to my son's Soccer match. Happiness does not depend upon getting into college, getting your promotion, or picking up your Christmas bonus. Happiness just depends upon you. Most people are externally controlled and can not permit themselves to feel happiness until some environment condition is just right. Others are too busy doing, too busy spinning their treadmill to feel happy. If you wait for happiness, it will never come your way. Being happy, is being happy in the "here and now," in the present. It does not depend on what came before, or what will come after. Relaxation exercises help you get into the present, into the here and now of happiness.

I feel TERRIFIC. Setting and reaching personal goals is terrific. You have to do more than think healthy thoughts and get into being happy. Success depends on striving to achieve, to accomplish, to actualize your individual potential. People who write down their goals and their plans are more apt to achieve their goals. Take a small step toward your goal each day and you will be off on your individual journey. As you take a step, set up your own schedule of reinforcement. Be terrific to yourself.

Healthy and **Happy** were redefined by modernists as intrinsic motivation techniques. **Terrific** became an external motivator. But, for the pre-modernist, these were self-motivators to take him/her beyond external control. Strengthening his mind to be more self-reliant.

David McClelland's Need for Achievement Stories

McClelland showed people pictures and had them write a five-minute story about what was going on each picture. He then analyzed the stories for achievement-oriented phrases, plots, and themes. "He tries his best to succeed." Pre-modern, like modern and postmodern stories are influential.

The Doctor Story

A boy is dreaming of being a doctor. He can see himself in the future. He is hoping that he can make the grade. It is more or less a fantasy. The boy has seen many pictures of doctors in books, and it has inspired him. He will try his best and hopes to become the best doctor in the country. He can see himself as a very important doctor. He is performing a very dangerous operation. He can see himself victorious and is proud of it. He gets world renown for it. He will become the best doctor in the U.S. He will be an honest man, too. His name will go down in medical history as one of the greatest men.[14]

Deconstruction

1. McClelland also analyzed children's stories in different cultures to determine which countries fed their children a steady diet of achievement themes. The highest scores were children from the U.S., Italy and India.

2. Achievement people like challenge, like the difficult operation. Achievement people prefer tasks that have some risk of failure, are somewhat difficult to master, and adventures that are somewhat challenging. They are competitive and seek setting in which they can test their skills against others.

3. *Stories.* What we want to understand is how do people use stories and conversation to influence each other. What is the process of influence? People are influenced and motivated and mobilized by stories. Stories define unmet needs, dissatisfactions as well as opportunities, challenges and the paths, scenarios, and plots to get to a new place. Stories influence by conveying the horrors that happen when needs do not get met, when opportunities and challenges are not addressed and what are the consequences of following negative scenarios and horrific plots. Stories influence. Since there are many influences, each influence perspective has its own stories.

❑ MODERN INFLUENCE ❑

Introduction

To make people comply, management uses scientific management, behavioral science, and even human relations theory. Human relationalists use peer group manipulation, administrative science uses surveillance, behaviorists use punishments and rewards to get men and women to be compliant parts in the machine. Modernist transforms persons into the "rational" animal, the "economic" man making rational choices, the "group" thinker.

The Modern Narrative. What is the story here? The narrative of modern influence is the story of rational compliance: teaching man categories, slicing man into categories, and using categories to control man.

Three Strands. In these stories, we find that pre-modern, modern, and postmodern motifs, dualities, themes, and values intermingle. There is a dialectic between the three strands. Modernist is taking over from pre-modernist. Pre-modern and postmodern resist and rebel.

Modernist Rationality uses division of labor to destruct the work community.

Modern Age Printers

I was told that back in Europe in the days of Gutenberg, printers were regarded highly. They were the purveyors of knowledge. And, I understand that in some countries they were allowed to carry a short sword. As we've progressed with the *modern age*, you have less and less of that. I can just see the change from when I worked at shops and it was somewhat of a community of men and then the guys before had a greater community and the people after now: the girls at the computers and phototypesetter. I would not even consider that community. You know? [Boje, 1983. ER-10].

People seek their community outside of work.

From Quality Attitude to Leisure Attitude

The attitude today is no one really cares to do a quality job. Young people for the most part, want to give you eight hours and then they want to leave and during the eight hours they're not necessarily overly interested in working hard. Some are, of course, but many are not. . . But still in all they live in a different world than the one we come from, when there was more stress on quality. They will give you quality because you demand it, not because they want to give it. [Boje, 1983. EL-13].

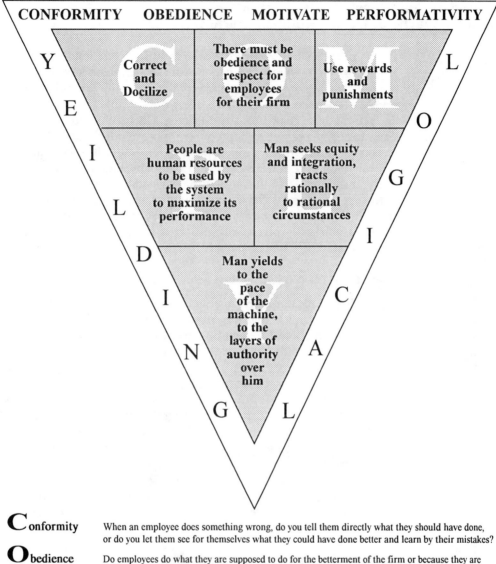

Conformity — When an employee does something wrong, do you tell them directly what they should have done, or do you let them see for themselves what they could have done better and learn by their mistakes?

Obedience — Do employees do what they are supposed to do for the betterment of the firm or because they are afraid what will happen to them if they don't do what they are supposed to do?

Motivate — How do you motivate your employees to do their best for the firm?

Performativity — Do you categorize each employee into a specific department according to his or her abilities?

Logical — Do you inform your employees as to the correct way to handle a situation, or do you let them judge for themselves?

Yielding — Do employees do just what management tells them to do, or do they step out of the bounds of their job because they want to try to help make the firm better?

Pre-modern Man Meets Postmodern Man:
The John Wayne & Dustin Hoffman Stories.

This is part of a transcript from a large utility company, we are calling, Edison. In the many stories presented, the characters are talking about, though this was not their agenda at the time, the transition of Edison from a Modern to a Postmodern organization. John Wayne represented the pre-modern character, the Masons, Mormons, and Naval Officers (See stories in previous chapters) are more modern, and the character of Dustin Hoffman personified postmodern man. In this grand histori- cal transition of a hundred year old company, the transition of the role of the individual and that individual's relationship to the organization is the central theme. The work ethic of the individual, and the corre- sponding type of organization necessary to accommodate the new breed of worker is necessarily different for pre-modern, modern, and postmodern fibers which thread their way through Edison history.

Scene One: Pre-Modern Utility: John Wayne meets Dustin Hoffman.

Mike "I think the heros of this company are the John Wayne char- acter. You know, the rugged individualistic. You know, when I came here I looked at the culture too and its got what I call a lot of old cowboys in it. And we even have a history book and it starts back in 1910 or something and its building some- thing like 57 miles of railroad through the Sierras to get the water down. You can imagine what was going on then and that kind of sacrifice and rugged outdoorsy. You know, and you look at the photographs. Look at the Edison News which comes out every payday. And it shows pictures of the line- men and so forth. Most of them I would say that most of those guys look like Daniel Boone. They have long hair, moustaches and beards, and plaid shirts. Its an image. Its a kind of a uniform type thing. And they like that. They made the company type thing."

Enter Dustin, the Postmodern Utility Man.

Ben "But I think they're running into problems now [Yeah, Oh Yeah] Because the John Waynes are running the company and the Dustin Hoffmans are being hired."

Mike "Also some of the Dustin Hoffmans are moving up into mid- dle management. Slowly and there may even be one of them who is a vice-President. An I think he will be forever seen as always being in short pants."

Sue "I think there are two areas in Edison that [have] been known for tough management. . . Power Supply and Customer

Service and the [second is] the macho of the Field People. Well, we've been doing a three phase training program with customer service starting with pre-supe[rvisor] and now we've got second level going and first level. And we've had the VP of customer service, a fairly new person saying: "Well there is a difference between leaders and bosses." And one of the people piped up and said: "You mean now we're going to start treating people like human beings around here." Because out there its always been very autocratic. You know! "Get your ass up the pole and do it." You know this is the job today. Today [its] more participate you know. They seem to be reacting positively in the classroom, but they're real skeptical that this is really going to come about in the field."

Boj ". . . What you're saying [is] there are some new role models coming into . . . Edison which connote some new values. What would those values be? What is a Dustin Hoffman character, in short pants?"

Mike "When I mentioned Dustin Hoffman—there are some in middle management—I was thinking more of a lineman who takes less pride in—slightly less pride in the macho image. And they do a job and they do it well and there is probably some macho to it, but at the end of eight hours, let's go home and crank up the RV. I think there is more personal dedication than there is to dedication to the company. And that's where the Waynes and the Hoffmans are having trouble".

Dick "I think in the older managers—it was job comes first and you do whatever it takes to complete the job. And the current middle management philosophy is more people oriented. I think its reflected very well in Morris Massey's book: *The People Puzzle.* He talks about the times people were born and those decades and the influence that they had on the way people perceived what they are doing."

Boj "There is a fellow named Stinchecombe with a hypothesis that says companies pick up their cultural identity at the time of their formation and that it stays with the company."

Doug "When he goes into that depression—We're a product of the depression and I see it in our newer managers and our supervisors are not necessarily a product of the depression. I mean they've heard these tales maybe from their parents, but we still have enough old line managers here who remember the day that they won't let you get a dime to go get an ice cream cone and there was no dime for it. You know? and they are—still are very conservative in their views. But, I think that's changing as you get away from that depression era. Those old tales.

Mike "I think one of the differences between the John Waynes and the Dustin Hoffmans has to do with management style and philosophy. It has to do with willingness to be influenced by someone else. The cliche in conversation: "allowing others the freedom to participate in what happens to their livelihood.""

Sue "I can give you an example of that where a district manager was called into a district where they had always grown their own and they'd always done what they'd wanted their way. Well they were violating some safety policies . . . and they knew that basically they were going to be held accountable to the district manager. And yet this person was very willing to meet with all these foremen—to work through and talk through what their concerns were and why. And getting them to understand his tion and why he said: "No you are not going to do it that way." . . .

Mike "Well these two guys came in on a Wednesday and they were having a meeting on Friday and they wanted some advice from us. And uggg about how they should handle these guys [the foremen who violated safety policies]"

Don "And the union reps brought grievance against them"

Mike "And we advised them—stick to your guns. You were right according to contract. The worst thing you could do was bend that contract. . . And then we went into how to handle confrontation. . . . we told them if you give on that one. And what I think we were doing was taking into account the [John Wayne] culture of the company. You know? The people who were grieving would not have respected those managers because of the culture of the company which says: "You're John Wayne. You stick to your guns when you know you are right!" So he did that, it was pretty difficult."

Boj "I'm excited to hear the emphasis on participation and on confrontation because I teach those values in my MBA class."

John Wayne: Pre-Modernist	Dustin Hoffman: Postmodernist
Hard nosed	NOT TOUGH:
Tyrannical, Dominant	The dude
Mean son of a bitch	Treat us like humans
Coercive, Cruel	People oriented
Have autocratic heros	Willing to listen
Tough management	Talks through concerns
Participation is abdication	Wears short pants
Abusive, intimidating	More participative
Brute of a person	Less macho image
Bull of the woods	Willing to be influenced by others
COWBOY DISCOURSE:	NOT COMPANY ORIENTED
Slow to pull the trigger	More personal than company dedication
Rugged Individualist	Educated (MBA, Law, or Engineering degree)
Old cowboy	Drives an RV
Notched ears (fast track)	Will not work overtime
Calf that's marked	Thinks half day is 9 to 5 instead of 9 to 9.
Cow tail to superiors	Has not clum.
Stick to your guns	Not part of Edison family.
Knock your block off	Not a "home growner"
Square Dealing	
Known for their drinking	
Hit the bar and went at it with two hands	
Hard living group	
Plays poker	

Table 4.5.

Scene Two: The Modern Masons Play Poker.

Mike "I wouldn't say there is an emphasis on it uh in fact some people are disappointed because they have been asked to participate. And if the person who is doing the asking doesn't like their participation or doesn't like what he hears he reverts back to the old [John Wayne] style. I tend to look at it in terms of personality theory. I think that the successful manager or executive in this company has a classical approach which means . . . that you dominate and abuse those below you and cow tail to those above. And it works and the job gets done. Some people don't like that. Particularly, younger folk from a different [Dustin Hoffman] generation. . . . old line managers do not understand difference between participation and abdication.

Doug Yeah but, your reward system, not so much now, but it was very prevalent where if you were one of the good ole boys, you did all right. Your reward for being a good ole boy was ultimately being promoted. Not necessarily based on your skills.

Mike	Didn't 20 or 30 years ago, or maybe not that long ago, being a member of the club meant being a Mason.
Doug	A member of the club meant playing poker. Now this fortunately was knocked off by a chairman of the board who had heard that promotions were being discussed and actually consummated by a group playing poker in an evening. "It's your turn to nominate a guy now."
Mike	"I'll see your raise and I'll throw in George."
Doug	"We have to promote your man now. He's due. In fact, we had an employee attitude survey sometime back. Our then President, Mr X, said that he wanted all of the department heads to read the results of that employee attitude survey as they pertained to his or her organization and . . . she was very conscious because she was very new . . . conscious of her image . . . she had each of her managers reporting to her come in and read them. And I remember—and this is directly true like Mike said. It said "why are the decisions made by the Masonic group?" An ugg, I don't have a chance to make it in the company because I'm not a Mason." And they actually zeroed in on that. Well then, this came to the attention of topside and uh certain things were taken care of. We could notice a few—at least I did, a few things go on.
Mike	"You don't wear a Masonic ring anymore do you?
Doug	Sorry, I stopped at De Molay [an organizations for boys sponsored by the Masonic Lodge]
Boj	Was it difficult to change that image of the Masonic order or poker game?
Doug	"The old poker game was knocked off. That was earlier. That was earlier. The John Waynes, the hard living—and incidentally, we had a vice president at that time who had been a former chief in the Navy and had not had a high school degree and would openly admit to this in a gathering of all of his department people. It was the largest company in the company . . . around 6,000 people . . . "there's a lot of opportunities for people in the company to grow and make it, I did. I'm a Vice President and I don't have a high school degree and by God I made it and so can you." Well you know, I mean you don't have any more Abraham Lincoln's around here anymore now. Our topside people have MBA's and law degrees and engineering degrees . . . but that was the style then. I made it, you can and we'll discuss this further at our poker party on Saturday night. Well that was gradually dissolved and done away with."

```
┌─────────────────────────────────────────────────────────┐
│                   MASONIC DISCOURSE                       │
├─────────────────────────────────────────────────────────┤
│ Masonic Order                                            │
│ Good old boys network                                    │
│ Members of the Club are Mason                            │
│ Members of the Club play poker                           │
│ I'm not a Mason                                          │
│ Masonic Ring                                            │
│ De Molay                                                │
└─────────────────────────────────────────────────────────┘
```

**Scene Three: The John Waynes Drink, the Mormons Don't.
The Transition to Postmodern.**

Mike   "What's behind this drinking controversy that's going on now? . . . For example, you can imagine that a lineman on a telephone pole who has a couple of beers with his lunch is not going to be as safe. You know compared to someone who hasn't had anything. So in part of the company now there is no drinking policy . . . You ain't allowed to drink period during working hours. Now another side of the company is saying that's poppycock and they are known for their drinking and so there is a corporate committee now formed to study this with all sides represented and they are due to come down with a recommendation for the policy on that. . . . I'm wondering that if a real strong thing in this company isn't something called fairness. Damn it, if the linemen can't drink at lunch, then the Vice Presidents can't either, and the staff people and personnel can't either. I don't know if that's behind it . . .

Sue   "I heard of two instances that might have kicked that off. One was where umm Mr M. was holding meetings out in the districts and one guy raised his hand and said: "I'm a lineman splicer and I'm sick and tired of going up the pole and having my life put on the line by these people who have been drinking and when are we going to stop this stupidity." And that's one story I heard. And, I don't know if its true. We're just hearing these things.

   The other one was where the crews—it was storm condition and the crew was entitled to a dinner. Went out to a dinner at a pizza parlor and were all having beer. . . . An operations supervisor came in an said: "Hey, we need you back out there." Something happened. And they kind of got into this scuffle or whatever. Those are the two things I heard that might have precipitate it, but I don't know.

Doug   "Well, there's a third one and that is the Chairman of the Board is a Mormon! So when you want to get promoted you issue an edict about not drinking and about several months later you become an executive vice president or a senior vice president when you were formerly a (long pause). Now that's the other one.

Sue "You know, I've heard the opte. I've heard the opte. I've heard that Mr M. was furious when he heard what Mr X had done, because he felt that . . . our chairman of the board being a Mormon is now trying to impose his own values and I think he was furious. . . . We're telling you stories of which you probably can't validate some of them.

Doug "We'd prefer not to believe that too.

Boj "I think what's important about the stories and why I pursue them as a topic is they do convey the values and if you put an ear to the wall and you listen to some of those stories, you can pick up what the current value tions are that the company wrestling with. . . .

MORMON DISCOURSE

Chairman of the Board is a Mormon
Issue an edict about not drinking and get promoted
The drinking controversy
Imposing his values on John Wayne

Scene Four: Modern Management is Transformed by Postmodern Discourse.

Mike "Now what happened with last revision is . . . uh the pronoun *he* was modified to include *she's* and there were more pictures of minorities and women. Before it was all white male. And it was each man has one boss type of philosophy. Well now they changed that to allow for something modern called matrix management and they tinkered with that phrase a little bit. But this is a very interesting book and it says a lot about the values of the company and what comes through to me is as Doug says: "old line, respectable, established, this kind of thing, square dealing, fairness" you know?

Doug "We attract a whole new employee [now] . . .

Boj "It might be nice if you have a series of those books to go back and look and see how they changed certain contents.

Mike "There's at least five revisions of this thing.

Don "But its always blue . . . and it only gets edited when there's a new CEO.

Doug   "And they still have courteous treatment for unions and blah, blah, blah.

Don   "And they do. It took two years to get that thing through and revised. It had to go to extraordinary levels to have it edited. And there must have been six or seven key people who read every word of it and deliberated it. It was like re-doing the Bible.

Mike   "When the vice-presidents and the top management—they have an annual offsite. And when one of them asked me to come up with a list of provocative questions that he could propose for discussion. Anyway, I referred to the motto. I gave him a list of I don't know, ten and he was going to pick three or four. And I referred to the motto: "Good service, Square dealing, and Courteous treatment." And I suggested the provocative question be: "Is that meant for the company's interface with its customers or is that also meant to apply inwardly, also toward the employees?" And this guy says: "Wow, you know I never thought of that." He didn't use that. . . .

REVISING MODERN DISCOURSE

Revisions versus nothing changes
Pronoun he modified to include she
More pictures of minorities
More pictures of women
Phrases like modern matrix organization
The faded motto: Good service, Square Dealing, and Courteous Treatment.
Motto getting redefined (remythologized).
Courteous treatment for unions
Fewer John Waynes, Navy Admirals, and more Dustins.
Dustin is not part of Edison Family.
Dustin listens, participates, and goes home early.

Deconstruction Points

1.   Diversity. As the American work place becomes, more diverse, the organizational machine is not able to homogenize people into precise cogs in the industrial machine. The modernist accommodation is to replace "he" with "she" and "I" with "us" while putting in more pictures of minorities and women in the company literature. In the postmodern organization, diversity is celebrated. The organization builds diversity as a strategy to compete more effectively in diverse global markets. In the postmodern organization, diversity is an asset.

2. Dustin Hoffman. Dustin personifies the postmodern man. Dustin does not form intimate, fraternal, familial attachments with the work organization. Dustin is not a company man. Dustin balances his life between leisure, family, and work. Work is a career, something he trained for in college. Dustin will network within the organization, but his attachment is less committed and Dustin will move on to work in many companies and he knows it.

How the Science of Human Relations Affects Modernist Influence?

The Hawthorne Studies. There were a series of studies in the Western Electric Plant in Hawthorne (Chicago) from 1924 to 1932: the illumination experiments, the relay-assembly test room experiments, and the bank wiring observation room experiments. Regardless of illumination changes, environmental changes, incentives were modified between a control group and the experimental group, but both groups increased performance to higher levels. Professor Elton Mayo explained it as "The Hawthorne Effect." If managers pay attention to their people, the people react by being more productive. It is not the money or the environmental lighting, seating, etc. that determines productivity. The Hawthorne effect was thought to explain Taylor's experiments at Bethlehem Steel. The Hawthorne experiments had discovered human relations as a factor that affects productivity. Informal work group norms for what is a fair day's work and group norms for what is the minimum and maximum daily output for a fair day's work controlled productivity levels.

A Critique of the Human Relations Movement as being Social Science Engineering. If Taylor was the mechanical engineer, the Human Relationalist became the social engineers: manipulating work group norms to engineer more productivity.

1. *Scientism.* Some social scientists believe there can be an exact science of man. People are treated as definite objects. Mathematics is used dogmatically to categorize, sort, and stereotype man into numbered cells. This section is a critique of those who measure personality, intelligence, group dynamics, and aptitude in order to plan man. The modernization of man has this agenda:

   More than ever, the world's greatest need is a science of human relationships and an art of human engineering based upon the laws of such science (Whyte, 1956: 27).

Scientism is the control of the human mind to plan and control and otherwise socially engineer the human machinery. Modernism is an age of social engineering. If Taylor represents the extremes of physical engineering, then the human relations movements represents the extreme of social engineering. Taylor seems too obvious in his applications of mechanical engineering to humans to be effectual. Human relationists put on the mantle of the good therapists and appear rather mild-looking and mild-mannered helpers.

Thoreau once said: "If you see a man approach you with the obvious intent of doing you good, you should run for your life."

2. *Evangelism.* Social engineers evangelize that it is possible and desirable to align the goals of man with the goals of organization. The father of Human Relations is Elton Mayo. His experiments at the Hawthorne, Illinois plant of Western Electric are reported in every management textbook. They were surprised to discover the Hawthorne Effect. When you change the illumination level in a production room and left it the same for a control group, production increased for both groups. A Harvard group repeated the experiments in a "relay assembly" test room. They introduced changes in lighting, rest periods, hours, and economic incentives. Output increased for the test group and also inexplicably for the control group.

The human relations experimenters had discovered that the workers were an informal social system. Like Taylor, they had discovered that the informal work groups controlled their output. The informal social system appreciated their ideas being solicited, their involvement in the experiments, and they responded with increased output. The Hawthorne effect was the battle cry of the human relations movement and was used to attack Frederick Taylor's scientific management principles. Taylor's changes in incentives and work planning were a Hawthorne effect.

3. *Harmony Groups.* In the pre-modernist period, back to the Middle Ages, people were disciplined by informal codes of behavior in the trade groups they belonged to. The scientific engineering by Taylorists, had split the work group apart by strict scheduling and planning clerks. Liberals were happy to see feudal group alliances breakdown, because this freed the individual to be an individual. Mayo, on the other hand, saw that man was most motivated by his group membership. What was good for the

work group was therefore good for the health of the individual. How can man enjoy the belongingness of pre-modern, feudal times, without the disadvantages pointed out by Taylor?

The science of human relations was the engineering of the harmonious work group.

1. *Interviews.* Mayo and his followers made the interview a management tool. Human relations scientists were hired by management to listen to worker troubles, dissatisfactions, and grievances. In this way the scientist adjusted man to his work group. The human relations psychiatrists understood gripes about an evil foreman who reminded them of their father or mother.

    I will be running down the list I will read aloud "married: seventeen years." Then I will read "children: none." I will let my eyebrows go up just a little and then pause thoughtfully. He is probably very sensitive on this point and in a few minutes he will begin to blurt out something about his wife or himself being sterile, and how maybe they have seen doctors about it. . . After several more minutes of stress I build him up again. Toward the end of the interview I usually smile and say, "Well, why don't we stop while we're ahead." That makes him relax and makes him think everything is going to work out all right. Then I shoot a really tough one at him. He is caught off guard" (Whyte, p. 206–7).

2. *Nondirective Sensitivity Counseling.* Nondirective counseling was used by Freudian followers to get workers to express the insensitivity of management to workers. Sensitivity training groups became popular in the 1950's, 60's and 70's. All group disharmonies were analyzed to adjust the individual to his or her work group.

3. *Personality Testing.* Personnel testing is not descended from the scientific management movement, it is descended from the human relations movement. Human relations scientists are more interested in harmony measures, than in productivity measures. Personality tests, IQ tests, GMAT tests to get into MBA programs allows the Human engineers to measure the whole man. The whole American Society is obsessed with testing and examining people by some yard stick of conformity. The shared fallacy is that these tests assume social scientists can measure minor variations in human beings so that their future behavior can be predicted.

If it can be predicted, it can then be planned. Plan the group by testing the personalities of the group for compatibility. Management uses psychological tests to weed out unqualified and disruptive workers. The happy man is part of a harmonious work group.

4. *Social Science Research.* There is a near-evangelical acceptance of social science research (Whyte, p. 48). The Human Relations movement wanted to break the efficiency, time and motion experts grip on the big corporation. They sought to sensitize CEO's to group dynamics, informal organization, and social psychology. The evangelical aspects can be seen in the rhetoric that America was on the brink of the great discovery of the science of the group. "Synergy" the whole is greater than the sum of its part— proved that groups were superior to individuals. Social Science research would unleash human creativity, problem solving, and group dynamics. It was a crusade against the authoritarianism of Taylorism to democratize the work place. "Down with the authoritarian Tyrants!"

5. *Group Dynamics Harmony.* Human relations experts could create a harmonious climate in the group and between groups in the organizations by imparting the science of group dynamics. Man could once again be socially secure and at the same time individually creative. Teaching management and organizational behavior from the 1950's to the 1970's meant stimulating discussion, group games, and non-directed learning bull sessions. The leaderless class and the leaderless group were imports from the Tavistock (England) school of human relations training. "In many institutions, as a consequence, the yardstick of a teacher's performance is the amount of interaction he develops in the group, and those who keep the students' focus on the discipline are apt to find themselves under censure" (Whyte, p. 56). The imitation of harmony is just as despotic as the imitation of mechanistic engineering principles onto man.

6. *Normalization.* With all the aptitude, psychological, psychiatry, group dynamic testing, measuring, and categorizing going on by the social scientists, it became possible to prescribe scientific norms for relating the individual to the group and planning her tion in the corporation. Individuals who depart from the norms of the majority are deviates. They are true individuals. Modern organization uses social science to dominate the individual by standardizing and formalizing the norms to which she must conform.

7. *Professionalization of Leadership.* In pre-modern times leaders were gutsy, authoritarian, self-assured, visionaries, on a mission to tame industry. They were ruthless. Now social scientists train them in the scientific arts to be professional executives. The entrepreneurial talent of the pre-modern executive has been channeled into administrative work. The hero of the modern, scientific organization is the bureaucrat. Instead of the dream of taming the frontier, higher quality products, better customer services—he dreams of his pension plan, the next ski trip, stock options, and the next corporation he will move to next quarter. The professional administrator works on a treadmill, without tangible goals for taming the frontier. Administrators compete for survival with other administrators in the professional rat race, rather than competing with other companies.

Modernist Taylor Note: For Taylor, and modernism, the leader was no longer a sovereign entitled position. Science could determine not only the worker's job, but that of the employer as well. Nevertheless, the worker was in his position because of his laziness, indolence, ignorance—surviving according to his fitness in the competitive struggle. The application of scientific principles allowed management to motivate to the worker to increase performance and reinforce strong work ethics.

> A long series of experiments, coupled with close observation, had demonstrated the fact that when workmen of this caliber are given a carefully measured task, which calls for a big day's work on their part, and that when in return for this extra effort they are paid wages up to 60 per cent. Beyond the wages usually paid, that this increase in wages tends to make them not only more thrifty but better men in every way; that they live rather better, begin to save money, become more sober, and work more steadily (Taylor, p. 74).

❑ POSTMODERN INFLUENCE ❑

Introduction

The postmodern influence is individual. The means that the individual de-centers organization influence. The individual is unconforming even to people's contradictory voices, caught in a web of fragmented and irrational participation, trying to affirm the self, to reclaim influence over the self. The postmodern person deconstructs the influence of other people's language, other people's stories, and does not act as an actor in other people's stories. The postmodern project is to reverse the binding and confining influences of modernism and pre-modernism.

❑ I-N-D-I-V-I-D-U-A-L ❑

I   *Independent:* Avoid domination, be private, seek freedom from collective influences. The postmodern project is the death of bureaucratic influence. Formal organization, as a modernist invention, took people's independence away. It is time to emancipate the individual, to liberate him/her from tyranny, from cults, from behavioral manipulation, and from peer groups. Avoid bureaucratic dependency by maintaining temporary commitment, by participating in multiple networks. Abolish the influence of hierarchy, especially surveillance. Much of the information you surrender is an invasion of your independent privacy. Dependence is dead.

N   *Narcissist:* In search of a self-image, self-will. The postmodern project resurrects the ego. Be your own hero. Follow your own bliss (Joseph Campbell). Loyalty to self is more important than loyalty to church, family, or work organization. The Chinese have a saying: "take care of your family before you take care of the world." The narcissist addition would be: "take care of yourself before you take care of your family or the world." Loyalty is dead.

D   *De-centered:* Person is a multiplicity of selves, practices many logics, dis-unified, not-centered. "—absence of anything at the center or any overriding truth. This means concentrating attention on the margins" (Rosenau, 1992: xi). In planning, it means de-centering planning so that there are many plans in many local groups instead of submitting to one grand central plan. In organizing, de-centering is getting away from a central hierarchy by networking across many diverse forms of organization. In influence, de-centering is getting away from one central truth, one central authority and working with a multiplicity of logics and authorities. In leadership, de-centering is de-throning a central leader and working out a network of leadership. In control, it is de-centering centralized control in favor of self-control. It is the death of the center.

I   *Individual:* Spontaneous (not planned or rehearsed), unique in thought and action. Not trapped by convention, tradition, or precedent. Not coopted by the competition of achievement. "The postmodern individual is relaxed and flexible, oriented toward feelings and emotions, interiorization, and holding a "be-yourself" attitude" (Rosenau, 1992: 53). Rigidity is dead.

V   *Voices:* Each person has many voices in them. Some have less influence, some have more. Bureaucracies are exclusively male-voices. It is gender-bound. There is a female and a male voice in each of us. The feminist project is to either balance the male and female voice or

Independent: Avoid domination, be private, seek freedom from collective influences.
*As a manager, do you influence the ways your employees
handle situations or do you leave it up to them?*

Narcissist: In search of self-image, self-will.
Does an employee with a strong self-image perform better than an employee with a weak self-image?

Decentered: Person is a multiplicity of selves, practicing many logics, dis-unified, not centered.
Are managers open-minded to all employee input?

Individual: Spontaneous (not planned or rehearsed), unique in thought and action.
Are spontaneous ideas as influential as set guidelines are to the daily operation of business?

Voices: Each person has many voices in them. Some have less influence -- some have more.
In training, are employees taught which voices to listen to when faced with a difficult situation?

Irrational: Fragmented, willing to participate in contrary causes and multiple realities.
Is there a "motto" for employees to follow as to what they base their action on?

Diversity: Discord and variety are balances to unity, conformity, and community.
Does the diversity of your employees help create a better business environment?

Unconforming: Self-disciplined rather than other disciplined; rebel against authority.
Does the company promote self-discipline or would they rather have employees carry out orders as told?

Affirming the Self: Self affirmatives like: "I feel Healthy, Happy, and Terrific!"
Does the company do anything to help employees affirm themselves?

Linguistic: Individuals influence by language, by categories, by storied personifications.
Have you found that the attitude of a manager affects employee performance and if so, how as a manager is this pressure handled?

to be quite radical and replace the male voice with a female, matriarchal voice. When you do not have a voice, you become marginal and peripheral to the conversation. There is an ethnic and racial voice in each of us. We use a different voice with different groups of people. There is a religious, agnostic, or atheist voice in each of us. There is a parent, adult, and child voice in each of us. The individual selects which voice to use with each utterance. When monarchs ruled over subjects, they also ruled over the voices we could safely exhibit. In postmodern psychology, the task is to de-throne the rational, unified view that people have only one voice. The role of psychoanalysis is to get people to drop their dependence on one voice, one story of who they are. If I have a multiplicity of voices, and I do, then I choose when to use which voice. To avoid modernist influence is to make my own voice decisions. Univocal is dead.

I   *Irrational:* Fragmented, willing to participate in contrary causes and multiple realities. Two opposing views can both be true. If life is fragmented then central planning leads to disorder, confusion, and the deterioration of life conditions (Rosenau, 1992: 131). Social science personality and style tests make people into objects, box people into categories, and write rational stories on their foreheads. If mass production is irrational, then abandon mass layout, mass-control of time and space and give people space they can control. Maybe experts do not know how to plan and organize better than locals because you can not successfully impose one reality over other realities. Postmodernism "reveals formal organization to be the ever-present expression of an autonomous power that masquerades as the supposedly rational constructions of modern institutions" (Cooper and Burrell, 1988: 110).[15] One rationality is not privileged over others. The pre-modernists believed in God. Modernist believed in the progress of technology, even after Naziism and Hiroshima. Modernist rationality replaced God with a machine, then a computer, and finally sugar-coated the substitution with humanism. Humanism replaced God with Marxism and Stalinism, then split into secular, liberal, enlightenment, Renaissance, and new age humanists. No wonder Skinner wants to put the world in a Skinnerian box and take away all individualism. Post-industrialism promised a higher quality of life, once we adopted the service economy. Postmodernist seeks to abolish all these grand narratives as competing rationalities. Rationality is dead.

D   *Diversity.* Discord and variety are balances to unity, conformity, and community. Division of labor practices invite people to see themselves as members of departmental groups. It is a simplistic category system to keep people divided and conquered. Unity of command is another plan to replace diversity with homogeneity. Hierarchy is out of phase with diversity. Hierarchy selects one power, one rationality, one voice and one whole. In diversity, there are many plans, many ways of organizing, and many influences. Superiority has no place in diversity. Diversity is participative. Diversity multiplies instead of making any one point of view dominant. Hierarchy is dead.

U   *Unconforming:* Self-disciplined rather than other-disciplined; rebel against authority; defy totalitarianism. Do not succumb to "technological" progress. Build your own plan, organize your own process, lead your own changes. Conformity is dead.

A   *Affirming the Self:* Self-affirmatives like: "**I feel healthy! I feel happy! I feel terrific!**" to gain personal control over mind (avoid outside influence and coercion), to promote the self, and retain freedom to choose feelings and actions. The mind is a tabla rasa and I can write my own influences onto it. "Healthy, happy, terrific" is one affirmation. Use it if you like. But it is better to develop your own.

L   *Linguistic:* Individuals influence by language, by categories, by storied personifications. The postmodern project is to break the shackles of oppressive language. Foucault and Derrida, for example, argue that the self is only a "position in language," a mere "effect of discourse" (Flax, 1990; Rosenau, 1992: 43). The administrative language of "productivity and efficiency" have more influence than words like "quality of life" and "ecology" People live up to their labels and categories. "He always stays overtime." "She puts the organization ahead of her family." "You know they will get the job done right." The individual is subordinated to the formal organization. Subordinate, superior, advisor, assistant, flunky, and imbecile. These are linguistic status categories. They locate you in a pyramid, hierarchy, or caste. The categories prescribe roles, relationships, and patterns of behavior. We are influenced by many diverse texts that prescribe a different characterization onto us. Some linguistic categories are more privileged than others. Categories are dead.

Cognitive Behavior Modification

In the 40's and 50's, the mind control movement took off. Writers like Norman Vincent Peale, Napoleon Hill and W. Clement Stone advocated *The Power of Positive Thinking*. The books were full of stories that people could read and enjoy to help them achieve a sense of self-control. In the 1960's and up to the 1990's, the power of positive thinking became the theory of cognitive behavior modification. If you control your thoughts, you can control your behavior. If you think for yourself, instead of playing out the tapes and scripts you learned from your parents, then self-control is possible. This line of influence is practice more by sales people and managers than by others in the firm. positive self talk increases PMA (Positive Mental Attitude). PMA uses positive reinforcement. Follow and precede a behavior you want to repeat with positive affirmations.

Cognitive behavior modification takes control of the mind away from the Skinner's environmental machine of reinforcements and gives the control to the individual. People can be self-disciplined rather than other-disciplined.

What are the borders, boundaries, limits being imposed on the individual? We have surrendered our self to bureaucratic control, how do we get our self back? Compulsive people are trained to be more compulsive and to exact more control over us when they graduate. The fast track is the fast track desire to exercise control over others, under the illusion that you get more freedom for your self. As Branden says!

> In denying human beings freedom of thought and action, statists and collectivist systems are anti-self-esteem by their very nature. Self-confident, self-respecting men and women are unlikely to accept the premise that they exist for the sake of others.[16]

Where is individual freedom in socialized medicine, orderly commerce, protected agriculture, housing projects?

Can the self-disciplined individual self-manage and self-regulate in the postmodern organization? Can the synergy of the whole be obtained by a lot of free thinking parts? Or, will people demand leadership, demand an oppressive system of control, and trade freedom for an imposed order? What does it mean to manage in a postmodern organization that is replete with temporary relationships and individuals who are not organization men and women?

Persuasion instead of coercion. Capitalism is not an imposed system of coercion, it is people competing with one another in a free market: free from big government and free from big corporation. What if the individual surrenders freedom of choice in exchange for economic incentives; accepts corporate slavery in exchange for a pay check?

Can we go beyond Maslow's self-actualization to unity-consciousness in which the dualism of the individual and the collective organization disappear? Most organizational attachments do not allow us to self-actualize. If we rid ourselves of dysfunctional attachments, coercive attachments, oppressive subjections—then can we rid ourselves of the dualistic boundary between people and organizations? Or, are we so caught up in a web of life relationships, a network of attachments, that individualism is an illusion? The individual mired in family, fraternal, industrial, educational, social, environmental, governmental, and other organizational relationships. At any given moment, individuality is surrendered to family crisis, hell week, meeting the quota, doing the examination, having a happening, going back to nature, or an audit by the IRS, marching in unity to military cadence.

Giving service to the environment, to the homeless, to the world. Service is a surrender of self to a greater good. It is a commitment to the whole. To serve is to put the other first, and the self last.

> Of course, what a life of selfless service means is far from obvious. Does it mean that we simply ask other people what they want us to do and proceed to do it? Does it mean that we decide what is best for other human beings and impose our vision on them? (Branden, p. 251).

With the advent of the customer-focused organization, the question of giving service to customers is critical. The customer is given more influence over the organization. The individual employee is given more freedom to serve. The serving person serves the internal and the external customer. The serving person has the integrity to give the person who receives his or her services "added value." There is a negotiation between the server and the customer about their shared vision for a particular service. I think you ask both the server and the customer what each wants, how each wants to proceed, and work to make this relationship productive and impactful for both parties. But, that influence has to be de-centered.

❑ SKEPTICAL INTERPRETATION OF POSTMODERN INFLUENCE ❑

The new industrial relations of TQM is supposed to increase worker control over their jobs, give workers more brain-involvement, and lead to long-term job security.

1. *Empowerment.* When is the last time someone tried to empower you?

   Boj: I went to a feminist conference and asked the question: How can I as a white, male empower women in my MBA classes? The response I got back, shocked me.

   Feminist: You! You can not empower women, they empower themselves.

   Empowerment implies that you have been disempowered. To be disempowered is to be on the margins, to be peripheral to power, and even to have access to power denied. We think much of what is called empowerment is very token. Is it empowering to be able to turn in a suggestion?

Usually when someone says: "I am going to empower you" it translates to: "I am going to abandon you and let you do all this work I did not want to do."

Boj: "Bob, I am gong to empower you to write this next chapter, while I go out for a beer!"

In Japan, workers are empowered by Toyota to live in dormitories, think about their job every waking minute, and meet in the evenings to write suggestions on ways to influence higher levels of performance. Workers are also empowered to work shifts that rotate day to evening from one week to the next so that the organization can balance the efficiency of production between shifts. It is good for the company, but over time individual's internal clocks go bonkers and the slow grind of fatigue and sleeplessness sets in. You do not know if it is day or night.

2. *Excellence and Postmodern Influence.* The excellence literature of Peters and Waterman, and Deal and Kennedy celebrates management massaging corporate culture to influence people to higher levels of quality performance. Instead of the employee becoming the little cog in the machine, the postmodern employee is the "little pledge in the fraternal corporate culture." "Management is urged to become directly and purposefully involved in determining what employees should think, believe or value" (Wilmott: 1992: 61). Autonomy and self-management are words used to induce people into gazing and influencing their own performance to meet corporate canons of excellence. Wilmott makes the point that as the corporate culture grows in strength, there is a de-differentiation of economy and culture through the calculated manipulation of celebration, ritual, fun, and "attaboys." The Nordstrom salesperson has become the "Nordie" who works through lunch and dinner to delivery packages, write birthday notes, and check the stock in the backroom.

3. *Under the Work Influence.* Americans are becoming a society of employed workaholics and unemployed homeless. Americans have recently surpassed the Japanese in number of working hours. While the Europeans are curbing their work hours to 35 and the Japanese are anticipating less work hours, American workers, particularly salaried workers are asked to stretch the work day.

4. *Theory Y.* McGregor (1960) argued that the way to influence people to higher levels of performativity was to fulfil their "higher order" needs for "self-esteem" and "self-actualization." The missing element is the employee's voice and point of view. Theory Y

focuses exclusively on manger's assumptions. Employees have no role to play in the process.

5. *Employee Involvement.* Workers get to participate in incresing their own workload and their own surveillance. Fewer layers of management save money as the worker self-supervises. Fewer inspectors saves money. Having the worker do time and motion studies of their own behavior lowers supervision and inspection costs. One mechanism for employee involvement is multi-skilling. The multi-skilled worker is said to have more influence over their work process and their flexible usage within the company. In reality, skilled jobs are done by team leaders, not by regular team members. But, few companies invest the training to so that people can do very professional skills. Multiskilling generally means that management can assign the worker to clean up, deliveries, preventative maintenance, or doing multiple unskilled assembly tasks within the same 60 second cycle time.

Toyota's idea of employee involvement is pre-involvement screening. Worker's who are very young and agile and all male are put on the Kyoto assembly teams. Only those young people who can potentially master the rapid pace practices and team culture of Toyota are selected. It is influence by selection.

6. *Racial Stereotypes.* America managers are doubtful that Japanese team methods could be used in the U.S. Racial stereotypes are the explanation. One stereotype said that Japanese are more "docile" and willing to follow orders unquestioningly. Another said that Japanese methods could be applied only in Japan because of its "homogeneous" culture, a culture which stresses values such as hard work and loyalty to the employer.

7. *MAD.* **The skeptical side of Healthy, Happy, Terrific (HHT) is Manipulated, Alienated, Damaged (MAD).** Positive mental attitudes are one thing, but people at all levels of the organizations are MAD. Lambs to the slaughter. Beware!

❑ SUMMARY ❑

Pre-modern man is illustrated by the self reliance of Ben Franklin and the discipline of the printing apprentice. Positive mental attitudes are apparent for both Ben and the apprentice. The influence of the craft, guild, and God are apparent.

Modern influence presents the "rational" animal who complies. The strictures of scientific management, the rewards and punishment, and the peer groups manipulation of human relationists are tools for compliance.

We bridge the modernist period with a visit with John Wayne and Dustin Hoffman where the pre-modern man meets the postmodern one. The key to the postmodern project is the individual—de-centered, fragmented, diverse. In response to many voices the individual is stronger, but in response to strong culture facets such as employee involvement, empowerment, and work influence the individual is often weakened. With stronger individualism, their is a ray of hope that their will be spin off benefits to the customer, organization, and community. But, beware postmodernism in pre-modern and modern disguises!

❑ NOTES ❑

1. *Notes and Queries*, 1888, Volume 4: 451.
2. Reprinted in *Gentleman's Magazine*, Vol. X (1740): p. 239–240. Original source: *The Craftsman*, Volume 24, May, 1740. By the 1800's Chapel rituals were outlawed in Germany because they encouraged drinking and hazing.
3. Chapels were organized into loosely coupled societies, with democratic meetings. The Chapel was the forerunner of trade unions and for owners, trade associations. See Boje, David, 1983 (ibid). Child, John 1967 *Industrial relations in the British Printing Industry*. London: George Allen and Urwin, Ltd.; Musson, A. E. 1954. *The Typographical Association* London: Oxford University Press; Powell, Leona Margaret 1926. *History of the United Typothetae of America.* University of Chicago Press.
4. Quote is from Oschilewski as cited in Thompson, Lawrence S. (1947). "The customs of the chapel." *Journal of American Folklore*, 60 (Oct.–Dec.) #238: 329–344. See Avis 1971 *The Early Printers' Chapel in England* London: F.C. Avis. See summary of these rituals in Boje, David. "The printer's eye: the Aesthetics of technology." UCLA working paper 12–83 (December, 1983): 8–11.
5. Franklin, Benjamin. 1806. *Franklin's Works.* Vol 1.
6. Cannon, I. C. 1968. "The roots of organizations among journeymen printers." *Journal of Printing Historical Society*, 4: 99–107.
7. Moxon, Joseph 1683. "Ancient customs used in a printing-house." IN Herbert Davis and Harry Carter (Eds.) *Mechanic Exercises on the Whole: Art of Printing* 1683–4. pp. 323–286. London: Oxford University Press, 1958 edition. See page 100.
8. Source: the *Autobiography of Benjamin Franklin* as cited in Napoleon Hill and W. Clement Stone *Success through a Positive Mental Attitude*, New York: Pocket Books, 1977: 124.
9. *Success through a Positive Mental Attitude* New York: Pocket Books, 1977: 49.
10. Ibid Most of these sayings are contained in Stone and Hill.
11. Based on Bettger's book: *How I raised myself from Failure to Success in Selling*, Prentice Hall. Quoted in Hill and Stone, p. 141–2.
12. Napoleon Hill and W. Clement Stone, 1987. New York: Pocket Books: 179–182.
13. Marcuse, Herbert. *One-Dimensional man* Boston: Beacon Press, 1964: ix.

14. Atkinson, J. W. "Towards experimental analysis of human motivation in terms of motives, expectancies, and incentives." In J. W. Atkinson (Ed.), *Motives in fantasy, action, and society*. Princeton, N.J.: Van Nostrand Reinhold. 1958: 193.

15. Cooper, Robert, and Gibson Burrell. 1988. "Modernism, Postmodernism and Organizational Analysis: An Introduction, Part I." *Organization Studies*, 9 (1): 91–112.

16. Nathaniel Branden, *Honoring the self: The psychology of confidence and respect*, Toronto: Bantam Books, 1985: 235.

17. McGregor, Douglas. 1960. *The Human Side of Enterprise*. New York: McGraw-Hill.

CHAPTER
5

LEADING STORIES

LEADERSHIP DEFINITIONS

Pre-Modern Leadership. Leaders are **Masters.**

M   *Master.* Head of the work institution. Owner of the slaves, serfs, and tools. Sometimes more skilled than others in a profession.

A   *Authoritarian.* Enforces unquestioning obedience to the leader's own authority.

S   *Slave Driver.* A leader oversees the work of others. A real taskmaster.

T   *Tyrant.* Sovereign and oppressive control over other people.

E   *Elite.* Leaders are regarded as the finest or most privileged class.

R   *Ruler.* Leaders govern and rule over other people.

Modernist Leadership. Leaders are **Panoptic.**

P   *Panoptic.* Leader does the gaze on everyone. Bertham's Principle: power should be visible and unverifiable.

A   *Authoritarian.* Final evaluator of performance and quality.

N   *Network of penal mechanisms.* Penal mechanisms are little courts for the investigation, monitoring, and correction of incorrect behavior and then the application of punishments & rewards to sustain normalcy.

O   *Organizational.* Lots of divisions, layers, specialties, and cubbyholes to cellularize people.

P   *Pyramid.* Leader sits at the top of the pyramid.

T   *Top.* The head boss, the top of the hill, and the highest ranking person.

I   *Inspector.* In charge of surveillance, inspection, and rating of everyone else.

C   *Centralist.* All information and decision flows up to the center and back down to the periphery.

Postmodern Leadership. Leaders are **Servants.**

S   *Servant.* The leader is the servant to the network. Leaders serve people who in turn serve customers. De-differentiates self from the people.

E   *Empowers.* The leader empowers participation in social and economic democracy.

R   *Recounter of Stories.* Tells the stories of company history, heros, and futures.

V   *Visionary.* Without vision the people perish.

A   *Androgynous.* Male and female voices.

N   *Networker.* Manage the transformation and configuration of the diverse network of teams spanning suppliers to customer.

T   *Team-builder.* Mobilize, lead, and detach a web-work of autonomous teams.

Table 5.1.

LEADERSHIP

SCORES	1 2	3 4	5
Master	Shops are run by more than one, skills are widely spread	Few tasks were delegated, the head of the shop tried to control everything	Head and owner of all work done More skilled than others
Authoritarian	Obedience is not present or enforced	Obedience begins to lean towards the leaders but with some question	Enforces unquestioning obedience to leader's authority
Slave Driver	No overseeing of work. No foreman present	Beginning to check work of others	A leader oversees the work of others. A real taskmaster
Tyrant	People are able to have control of themselves and their work	Cut backs were taken of people's freedom	Sovereign and oppressive control over other people
Elite	Leaders get no special treatment of benefits	Leaders are given special treatment in certain situations	Leaders are regarded as the finest or most privileged
Ruler	Few rules are present to oppress people	Certain rights and freedoms are governed by the leader's standards	Leaders govern and rule over the other people
Panoptic	No devices or actions taken to watch over the workers	A hint of the gaze is present, but freedom is still alive	Leader does the gaze on everyone
Authoritarian	No ending evaluations of work	Evaluated by others in the workplace	Final evaluator of performance and quality
Penal Mechanisms	Discipline is given by each particular worker	No balance between rewards and punishments	Penal mechanisms, punishments & rewards to sustain normalcy
Organizational	Everyone has the same skills and is on the same level	Segments of the workforce begin to emerge	Lots of divisions to celluarize people
Pyramid	Many district heads (vp) are in control of all situations	Few people sit on the top to make the decisions	Leader sits at the top of the pyramid
Top	Input by the employee is prevalent	Input is quartered off and given to only a few	The head boss is the highest ranking person

LEADERSHIP

SCORES	1 2	3 4	5
Inspector	Workers are expected to inspect all of their own work	A foreman is hired to survey and inspect the work and workers	In charge of surveillance, inspection, and ratings
Centralist	Information is known by all within the company	Information and decisions are made only by a few select people	All information and decisions flow up to the center and back
Servant	Leader serves himself	Service is given to few within the network	The leader is the servant to the network.
Empowers	Leader enpowers participation in the pyramid	Leaders are empowering at each level to a degree	The leader empowers participation in social and economic democracy
Recounter of stories	A couple stories here and there.	Stories are used at most levels	Tells stories to company history, heroes and futures
Visionary	Some vision	Vision for the people is seen	Without vision people perish
Androgenous	Mostly male voices but some female	Males voices are dominant yet the females' are finally heard	Male and female voices
Networker	Teams configurations are limited and are growing	Diverse network of teams including suppliers to customers	Manage configurations of the networks extremely well
Team-builder	Some autonomous teams are beginning	The web-work of autonomous teams is prevailing	Mobilize, lead and detach web-work of autonomous teams

	PRE-MOD	MOD	POST-MOD
Q1: What kinds of people do you hire?	N/A	Segments of the work force are beginning to emerge. Each employee does not have the same amount of skill or is on the same level. pan O ptic 4	The web-work of autonomous teams are being formed. Carl's does not discriminate and hires a mixture of people. servan T 3
	0%	57%	43%
Q2: What roles do under-represented groups play in the company?	N/A	Employees are limited to lower level positions by a language barrier. Carl's does not provide bi-lingual training manuals for upper management positions. Each employee does not have the same amount of skill or is on the same level. pan O ptic 2	Carl's requires that their employees work well with all types of people. They know that this is essential when hiring in order to build effective teams. servan T
	0%	40%	60%
Q3: How do you motivate upper level management to maintain creativity and a Positive Mental Attitude?	The leaders of Carl's do not get any special benefits or treatment. They are motivated by the same factors as the other employees. mast E r 2	There is some evidence of segmentation if Carl's. He states that the management is more influenced so that they can lead the rest. pan O ptic 3	A vision for the people is seen. Carl's wants the organization to have a family atmosphere for the employees. ser V ant 4
	22%	33%	45%
Q4: What sort of leadership actions does the owner exhibit to the employees?	Certain rights and freedoms are governed by the leader's standards. Carl has broken this by being personable; some of them are still present. maste R 3	A hint of the gaze is present, Carl visits his stores often. Freedom is still alive and encouraged by Carl's friendly attitude. P anoptic 3	Carl is truly a servant to the network. He has shown to the employees that he is a part of the organization, not a ruler. S ervant 5
	27%	27%	46%
AVERAGE	12.3%	39.3%	48.5%

servanT:
Team-builder (3) 43%
The web-work of autonomous teams are being formed. Carl's does not discriminate and hires a mixture of people.

panOptic:
Organizational (4) 57%
Segments of the workforce are beginning to emerge. Each employee does not have the same amount of skill or is on the same level.

servanT:
Team-builder (3) 60%
Carl's requires that their employees work well with all types of people. They know that this is essential when hiring in order to build effective teams.
panOptic:

Organizational (2) 40%
Employees are limited to lower level positions by a language barrier. Carl's does not provide bilingual training manuals for upper management positions. Each employee does not have the same amount of skill or is on the same level.

Q1: What kinds of people do you hire?

A1: That is somewhat of a loaded question. If you are referring to race we make no discriminations. Of course we want to hire responsible persons who will do quality work. It is also important to hire those who we believe will stay with Carl's for a while. It is wasteful to hire and train an employee who will not be with the organization for a fair amount of time. Each employee goes through a training period that is unique, if a new employee plans to progress through Carl's they can receive the appropriate amount of training necessary. If someone is going to be hired for a part-time job, or even for summertime work, they will probably not receive training in order to become a store manager. The kind of person that is to be hired is not important, it is the employee that they will be.

Q2: What roles do under-represented groups play in the company?

A2: I guess you mean minorities when you say "under-represented". As I stated before we make no discrimination of race or sex when hiring individuals. When we evaluate potential employees for hiring we want someone who will be able to work with all types of people, no matter what their color or sex is. All of our entry level training manuals are presented in English as well as Spanish. Eventually I would like to see all levels of our training manuals to be provided in Spanish as well as English, but at the moment this is not the case. We do not require our employees to be multilingual, but I believe that it is appropriate in some areas.

mastEr:
Elite (2) 22%
The leaders of Carl's do not get any special benefits or treatment. They are motivated by the same factors as the other employees.

panOptic:
Organizational (3) 33%
There is some evidence of segmentation in Carl's. He states that the management is more influenced so that they can lead the rest.

serVant:
Visonary (4) 45%
A vision for the people is seen. Carl's wants the organization to have a family atmosphere for the employees.

masteR:
Ruler (3) 27%
Certain rights and freedoms are governed by the leaders standards. Carl has broken this by being personable, some of them are still present.

Panoptic:
Panoptic (3) 27%
A hint of the gaze is present, Carl visits his stores often. Freedom is still alive and is encouraged by Carl's friendly attitude.

Servant:
Servant (5) 46%
Carl is truly a servant to the network. He has shown to the employees that he is a part of the organization, not a ruler.

Q3: How do you motivate upper level management to maintain creativity and a Positive Mental Attitude?

A3: Within the restaurants the managers are motivated in the same manner as the entry level employees are and that is through a family atmosphere. This is something that is emphasized greatly in Carl's, you could say that it is stressed more with management since they are the ones who portray it to the rest of the work force. Without this atmosphere I think that Carl's would not be as successful.

Q4: What sort of leadership action does the owner exhibit to the employees?

A4: When I first started in the company I went to a regional manager meeting, there were probably 30 or 40 individual managers there. Carl Karcher spoke at the meeting, telling the story of Carl's Jr. and how he once sold hot dogs out of a portable stand. Anyway, at the end of the meeting we were to get our nametags from a table at the front of the room. Carl stood at the table and handed the nametags out to the new managers one by one. He had met each person once and shook their hand, but he had no other contact with the person or way of knowing their names so well. I thought that this was neat, but just a name trick like you see on late night television. Well, probably three years from that day I was waiting in line at the Carl's out in front here. Carl was standing in front of me, but I didn't want to bother him thinking that he would not have remembered me. He turned around, asked by name how I've been, and shook my hand. I was astounded. I found out later that he is that friendly with all of his employees, and he knows the majority of them on a first name basis. It really shows the individual employees that he cares.

THE CARL'S JR. LEADERSHIP SUGGESTION BOX

AREAS THAT THE NAVY BLUE TEAM LIKED:

- ❑ Carl's does not racially discriminate when recruiting employees.
- ❑ The entry level training manuals are printed in Spanish as well as English.
- ❑ Carl's motivates their employees through a family atmosphere.
- ❑ The management of Carl's Jr. are motivated in the same manner as the entry level employees.
- ❑ Carl Karcher is very personable with all of his employees, no matter what level they are.

SUGGESTIONS FROM THE NAVY BLUE TEAM:

- ❑ All training manuals need to be printed in Spanish as well as English.
- ❑ Upper level management needs to influence the entry level employees more directly, not solely through the restaurant managers.
- ❑ There is evidence of a panoptic gaze, this could lead employees to think that Carl is checking up on them when visits the restaurants. This should be examined and eliminated where appropriate.

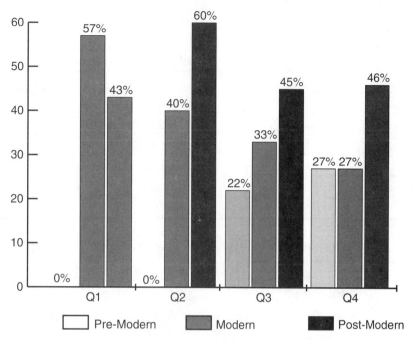

CARL'S JR. LEADERSHIP ANSWERS

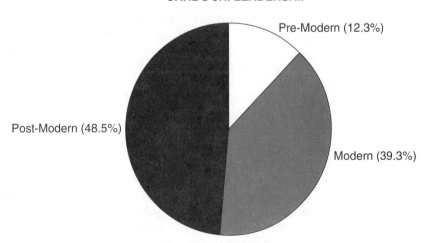

CARL'S JR. LEADERSHIP

MANAGER	LEADER
PMA is situational	PMA is inspirational
Do the things right!	Do the right thing
Performs	Transforms by Example
Reaches Objectives	Visionary
Plays the Game	Designs the Game
Authorizes, Scapegoats	Empowers, Trusts, Delegates
Status holder, Self-focus	Servant to others, Vision-focus
Status Quo, Secrets	Change Agent, Opens paths
Gives out data	Tells Stories
Talk Talk	Listen Listen

Table 5.2. *Differences Between Managers and Leaders.* I want you to get beyond management to the essentials of leadership.

Introduction

From the whips to the gaze and then to the storyteller, we will explore pre-modern, modern, postmodern leadership.

Rebelling Against Traditional Management/Leadership Theory.

Boj   Usually the instructor sets up leadership by saying that the field of leadership studied great *men* of leadership and could not find any philosophies, values, or behavior traits that could be taught to the **"now"** generation. This line of inquiry was abandoned. Then leadership pioneers at Ohio State and Michigan State began to identify initiating structure (planning and organizing) and consideration (human resource stuff). You know, the managerial grid, be the 9,9 leader who does both. Finally, after 40 years of no correlation between these two behaviors and performance, the contingency leadership theorists came along. Contingency people say a leader needs to be flexible: be autocratic and initiating in some situations, then be kind and humanistic in other situations. The current books out on the leadership market talk about empowering followers with grand visions, getting out of the leader office and visiting a customer or dock worker, and doing some alignment. But, to me, vision is just another word for superordinate goals and modernist planning. Empowerment is the old concept of delegation in a new cloak. Visiting workers is token participation. We need to look at how this "modern" leadership is just a lot of show, a new form of the gaze, and new plot to get people without a voice to adopt *one* vision and *one* logic for some grand narrative. I say the whole field is a pile of "cow maneuver." What if we start over, maybe we should go back and look at great leaders.

Bob Let's look at the stories of some leaders. Let's trace their rise to leadership. What did they experience? What was happening in their lives? What was going on around them? What crisis were they experiencing? What expectation did they have of themselves? What did others expect of them? What patterns emerge? What concepts of leadership seem to be suggested? Let's look at the struggle leaders experience and see what we can learn!

Leaders and History

We have images of leaders from the fact and fiction. These images in turn, affect our beliefs about today's leaders. Joseph Campbell has provided us with the tale of the leader as a hero on a journey.[1] (Unfortunately Campbell is less enlightening on the pictures of heroines).

Joseph Campbell tells us the hero goes on a journey with three episodes: separation, initiation, and return.

	SEPARATION	INITIATION	RETURN
HANS SOLO	Begins as mercenary & materialist	Comes in late to save Luke Skywalker	Transformed to hero who has found he is compassionate human being
DON QUIXOTE	Rode out to encounter giants	Found windmills at time Mechanistic/machine interpretation of world was coming in vogue	Invents a magician who had transformed his giants.
DAEDALUS	Master technician put wings on his son, Icarus	Fly out and escape the labyrinth he had invented. "Fly the middle way" but the son flew into the sun.	Daedalus did fly the middle way. Danger of too much enthusiasm when going a new way.
BEATLES	John Lennon et. al innovate music.	Became sensitive to needs of the time. Explored Oriental music forms.	In tune with their time and brought new spiritual depth to pop music.
MOSES	Ascends mountain summit	Meets with Yahweh	Comes back with the rules to form a whole new society
BUDDHA	Went on quest to get beyond world suffering	Found solitude beneath the Banyan tree of knowledge where he received illumination	Enlightened all of Asia
JESUS	Went into desert for 40 days	Desert quest saw encounter with 3 temptations and then crucifixion	Transcended all pains of earth to show the way.
MOHAMMED	Camel driver goes to a cave each day	Meditates and a voice says "write this down."	Brings teaching to middle east
DARTH VADER	Mask put over his evil monster	When mask removed we see a man that is unformed, not developed. Balance of the force and the darkside	Darth is the bureaucrat living not for the self, but for an imposed MODERNIST system.

Table 5.3. The Hero's Journey.

Pre-Modern Heroes	Modernist Heroes	Postmodern Heroes
❑ Slays different monsters to shape the world out of unshaped wilderness	❑ Cookie molding of people to fit in the big mechanistic machine.	❑ Magic Johnson is a hero on the court and is being tested on a new journey
❑ Like Moses who ascends mountain, meets with God and comes back with rules for whole society.	❑ Follow precise paths with precise terms	❑ Star Wars monster masks represent real monster forces in the modern world. Vader's mask removed to show unformed man, undeveloped human
❑ Legendary hero is founder of something or of a new way of life	❑ Manhattan project. Big quest into unknown to bring back evil	❑ Vader was the modernist bureaucrat.
❑ Leaves on a quest to discover the seed idea	❑ Feelings are overcome and controlled. i.e. Darth Vader did not listen to his own heart till there very end.	❑ Luke Skywalker rejects the system's impersonal claims on him.
❑ Spiritual quest	❑ Mirror mirror on the wall who is the highest paid CEO of all?	❑ Luke "turn off your computer, turn off your machine . . . following . . . follow your feeling"
❑ Transitions to maturiy	❑ Greed is good, Fear is good.	❑ May the Force be with you." Pour the energy into life, not programmed, political intentions
❑ Slay dragon drink its blood to draw its power	❑ Man is the modernist robot working in the bureaucratic system. The warriors have Vader masks.	

Table 5.4. Contrast of Hero Journey's in Pre-Modern, Modern, and Post Modern Eras.

So What? In pre, mod, and post stories of leaders, there is a journey of separation, initiation, and return. The leader brings back new rules to play by, new visions to share, new stories to tell, and the people respond. We are not looking at the traits and behaviors of the leaders, we are looking at the process of transformation that happened during the journey of the leaders. What can we extract from the journey's that can give us insight into our own leadership challenges?

The Story of Miliken

Introduction

In order to survive, firms that once flourished despite their thick-porridge bureaucracies have had to become sensitive to technological pressures, flexible enough to respond to those pressures. Perhaps the most responsive firm in the textile industry is Miliken & Co., headquartered in Spartanburg, SC. It has not always been so responsive.

Premodern and Modern: Before the Revolution

Prior to 1981, Miliken & Co. was run as a dictatorship. Roger Miliken ran the total show. His raging impatience for dissidence and inaction wreaked terror among his managers. His despotism showed up when he summarily fired 600 managers under the premise that Parkinson's law had been in effect long enough. His ultra-conservatism became ultra clear when he ordered all Xerox machines removed from every Miliken office on the day after Xerox-sponsored documentary on civil rights appeared on TV. People were proud to work for Miliken, but tired. Not many people could work the expected 60 to 70 hours a week.

Roger Miliken loved bricks, mortar, and machines, but distrusted people and the market place. He did not feel comfortable allowing customers to help set his direction. He frequently became involved in minute details. Secrecy was important. The goals of efficiency and productivity required long production runs with few changes, tight control of *incoming* inventories and suppliers, and inflexibility for *outgoing* product and customers. "Never do anything in small runs". Relationships with suppliers were adversarial, stiff at best. The structure was hierarchical and militaristic.

Paradoxically, despite the seemingly short term philosophy, Miliken & Co. had a huge R&D facility and may have spent more on R&D than rest of the textile industry combined. Further, Mr. Miliken showed a fetish-like interest in the latest management tools: long-term planning, computerized MIS, quantitative techniques, and a 7-week training course for managers.

Enter Postmodern: Come the Revolution ("Pursuit Of Excellence-POE")

Most revolutions are perpetrated by outsiders with little to lose and much to gain. This one was completely driven by Roger Miliken himself as a result of two realizations. The first realization was that *past paradigms were not acceptable*. The comfort afforded by old accepted beliefs and ways of doing things (such as, "Quality is a luxury") was primarily responsible for failure to improve, and ultimately failure of the firm. Miliken realized that the firm's survival depended on avoiding this "paradigm paralysis" and accepting new paradigms (such as, "Quality is expected by everyone").

The second realization was that *management was a problem.* Mr. Miliken stood up on a table and explicitly admitted that *he* was the problem. He realized that quality was attained with people, not out of people. He then began to reverse his leadership style 180 degrees. He empowered employees (renamed "associates") and adopted a team approach to production with cross-functional teams including suppliers. He continued the massive training programs including training for suppliers. He, the CEO, (not just his first-line supervisors) attended Crosby's Quality College. Thus, Miliken mounted a cultural revolution.

Postmodern Continues: Come the Second Revolution (Total Customer Responsiveness-TCR)

Miliken & Co.'s focus on the customer began when Roger Miliken forced his foot-dragging salespeople to become involved in quality program. The driving energy of TCR comes from cross functional Customer Action Teams, including representatives from customers, manufacturing, sales, finance, and marketing. The purpose of these teams is to solve problems on how to serve current markets and create better ones.

For example, Miliken and Levi Strauss have joined together in a 'Partners for Profit Program". This program gives the two firms the advantages of vertical integration without being vertically integrated. In effect, the programs uses JIT as a marketing strategy by linking it forward to the customer. The JIT partnership is implemented with five steps.

1. Miliken uses SPC to manufacture high quality fabric according to Levi's standards of color and roll sizes.

2. Computer/telecommunication linkages between Miliken and Levi provide for precise electronic coding and tell Miliken exactly how to load their trucks.

3. Miliken ship directly to Levi.

4. The fabric is unloaded at Levi's docks exactly when, how, and where Levi wants it.

5. Levi omits inspection, sorting, and storage of incoming Miliken fabric.

The result is a reduction in cycle times. Speed (timeliness) is an aspect of quality. It once took *six weeks* to have a customer agree on a sample, set up, produce, and deliver. Now that takes *five days*.

A more highly publicized result is that Miliken won the Malcolm Baldridge National Quality Award in 1989. Their primary areas of excellence in winning this award were their improvement of customer satisfaction and their "Ten Four" goals, striving for improving quality indexes tenfold in four years.[2]

❏ PRE-MODERN LEADERSHIP ❏

Leaders in pre-modern times were the masters. Serfs, indentured servants, and slaves worked with craftsmen in the fields and shops. Even craftsmen were tied to their master's shop and could not just up and leave of their own accord to enter the service of another master. Pre-mod leadership has roots in the military organization, the university, religious orders, and as we have discussed, even fraternities and sororities. There are many pre-mod leaders such as Napoleon, Gandhi, Thomas Jefferson, and Moses. To get an idea of the deep roots of pre-modern leadership we will look at Sun Tzu and Attila the Hun.

The Chinese Emperor's New Leader

Ho-Lu (King of Wu) said, " . . . Can you conduct a minor experiment in control of the movement of troops . . . Can you conduct this test using women?"

Sun Tzu replied, "I can."

The King thereupon agreed and sent from the palace one hundred and eighty beautiful women.

Sun Tzu divided them into two companies and put the King's two favorite concubines in command. He instructed them all how to hold halberds. He then said, "Do you know where the heart is, and where the right and left hands and the back are?"

The women said, "We know."

Sun Tzu said, "When I give the order "Front," face in the direction of the heart; when I say "Left," face toward the left hand; when I say "Right" toward the right; when I say "Rear," face in the direction of your backs."

The women said, "We understand."

When these regulations had been announced the executioner's weapons were arranged.

Sun Tzu then gave the orders three times and explained them five times, after which he beat on the drum the signal "Face Right." The women all roared with laughter.

Sun Tzu said, "If instructions are not clear and commands not explicit, it is the commander's fault. But when they have been made clear, and are not carried out in accordance with military law, it is a crime on the part of the officers." Then he ordered that the commanders of the right and left ranks be beheaded.

The King of Wu . . . saw that his two beloved concubines were about to be executed. . . . "I already know that the General is able to employ troops. Without these two concubines my food will not taste sweet. It is my desire that they be not executed.

Sun Tzu replied: "Your servant has already received your appointment as Commander and when the commander is at the head of the army he need not accept all the sovereign's orders."

Consequently he ordered that the two women who had commanded the ranks be executed as an example. He then used the next seniors as company commanders.

Thereupon he repeated the signals on the drum, and the women faced left, right, to the front, to the rear, knelt and rose all in strict accordance with the prescribed drill. All without a giggle.

Sun Tzu then sent a messenger to the King and informed him: "The troops are now in good order. The King may descend to review and inspect them. They may be employed as the King desires, even to the extent of going through fire and water."

Ho-Lu then realized Sun Tzu's capacity as a commander, and eventually made him a general.[3]

Deconstruction Points

1. *Master Leaders.* In this feudal time, around 300 B.C., the leader ruled supreme. Both the general, Sun Tzu and the King were elite rulers and masters over all their subjects.

2. *Gender.* It is interesting that the minor exercise led to the be-heading of females.

3. *Fear Management.* Leadership is by fear and intimidation. A public show of force gets the troops in order.

4. *Strategic Choices.* The general seized upon an opportunity to impress the king with his skills at disciplining troops.

Attila the Hun Story

As the story goes, a Gallic monk, provoked either by the horror of Attila's ambition or by a taste for martyrdom, created a new title for him. The monk hailed Attila not as "King of Huns" but as "the Scourge of God."

Attila, sensing the power this newly acquired title would yield on the battlefield and in negotiations, was quick to adopt it, for he knew the sobriquet would have the influence of an army of 100,000.

Attila pressed the advantage of his reputations as "the Scourge of God," . . . In the year A.D. 446, Attila, preparing to launch his march on the empire, needed money to gain the supplies and material essential for the expansion of his army. So he invaded Thessaly. . . .

Selecting the most vicious and ferocious-looking warriors from his army, Attila ordered them to wear garb of rough fur and leather, to eat only raw meat and to inflict the most horrible tortures on their prisoners. All of this planned fury was for the sake of perpetuating a legend.

. . . Theodosius allowed the utter destruction of more than seventy villages before he sought to make a truce at Thermopylae.

Because of Theodosius' earlier resistance and now his meek submission of the Eastern Roman Empire, Attila raised the price of peace. Roman prisoners were to be freed at a new cost of twelve pieces of gold instead of the usual eight.

Attila could have demanded much more. However, he knew the Romans would simply slap their subjects with new taxes to recoup the moneys. Attila had no wish to burden the peasants, merchants, artisans, plebeians or subjects of the empire, he simply sought to conquer its corrupt leaders.[4]

Deconstruction Points

1. *Fear.* Respect for authority is born of fear. But, if you push fear too far, the result is resistance, low morale, and sabotage (p. 46).

2. *Privilege.* The privileges of leadership are respected by the people so long as no harm comes to the people. Attila obtained tribute and ransom which he shared with his subordinates.

3. *Respect.* "Always pay proper courtesy to your subordinate leaders. Should you fail to accord them respect, so will their subordinates" (p. 48).

4. *Delegation.* "Even I, Attila, cannot accomplish for you what you are not willing to accomplish for yourselves. You must be willing to accept the responsibilities that I choose to delegate to you. . . . You must trust to your subordinate leaders those responsibilities that fit their office" (p. 73).

Once a chieftain has delegated responsibilities, he should never interfere, lest his subordinates come to believe that the duties are not truly theirs. Such superficial delegation yields fury in the hearts of subordinates (p. 74).

A competent chieftain will delegate important assignments to even inexperienced subordinates in order that he might accomplish his mission, develop his subordinates' skills and demonstrate loyalty for and trust in his subordinates (p. 75).

Master: Head of work institution. Owner of the slaves, serfs, and tools.
Sometimes more skilled than others in a profession.

Do feel that you manager is more skilled than you are?
Do you feel that you can do a better job than he/she can?

Authoritarian: **Enforces unquestioning obedience to the leader's own authority.**

Would you go over your manager's head in order to get something done
or would you go directly to him/her? Are you afraid of him/her?

Slave Driver: **A Leader oversees the work of others. A real taskmaster.**

Do you feel that your manager assigns too many tasks for you to do?

Tyrant: Sovereign and oppressive control over people.

Is your manager hard to work with? Does he/she overstep the boundaries
of their position?

Elite: Leaders are regarded as the finest and most privileged class.

Do you feel that a position in management is one of prestige or privilege?

Ruler: Leaders govern and rule over other people.

Do the managers of different departments tell other employees what
to do or do they just keep in their own area?

5. *Self.* "Seldom are self-centered, conceited and self-admiring chieftains great leaders, but they are great idolizers of themselves (p. 102).

6. *Positive Mental Attitude.* "A wise chieftain never depends on luck. Rather, he always trusts his future to hard work, stamina, tenacity and a positive attitude" (p. 107).

For comparison, we have made up a table of leadership skills from Sun Tzu and Attila the Hun.[5]

Sun Tzu Leader Skills	Attila the Hun Leader Skills
❑ **Moral Influence**—cause the people to be in harmony with their leaders, so that they will accompany them in life and unto death without fear of mortal peril (p. 64, 102). ❑ **Command**—The general's qualities of wisdom, sincerity, humanity, courage, and strictness (p. 65). ❑ **Doctrine**—Organization, control, assignment of appropriate ranks to officers, regulation of supply routes, and the provision of principal items used by the army (p. 65). ❑ **Balance**—Act expediently in accordance with what is advantageous and so control the balance (p. 66). A skilled commander seeks victory from the situation and does not demand it of his subordinates (p. 93, 101). ❑ **Deception**—Feign disorder, feign incapacity, avoid him where he is strong, anger his general and confuse him, pretend inferiority ❑ **Foreknowledge**—Use secret agents to assess enemy situation (p. 144–149).	❑ **Loyalty**—Listen to the loyal and remove the disloyal (p. 17). ❑ **Courage**—Accepts risks of leadership. Not bewildered by adversity. Confident in times of uncertainty (p. 17–8). ❑ **Desire**—Wants to lead (p. 17); Competitive desire to win (p. 19–20). ❑ **Emotional Stamina**—To recover from disappointment (p. 18). ❑ **Decisiveness**—Knowing when to act and when not to act. Not vacillating or procrastinating (p. 19). ❑ **Anticipation**—Learning by observation and through instincts to anticipate thoughts, actions and consequences (p. 19). ❑ **Timing**—One often learns this skill by applying the lessons learned through failure (p. 19). ❑ **Self-Confidence**—Personal feeling of assurance to meet challenges of leadership (p. 20).

Table 5.5.

❑ MODERNIST LEADERS ❑

Introduction

As the industrial revolution model of the factory bureaucracy became the dominant form of organization, the modernist leaders implemented grand systems for linking people to machines or to service bureaucracies. The factory bureaucracy was supposed to also control the dysfunctions of leaders like J. P. Morgan and others who accumulated massive wealth at the exploitation of everyone else. In the age of the machine, John Patterson was a ruthless king divinely appointed to make cash registers.

John Patterson's Story (NCR)

Patterson's dictum was simple: "When a man becomes indispensable, let's fire him." Rarely did he wait that long. Between 1910 and 1930 one-sixth of the nation's top executives had been trained—and fired—by Patterson. Dismissal came without warning or recourse. "There are just two things," Patterson would tell the soon-to-be-discharged. "Everything you say is wrong. Everything you do is wrong."

Those who remained were hardly unscathed. When executives were absent, Patterson periodically dumped the contents of their desks into the trash, permitting them, as he put it, "to start clean." When executives were present, they were subject to an unceasing flow of presidential memorandums by which Patterson sought to regulate their behavior, from the width of their ties to the percentage of the tips they gave.

Few areas of life escaped Patterson's attention. . . . If horsemanship helped to develop a sense of mastery, then all company executives would be roused before 6 A.M. for a morning trot. . . . Male employees at NCR had a fully equipped gym and exercised every day—part of the company's program to enhance job performance. . . . By 1905, 500 women worked at "The Cash." Exercise was part of their routine. . . .

Patterson, a contemporary said, "thought himself divinely appointed to make cash registers." The efficiency of his factory and the diligence of his sales force brought him the bulk of the cash register business, but he wanted all of it. . . . One of his approaches to competition was lordly. A competitor would be invited to Dayton, all expenses paid, to tour NCR and be overwhelmed by the strength of the giant he was challenging. Tours ended in the Historical or "Gloom" Room, where cash registers built by then defunct challengers were piled; a buy out offer generally followed. Another

PANOPTIC

Leader does the gaze on everyone. Bertham's Principle: Power should be visible and unverifiable.

Final evaluator of performance and quality

Penal Mechanisms are little courts for investigation, monitoring, and correction of incorrect behavior and then the application of rewards to sustain normalcy.

Lots of divisions, layers, specialties, and cubbyholes to cellularize people

Leader sits at the top of the pyramid

The head boss, the top of the hill, and the highest ranking person.

Panoptic - *Do you feel that management is constantly looking over your shoulder?*

Authoritarian - *Does your manager evaluate each employee on a timely basis?*

Network of Mechanisms - *Does your company investigate, monitor, and correct the incorrect behavior of employees?*

Organizational Layers - *Do you find yourself separated from everyone else in the workplace?*

In charge of surveillance, inspection and rating of everyone else

All information and decision flows up to the center and back down to the periphery.

Pyramid Surveillance - *Do you see yourself at the top of the pyramid?*

Top - *How far can one get in this company and how long does it usually take to get there?*

Inspector - *Do you have periodic inspections by the "central" office which inspects each individual department?*

Centralist - *Does decision making flow horizontally or vertically?*

TOWER

approach was to flood an opponent with lawsuits which absorbed his time, drained his treasury and disrupted his plans. . . .

In 1901, Patterson, angered that small firms were making money selling secondhand NCR cash registers, set up a dummy operation to drive them from the field. Backed with a $1 million budget, it undersold, undermined and bought out competitors. Meanwhile, the in-house competition department at NCR trained representatives known as "knockout men." Standard tactics included the following: if a customer was considering purchase of a competing machine, a knockout man would claim that the machine violated NCR patents and that the retailer would end up in court; the NCR man would offer to cover the legal expenses involved in reneging on the agreement.

One individual who was fired from NCR vowed "to build a bigger business than John H. Patterson has." Which, at IBM—the very model of the modern corporation—is exactly what Thomas J. Watson did.[6]

Deconstruction

1. *Fear.* Paterson ruled by fear.

2. *Central Control.* Patterson micro-managed his employees, including their personal habits. He fired anyone that got too powerful in his pyramid.

3. *Authoritarian.* He was the ultimate authority and had the last word.

4. *Total Control.* Patterson sought to control the entire life space of each employee as exemplified by the gym exercise requirements.

5. *Competing Voices.* His style was to destroy the external competition and to fire any competing voices, such as Thomas J. Watson. There was one voice, one logic, one way, and that was Patterson's.

6. *Anti-bureaucratic.* You do not find a heavy emphasis on bureaucratic layers and committees. Patterson moves about his domain with the determination of the pioneering entrepreneur who keeps all the reins in his own hands.

❑ WALT DISNEY ❑

Some Background on Walt. Walter Elias Disney was born December 5, 1901. He was a cartoonist until 1926. After 1926, he did not do a single cartoon drawing, but he did perform as a storyteller and controlled story production.

Most people have an image of Walt as a kindly gentleman they watched on Sunday evenings. The public relations department accounts of Walt are part of the commodification of the Walt legend for profit and survival. The PR account is one grand story, but what we want to introduce here are differences in story accounts. There are many sides to this leader and the PR appearances can be deceiving. Walt was a control freak who ruled paternalistically. He was the innovator and the tinker. He fired as many people as Patterson. Walt wrote his story onto the world in such a dominant manner, that it is difficult to find skeptical accounts of the grand Walt legend.

Good leaders are good storytellers and Walt was a master storyteller.

Roy Disney recalls Walt's Story Style

I was eight or nine years and . . . I was upstairs in bed sick and it was a Sunday. And Walt and Lilly came over to have dinner with my mother and dad. And they came up and said hello to me. And Walt—(and Lilly went back down stairs) kind of cocked his eyebrow and stayed and said: "we're working on a story I want to tell you." And he sat down there on the edge of the bed. And he must have been there half an hour. And told me Pinocchio from end to end. With all the gestures and wonderful—he had a way of absolutely hypnotizing you when he told a story. And I sat there absolutely enthralled. And, I couldn't wait for that movie to come out.

What he did with me that night and what he always did with everyone when he was working on a story—he was testing it. He'd tell you this story and then if he saw a place that wasn't quite working, the next time he'd tell it he'd of changed it a little bit. And stories evolved with him that way (Transcription of Benson video, 1989).[7]

Walt's animated films did not carry screen credits. The animators had no voice or signature for their work. According to Kinney (1988: 9) most of the general public thought Walt wrote the stories, made the drawings, did the layout, voices, and sound effects.[8] Jack Kinney, worked for Walt from 1931 until 1957. He was among the legions of who drew thousands of toons for hundreds of pictures, but in and out of Walt's organization had no voice.

Sometime after Walt's death, Ron Miller, Walt's Son-In-Law become CEO. His background was finance and he managed Disney with numbers instead of with stories. He did not tamper with the Disney machine, except to add a few more layers and a lot more committees.

Walt was a control freak; obsessed with control. These next stories gives some glimpses of the journey Walt traveled to become a control freak.

Sleeping Beauty Story

Once upon a time there was a Sleeping Beauty performer, who was late for the parade. She was fussing with the snaps on the back of her costume as she hurried by the Disney theme park guests. The rules said she was supposed to be fully dressed before she was to appear before any guests, in order not to spoil the illusion. Walt saw her and fired her on the spot without a comment. (Boje, 1990 interview).

The Security Guard Story

Walt was coming into the park one day. He approached the park entrance and the security guard asked to see Walt's pass.

Walt: I left it at home. I'm Walt Disney.

Guard: I'm sorry but you can not enter without a pass.

Walt: What is your name?

Guard: Dave Smith.

Walt: I am going to buy a ticket, but I'd like you to come to my office at noon.

Guard: Yes, Mr. Disney

The story ends with Walt promoting the guard to manager of all the park entrance shifts. Walt admired people who followed the rules (Boje, 1990 interview).

Charles Shows, Disney Writer

For instance, I was quite prolific at coming up with ideas for new television shows, and Walt needed ideas. According to studio policy, when I wrote up an idea for a new show, I was to submit it to one of the producers. However, the producer I worked under lived in a state of stark, naked fear! When I would submit a new show idea to him, he was so afraid Walt wouldn't like it that he would throw the show proposal into his wastebasket. He figured it was better that Walt didn't see the idea—than to have Walt see it and not like it!

After wasting precious weeks of time creating new ideas for television shows—only to have them discarded—I decided to bypass the barrier by using the "fear system." Neatly, I typed my ideas on studio stationary and at the top wrote the magic words: "Carbon copy to Walt Disney." My fearful supervisor now was afraid Walt might see my idea and like it—and fire him for failing to submit a good idea" (Shows, 1979: 75–76).[9]

Walt had Charisma. He was an autocratic and a fanatical perfectionist who controlled every facet of the business. While he surrounded himself with the best talent, he retained absolute sovereign control over every phase of every project. If a project did not met his personal standards for perfection, it was shelved. Charismatic leader tell stories and Walt was perhaps the finest storyteller of all time. Followers imitated his storytelling style.

Pre-modern Animation. Before Walt Disney, animation was a cottage industry, controlled by craftsmen and their apprentices. It was an art form and the artist sketched and designed and planned and crafted his art medium. In the pre-modern phase of animation, a support system of animators got together around each new project. Walt created the studio system that would keep artists and artisans fully employed by moving them from a piece of one project to a piece of another project, and so on. He put craftsman into functional teams, and kept them employed year-round. Before Walt, animators and story men were subject to seasonal employment.

Mickey Mouse

In 1927, Walt launched a cartoon series with Oswald the Lucky Rabbit as the main character. Oswald had many of the soft-cured physical features of his future character: Mickey Mouse. Charles Mintz, the distributor for the toons, tried to cut Walt out in order to reduce his costs. He hired away several of Walt's best animators and claimed Oswald the Lucky Rabbit belonged to him. Mintz copyrighted the name of the character. Walt was furious. He developed a new character called: Mortimer the Mouse and he never, ever let anyone copyright or control anything Disney ever again. Walt's wife thought Mortimer was a pretentious name for a mouse and suggested: Mickey Mouse. The rest is history.

In 1930, Ub Iwerks, who had worked with Walt since Kansas City, doing short cartoon features, was lured away by one Pat Powers, who Walt had contracted to distribute his Mickey Mouse cartoons. Pat being a finagler, did not give Walt detailed financial reports and would send Walt a few dollars from time to time. Iwerks could do 700 drawings a day. Powers used Iwerks to try to squeeze a $2500 a week distribution contract out of Walt. Walt turned Powers down and gave his distribution contract to Columbia pictures and hired a whole staff of New York animators to replace Iwerks.

After these incidents, Walt made it a habit to keep his plan for each project in his head, assembling a project part by part, team by team, keeping central control until his empire was visible for all to see and for him to possess.

The Transition to Modern Management.

Walt institutionalized a control process that consisted of departmentalizing the production process phases from story plot department to dialogue and sketch departments, music departments, inking departments, background painting departments, voice departments, and the like. Walt had bureaucratized tooning. Walt attended story performance meetings and assessed the weakness of plots, dialogue, sketches, and the like. Walt's stenographer recorded the meetings.

In 1952, Walt set out to make his vision of twenty years a reality. His story department sketched and built models of his theme park. Main Street, for example, was Walt's vision of the heart of a small Midwestern town that Walt knew as a boy and calculated to correspond to his archetype of the American town. The Disney Sunday night TV show helped Walt to give his vision of Disneyland theme park maximum public exposure. Walt's toons, movies, and theme parks had an appeal to the emotions of millions of people. In 1958 Walt said: "Dream, diversity and never miss an angle."

Disney's empire was a story processing machine, where every element was carefully related to each other element. His movies, shows, and parks were clean, simple and highly controlled. Walt centralized all project planning and operation decisions. Walt was at the top of the Sleeping Beauty Castle, and everyone that worked for him, was at the bottom. There was a clean and tidy place for everyone and everyone kept in their place. Every element was preplanned to be noncompetitive with every other element. The films, TV shows, and theme parks were complementary elements in the overall Disney empire. These were backed up by training, research, and an elaborate infra-structure. He was not a theory "Y" leader. He ruled by fear. It was a flat structure. There was no "real" middle management, just Walt at the top.

Walt died on December 15, 1966 at St. Joseph Hospital in Burbank, across the street from his studio. While the Disney production system was institutionalized, Walt's creative imagination and decisive control was not. When Walt died, gross earnings were $120 million, they floundered in the early 1980's and they now exceed one billion.

Ron Miller Inherits the Modernist Story Machine.

Ron Miller, Walt's son-in-law became CEO. He was a finance guy and managed Disney with numbers. He did not tamper with the Disney machine. There was a lot of pressure to get into the PG-13 and R movie markets. Films like Pete's Dragon and The Black Hole did not do well at the box office, but Disney animated files like The Jungle Book, The Aristocrats, Robin Hood, The Rescuers, and the

Fox and the Hound did OK. Even a 1984 rerelease of the Jungle Book netted $15 million. It was Miller who launched Touchstone pictures and released Splash as a strategy to keep the Disney family image uncontaminated by PG-13 and R movies. Kids thought it uncool to go to G movies anymore. After Vietnam, people wanted movies like M*A*S*H, Easy Rider, and 2001: A Space Odyssey, American Graffiti and The Graduate. But, few creative geniuses were willing to work in the Disney method of film production.

Committees in the Mouse Museum. Ron Miller did not get into the details of production planning, project selection, and project management. He left decisions to a committee system that evolved after Walt's death. People asked: "What would Walt do?" The committee system kept Disney a conservative and risk-averse company.

Corporate Raider. Saul Steinberg, the corporate raider, smelled a victim and bought up Disney stock with the goal of carving up the Disney empire into bite size pieces that could be sold off, leaving an empty corporate shell. Ron Miller fought back by buying real estate and businesses to dilute Steinberg's ownership. Miller threatened Steinberg with the poison pill tactic: a leveraged buy back of Disney stock at a price that would put Disney too far in debt for Steinberg to be able to sell off the pieces of the empire. Finally, Ron Miller paid greenmail to Steinberg and an imitative second raider: Irwin Jacobs. Roy Disney Jr., son of Walt's brother Roy, lead the charge to oust Ron Miller.

Enter the Postmodern White Knight.

In 1984, Michael Eisner succeeded Ron Miller as CEO. Eisner and his knight, Frank Wells awakened Sleeping Beauty in her castle and with the help of the princely Bass brothers and their money, drove away the takeover artists. Eisner brought in the creative wizards: George Lucas and Francis Ford Coppola to build some new attractions like Star Tours and Captain EO. Eisner's style of leadership was not rooted in the storytelling style and story-control processes that Walt had used to control his empire. Walt had been a visual man, a cartoonist who liked each of his project made visual. Eisner was from the movie industry, where scripts were written down. Whereas Disney had sketches made and pinned to the wall for his inspection and approval, Eisner and friends transformed the "mouse museum" into a major film studio, multiplied the theme parks, and kept the Disney Empire together (Boje, 1990).[10]

Deconstructing the Disney Legend.

We organized the stories according to voices, totalism, universalism, essentialism, and panoptic gaze. We will look at three leaders: Walt Disney who invented Disney and took animation from the pre-mod to modern; Ron Miller who symbolizes the bureaucratic, modern manager of the Mickey Mouse museum; Michael Eisner, who rode in on a white horse to rescue Disney Corporation from its bureaucratic cage as well as a hostile takeover and symbolizes, to us, the initial transition to postmodern leadership.

Voices. As you read the Disney stories, deconstruct the "voices." Who gets a voice in the Walt stories, whose voice is marginal, who guests no voice at all? In Walt's stories there is typically *one* voice and it is Walt's. Walt rarely allowed any "voice" other than his own to be heard. Walt refers to his wife, Lilly, as "Mrs. Disney." Perhaps a formality of his generation, but a signal of possession none the less. Walt took ownership of everything about Disney. Musicians and composers of the musical accompaniment for Disney's movies and short were referred to as "my musicians". Cartoonists were "my artists". "My brother, my uncle, my father, my daughter, my pal" are all references to people made by Walt, but none of whom was ever given a more personal reference by name. Certainly none were ever the voices of Disney's storytelling organization. There is one exception to Walt's possession of people and their talents; his characters. Mickey Mouse, Donald Duck, Tico Tico, Goofy, Jose Carioca (a parrot), all are allowed a voice in the Disney organization; mostly because they **are** the Disney organization. Walt recognized this.

When we looked at the Eisner stories, the deconstruction process shows how he gives identity to the many voices that are present at Disney. George Lucas, Michael Jackson, and Walt all have stories as actors and participants in the Disney organization. Whereas Walt uses personal experience narratives, Michael Eisner tells more third person stories through a narrative style. For example:

> Actually on the 30th Anniversary night, I came down here with Frank and the writer from New York Times and I was proudly telling about all the things we were doing at Disneyland and I got to the George Lucas-Star Wars rides and having heard from Dick and other people the attractive attraction which Disneyland ever had was during Inner Space, I told her we were replacing it. We're going to put in this great Star Wars attraction with technology that has never been seen before. It's gonna be the attraction that's going to replace that "dog" Inner Space. She said, "How can you say—that Dog? That's the most brilliant attraction ever at Disney. Walt Disney himself designed it. How can you ruin Disney?" She then dragged me to go over on it. We rode it twice. She called me a monster. And I haven't told anybody it's a dog. So it's not my fault. I just want you to know that it's not gonna be as good as the Star Wars attraction will be. (line 898–913, VT699; Boje 1992).

Totalism. In deconstruction, a totalism is an historical account which privileges one particular and rather narrow point of view. To deconstruct, we look at the stories that are not told as part of the grand story of Disney. As part of Walt's dominating voice at Disney is the history of Disney . . . as told by Walt. History is a recount of events as seen and enacted by participant observers. Disney's "official" history was told by one man from one perspective. The Disney story is a commodification as well as a control device. It is commodification because Walt is himself one of the characters of Disney, the way that Mickey Mouse is a character of Disney. Walt's story is control because it contains the embellishment of the Disney philosophy, the one man logic of what to do, what to say, how to walk the Disney walk. The story contains the Disney focus on neatness, order, the enactment of life in the Midwest town.

For Ron Miller, even though I did not record any of his storytelling, I do know the ghost of Walt remained at the helm. In the many committees that reproduced during Miller's administration, people would often say: "what would Walt have done?" They would tell the story of how Walt handled a similar situation and then do it that way. People called Disney the Mouse Museum referencing their traditional Walt-Midwestern values, their conservative deals—people who took on Disney film projects got paid less than industry standards. Walt's story of Disney was continuing its life force without Walt peering out of the castle tower at his expanding empire. I think there was no room at the top of Disney for both Ron and Walt.

When I look at Eisner's approach to totalisms, I see more paradoxical accounts. The paradox is Eisner could both reference Walt's history and attack Walt's strategy as out of date for Disney in the same discourse. For example, while Eisner would invoke the Walt legend to bridge into his own strategies "This is how Walt did it" he would then challenge the Walt legend "but, this is where Walt and I part company."

> I couldn't follow it (said Eisner). I'd go down there and they'd go through the story boards. And you go through one story board and they'd bring in another story board. And, I'd sit there for hours and I couldn't remember what was in the first story board. And, it was a hard process for me to deal with. I'd been used to working in the script area.

> And, I was a little critical of some of our animated films that had been done before Walt died. Because I think there were great scenes but a lot of scenes put together. But, sometimes the art of the story (as he motions his hands back and forth in an art in the air) didn't follow the way I was used to thinking about stories, or what I learned in school about the construction of—the stories and all that. And I'd keep thinking about this.

> And every time I'd say: "How was it done in the past?" And I'd hear about Walt. He'd just be there and he'd jump up and down and he'd go back and between things and so forth. And Roy Disney (Jr.) told me a story about how he sat on his bed when he had the flu or the

mumps or something and told the entire story of Pinocchio in the bed. And, I finally discovered they did have a script (emphasized).

And the script was in Walt Disney's head. We didn't have Walt Disney. And therefore we didn't have a single mind, tracking the entire movie. We had (a) committee of minds. And that was the problem. And now we do scripts (Lines 2817 to 2942; Benson, 1989 Video; also in Boje, 1992).

Eisner is telling his story in a way that destructs the Walt Disney Story. He is pulling on one of the strings of the story's fabric, and in the process, unraveling the grand account. Walt's control over the storytelling process of Disney is going to change to allow Eisner to get scripts instead of story boards, to have script meetings instead of story board meetings. Eisner is also using the stories he hears of Walt as an inquiry into the Disney system. Eisner is not postmodern man. Rather, he is opening up the modernist account that Disney has been living out for many generations to other interpretations. The history of animation that is Disney, still does not give much voice to the legions of artists and technicians that made Disney. For these stories look to Charles Shows (1979) who was a script writer for the TV shows and movies and tells his side of working with Walt. See Jack Kinney's (1988) side of the story of animators, how the animator's lived in the most marginal quarters, away from the main lot in a dilapidated apartment building, not getting their names on their work. Schickel (1985) tells the tale of Disney commerce and art.[11] Finally John Taylor's (1987) account of *Storming the Magic Kingdom* tells the multi-facets stories of how Disney transitioned from Walt to Miller and then to Eisner leadership.[12]

Universalisms. A universal is a grand and macro principle, a sweeping statement to gloss over a lot of differences in the local accounts. Walt advocated, for example, that Disney stay with the "G" movie market. He felt that it would be bad for business to get his cartoons, TV show, and theme park associated with "R" films, even though it was clear that the youth market was increasingly repelled by the idea of being caught dead at a "PG" let alone, the staple of Disney, the "G" movie. In this next story, we get a story of a story. Eisner, speaking at the 1984 stockholder's meeting is recounting a portion of a speech (a story) that Walt once gave (Walt's story).

Take A Chance

And I quote (says Eisner).

When I was 21, I went broke for the first time. I slept in chair cushions in my studio in Kansas City and ate cold beans out of the can. I took another look at my dream and set out to Hollywood. Foolish? Not as a youngster. An older person might have had too much common sense to do it. Sometimes I wonder if common sense isn't another way of saying, fear. And fear too often spells failure. In the lexicon of youth there is no such word as fail. Remember the story about the boy who wanted to march in the circus parade. The band master needed a trombonist so the boy signed up. He hadn't marched a block before the band master demanded, "Why didn't you tell me you couldn't play the trombone?" The boy said, "How would I know? I never tried it before." (line 195–207)

Of course the speech was given by Walt Disney and it was entitled: "Take a Chance." Walt was already a grandfather at that time and concluded the speech this way:

"If I am no longer young in age I hope to stay young enough in spirit never to fear failure, young enough still to take a chance and march in the parade." (line 209–212; Boje, 1992)

This is one of many places in this stockholder meeting that Eisner invokes the Disney legend.

"In 1923, Walt arrived in Hollywood with drawing materials under his arm, $40 in his pocket, and a dream. Waiting for him at Union Station was his brother Roy who would dedicate his life to making Walt's dream come true. Together with their wives: Lily and Universalism, working alongside them at night around the kitchen table, they struggled to keep a tiny studio alive (lines 223–229; Boje, 1992).

There is an official discourse and there are many marginalized discourses in every organization. What is interesting, is that though Roy and Walt were partners, Roy has no character and no voice at all in the Disney account. Here is Eisner giving Roy a characterization, that was not in Walt's egoist account of the founding of Disney. For Walt, it was Walt Disney alone who developed the Disney machine of Walt Disney Productions. Look at how animator and author, Jack Kinney renders the account:

It was a lovely spring evening in Paris. Roy Disney, Sr., and Jack Cutting had just finished a fine dinner and were taking a stroll. They talked of various subjects related to the studio, mixed with general small talk. They were relaxed and in a reminiscent mood, and finally Jack asked, "Roy, now that Walt is gone, why don't you take some of the credit for the development of the studio since the early days?" Roy stopped Jack with a hand on his arm and said, "Let me tell you a story.

When Walt and I first started in business, we had a little studio on Vermont Avenue—really a storefront, with a gold-leaf sign on the front window reading 'Disney Brothers Productions.' As we prospered, we needed larger quarters and we found them in a building on Hyperion Avenue, close to our original store. One evening when Walt and I were discussing our move, Walt said to me, 'Roy, when we move to Hyperion, I'm going to have a large neon sign erected, reading "Walt Disney Studios, Home of Mickey Mouse and Silly Symphonies." He looked at me as if expecting an argument. I said, 'If that's the way you want it.' And Walt said, 'That's the way I want it and that's the way it will be!' And that's the way it was. So you see, Jack, I think it's a little late now, and besides, that's the way Walt would have wanted it." (Kinney, p. 198)

Eisner, goes on in his stockholder speech to further turn on the legend:

"No one was more sensitive to change nor more attuned to its possibilities than Disney himself. I believe that Walt would take great pride in announcing with me today that our company has concluded an arrangement with George Lucas whose film-making innovations have created the Indiana Jones and Star Wars series of movie. . . . I don't know if Walt would be more pleased with this announcement because George today comes closest to the creative level of Walt himself or because George as a child was there 39 years ago at the opening day of Disneyland. . . . In **Disney's** business the fundamental idea can apply to a motion picture, a Disney Channel, or network TV show, a new pavilion, a theme park attraction, or a merchandise offering" (lines 237–256; Boje, 1992).

The universal's here are the ways in which the story of Walt is reshaped by Eisner to fit his particular vision of how Disney, the Corporation, is to react to change; how Disney the man, would have welcomed the creative genius of George Lucas; how Disney the spirit lives on in the merchandise. Eisner is like Gorbachev, reshaping the Marxian Grand Narrative to sent the Soviet Union down a new path. In Eisner's case, he is opening the doors of the Disney museum and letting new curators rearrange the exhibits. It is still the same story, but the base of participation is being widened by Eisner.

Walt had a universal vision of a vast empire in which his cartoons, characters, TV shows, and films would culminate in the production of Disneyland Theme Park. The theme park was based on Walt's vision of a small Midwestern town, the one Walt knew as a boy. Disneyland is Walt's archetype of an ideal American town. All facets of the Disney operation "synergized." The toons and movies produced the characters which became theme rides and exhibits and walking characters in the theme park. The TV show, movies, and toons told the Disney characters and the TV series sold the concept of a theme park.

To deconstruct Disney is to look at the stories that get marginalized by the official Disney legend: the account to Walt's founding story and his triumphs in animation, theme parks, and merchandising.

Essentialism. An essentialism, is similar to a universal, except that it is a micro theory, an appeal to a foundation essential of human character. We have seen several already, in the accounts of Eisner about

Walt. Walt has the character to "accept the risk," "make the change" "act like a young man," "be the creative genius." These norms are held out to the flock.

If you read the lesser accounts of Walt, such as those of Kinney and Shows, then you hear Walt referred to as "Der Fuhrer" and "Mr. Fear." In the office art, one a set of drawings called "the Seven Faces of Walt" circulated (Kinney, p. 157) Walt was Simon Legree, Der Fuhrer, The Bountiful Angel, Mr Nice Guy, Ebeneezer Scrooge, Beezelbub the Devil, and of course Mickey Mouse (with a dollar sign as the s in mouse ("mou$e"). Jones (1991) has suggested that people tell these informal accounts when the strong ideation system of the organization does not allow for people to speak up about the oppression they are enduring.[13]

By most non-official accounts, Walt is said to have ruled with an iron fist. If you disagreed with Walt, you could get fired. If you broke a rule of Walt's you would be fired. Everything was owned by Walt Disney Productions. Walt was everything, including all people.

> Frustrated by the noise of a lawn mower outside the conference room window. . . . He opened it, and yelled at the top of his voice, "Shut off that goddamned machine and get the hell away from here, you stupid son-of-a-bitch!"
>
> The roar of the power mower stopped abruptly. Once again, all was quiet. The Disney executives resumed their meeting.
>
> Ten minutes later the session was interrupted again, by a phone call. It was Disney [Walt]. His tone was stern. He ordered Harry to come to his office "at once".
>
> "Harry," Walt growled, appraising him, "I understand you just raised hell with one of my gardeners."
>
> "I'm sorry, Walt," Harry shifted uneasily. "I guess I lost my cool."
>
> Walt glared at him. "That old man has been with me twenty-two years," he snapped, "and if I ever hear of you cussing him out again—I'll fire your ass!"
>
> "I'm sorry, Walt," Harry murmured, shaken. "It won't happen again—I promise." and he started toward the door.
>
> But Walt stopped him in his tracks. "And another thing," he barked "Always remember this—I'm the only son-of-a-bitch around this studio!" (Shows, p. 70)

Walt was very intense and moody and was not above using scare tactics in his meetings. He had strong likes and dislikes and held a grudge forever. What is interesting about this observation and the next story is the way in which the grand story of Disney and the public personification of Walt is the nice guy who made it big by being creative and enterprising. It is as if you are dealing with a family that is in denial, that they have a perfectionistic, workaholic addict that often uses temper to keep the family in line. Schaef (1987) has written about the ways in which organizations exhibit process addictions and behave much the same as substance-abuse families.[14] No matter what daddy does, tell the right cover (up) story to everyone. Look at the dysfunctional games below.

> Walt roamed his domain with a hard-heeled stride that, along with his distinctive cough, warned us of his arrival. He'd crash through the door, stride to a chair, sit down, and tap his fingers on the arm until one of the guys grabbed a pointer and proceeded to tell the story.

> He'd usually allow the guy to finish, then all the boys would hold their breath until he started talking. We studied him the way he studied the boards. If he coughed, you knew you'd lost his attention. A slow tap meant he was just thinking, but a fast tap meant he was loosing his cool. . . . If you had something good, Walt usually said he liked it right out. Then everybody could relax and get on with the meeting. Sometimes he could be very enthusiastic, and all the guys would fly high around the room and pitch in to use his suggestions for tightening the stuff up, then help move the boards into the director's room and into production.

> If he didn't like it, he'd want to get out before any more money was spent. He'd stomp from the room, leaving the poor guys responsible with egg on their faces. (Kinney, p. 151)

> Suddenly I heard the unit door bang open, and with a few coughs, Walt made his appearance, quickly sitting in front of the boards and immediately starting to drum his fingers on the chair arm. This was a surefire tip that he was in one of his gorilla moods. Frowning at the empty chairs, he lit a cigarette and said, "Okay, Jack, let's get going. What are you waiting for?"

> So I started telling the story . . . as each of the various groups gathered, they realized that "man was in the forest" (a line from Bambi) as they quietly seated themselves. (Kinney, p. 93)

Walt also made it a habit to keep his plans in his head, assemble each project part by part, team by team, while keeping central control. Walt moved animation away from a system of seasonal employment for skilled animators and in its place concocted a system of departments, production phases, and interorganizational contracts. Instead of a skilled craftsmen doing a job from story to drawings to inking to background, Walt split the production process into phases, put a department over each phase, appointed a department head, and in the end bureaucratized cartooning. In story meetings, Walt would listen to story plot ideas, give the OK to some and shelve the rest.

Walt was the king of his Sleeping Beauty Castle. Everyone that worked for Walt was his subject. It was a clean and tidy place, with a place for everyone, and everyone kept in their place. Every element was pre-planned to be noncompetitive with every other element. Walt, by all accounts (Kinney, 1988; Shows, 1979) ruled by fear. There was not much middle management. It was the ideal flat structure with just enough layers to be efficient and to leave Walt in control.

Walt's Panoptic Gaze. In an organization that commodifies stories by buying up options for children's stories at low prices, putting the story through the Disney machine, and out-putting it as cartoons or movies, followed by merchandising, and then theme park exhibition, it is no surprise that storytelling is itself a valued commodity at Disney. Walt prefer "G" rated stories. But, Walt used the process of story-telling as a process of control.

It all began when Webb Smith, around 1931 pioneered the process of story boarding. Webb, it seems, was a hell of an artist, but a bit messy for Walt's taste. Webb had the nasty habit of sketching gag sequences instead of writing them down, and then tossing them in (to others) a rather confusing mess all over the floor of his office. To avoid Walt's penalties for being uncleanly, Webb took to pinning his sketches on the walls. Walt was initially quite furious: "the holes will ruin the walls, that I spent good money redecorating" (Schieckel, 1985: 148; Kinney, 1988: 62). Webb began pinning his rough sketches to 2 by 8 foot and later 4 by 6 foot boards. He could easily reposition the sketches until the continuity of the story scenes had been achieved. Scene backgrounds and dialogue could then be pinned to the sketches. Hundreds of drawings on Webb's story boards would get repositioned until the story was ready for telling at a story meeting. The idea spread, with Walt's advocacy, and every story meeting, every project, and over the years every film, every theme ride, every layout was story boarded. A group could work with the story board, perfect the story, and use the boards to coordinate production. Walt took the process a step further.

Walt's Gaze. Walt, it seems was an obsessive control snoop. He made it his habit to roam the halls at night so he could take a peek at the progress of every project in his domain. Unit managers ("straw bosses") would also snoop and run back and forth to report the progress of each project to Walt. Foucault (1977: 175–180) defines the panoptic gaze as a multiple, automatic, continuous, hierarchical, and anonymous power functioning in a network of relations from top to bottom, from bottom to top, as well as laterally to hold the enterprise together with no shade anywhere to hade from the eternal gaze.[15] Walt could roam his kingdom and literally gaze his empire's projects through the story boards and thereby look at the workings of each departmental cell. Biographies, such as Kinney's, report that Disney people learned to internalize the gaze. They would behave as if Walt had actually visited last night, inspected what they were doing, and was getting ready to raise hell. Foucault refers to this internalized gaze as Bertham's Principle: power should be visible and unverifiable (p. 203). Actually Disney's was a less than perfect cage of subjection. People knew the signs to look for to discern Walt's gazing rituals. If Walt had come in the night, then Chesterfield cigarette butts would be everywhere since Walt was a chain smoker. Walt could also not resist messing with the boards.

As mentioned above, Walt had a stenographer record story meetings. A typical story performance session could last from one to three hours and involve as many as twenty people. Walt not only gazed the story plots for sellability, he assessed the neatness of the boards. Kinney's (1988) story of Walt's leadership style gives us insight into how Walt had constructed his cartoon machine. Before reading the story, I need to insert that what is postmodern about this story of Walt is that we are getting one of the very few glimpses of the non-official story of Walt. Kinney is a marginalized character at Disney, an artist who does not get to sign his own work, by his account someone paid less than fair market value for art that is sold for millions. A single frame of a thousand frame cartoon drawn by Jack Kinney now commands thousands of dollars. In looking at Kinney's story, we are deconstructing Walt and Disney's side of the Disney monologue.

Eisner's Gaze is the Script. Instead of storyboard sessions, there are now script meetings. Instead of a visual blueprint, there is a written narrative blueprint. The difference being the script is not quite the control mechanism that the storyboard system was. Walt could walk the corridors of his empire and visually examine the progress of each department by inspecting their storyboards. The script is not so perfect a cage as a network of storyboards in every aspect of the empire. Storyboards give more surveillance opportunities than scripts. Storyboards also give more direct control over production by a central leader. Walt could control and monitor the juxtaposition of dialogue, music, scene design, and scene sketching.

Story Man. People in the story department, mostly men, were called "story men." Story men had their own story telling styles. Kinney catalogued four styles: cool, violent, emotional, and irreverent.

The Storyboard Gaze	The Script Gaze
1. Animators drive the story process. 2. Plot gets re-worked in sessions as Walt tells the story to get it ready for an audience. 3. Characters get re-developed with input in story sessions. 4. Sequence re-worked to improve continuity and gags. 5. Control over one department to the next in the chain of production. 6. Focus on final visual impact of the customer. 7. Plot is in Walt's mind, not available for debate. 8. Pace and continuity of action is tightened in pre-planning sessions before they go to full production.	1. Writers drive the story process. 2. Plot is in tact. 3. Character left in tact with little input. 4. Sequence left in tact and gags left in tact. 5. Control by Script team at get go, then delegated to production people. 6. Customer focus. How will customers go for it? 7. Plot is in the script. 8. Dialogue is tightened as the production progresses.

Table 5.6.

Four Storyman Styles
Cool Style   Each guy had his own style of presenting. Some tried to "cool" approach, "acting a wee bit above it all" but that was really just a cover-up for incompetence. The best story guys could act up a story, laugh uproariously at their favorite gags, and outshout everyone, while using a wooden pointer to emphasize the main elements.
Violent Style   Roy Williams added his own nuances with the "violent approach," kicking the boards and beating them to bits while he told the story. That was crazy to watch. He always had us in the palm of his hand just like a used-car salesman.
Emotional Style   Then there was the "emotional approach," typified by Homer Brightman. Homer was a real ham actor. One time he made a particularly dramatic exit with the line ". . . quack, quack, quack." One of the boys got up and locked the door after him. He left him banging on the door and broke for lunch.

Table 5.7.

Four Storyman Styles

Irreverent Style

It was Mike's debut in front of all the hard-nosed, experienced story guys. His story starred Donald Duck and Pluto. Mike took his position in front of the eight-by-four foot storyboards filled with continuity drawings and a hush fell over the assembled group. . . .

"Well, we open on Donald Duck's house, it's early morning. The f___in' sun's just peekin' over another f___in' rooster, and boids atart whistlin'. A cat yowls, Pluto wakes up an' starts chain' the goddam cat, leaps outta bed maddr'n a goddam harnit. He trips over a pair of shoes and falls on his ass, then the f___in' tree, raisin' hell with that f___in' cat. Then the f___in' duck runs on, at ol' Pluto, his f___in' underwear, a goddam nightshirt, anna lotta socks and other f___in' stuff, the f___in' duck gets hisself all f___ed up with all the goddam clothes offa the f___in' line an' he trips an' falls on his f___in' ass again. . . . "

The guys are now laughing up a hurricane at Mike's recitation.

"Hold it!" yells Dave [the Manager], over the uproar. "Hold it!! Mike, hold it," he shouts. Mike stops and says: "What the f___ for, I'm just gettin' started!"

"Yeah," says Dave, "but you can't tell a story like that!"

"Why the f___in' hell not?" says Mike.

"You gotta clean up your dialogue," Dave answers. "Walt won't hold still for you referring to Donald as "that f___in' duck.". . . . . [Adapted from Kinney, p. 63–5]

Table 5.7. *Continued*

Deconstruction.

1. *Style.* Each style has a distinct story performance style and relationship between teller and audience.

2. *Supervision.* During the ritual storyboard events, there was a supervisor approval process that depended up the story man's story performance skills.

3. *Formality.* The storytelling style was less formal when Walt was not around, and more formal when he was present. Story men did not insult the Duck or the Mouse when Walt was around.

4. *Circulating Fear Stories.* Walt took actions that circulated stories of fear throughout his kingdom. The story's recipe was: if you do things Walt's way, you are treated like royalty by Walt. If you cross him or break the rules, then you are gone. People did things the way they heard that Walt would want them done.

5. *Walt after Death.* After his death, people shared stories about Walt to answer the central question: "What would Walt have done?" Then people would recount a story of how Walt had responded to an analogous situation. In fact, training for new cast members at the Disney Theme Parks is informally handled by a mentor. After a brief tour of the facility, the mentor tells stories. And, who could argue with these stories. After Walt's death revenues increased by 230 percent and profits by 285 percent.

6. *Sequencing.* In the case of rides, the storyboard unfolded the ride like the sequences in a toon. A set of pre-planned visual events where the audience is the camera moving on rails through the events of the story line as they walk or are carried through the theme park. You walk up Main Street (the Midwestern Town scene) then your eye catches sight of the Sleeping Beauty Castle. Reaching the Castle, at the center of the park, the themes are arranged clockwise around the castle tower: Adventureland, Frontierland, Fantasyland, and Tomorrowland. A railroad, monorail, and other rides are to take the visitor from one setting to the next, in a sequence that tells Walt's story, unfolded in the very design of the park as a whole. It is a calculated sequence of visual events.

7. *Harmony.* Taylor, Mayo, Skinner and other utopians had their vision of how to create harmony between the individual and the organization. Walt's harmony was fashioned on a story board as a set of continuity sketches to perfect his particular vision of a corporate structure. Walt deconstructed and reconstructed the continuity of each project in his empire by storytelling and story boarding. He had a sense of harmony that was pleasing to the common man and revolting to intellectuals. Each action, each sketch, each voice contributed directly to the whole design. There was no clutter, no waste, and there was a place for everything and everything and every body was in their place.

8. *Leadership through Quality.* Walt's production machine was fabricated quality products and services.

9. *Storytelling as Inquiry.* For example, as Michael Eisner tells his story, he is making sense of how the pieces fit together. He is culling the stories of Roy Jr. and other Disney people to find out what is going on at Disney. Why does it not make sense to him? Eisner is using his story as an inquiry system to discover that the script is in the mind of Walt and Walt is no longer here. Eisner and his recruit: Katzenberg use scripts to discuss, select, and then product stories.

Mr. Fear Story

Once upon a time the MiniScribe Corporation, a computer disk-drive manufacturer, hired Mr. Q.T. Wiles to be their CEO. Everyone was so afraid of Q.T. that they faked financial statements and went through hell to falsify sales and inventory records.

"In one instance, the company shipped bricks to distributors and marked them down as computer component sales. In another, repackaged scrap metal and obsolete parts were made to appear to be new products."[16]

For division managers, their life depended upon reaching the goals set by Q.T.

Dash Meetings Q.T. held court in his "dash meetings." "At one of the first such meetings he attended says a former division manager, Mr. Wiles demanded that two controllers stand, and then he fired them on the spot, saying to everyone, "That's just to show everyone I'm in control of the company."

"At each dash meeting, division managers had to present and defend their "dash books," Mr. Wile's term for business plans that had to conform to a set formula. Invariably Mr. Wiles would find such plans deficient and would berate their authors in front of their peers. A former controller said Mr. Wiles would throw, kick and rip dash books that displeased him, showering his intimidated audience with paper while yelling, "Why don't you understand how to do this?"

Q.T. and the executives he brought with him to run MiniScribe became known as "the VC" derived from "venture capitalists."

"Basically," a former MiniScribe accountant says, "Q.T. was saying, "This is the number we want to hit first quarter, second quarter, third quarter and so on, and it was amazing to see how close they could get to the number they wanted to hit."

. . . On one occasion, an analyst relates, it shipped more than twice as many disk drives to a computer manufacturer as had been ordered . . . the excess shipment was worth about $9 million.

. . . "Everyone wanted to do good by Q.T.," says a customer representative, describing how division reports would be doctored as they rose from one bureaucratic level to the next.

Before long, the accounting gimmickry became increasingly brazen. Division managers were told to "force the numbers," . . . one division controller . . . quit when ordered by a vice president to lie about financial results. In this tense atmosphere, wild rumors abounded. Workers whispered that bricks were being shipped just so a division could claim to have met its quota. Others joked that unwanted disk drives were being shipped and returned so often that they had to be repackaged because the boxes were worn out."

. . . "It was almost like a fraternity party, with everybody huddling together to figure out how to keep the house dad from knowing what was going on."

Q.T.'s Denial. The house dad may not have wanted to know. After investigators showed him several memos that had been distributed at a meeting he attended, Mr. Wiles acknowledged that they "indicated the opposite of what he had previously been told." He denied having seen them and noted that if he had seen one particular memo, "he would have certainly read it as saying 'somebody's cheating.'"

After the scam was exposed, stocks dropped from $15 a share to $3 a share. Before the news broke, MiniScribe executives collectively sold 350,000 shares.

As the story goes, Q.T. "abruptly resigned, telling board members that the company's problems were far more pervasive than he had realized."

Deconstruction Points.

1. *Addicted System.* An addicted system is an addict (Q.T. Wiles) and an entourage of *co-dependents* (the executives and managers of MiniScribe). Addictive systems always have these two components: addict and co-dependents.

2. *Illusion of Control.* Q.T. tried to control by fear in order to stay in control. His "Dash Reports" were designed to do the *Gaze*, to monitor and control the executive's performance. But, the co-dependent, executives just told Q.T. what he wanted to hear.

3. *White Male Myths:* Q.T. was a God and everyone else was his subject. There was no women's reality, no accounting story, no black reality. There was only Q.T. reality.[17]

   ❑ **Myth # 1.** The White Male System is the only thing that exists. Q.T. was the only person who understood reality.
   ❑ **Myth # 2.** The White Male System is innately superior. Anyone not using Q.T.'s system was innately inferior.
   ❑ **Myth # 3.** The White Male System knows and understands everything. Anything outside Q.T.'s system did not exist.
   ❑ **Myth # 4.** It is possible to be totally logical, rational, and objective. Q.T. believed by being fearful people would reach the numbers.

4. *Process Addiction.* What kind of addict was Q.T. By all accounts he is addicted to work and addicted to his own system of fear. These are process addictions as opposed to substance addictions. Like any addiction, the addict lives in a perpetual state of denial, compulsive-perfectionism, dependency, and crisis. The role of his co-dependents is to keep everything all right by perpetuating the denial even if it means deception, lies, and loss of self.[18]

Leadership Archetypes. An archetype is a characterization, a metaphor, a story theme that frames relationships. For example, Q.T. Wiles archetype was "V.C." (Viet Cong) because of his system of fear and dependency. Walt Disney has many archetypes in his stories: from rags to riches, Gestapo, to fear. Michael Eisner's archetype is the Prince in the Sleeping Beauty theme. Eisner rescued Sleeping Beauty from the

Mouse Museum and with the help of the princely Bass Brothers from Texas drove away the evil take-over knight. Sleeping Beauty got some new rides. Eisner brought in George Lucas and other geniuses to once again do the Disney Magic. The Disney magic is a package approach to marketing. You do a film with Speilberg like Roger Rabbit. Then you franchise the dolls, build the theme rides, and fold the characters into the park. You bring in Michael Jackson and create Captain EO. They are working on folding all aspects of "Honey, I Shrunk the Kids" into the Disneyrama.

Keep the notion of the hero's archetypes (good or bad hero) in mind in the next stories.

Modernist Leadership in the Edison Utility

SCENE One: Carbon Copy Heroes and Customer Service Rediscovered.

In this next part of the transcript, I ask the group about corporate heroes.

Boj   "Who are the heroes of Edison?

Mike   "We don't have any strong heroes, if anything it is a hero committee that makes the decisions.

Rich   "If anything the hero is a faded image, an image that has been photocopied too many times.

Doug   "I think wherever Watson went, Wood would ever go. He would probably do the same things that he did at IBM. But, I guess I go back to the old line company. Maybe its not a person, but its a square-dealing, courteous treatment thing that we tattooed on our wall. What is it? Square dealing, courteous treatment and (pause)

Mike   "I always forget the third part.

Rich   "Good Service.

Mike   "Ok, then its the courteous treatment I always forget (lots of sustained group laughter at this inside joke) . . . they used to have these great big signs you know? Square dealing, courteous treatment, and good service. You know? And I dare say, the company does pride itself on that still. And there is nothing wrong with that. That's good.

Boj   "What about the heroes?"

Doug   "Its the legendary officers, each one of them, a carbon copy of the one before that kind of define the company.

Boj   "It's interesting that there is no hero. No, there is no person now you would define as hero.

Rich	"But follow the carbon copies. You get the eighteenth generation carbon and you loose resolution.
Mike	"You loose some of the clarity of the image (said with humorous tone) [Group chimes in many voices in many ways to say "Right, I think that's it."]
Rich	"And [still laughter in group] I don't know about the real early leaders, but to come up with a third of a slogan that says "square dealing" that's faded to me.
Mike	"Yeah.
Rich	"And although we may try to apply the principles of what we are saying. I don't know that any employee would say those three things with a straight face.
Mike	"Rich, notice how we laugh.
Doug	"There's the customer too. It's not that I'm a square dealer with you Rich, but I am a square dealer with the customer. That's the company motto or credo was that—dealing with the customer, good service, square dealing—but, that doesn't mean we, but that's what you're talking about.
Mike	"In effect, in the last couple of years they've made a big effort to go back to that original motto. Remind everybody to put out statements like corporate goals. That sort of sign that some people feel that people have forgotten about it—that was the way we did it. . . .
Boj	"Hum, I'm sort of intrigued with the hypothesis that maybe we've Xeroxed too many copies and the image has gotten a little diffused.
Doug	"That's a goodie.
Mike	"Because the leadership of this company is really truly a corporate body, not an individual. Mr. G., they say, rules with an iron hand in a very subtle way. I don't believe that entirely. Because I think this operation is so immense, so massive and so diverse that it can't be headed by one person anymore than a government can and I think that as CEO we have statesmen. As president we have politician. And both of them are superb at that and they are not in the same body. Up in there we have a couple of financial geniuses, at least one, which the other statesmen and the politician aren't. And the company is structurally organized for participative management. Even right from the top. We have a management committee. I don't think they function as a team.
Doug	"But they still function as a committee.

Mike   "They function as a committee but not as a team in an interpersonal way. And a lot of the stories that I hear in my work—you know—are the interpersonal you know? Unfortunate games that get played at that level and they are very costly.

SCENE Two: Revising the System Reproduces the Same System.

Rich   "If you wanted to do a content analysis of this little book (he had gone next door to get the history book of Edison sometime after discussion of the faded motto started) It would tell you something about the values of the company. This is our management guide. This a credo, the corporate philosophy. First edition, 1956, and it has been revised five or six times since then.

Doug   "Every time there is a new president.

Boj   "They revise it?

Mike   "But nothing changes.

Doug   "Nothing changes! (with emphasis on the word nothing) {lots of group laughter ensues].

DISCOURSE ABOUT THE FADING OF THE MODERN HERO IMAGE

Leaders are weak carbon copies
Follow the carbon copies, to the 18th generation
They are a corporate body, not individual heroes
It is a committee, not a team
The top is a committee, not one strong hero
Our motto has lost its resolution, its faded, too many copies.
We must recover, rediscover, find our motto

❑ SUMMARY ❑

As we began looking at modernist leaders such as Patterson of NCR, Walt Disney, and Q.T. Wiles, we found very forceful and authoritarian leaders who ruled their organizations with a controlling hand. As the modernist era became increasingly bureaucratic, leaders like Ron Miller of Disney and the carbon copy leaders of Edison Utility were not nearly as swashbuckling and decisive or pivotal. They were more the manager-types, stuck a top a pyramid, part of the panoptic strings and levers that is the bureaucratic machine, but far less impactful on changing the rules or the game. We think that this transition to carbon copy leaders, with less heroic journeys, has become the role model and prescription for too much of today's writing on leadership, as well as the sacred text of traditional management texts.

❑ POSTMODERN LEADING ❑

The Journey via Storytelling. Leaders lead us on the journey. They tell the story of how life will be when we reach the next port, cross the next bridge, and win the next battle. We see ourselves on the ocean tacking and hauling canvas; we see ourselves laying the planks for the bridge; we see ourselves gathering the hay to feed the horses, polishing the armor, and mounting our steeds to head for the battle field. The leader is the storyteller of our future. We see ourselves playing valuable roles in some realizable future. Gifted leaders are able to see how diverse, talented, and unique people can have supporting story lines that contribute to the grand vision. The leader does not mount a stage and walk to the microphone to convince in a few minutes, with a few home spun phrases, an entire organization to tackle the next mountain. Each day, each meeting, each golf game, each drive is an opportunity to get one person's story line in the open and figure out how it will contribute to his own campaign. Instead of cloning, he is diverging. Instead of taming, she is unleashing. Instead of manipulating, he is understanding. Instead of preaching, he is listening. They are co-producing the story line that will bring the future into the present. Together, they go off on the hero's journey.

Two legendary organizational story tellers are Sam Walton of Walmart and Fredrick C. Crawford of TRW. Both were spellbinders. Crawford was self-effacing with his success. "I could never fully accept the fact that I was head of a business. It seemed a mistake. I know people in their forties are supposed to be serious and grown up, but I never felt that way. That's why I love stories."[19]

Jack Welch, CEO, of General Electric is another accomplished storyteller. Bob observed Welch in the Pit-lecture-hall at the Management Development Institute. Welch could not only captivate the audience for hours with his stories of speed, simplicity and self-confidence but was also adept at drawing out stories from the listeners. The dialogue became a real working session.

When John Thorbeck assumed the presidency of Bass Shoe Company in 1987 he recognized the value of stories in the 111 year old company. He began resurrecting stories about George Henry Bass, who founded the company in 1876 and about the shoes made for Admiral Byrd and Charles Lindberg. He also hired an archivist to put together a company history. By identifying the company's personality, values, and idiosyncrasies, he would then try to match them with new market realities. The archivist uncovered a loyal work force who closely associated with the hallmark of quality of the original Bass family. There was, in short, a set of historical organizational values that could be used to make a whole framework out of manufacturing, marketing, sales, and accounting.[20]

The Leader's Role in Diversity Storytelling. What kills diversity is not knowing the stories of others who are different from you, who think different from you, who act different from you. The leader's job is to get other people to learn stories about diversity. People fear and do not trust what they do not apprehend. Stories are windows into the differences that make people unique and the similarities that derive from being on the same planet. Before people can celebrate and value diversity, they have to hear the stories. Leaders need to evaluate people on their understanding of diversity. The best thing the leader can do is clear away some bureaucracy to create some space where the storytellers can do their educational thing. Report the successes that come from diverse teams of folks getting a new idea to market, toppling an obstacle to performance, finding a synergistic path to quality. Stories get people past their entrenched opposition and their distrust for differences. The leader's job is to increase diversity by creating story sharing times.

Servant Leadership. To summarize what we know this far from our chapter sections on planning, organizing, and influence—the postmodern organization will be a network with many nodes, flatter than before, more skilled than its bureaucratic predecessor. The periphery will consist of many semi-autonomous working units, there will be a high proportion of minorities, and there will be an equal mix of males and females. What will leadership look like in a postmodern setting?

Postmodern leadership is usually defined in terms of telling a "vision" of the future to teams of people, empowered to achieve that vision.[21] We would like to expand the postmodern concept of leadership by looking at servanthood and networking as leadership constructs.

De-Differentiation. One answer is that it will not be Theory X, like Walt, nor will it be the Theory Y of Human Relations theory. The answer lies in *de-differentiating people and their leaders.* De-differentiating means getting rid of status differences. That includes privileged parking, separate dining and washrooms, and glutinous salaries. Why should executives in the US be the most highly paid in all the world, while they lay off more people than their lower paid counterparts in Japan, West Germany, and Sweden? Leaders are farthest away from the productive action of the firm, and have all the privileges and make all the money too. De-differentiation means moving the worker closer to the leader. Let the worker plan, organize, influence, control, and even lead. Lessen the manager's authoritarian monopoly. This means training and skilling the worker to think. De-differentiation is a rebalancing of power between leader and follower. The leader gets a little less status, money and managerial prerogative. The worker gets a little more.

Servanthood. After de-differentiation, the next task is servanthood. The role of the leader will be to serve customers by serving the people in the network of relationships. Peter Drucker and Tom Peters both advocate that the purpose of business is to create and to maintain a customer. One of the silent customers is the environment. The role of the leader is to empower people to make a value-added difference for the customer. The servant leader pays attention to customers, supplier, people at the core, and people at the periphery.

The servant leader is setting an example. Being courteous to customers requires being courteous to people. If the network is customer

Servant

The leader is the servant to the network. Leaders serve people who in turn serve customers.
Are managers viewed as leaders or managers in this company?

Empowers

The leader empowers participation in social and economic democracy.
How does a manager encourage employees to participate in specific tasks and events.

Recounter of Stories

Tells the stories of company history, heroes, and futures.
How are stories and traditions of the company used to inform company employees?

Visionary

Without vision, the people perish.
Are employees constantly aware of the future and their future in the company?

Androgenous

Male and female voices.
Is there any discrimination against women in the company?

Networker

Manage the transformation and configuration of the diverse network of teams spanning suppliers to customers.
How do the different departments offer their services to the customers?

Team-Builder

Mobilize, lead, and detach a web-work of autonomous teams.
How do all the different departments come together to reach company goals?

focused, then the leader puts the customers and the peoples interests ahead of his or her own. In the age of Michael Milken and Mr. Keating's Lincoln Savings and Loan, this is a radical ethic. These leaders sought to be served and to serve themselves, not to serve the interests of others.

In Matthew 20:26 the verse reads "whoever would be first among you must be your servant." The concept of servant leader has therefore existed since the time of Christ. The servant leader does not take maximum bonus for him/herself when the people are being laid off, as in the case of Chrysler's Lee Iaccoca.

Those customers, vendors, and network workers affected by a decision should participate. Instead, the status leaders seek to impose their will on others, to "lord if over them." In pre-modern times, the sovereign ruler ruled over the people. In modern times, the bureaucratic manager lead from a position of authority. The military leaders issued commands that were to be obeyed without question. The recent books on leadership by Bennis and Nanus (1985) and Peters (1987) advocate that leaders communicate a vision that inspires people to follow, rather than relying on orders, commands, rules, and rights. In the postmodern networks, the leader will not have the power to coerce that s/he has enjoyed these past centuries. The vision must be attractive and reasonable and inspiring to the participants in the network. Without vision the people perish; without vision the network perishes. The job of the leader is to help people in the network fashion the vision that will take them forward. Vision gives order to the transition to the future. Vision lets people focus on what needs to be changed. This duality is expressed by Whitehead:

> The art of progress is to preserve order amid change and to preserve change amid order.
> —Alfred North Whitehead

Precision Lenscrafters Story

Precision Lenscrafter, a division of the United States Shoe Corporation, opened its first store in 1983. Since then it has grown to over 250 stores throughout the United States, Canada, and Puerto Rico and is quickly becoming the number one super-optical in this country. The guiding theme of Lenscrafters is complete customer satisfaction. Not only are the highest quality lenses and frames guaranteed, but a commitment to make the glasses in about one hour provides the basis for customer service. This common goal is attained through the joint efforts of the Lenscrafters associates including: frame stylists, cashiers, lab technicians and opticians, all coordinated under the General Manager (GM). The GM of the store #153 in Yonkers is a Mr. Smith.

On an average Saturday, in a 11 hour period, store #153 can have as many as 75–100 jobs to complete. On hectic days like these, the one hour service is put to a vigorous test and tensions occasionally flare among customers and associates alike. The one hour service, working on the basis of an assembly line, is very affected by unpredicted absences. One Saturday two lab technicians called in sick leaving four to do the work of six. By 2:00 P.M. the store was filled with customers expecting to receive their glasses in one hour. One customer, an elderly lady with a very high bifocal prescription, had her frame and lenses sent into the lab at 3:00 P.M. The frame stylist failed to realize that due to the help shortage the job may be delayed. The lady, returning at 4:00 P.M., grew quite irate when she learned her glasses were not started yet. An argument broke out between the frame stylist and the lab technicians which resulted in all jobs being put on hold. The one hour service was thrown into disarray. Mr. Smith witnessing the growing hostility in the lab, rushed in to resolve the conflict. He stated that arguing would not get the glasses done and that they all should calm down. The lab was under a lot of pressure and in desperate need of assistance with the jobs. Mr. Smith put on a lab coat and started cutting lenses in addition to working on the floor dispensing eyewear. Using his laboratory skills he made and dispensed the elderly lady's difficult prescription in 45 minutes. Although quite upset at first, she grew very satisfied when she witnessed the personal care and attention received.

Later that evening when the crowds diminished and everyone was a bit more relaxed, Mr. Smith held a store meeting. He congratulated the lab on its efforts to keep up the one hour service even when they were short handed. In order to avoid a similar situation in the future all frame stylists were told to inform the lab on any more difficult jobs so a proper completion time can be passed to the customer. Mr. Smith also proposed an idea of cross-training associates. Lab technicians would be taught selling techniques and customer service while frame stylists would be trained basic lab skills as cutting and grinding. This way a shortage in the lab or on the floor would be avoided by utilizing idle labor.

DECONSTRUCTION

1. *Vision.* Smith articulated his vision of the eyewear production from choosing the frame to dispensing the final product.

2. *Servant.* He was servant to the network by coordinating the activities of frame stylists, cashiers, lab technicians, and opticians.

3. *Networker.* He acts as liaison between the lab and the floor to insure one hour service.

4. *Empowers.* To anticipate problems, closer links were drawn between the frame stylists and lab technicians.

5. *Team-builder.* Cross-training of lab technicians and frame stylists would provide complementary skills.

6. *Voyager.* The leader must voyage into the network, visit all its participants, and listen to what is going on. The servant works with the people on the firing line, at the point of contact with the customer, and the people that are adding value to the customer's products and services. As the leader encounters the vital point in the network, s/he learns what makes the network work, instead of assuming that s/he knows what makes it work, or worse, that what made it work last year is what will make it work effectively this year.

New York Stock Exchange Story

The scene is downtown Manhattan-Wall street to be exact. Mr. Gallo is walking towards his office from the subway station. On the way, he stops to talk to Jerry Campbell, a construction superintendent, about a job that has recently been completed. It is Mr. Gallo's responsibility to see that all constructions projects for the New York Stock Exchange are architecturally sound since he is both a project manager and a licensed architect for the corporation.

At the office, he begins to make arrangements for a meeting at Metrotech with representatives from SIAC and the NYSE. A few months ago, Mr. Fearon, V.P. for Recovery and Planning conceived the idea of having a contingency trading site for the NYSE. This site would need to be totally independent of trading floor on Wall Street. Since Mr. Fearon did not have a strong background with projects of this magnitude, he was forced to rely upon the skills of others. For all practical purposes, the job of finding a site was given to Mr. Gallo.

After a great deal of consideration, Mr. Gallo found the Metrotech building to be a suitable site. The only problem was that the building already had an existing tenant. The Securities Industry Automation Corp. (SIAC), a subsidiary of the NYSE was already established in the building. SAIC was resistant because there was nothing for them to gain and they stand to lose approximately

20,000 sq. ft. of office space and control over their electric, heating, ventilation, air conditioning and telephone systems.

There has not only been a problem with the terms of the proposal, but also with the way the negotiations were being handled. Due to his lack of experience, Mr. Fearon has hindered the progress of the project. Instead of holding group meeting with the outside architectural firm, engineering firm, construction consultant and Mr. Gallo, Mr. Fearon had held his own separate meetings with the individual parties where he was unable to work effectively and efficiently. Mr. Gallo has since brought the team together. He has brought all of the outside consultants together with the representatives from SIAC and the NYSE to try and come to a compromise. Through these meetings, SIAC has come to the realization that the NYSE is going to follow through on their projects. SIAC is not entirely pleased with the arrangement, but they have agreed to work with the NYSE in accomplishing their goal.

DECONSTRUCTION

1. *Servant.* Gallo successfully coordinated the activities of the consultants, SIAC, and NYSE.

2. *Networker.* A deteriorating situation was turned around by deft interpersonal skills.

3. *Vision.* Gallo has a clear picture of the final outcome and facilitated the final outcome.

4. *Team-builder.* SIAC is a reluctant participant, but it showed sufficient commitment to work with the other members.

5. *Celebrator.* Celebrate successful customer service, successful product improvement, successful cost savings, and failure. People need to be celebrated for taking a risk, trying something out, finding out what does not work.

Almost Always Instant Pants Story

I work at a men's clothing store in the Galleria Mall in White Plains. The majority of our clothing consists of finer men's clothes and suits, on which we offer expert tailoring at no additional charge. In front of the store there is a sign which reads "Instant Pants"—referring to our better dress pants which all have unfinished bottoms and require tailoring. The tailoring is done right on the premises and our tailor, Alex Hernandez, ranks among the best in his field. Our objective is complete customer service and satisfaction.

On an average day, the tailor does approximately six to eight of these "Instant Pants" while the customer waits. In addition to this,

Alex has other suits and garments sold previously and promised for specific days. A day filled with several requests for pants-while-you-wait, therefore, can hinder the already promised work and set the tailor behind schedule.

One particular Sunday a customer came into the store to pick up a suit which he was to wear that same day at a wedding. After the customer tried the suit on, it was obvious the pants were substantially mismarked and far too short. Alex does not work on Wednesday or Sunday which presented a big problem. The customer demanded the pants to be either replaced or re-altered. We assured him that the situation would be rectified as soon as possible, yet explained there was no tailor available on a Sunday. The customer referred to the "Instant Pants" sign out front and demanded an explanation. At the bottom of the sign it read, in considerably smaller letters, "almost always". By this time the customer became quite irate and an argument broke out between the customer and the salesman. At this time Jerry Aaron, the store manager, witnessing the growing hostility rushed over to attempt to resolve the conflict. Jerry took the pants downstairs to Field Brothers, a competitive store, to see if their tailor would help him out and correct the bottoms in time for the gentleman to attend his wedding. As it turns out Field Brothers does not have a tailor on Sunday's either, but their store manager is trained to perform simple alterations such as plain bottoms on pants. Understanding the predicament Jerry was in Field Brothers corrected bottoms.

The following day Jerry contacted our district manager Ed Dobson and informed him of the transactions which transpired the previous day. Ed agreed that cross-training the store manager and assistant manager to perform simple alterations on pants would help dissolve many conflicts which arise. Very often customers who need pants while they wait are turned away on Wednesday and Sunday and hiring a part time tailor for those two days would prove to be rather expensive.

In this particular business, the tailor shop's relationship with the sales crew is extremely important. One cannot function without the other. Ed congratulated Jerry and the staff on their efforts to maintain customer service during this rather unpleasant incident. In order to avoid a similar situation in future, the manager and assistant manager were taught to perform simple alterations using the blind stitch machine. The task is not difficult and would be limited to situations when customer service is threatened. Discussions are still in process regarding the validity of the "Instant Pants" sign and the repercussions of having "almost always" in such small print.

DECONSTRUCTION

1. *Servant.* Jerry knew that the customer should be served. He took the unusual step of using a competitor's facility to accomplish the feat.

2. *Empowers.* Jerry did not hesitate to do the right thing. Ed Dobson had set a climate for the proper activity.

3. *Recognition.* Ed congratulated the team for their superior performance under adverse conditions.

4. *Beaming.* The staff congratulated itself for outstanding customer service.

The Third Dimension of Power. Steven Lukes (1974) defines it as the power to shape perceptions, cognitions and even preferences in ways which promote the interests of one group over another. People are complicit in their own oppression and accept the status quo; some groups are even aware of their oppression over other groups of people. In pre-modern times one groups subordination to another group was ordained by God. In modern times it is merely survival of the fittest. The advancement of these claims by one group versus another is itself an exercise of power.

The New Leader. The new leader cultivates uniqueness and diversity. Each person is the hero of their own journey and the leader's role is to help each person along their individual journey. Rather than put people into normalized categories, find out unique ways each person can serve customers and add value. Clear the field of bureaucratic barriers so each individual can assert their uniqueness. Jack Welch of GE claims that leaders have a passion for excellence and hate bureaucracy and as well as all other nonsense that comes with it.[22] Help everyone tell their story in a way that gains respectability in the organizational community. Give them their voice, rather than having them mimic the bureaucratic monologue.

The leader's role is to get the person's success story broadcasted. The system adapts to its heros. The leader can find the heros that others in the system need to model. Get the individuals to tell their story. Xerox, once a year has "Team Xerox" day. Teams of innovating people, who have innovated, improved quality, fashioned a new service, saved money—are brought on stage and televised to Xerox audiences around the world. Each team tells its success story and receives the attention of everyone at Xerox.

LEADERSHIP BY VISION

Martin Luther King, Jr. (1929–1968)

"I Have A Dream"

. . . I say to you today, my friends, that in spite of the difficulties and frustrations of the moment I still have a dream. It is a dream deeply rooted in the American dream.

I have a dream that one day this nation will rise up and live out the true meaning of its creed: "We hold these truths to be self-evident: that all men are created equal.":

I have a dream that one day on the red hills of Georgia the sons of former slaves and the sons of former slave owners will be able to sit down together at the table of brotherhood.

I have a dream that one day even the state of Mississippi, a desert state sweltering with the heat of injustice and oppression, will be transformed into an oasis of freedom and justice.

I have a dream that my four little children will one day live in a nation where they will not be judged by the color of their skin but by the content of their character.

I have a dream today.

I have a dream that one day the state of Alabama, whose governor's lips are presently dripping with the words of interposition and nullification, will be transformed into a situation where little black boys and black girls will be able to join hands with little white boys and white girls and walk together as sisters and brothers.

I have a dream today.

I have a dream that one day every valley shall be exalted, every hill and mountain shall be made low, the rough places will be made plains, and the crooked places will be made straight, and the glory of the Lord shall be revealed, and all flesh shall see it together.

This is our hope. This is the faith with which I return to the South. With this faith we will be able to transform the jangling discords of our nation into a beautiful symphony of brotherhood. With this faith we will be able to work together, to pray together, to struggle together, to go to jail together, to stand up for freedom together, knowing that we will be free one day.

This will be the day when all of God's children will be able to sing with new meaning "My country 'tis of thee, sweet land of liberty, of thee I sing. Land where my fathers died, land of the pilgrim's pride, from every mountainside, let freedom ring."

And if America is to be a great nation this must become true. So let freedom ring from the prodigious hilltops of New Hampshire. Let freedom ring from the mighty mountains of New York. Let freedom ring from the heightening Alleghenies of Pennsylvania!

Let freedom ring from the snowcapped Rockies of Colorado!
Let freedom ring from the curvaceous peaks of California!
But not only that: let freedom ring from Stone Mountain of Georgia!
Let freedom ring from every hill and molehill of Mississippi. From every mountainside, let freedom ring.

When we let freedom ring, when we let it ring from every village and every hamlet, from every state and every city, we will be able to speed up that day when all of God's children, black men and white men, Jews and Gentiles, protestants and Catholics, will be able to join hands and sing in the words of that old Negro spiritual, "Free at last! Free at last! Thank God almighty, we are free at last!" (Civil Rights demonstration, Washington, D.C., in 1963).

Deconstruction

1. *Vision.* Martin Luther King, Jr. had a vision for America. A vision is a story of the future that empowers people to take action. His vision was persuasive. It recommends a particular course of action.

2. *Equality.* Aristotle wrote, "Equality consists in the same treatment of similar persons."

LEADERSHIP AND STORYTELLING

Symbolize Vision
Persuade Change
Point to Values & Priorities
Point to Precedents
Teach
Enthuse

STORY SKILLS

Telling them
Hearing them
Crafting them (by priority; by vision; by policy)
(Storyboarding)
Scripting new heroes
Systematic Collection
Assessing: "What is the story around here?"
Control over your own storyline (Role & Destiny)
Revisionism (New slant to history)
New positioning of stories that support change

> ### *General George S. Patton*
>
> Never tell people how to do things. Tell them what to do and they will surprise you with their ingenuity.[23]

Donald Peterson at Ford—Leading By Listening & Empowering

As the story goes, in 1980, there was an unannounced visit to the automotive design center and the visitor tapped design chief Jack Telnack on the shoulder.

"You're a professional designer. You're far and away the most knowledgeable person there is about what we ought to do," the visitor said. "Do you like these cars? Do you feel proud of them? Would you park one of these cars in your driveway?"

Telnack wasn't quite sure what to make of it. You see, the visitor was Donald Peterson, the company's president and chief operating officer. At first, Telnack was tempted to stand by the company's plan. But he saw an honesty in Peterson's inquisitive face that he couldn't ignore.

"Actually, no, I don't like these designs," Telnack told him.

Peterson granted Telnack a few weeks to come up with a new model. Telnack sketched the kind of car he'd personally love to own—a sleek, aerodynamic model with features similar to the European styling found in Mercedes-Benz's and BMW's. Telnack didn't realize it at the time, but the sketch he had just made . . . Ford Taurus, destined to become the best-selling midsize car in the United States.

"That one conversation turned everything around," says Telnack.[24]

Deconstruction.

1. *Empower.* Don Peterson empowered Telnack to do the design he wanted without worrying about bureaucratic B.S. Telnack already knew how to design a better car. He just need to be empowered to self-define his job.

2. *Listen.* Don Peterson heard Telnack's story. He diagnosed the story and the rest is Taurus history.

3. *De-bureaucratize.* If you know Ford, you know that the designer is at the mercy of bureaucratic review and monitor and approval committees. Peterson cut through all that by making Telnack the

champion of the new design. The enemy is not the Japanese flexible manufacturing system, it is the American bureaucratic pyramid!

4. *Leadership by Dialogue.* Peterson's simple conversation was transformational because it opened the door to moving out of the pyramid and into team work.

5. *Customers.* Telnack was thinking like a customer.

6. *Servant.* Peterson got out of his office and went down to the trenches to see how he could serve his people. A servant asks other how to improve the job, how to make things better, how to become more successful. The people doing the work know more than the high-priced experts.

7. *Implement Suggestions.* By 1984 employees of Ford Tempo and Mercury Topaz made 666 suggestions and implements three fourths of them (p. 76). It is not as impressive as Toyota's hundreds of thousands of suggestions with 95% implemented, but it is a damn good start.

Peterson & Deming

After watching a TV documentary on what Deming did for Japan after World War II, Peterson spent the next five months trying to convince Deming to visit Ford.

"Deming wouldn't come until Peterson got on the phone and assured him that he personally would listen to what Deming had to say. When Deming arrived in January 1981, he went straight to Peterson's office. What he offered was a statistical system that ensured that products would be built right the first time—without defects that would have to be repaired afterward. . . . What he preached was "continuous improvement."

. . . In meetings at Ford he came on strong, ridiculing management for what they'd done to Ford employees. Deming says that 80 percent of quality problems are caused not by hourly workers but by poor management" (p. 79–81).

Networking Leadership. Clegg (1990) thinks Japan has postmodern organizations because their structure is more flexible and flatter (in number of layers) than the Western model. Further, the ringi-ko decision making structure focuses on wide participation and consensus processes. The networking of suppliers, enterprise, and government is part of network leadership in Japan (zibatsu). Japanese workers trust their leaders to make decisions for the benefit of the enterprise which will also benefit the people of that enterprise.

Postmodern Japan. A post-Weberian and post-Fordist rationality is in place in Japan. Where Japan falls short is in the restricted role of women in Japan and in the U.S. the restricted role of minorities. Women and minorities attain only the more peripheral leadership positions. In that peripheral position skills and wages are less than in core (central) positions. Japan has gone beyond Fordism (modernism) by reintegrating the workers' skill, knowledge and creative thinking back into the production process.

Flexible manufacturing system. While Japan uses flexible manufacturing systems (FMS) to produce niche products the U.S. uses FMS to further control the worker. While Japan is using FMS to produce a higher variety of output in many niches, the U.S. is using FMS to produce larger batches of standardized products with de-skilled workers (Clegg, 1990: 213). According to case studies by Shaiken, Herzenberg and Kuhn (1986) FMS is being used to diminish worker autonomy and responsibility for planning. In Japan, workers are part of multi-skilled work teams using KAIZEN systems to continuously improve production processes. The U.S. is still using the modernist strategy of using capital to buy fancy robotics as a way of getting rid of skilled workers so they can show short term profit.

Building Worker Skill. While West German auto production has focused on building worker skill and increasing their participation, the U.S. auto industry has de-skilled the auto worker. According to Clegg's (1990: 215–216) review of West German organization studies, the automotive, machine tool and chemical industries have stayed focused on worker skill training, while trying to find ways to treat workers as an intelligent part of the production system. Production is being re-organized to allow for more multi-skilled workers to be utilized. One of the added skills, is the ability to work on the production system itself, rather than relying on experts. The final result is that the division and specialization of the work force is being lessened. This development allows for more sophisticated technologies to be implemented with a more and more skilled workforce. The problem is, that the workers who do not get on the training bandwagon are being left behind (displaced). They will find that their lack of skill or multi-skills will keep them out of higher paying jobs. In the U.S. automotive jobs are dumbified so de-skilled workers can perform the jobs at lesser rates of pay. This de-skilling is relevant to leadership, because it increases the gap between leaders and the people doing the work in America.

Working Partner. While the Swedish Automotive industry has focused on making the worker a more democratic & economic partner in the enterprise, the American Automotive industry is still de-skilling the worker. Within Sweden, workers participate in the capital ownership of the firm by the investment of "wage earner funds." And why not? Why should U.S. executives get stock participation and ownership incentives, but those same opportunities are denied to American workers? The division of labor between menial and manual work versus brain work is less in Sweden than in the U.S. Can participating in capitalism be opened up beyond just the behind-the-scene investor to the worker? In Sweden, labor has a high profile in economic management: investment and labor planning, decision-making, and control. In Sweden the problem is not defined as "unemployment." Instead it is defined as labor "redeployment."[25]

> A series of statutes, known as the Aman laws, redefined the rights of shop stewards, safety committees and employees in general, as well as imposing obligations on employers to accept worker directors and to disclose and negotiate over all corporate plans affecting their workforces (p. 231).

Exclusionary versus Inclusionary Postmodern Leadership. The metaphor of the brains versus the hands fits here. In the U.S, the postmodern movement is being stalled, in comparison to both Japan, West Germany, and Sweden because in the U.S. leaders are investing in themselves first, then in capital & technology, and least in skilling the workers. Japan's postmodernism is exclusionary, while Sweden's and West Germany's is inclusionary. American postmodernism is a dream. It is a dream because American leaders do not want to increase worker skills or to grant democratic participation in capital control. Why should they? As Clegg (1991: 234) suggests, leaders participate in the "enclaves of privilege" which are barred to workers. American leaders would rather take their fat bonus, row off to shore, and watch their ship sink.

> **Nothing great was ever achieved without enthusiasm.**
> —Ralph Waldo Emerson

Enthusiasm. Select the leader who is enthusiastic about bringing the network's vision into being. Be enthusiastic about quality improvements. If a leader can locate quality improvements and spread the story of quality improvement to the rest of the network, then that leader is a servant to the entire network. That leader is affecting the positive growth of the network by being enthusiastic about change and innovation and quality. A leader who is enthusiastic about customer service is a servant to the customers of the network. Networks survive because they effectively meet customer needs. Enthusiasm is contagious.

Skeptical Analysis of Postmodern Leadership

1. *Servant.* Take the case of H. Ross Perot. In his speeches, he typifies himself as a "servant to the people." He says he will create electronic town hall meetings to allow people to vote their preferences on policies he is considering. He is not going to run unless people in every state collect signatures to put his name on the ballot. Is H. Ross Perot a servant leader? Certainly, General Motors' Board of Directors does not think so. It is one thing to use the rhetoric of being the servant to the people and quite another to be that servant.

   Bureaucrats will often say that have been appointed to serve the people. The motto of the Los Angeles police force is "to serve and to protect." The Los Angeles riots suggest that there has not been enough serving.

2. *Empower.* How can leaders empower anyone but themselves? Can another individual empower you or do you have to empower yourself? Empowerment means that you were somehow disempowered. In fact, when someone says "I empower you" they usually hand you a stack of work to do. Is putting a suggestion into a sealed box empowering? Jack Kemp wants to economically empower the people of housing projects across America to self-manage their own buildings, to take on jobs running their own community from which they had been excluded, and to even get into apartment ownership. But are these people really empowered? To be empowered, the people of public housing developments would have to be let off their reservations and made powerful participants in white, middle class society. To be empowered is not to be on the margin or periphery of a society, corralled into a housing development, while armed and dangerous Los Angeles police patrol cars keep poor people away from non-poor neighborhoods. Is this empowerment or containment? There is a language game in the empowerment approach to leadership. Political leaders promise empowerment, but people are losing power.

3. *Recounter of Stories.* In the Michael Eisner stories, as he took over Disneyland, he revised the Walt legends to empower his own vision of command and control. Telling stories of history, heros, and the future options does not mean it is a postmodern leadership approach. The thing that Eisner did do that was postmodern was to put in more voices and points of view into his stories of Disney. In this way he de-centered his own voice and became somewhat more responsive to the many voices of Disney.

4. *Visionary*. Martin Luther King's speech was empowering and captured an agenda for our times. However, now every executive and bureaucrat and college dean across the country is using the word vision on top of every planning and control document that is reviewed by countless committees in countless retreats. Surely calling something a vision does not make it postmodern. Some visions are worthy, others are holocausts, bureaucratic control strategies, and most are fluff without connection to the ethics and dynamics of corporate life. The question to ask is who participates in the vision? Who is privileged and marginalized by the vision? Who implements the vision? How does the vision change or reinforce the status quo? Does it open up or narrow participation? Is there more or less exploitation? The British had a vision of the U.S. as a colony. We responded with the American Revolution. This means that there can be a conflict of visions and that leadership is helping people sort through that diversity.

5. *Androgynous*. There is a male and a female voice. The male voice dominated pre-modern and modern discourse. It also dominates in postmodern discourse. The female voice has been socialized to be weak: to please, to mother, to agree, to relate, to listen, to empathize, to appreciate, to follow, to show empathy. The male voice has been socialized to be strong: to command, to tell, to father, to direct, to dominate, to lead, to be rational. For women, the choice is to fit in by using a weak and subordinated voice or to be self-assertive and to adopt a stronger voice.

> In the postmodern organization, both voices are viable and worthy. Both genders can use both voices without getting stuck in one or the other linguistic practice.

Real androgyny, defined not as simply adding together the misshapen halves of male and female, but rather as a complex process of calling out that which is valuable in each gender and carefully disentangling if from that which is riddled with the effects of power, is a political struggle" (Kathy Ferguson).[26]
In a centralized leadership system, American organizations adopt a White Male Voice. Everyone on the periphery of the core White Male structure adopts a subordinate and decidedly female voice. De-centering and de-differentiating leadership as we move to flatter, more networked, more equalized patterns of organizing—will mean more self-defined, self-managed, and self-directed human action. Female skills for relating, nurturing, opening, expanding, and inviting in will be more valuable than male skills of pyramiding, demanding, closing, excluding, and expelling. As power balances shift, the gender skill needs will also shift.

Dominance is more a characteristic of pyramid and bureaucratic life than of network life. The leadership of post-bureaucratic organizations will necessitate androgynous voices.

Women need power in order to change society, but power within bureaucracies is not change-making power. The organizational forms and discourse of bureaucratic capitalism institutionalize modes of domination that recreate the very patterns of oppression that feminism arose to combat. . . . Bureaucratic discourse both creates and reflects the masculine notion of the subject, then posits that version of subjectivity as universal. But women's experience provides a vision of human relatedness and autonomy in which subjectivity is rooted in relatedness and autonomy . . . Feminist discourse would insist upon judging technology in light of the standards of autonomy and community named in the discourse. Many kinds of modern technologies . . . are compatible with decentralized and participatory decision-making. . . . Under the value system named in feminist discourse, calculations of efficiency and productivity would include an ongoing concern for the development of the individual, the needs of the community, and the requirements of nature (p. 203–5)

6. *Networker.* Just because we move from pyramid builder to a networker approach to leadership does not mean that it is postmodern. Electronic surveillance can be used in very flat networks to achieve leadership command and control in ways that are confining and exploitative. It is not the configuration or the global span of the network that makes it postmodern, it is how it equalizes and de-centers the power relationships and privileges.

7. *Team-builder.* Most of the postmodern teams are in fact, just bureaucratic committees by another name. For the Japanese, as we have discussed at length, the team concept in manufacturing makes every worker a generalist, while denying that specialist brought into synergistic relation as on a baseball or football team is a viable model. Putting people in teams is not all that positive. Students, working in student project teams, know that when you are dependent on one another, the team members and the team leader can exploit the allocation of work loads, scheduling, and the administration of rewards for results. Teams are often not too empowering. Maybe it would be more postmodern to recommend fewer teams and a return to an emphasis on individualism.

Postmodern Leadership Summary. The postmodern project is to de-hierarchize, de-centralize, and de-differentiate bureaucratic division of labor. In planning we looked at the re-integration of planning and doing. In organizing, we looked at network patterns that move from vertical divisions of labor to horizontal arrangements. In influencing, we looked at self-discipline and self-initiative. In leading, we have looked at post-white male leading. In leading, we substituted service for dominance. To lead is to empower the network to participate, to coordinate, to reconfigure, to invite diversity, to enlighten discourse, to envision alternative to bureaucratic life, to equalize participation, and to get a dialogue of many voices with many stories to happen.

❑ SUMMARY ❑

Sun Tsz, the elite master, intimidates the troops. Attila the Hun, the self-centered tyrant, displays his control through fear. Remnants of these premodern leaders exist today's organizations.

Modernist leaders are illustrated in the John Patterson's authoritarian control at the NCR pyramid and Walt Disney's storytelling gaze.

The visionary, networking, team-building, empowering postmodern leader serves and tells stories. This leader is particularly sensitive to both male and female voice. Examples range from Lenscrafters to the New York Stock Exchange, and from the United States to Sweden, Japan, and Germany.

NOTES

1. Campbell, Joseph *The Hero with a Thousand Faces*. Princeton, NJ: Princeton University Press, 1949; *Joseph Campbell: The Power of Myth* with Bill Moyers, New York: Doubleday, 1988; Also see Bly, Robert *Iron Man: A Book About Men*. Reading, Mass.: Addison-Wesley, 1990.
2. *Business Week*, (1981). How Roger Miliken Runs textiles' performer, January 19, pp. 62–73. Main, J. (1990). How to win the Baldridge award. *Fortune*, April 23, pp. 101–116.
3. Griffith, Samuel B. *Sun Tzu: The Art of War*. Translated by Samuel B. Griffith. Oxford: Oxford University Press, 1963: 57–59.
4. Roberts, Wess *Leadership Secrets of Attila the Hun*. New York: Warner Books, 1958: 45–6. Reprinted with permission.
5. Griffith, Samuel B. *Sun Tzu: The Art of war*. Translated by Samuel B. Griffith. London: Oxford University Press, 1963.; Roberts, Wess. *Leadership Secrets of Attila the Hun*. New York: Warner Books, 1985.
6. Adapted from Bernstein, Mark "John Patterson rang up success with the Incorruptible Cashier." *Smithstonian Magazine*, around 1990: 150–166.
7. Boje, David M. 1992 "A Postmodern analysis of Disney leadership: The story of storytelling organization sucsession from feudal and bureaucratic to 'Tamara-land' discourses." Invited paper to the 1992, New England Symposia: Narrative Studies in the Social Sciences, hosted by Harvard, MIT, and Boston Universities (May 9th).

8. Kinney, Jack. 1988. *Walt Disney and Assorted Other Characters: An Unauthorized Account of the Early Years at Disney's.* New York: Harmony Books.

9. Shows, Charles, Charles. 1979. *Walt: Backstage adventures with Walt Disney.* Huntington Beach, CA: Windsong Books International.

10. Boje, David M. "Storytelling is the business of Disney." LMU working paper (August) 1990. The story is a compilation of facts and experiences from a number of sources: Benson, Alan 1989 "The Walt Disney Story." G-Man Video Production. Burbank: Walt Disney Company; Finch, Christopher 1973 *The Art of Walt Disney: From Mickey Mouse to the Magic Kingdom.* Burbank, CA: Walt Disney Productions; Kinney, Jack 1988 *Walt Disney and assorted other characters: An unauthorized account of the early years at Disney's.* New York: Harmony Books; Schickel, Richard 1985 *The Disney version: The life, times, art and commerce of Walt Disney.* (Revised). New York: Simon & Schuster, Inc.; Shows, Charles 1979. *Walt: Backstage adventures with Walt Disney.* Huntington Beach, CA: Windsong Books International; Taylor, John 1987. *Storming the Magic Kingdom: Wall Street raiders and the battle for Disney.* New York: Alfred A. Knopf, Inc.

11. Schickel, Richard. 1985. *The Disney version: The life, times, art and commerce of Walt Disney* (Revised). New York: Simon & Schuster, Inc.

12. Taylor, John, 1987 Storming the Magic Kingdom: Wall Street raiders and the battle for Disney. New York: Alfred A. Knopf, Inc.

13. Jones, Michael O. 1991. "What if stories don't tally with the culture?" *Journal of Organizational Change Management,* 4(3): 27–34.

14. Schaef, A. W. 1987. *When Society Becomes an Addict.* San Francisco: Harper & Row. Also see Schaef, A. W. and D. Fassel. 1988. *The Addictive Organization* San Francisco: Harper & Row.

15. Foucault, Michel. 1977. *Discipline and Punish: The birth of the prison.* New York: Vintage.

16. The story is derived from these sources: Reuters, From. "Panel Alleges 'Massive Fraud' Committed by ExMiniScribe Officials." *Los Angeles Times* September 13, 1989.; Zipser, Andy. "Cooking the Books: How pressure to raise sales Led MiniScribe to Falsify Numbers." *The Wall Street Journal.* September 11, 1989.

17. Schaef, Anne Wilson *When Society Becomes an Addict* New York: Harper & Row. 1987.

18. Besides Schaef's work, see: Beattie, Melody *Co-dependent NO MORE.* Center City, MN: Hazelden, 1987; Wolititz, Janet G. *The Self-Sabotage Syndrome: Adult Children in the Workplace.* Deerfield Beach, Florida: Health Communications, Inc. 1987.; Harvey, Jerry B. "Organizations as Phrog Farms," *Organizational Dynamics* (spring) 1977.

19. Dyer Davis. "A voice of experience. An interview with TRW's Fredrick C. Crawford" *Harvard Business Review,* Nov/Dec 1991. pp. 115–126.

20. Thorbeck, John 1991. "The turnaround of value of values." *Harvard Business Review* (Jan/Feb): 52–61.

21. Clegg, Stewart, *Modern Organizations: Organization Studies in the Postmodern World,* London: Sage. 1990: 201; Kotter, J. P. *The Leadership Factor,* New York: Free Press. 1988.; Peters, Tom *Thriving on Chaos.*; Bennis, Warren & Burt Nanus, *Leaders: Strategies for Taking Charge,* New York: Harper & Row. 1985: 87–109. and many others.

22. GE Annual Report, 1991.
23. From *War As I knew It* Houghton Mifflin.
24. Hillkirk and Gary Jacobson, *Grit, Guts, and Genius: True Tales of Mega-Success: Who Made them Happen and How they did it.* Boston: Houghton Mifflin Company, 1990: 73–4.
25. Clegg, 1992: 224–8.
26. Ferguson, Kathy E. *The Feminist Cast against Bureaucracy* Philadelphia: Temple University Press, 1984: 170.

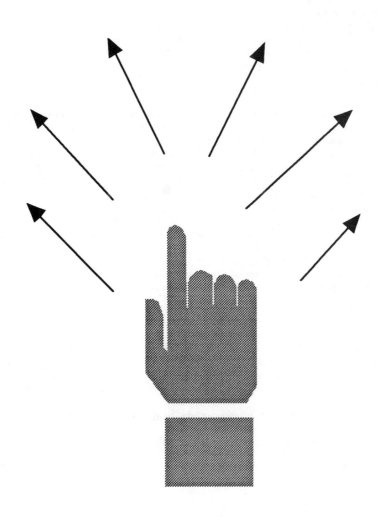

CONTROLLING STORIES

Control Definitions

Pre-Modern Control

Control is **Slave.**

S *Slavery.* Before the Civil War slavery was a way for masters to control. Many of the founding fathers were slave owners. It was a patrimonial system of control.

L *Levels.* Each class has privileges, status, and rights a lower class does not possess. In "Sultanism," absolute control is maximized. In each case, an elite controlled a staff of slaves, conscripts, and kin. Knights and nobles were part of a more decentralized patrimonial control system. These social groups were more privileged and could control some of their own lands, tools, and local governance structures. The more privileged your group, the more independent control you attained in the feudal system.

A *Arbitrariness.* People controlled according to their personal likes and dislikes. Promotion was the arbitrary choice of the patriarch, monarch, or master. With total control, the arbitrary use of force was deemed proper.

V *Venal.* Control was corruptible by bribes.

E *Elders.* Control by age. In "gerontocracy," the "elders" controlled the younger generations. In "Patriarchalism" people could be inherited by other people. It is partly economic and partly kinship-control. Older people had more dignity in the community.

Modern Control

Control is **Inspect.**

I *Impersonal.* People blindly obey the directives of anyone who occupies a particular office. Obedience is to the office. Control without affirmation or enthusiasm. It is without reference to family ties or slave-status.

N *Normative.* Control of the social and productive order is by normative rules, procedures, and directives. Normative rules are applied to particular cases. Norms come from the governing (controlling) executives and managers. Organizations condition people to behave within hierarchically approved norms of conduct.

S *Short-term Goals.* Control is toward short-term profit.

P *Pyramid of Surveillance.* Bureaucratic pyramids are a (supposedly) rational ordering of offices. A hierarchy of positions to monitor and inspect action. Each lower office is under the control of a higher one.

E *Externally-driven.* All sorts of controls are legally mandated.

C *Conform to Rigid Standards.* Social Science has been used to standardize human beings.

T *Technical Gaze.* Electronic surveillance mechanisms.

Postmodern Control

Control is **Choice.**

C *Choices.* The fundamental right of people to make choices.

H *Heterogeneity.* Diversity is an asset. Control is de-differentiated and de-centered so there is not as much gap between leaders and workers.

O *Oppositional.* With multiple voices, multiple logics, and multiple perspectives.

I *Individualism.* Doctrine of individual freedom in economic enterprise. Participation in corporate governance.

C *Co-Responsibility.* People are co-responsible for networking toward value-added and convergent purposes.

E *Environmental Audit.* A revised definition of efficiency and effectiveness that includes environmental and social audits.

Table 6.1.

CONTROL

SCORES	1 2	3 4	5
Slavery	Slaves have some rights	Master 50%, Slave 50%	Master has absolute power
Levels-classes	Lower class has rights and privileges	Few rights and privileges were experienced	Higher class has all the rights and privileges
Arbitrariness	Minorities, lower class know what they want	The minorities have limited choices	Promotion is arbitrary choice of masters only
Venal	People realizing control cannot be paid for	Brides could get control of you	Control corruptible by bribes
Elders	Control can be gained by hard work no matter the age	All groups have dignity in the community	Elders always control the younger
Impersonal	People rely on initiative and enthusiasm	People begin to use their initiative	People do exactly what they are told, no questions asked
Normative	Workers establish some norms	Managers are willing to hear few worker suggestions	Management establishes norms
Short-term goals	Various goals are a concern	Short-term goals are the main concern, but still some other goals are implemented	Short-term profit is the main concern
Pyramid of surveillance	Lower and middle class have few restrictions	Middle management has some say	Strict bureaucracy
Externally driven	Policies are shaped and altered	Signs of being able to bend some policies	Company policies are the law
Conform to standards	Showing some individuality and creativity	Little individuality and creativity	Robotic like figures, no creativity
Technical gaze	Slaves did all the work by hand	Machines are starting to develop to do the work	Electronic surveillance mechanisms

CONTROL—*Continued*

SCORES	1 2	3 4	5
Choices	Few people make the choices for all	Few groups are selected to make all the choices	People make all the choices on their own
Heterogeneity	A small gap between the leaders and the workers	Diversity is becoming an asset	Control de-centered, gap between two has disappeared
Oppositional	One voice, one logic, one perspective about to expand	Different people beginning to voice their thoughts	Multiple voices, multiple logic, multiple perspectives
Individualism	Little freedom in economic enterprise	Signs of freedom	Participation in corporate governance
Co-responsible	Individual responsibility is main concern still	People are co-responsible, but working towards same goal	People co-responsible for attitude towards adding values
Environmental audit	One or two auditors	Select group audits efficiency and effectively.	Efficiency includes environmental and social audits

	PRE-MOD	MOD	POST-MOD
Q1: How do you control the flow of customers?	N/A	The sixty seconds electronic timer at the drive-thru window represents an electronic surveillance mechanism. Carl's Jr. places the electronic device for the purpose of monitoring the efficiency of its workers. inspec T 5	The kitchen in the back must be in sinch with the servers in the front for maximum efficiency in order to beat the sixty second time limit. choi C e 3
	0%	63%	37%
Q2: What is your employee turnover rate?	Since a family atmosphere is generated and higher management judges raises and promotions, there is a patriarch involved. slav E 4	N/A	Employees choose not to leave because of the family atmosphere. This is why Carl's Jr. employee turnover rate is below traditional norms. C hoice 4
	50%	0%	50%
Q3: How is each store evaluated?	N/A	In order for a store to win the President's Award, they must follow the norm of things properly, that is, everything must be properly. i N spect 3	The President does not have the final say in the President award. Rather each store is judged by various people, such as two corporate level employees, an operations consultant, and an independent auditor. choic E 3
	0%	50%	50%
Q4: How has environmentalism been addressed?	According to the public's likes and dislikes, they decide if the foam coverings should stay or go. As in the case for Carl's Jr., the foam was out and foil is in. sl A ve 2	N/A	Carl's Jr. had to change with the times. One can say they had to diversify by changing to the foil wrapping to satisfy the public. c H oice 3
	40%	0%	60%
AVERAGE	22.5%	28.3%	49.3%

inspecT:
Technical gaze (5) 63%
The sixty seconds electronic timer at the drive-thru window represents an electronic surveillance mechanism. Carl's Jr. places the electronic device for the purpose of monitoring the efficiency of its workers.

choiCe:
Co-responsibility (3) 37%
The kitchen in the back must work in synch with the servers in the front for maximum efficiency in order to beat the sixty second time limit.

slavE:
Elders (4) 50%
Since a family atmosphere is generated and higher management judges the raises and promotions, then there is a "Patriarch" involved.

Choice:
Choices (4) 50%
Employees choose not to leave because of the family atmosphere. This is why Carl's Jr.'s employees turnover rate is below the traditional norms.

Q1: How do you control the flow of customers?

A1: Obviously like all fast food services, we try to serve our guests as soon as possible. Our standard time to take an order from a customer at the counter is three to five seconds, that is, we do not want a customer to wait more than five seconds to be served. As for the drive-thru, we have an electronic clock placed by the service window, and once a car pulls up to the window, the clock begins. Once the clock begins, we have sixty seconds to serve the customer. The clock buzzes as it passes sixty seconds, and is charted in the computer. This tells us that we need to improve our drive-thru work efficiency.

Q2: What is your employee turnover rate?

A2: Our turnover rate is probably one of the lowest in the industry if not the lowest for employees. I think we are on 114% to 115%, while traditionally, fast food is around 200% to 300%. I think part of the retention rate is due to certainly training, but more than anything I call it creating the environment you work in or care feeding your employees. You really get a family atmosphere.

iNspect:
Normative (3) 50%
In order for a store to win the President's Award, they must follow the norm of things properly, that is, everything must be done properly.

choicE:
Environmental audit (3) 50%
The president does not have the final say in the President's Award. Rather each store is judged by various people, such as two corporate level employees, an operation consultant, and independent auditors.

slAve:
Arbitrariness (2) 40%
According to the public's likes and dislikes, they decide if the foam coverage should stay or go. As in the case for Carl's Jr., the foam is out and the foils is in.

cHoice:
Heterogeneity (3) 60%
Carl's Jr. had to change with the times. One can say they had to diversify by changing to the foil wrappings to satisfy the public.

Q3: How is each store evaluated?

A3: We replaced the philosophy of 'let us catch you doing something wrong' with the idea that we should reward everyone. We are constantly expanding our programs to implement this idea. One of the highest awards we give is the President Award. A team of two corporate level employees, an operations consultant, and independent auditors go out and visit each store during a two month period. They conduct a three hour measurement covering everything from guest relations to employee attitude to the condition of the paint on the walls. They just cover everything. Only twenty-five percent of the stores are considered for the award. The counter people get gift certificates and the manager get a ring. Also each time they win the award, the managers get another diamond on their ring. Top executives attend the ceremony and hand out the awards.

Q4: How has environmentalism been addressed?

A4: As for health reasons, you know that we use the finest meats and freshest vegetables. We believe that the quality of the product is most important. And when a person asks me why Carl's Jr. costs more, I just reply, 'You get what you pay for.' As for the environmental issues beyond health, you probably have seen that we changed from foam to the aluminum foil wrappings. It is a shame because foam does not generate any CFC onto the food and also it is recyclable while the paper and aluminum foil isn't. We tried to educate the public, but they seem to be really stubborn. McDonald's poured millions and millions of dollars each day on advertisements to change the view on foam coverings, and you know where it got them. Right! No where! So if McDonald's can't even do anything about it, what possibly can we do if the public doesn't want to listen. However, if the public insists that foam generates CFC onto the food, then realistically we too must change with the public because they are the ones who buy our food.

THE IN-N-OUT BURGER
CONTROL SUGGESTION BOX

AREAS THAT THE NAVY BLUE TEAM LIKED:

- ❑ The televisions that are provided for waiting customers in some restaurants.
- ❑ The thirteen "periods" in which the restaurants are evaluated.
- ❑ IN-N-OUT is concerned with minimizing safety hazards and maintaining good employee interaction.
- ❑ IN-N-OUT is very environmentally conscious, even their bumperstickers are biodegradable.

SUGGESTIONS FROM THE NAVY BLUE TEAM:

- ❑ Standards should be set to ensure a quick flow of customers.
- ❑ More employee incentives should be implemented beyond the standard medical and dental.
- ❑ Those who conduct the "QFC Inspection" should be careful not to portray a panoptic gaze.

CARL'S JR. CONTROL ANSWERS

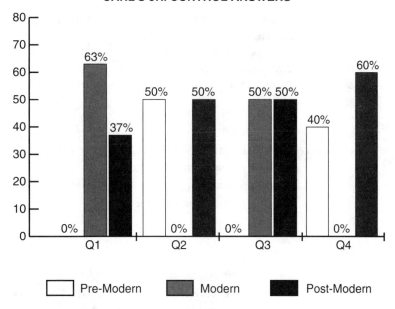

☐ Pre-Modern   ▨ Modern   ■ Post-Modern

CARL'S JR. CONTROL

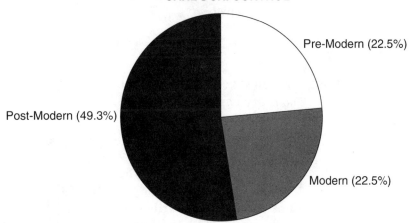

Pre-Modern (22.5%)

Modern (22.5%)

Post-Modern (49.3%)

INTRODUCTION

By this chapter it should be obvious to you at this point of the book that pre-modern, modern, and postmodern themes co-mingle and compete in the corporation. Sectors of one company can be pre-modern crew and craft cultures practicing the A, B, C's of management: Abusive, Belligerent, and Cruel; another can be a bureaucratic machine

SLAVERY

 S

Before the Civil War slavery was a way for masters to control. It was a patrimonial system of control.

Was this company formed from a patrimonial system of control? If not, how was it formed?

LEVELS

L

Each class has privileges, status, and right a lower class does not possess. The more independent your group, the more independent control you attained in the feudal system.

How many levels of control do you have? What are some of their names and what are the differing privileges or procedures involved.

ARBITRARINESS

 A

People controlled according to their likes and dislikes.

Who is in charge of promotions within the company?

VENAL

 V

Control was corruptible by bribes.

Has the source of control ever been corruptible by bribes?

ELDERS

 E

Control by age. Older people had more dignity in the community.

Does the age of a person affect the way they are promoted, paid or titled in the company?

with gentle people in cozy little cells doing electronic surveillance; and a third can be a flexible and spontaneous sub-contracting network of value-added customer-oriented relationships in small businesses and autonomous skunkworks. Any organization can have enclaves of the three control-rationalities. Instead of mono-control, Organization 2000 is poly-control.

We want the stories in this chapter to shock you, make you mad, and get you into a postmodern mind set about control.

❑ PRE-MODERN CONTROL ❑

A, B, C Management: Abusive, Belligerent, and Cruel. Control of one man over another has deep historical roots that are often oppressive, bloody, and catastrophic. The control stories that follow are graphic in their brutality because that is how it was and in some cases that is how it still is. Here are a few stories we did not learn in my high school Western Civilization class.

Serf Control. With 90% of the medieval population engaged in agriculture, serfdom was a ubiquitous feature of feudal medieval organization. Serfs and slaves were peripheral to the social order of kings, nobles, masters, and free men. Yet, believe it or not, free men would often chose to become serfs. In exchange for volunteering so many hours of labor, the Masters, Nobles and Lords would provide lodging and some protection against famine. Serfs were very controlled by ownership and had to seek permission to marry, to move, to grow this crop or that. The feudal manors maintained loose ties with any central king or church control.[1]

Caution. This next story contains graphic acts of control not suitable for reading by people with sensitive stomachs. If you dare, read the story to see how A, B, C control works in practice.

The Story of Damien's Torture

On 2 March 1757 Damien . . . was condemned . . . before the main door of the Church of Paris, where he was to be 'taken and conveyed in a cart, wearing nothing but a shirt . . . to the Place de Greve, where, on a scaffold that will be erected there, the flesh will be torn from his breasts, arms, thighs and calves with red-hot pincers, his right hand, holding the knife with which he committed the said parricide, burnt with sulphur, and, on those place where the flesh will be torn away, poured molten lead, boiling oil, burning resin, wax and sulphur melted together and then his body drawn

and quartered by four horses and his limbs and body consumed by fire, reduced to ashes and his ashes thrown to the winds . . .

Interspersed among the horrible cries, Damien often repeated: "My God, have pity on me! Jesus, help me!" He succumbed uttering: "Pardon, Lord".

Finally, he was quartered . . . After two or three attempts by the horses harnessed to Damien's limbs, the executioner Samson drew out a knife and cut the body at the thighs instead of severing the legs at the joints; the four horses gave a tug and carried off two thighs after them, then the same was done to the arms, the shoulders, the arm-pits and the four limbs; the flesh had to be cut almost to the bone, the horses pulling hard carried off the right arm first and the other afterwards.[2]

Pre-Modern Control. In feudal times, control was a public spectacle. People did inflict this torture on other people because they owned them, because the master had total control over the body of the slave, because the sovereign ruler had total control over the body of the accused, because the patriarch had total control over the bodies of his family, but mostly because torture as we shall reveal was part of the economic order of business. Torture kept the slave, the serf, and cheap free man labor productive.

Not Just Europeans. There were equally disgusting scenes in early American history. In the old west, for example, hangings were scheduled early, so people could bring a lunch, enjoy the scene, and be home by dark. Torture was public entertainment.

A good draw and quarter could last eight to ten hours. The violence of public punishment was contrived by the sovereigns to discourage defiance against authority. Gallows, pillory, scaffold, flogging, branding, and burning at the stake were a part of early American history.

Control has its rules. There were rules, for example, about the number of lashes of the whip and the types of mutilation to be used. During the torture ceremony the accused was expected to admit and repent his/her crime publicly. The spectacle played out the story of man, God and the hereafter. As the man struggles in his pain, he is living out on earth, the struggle he will face in hell. If an executioner screwed up, it could be a sign from God that the accused was innocent, after all.

Damien's Story Continues . . .

" . . . Damien's executioner who, being unable to quarter his patient according to the rules, had to cut him with a knife; as a result, Damien's hair, which had been promised to him, was confiscated and the money obtained from the sale given to the poor . . . And, behind this punishment of the unskillful executioner, stands a tradition, which is still close to us, according to which the condemned man would be pardoned if the execution happened to fail . . . In his confrontation with the condemned man, the executioner was a little like the king's champion . . . the king's sword . . . (p. 52).

Deconstruction

1. Control is a sovereign act, a rite of power, that preserves order that the people could see with their own eyes. The sovereign had the right to torture, confine, reprieve, and otherwise control subjects.

2. Pre-modern control is physical control. Masters had total control of the body of their subject.

3. For Foucault (1977), torture is a political act, and an instrument of naked power over the body to capture the soul. As Damien's torture ceremony played out, the Clergy and the Crown (in the role of the executioners) dialogued with the victim to get him to admit publicly his rehabilitation and to acclaim his remorse.

While torture and public punishment grew out of favor, the dominating control of humans by other human has been a central part of business and commerce for thousands of years. Torture was a major part of the control of labor in the pre-modern period. As long as torture made workers more productive and efficient, its use continued.

Torturing The First Americans

"How can Columbus discover people who were already there?" is a common Indian question each Columbus Day. When Columbus arrived in the "new" world, there were 10 million American and Canadian Indians, 15 million Mexican Indians, millions of West Indies Indians, and millions of South American Indians already there. 12,000 years ago, Asians had crossed a glacial land bridge between Siberia and Alaska. By the time the 500th anniversary of Columbus's Discovery comes and goes, Columbus will be remembered as the man who brought the institution of mass torture, diseases that wiped out 50 million Indians, along with the whole institution of slavery to the Indies, South & Central America, Mexico, and finally to the colonies of the United States. Columbus is no Hero to the Indians.

Land of the Free. As with other cultures, the American Indian had to be portrayed as beastly and sub-human to rationalize his/her control and to strip away his/her lands. This was not easy since the Indians were quite socially advanced. For example, centuries before the U.S. Constitution and the Continental Congress, the Iroquois League had its own congress, used veto power, and advocated freedom of speech, and a classless society. While women were denied leadership in many tribes, women would be chiefs in others. In 1540, Hernando de Soto, for example, kidnapped the female chief, "Lady of Cofitachequi."

Pueblos. Long before Columbus, millions of Americans: "Indians" were a diverse, peaceful, and prospering society. The Pueblo Indians have maintained a desert city for over 1000 years. The Pueblo city is twice as old as St. Augustine, Florida, the city white Americans celebrate as their nation's oldest community. In the 12th century, the ancient Cahokia had a city across from present-day St. Louis that had as many residents (20,000 to 30,000) as London at that time. Their trading network stretched from the Gulf of Mexico to the Great Lakes.

Pueblos and Environmentalism. The Pueblos are a 2000 year old civilization who saw themselves as a harmonious part of the earth. They wanted to blend their culture into the earth, while Europeans wanted to own and rape the earth. In May, 1539, the first white man scout, a black slave, encountered the Zuni tribe of New Mexico. A story of gold-lined streets and gold utensils reached the Spaniard Francisco Vazquez De Coronado. The story was false, but Spanish greed for gold had caused the massacre of several Zuni communities. As many as 200 Indian men, women, and children were publicly mounted on stakes at one time and burned alive. Towns were torched, women raped, and children dashed on the rocks as the cruel and greedy search for gold continued. With no gold to fuel the debauchery, the Spaniards left.

How did this Greed for Gold First Come to the Americas? Columbus began enslaving West Indies Indians and taking them back to Spain after he could not locate enough gold to make his venture profitable. These were the same Indians that showered Columbus with birds, cloth, fish, turkeys, corn, persimmon bread, and other gifts. Columbus and the Colonists interpreted Indian gift-giving as evidence that they were child-like. "If they gave gifts," they reasoned, "the Indians must be lazy." When Columbus could not obtain as much gold as he wanted, he told the Queen and King of Spain that the Indians were beastly sub-humans and that slavery could make them fit to be Christians. If he could not get the Indians to dig effectively for Gold he would turn Indians into Gold.

Gold Fever and Torture. Columbus's gold business needed the slave labor to mine gold. When he could not mine enough gold fast enough he proposed that slaves be taken back to Spain and sold for gold. At first the queen said no, but then relented.

One of the things I was not taught in school was the fact that the colonizers, being immune to small pox and other plagues, had been carriers of these diseases to the New World. Since the West Indies people had not encountered these diseases, whole populations of Indians throughout North and South America and the Caribbean were wiped out. In Haiti, for example a population of 500,000 became 500. It was disease, not the sword that defeated the Mexicans. Their population went from 15 million to 1.5 million, making it the biggest massacre of all time. In the United States entire tribes would be wiped out. I can see why Columbus Day is not a holiday Indians relish.

The Black Legend

As slaves were used to pan and dig for gold, and as they were sold and resold, the Catholic church got involved. At first, the church allowed for slavery if each colonist would agree to convert the slave to Christianity. Then, as stories of the mass torture, abuse, and murder of Indians began to circulate through Europe, a few members of the church began to ask "by what right does one man enslave and torture another man for economic gain?" Each man is God's child. As the story goes, the Church would only allow people to be enslaved if they ran away from a commitment to God. The colonists interpreted this to mean any Indian, upon being read what came to be called "The Regulation" that did not immediately swear allegiance to Christ was enslaved. Even if "The Regulation" was read to them in a foreign tongue or even if the concepts were not understood in their own tongue.

"The Black Legend" is from a book of stories by Father Bartolomeo de las Casas. Upon visiting the Spanish colonies he was so outraged by massacre of millions of Indians that he wrote of book of stories. The gold business and subsequently the plantation business destroyed whole continents of Indians.

THE BLACK LEGEND

[Translating from the Old English text.]

" . . . An historical and true account of the cruel massacres and slaughters of over twenty millions of innocent people; committed by the Spaniards in the islands of Haiti, Cuba, Jamaica, etc. As also, in the Continent of Mexico, Peru, and other places of the West Indies, to the total destruction of those countries . . . .

'To these quiet Lambs, endured with such blessed qualities, came the Spaniards like most cruel Tigers, Wolves, and Lions, enraged with a sharp and tedious hunger . . . they have cruelly and inhumanely butchered, that of three millions of people which Haiti itself did contain, there are left remaining alive three hundred persons . . . The island of Jamaica lay desolate . . . Cuba and Haiti . . . now totally unpeopled and destroyed . . . partly killed, and partly forced away to work in other places . . .

'Now to come to the Continent (Mexico) . . . souls, women and children being numbered in this lot . . . fifty millions were consumed in this massacre . . .

The Spaniards were not sent from heaven . . . neither was their cruelty piety–Women with child, whole bellies they would rip up, taking out the infant to hew it in pieces. They would often lay wagers who could with most dexterity either cleave or cut a man in the middle, or who could at one blow struck cut off his head. The children they would take by the feet and dash their innocent heads against the rocks and when they were fallen into the water, with a strange and cruel mouth they would call upon them to swim. . . .

"They erected certain Gallows, that were broad but low, that the tormented creatures might touch the ground with their feet, upon every one of which they would hang thirteen persons, blasphemously affirming they did it in honor of our Redeemer and his Apostles and then putting fire under them, they burnt the poor wretches alive . . .

"I have been an eye-witness . . . they hunted them with their Hounds, whom they bred up and taught to pull down and tear the Indians like beasts . . . the Spaniards made a Law among themselves, that for one Spaniard slain, they would kill a hundred Indians . . .

"The men perished in the Gold Mines with hunger and labor, the women perished in the fields, being tired out with the same calamities: and thus was a vast number of the inhabitants of this island wholly exterminated . . . And as for blows which they gave them with whips, cudgels and their fists, wherewith they continually tormented them in their labor, I could be hardly able to find either the time or paper to make a narration large enough of those things . . .

Tyrant. . . . in the Providence of New Spain, there came another cruel and furious Tyrant . . . who having perpetrated many heinous inequities, and sent great numbers of the Natives to be sold in the Countries of Spain . . . once it happened that they used eight hundred of the Indians instead of a team to draw their carriages, as if they had been mere beasts and irrational creatures. He was afterwards made President of the City of Mexico, and with him many other fellow tyrants advanced to the office of Auditors; which Offices they contaminated with so many impieties and abominations, that it is hardly to be imagined . . . he went further into the Country, that he might exercise his cruelties with more liberty, and caused fifteen or twenty thousand of the Indians to follow and carry the burdens of the Spaniards, of whom scarcely two hundred returned alive, the rest being all destroyed . . .

"the [Indian] king coming to meet him with all . . . honor, they put in prison because he was reported to be very rich: which that they might get from him, they thus tormented him; having put his feet in a kind of stock, and stretching out his body, they tied his hand to a stake, and then putting fire to his feet, while a boy was set to bath them with oil, that they might roast the better; there stood another also with dogs behind him, threatening to set them upon him . . . At length there came a Franciscan Friar who freed him from his torments, but not from death . . . With this kind of torture they put to death many other of the Princes and Noblemen of the Country . . .

"I Friar Bartolomeo de las Casas, of the Order of St. Dominic, who went to these parts through the mercy of God, desiring the salvation of the Indians, that so many precious souls redeemed with the blood of Christ might not perish, wishing with my whole heart, that they might through knowledge of their Creator live eternally.[3]

Deconstruction

1. *Control.* The Indians, Africans, and other peoples were controlled by fear of torture.

2. *Story.* These stories had a powerful impact on Spanish leadership. Not powerful enough to abolish slavery, but the stories of the horrors led to some new Church and Spanish rules to control slavery.

3. *Markets.* Slavery flourished as colonizing countries used slaves to plunder peaceful countries of their resources. The social and political economy of pre-modern times supported slavery as a means of controlling labor. Slave prices depended upon laws of supply and demand. As the supply of slaves became exhausted and as production became more skilled, the demand for slaves dropped off.

4. *Slavery Tradition.* For centuries production was organized around slavery, as an institution of human control. You could enslave anyone who was not civilized or anyone who was "beast-like." Slavery did not stop because of the excesses. Only when the slave population died out and thereby ceased to be an economic alternative did slavery cease to be a control option.[4]

5. *Abolition Myth.* America and Europe did their best to avoid abolition. "Abolition was eventually achieved not so much because of the desire of one party to end slavery but because the modern industrial system and a slave-based social formation were incompatible" (Lovejoy, p. 247). Slavery was cheaper than debt-bondage or paid wages. Abolition Laws were only enforced and with much reluctance when the business economy no longer had need of slave labor.

6. *Control of Production.* Gold mining, agriculture, livestock breeding, handicrafts, house-servants, military conscripts, and portage (carrying stuff) businesses depended upon the social control of slavery. As long as these businesses used hand labor (low level technology) slavery flourished. Social control is based upon continuing a class system (social division of labor) in which the upper class has enslavement privileges. There was also a sexual division of slave labor fueled in part, by the master's sexual appetites. The economy is therefore dependent upon slave control. To control production, you had to control the mechanisms of enslavement, slave distribution, and slave supervision.

7. *Transition from Pre-Modern to Modern.* It is the transition in the mode of production, more than anything, else, in my opinion that brought an end to slavery. It is when the political–industrial–military–

social economy shifted to modern production that slavery was no longer the center of that universe.

U.S. Slavery.

The colonization of America and Slavery were bed fellows. Dutch traders in 1619 were the first to introduce slaves on a grand scale to North America. As in Europe, slaves were owned and could be passed from father to eldest son as inheritance. By the revolution, there were 500,000 slaves in America (20% of the American population at that time). By 1720, 70% of South Carolinians were slaves, working the rice crops. Others worked tobacco. In Jamestown, the Indians were systematically exterminated, crops and villages torched—so Colonists could control and confiscate their lands to grow more tobacco.[5]

Slavery and Thomas Jefferson. Thomas Jefferson kept slaves at his Monticello estate.

> "When he was five years old, a slave named Eve on a plantation in nearby Orange County, accused of poisoning her master, was burned at the stake. It was not a lynching; the sheriff carried out the order of the local court. Children on plantations everywhere became aware of the subtle hierarchies of power without conscious teaching, and Jefferson learned very early that whites ruled over blacks even as children.[6]

At age 24, Jefferson's first legislative act in the Virginia legislature was a proclamation that any Virginia slaveholder, if he wanted to do so, could free their slaves. It was rejected. Within five years, Jefferson was denouncing slavery as "an infamous practice." Yet, Jefferson's personal conduct towards slaves was another matter.

> " . . . a mulatto shoemaker and carpenter belonging to him named Sandy stole one of his horses and ran away. The escape did, to be sure, involve a theft. Still, Jefferson in the *Virginia Gazette* of September 7, 1769, offered a reward for his capture-forty shillings if he were taken in Albemarle County and (pounds) 10 if caught in another colony . . . Sandy was caught, and three years later Jefferson sold him for (pounds) 100. (p. 103–4).

Masters had concubines. Sally Hemings, a slave, was Jefferson's concubine (p. 293).

> "Jefferson did free Sally's brother Robert Hemings, this in the same year he sold her sister Thenia. Robert had fallen in love with a slave woman belonging to George Frederick Strauss in Richmond, and had had a child by her. Strauss advanced (pounds) 60 to Robert to pay for his freedom, and Jefferson signed the manumission papers on Christmas Eve 1794 (p. 379–80).

People could, in some cases, purchase their freedom, but for every slave freed, 300 more were born in slavery.[7] In 1831, The Nat Turner slave insurrection happened: 55 whites and over 100 blacks were slaughtered in Virginia. Abolitionists were treated as dangerous fanatics. There had been stories of slave revolts in the Indies in which whites were murdered. After slavery was no longer as profitable as other pre-industrial modes of production, slavery would persist because of white man's fear about blacks massing to take over white society. Slaves could no longer be marginalized and excluded, or could they?

Abolitionists

"Abolitionists hold that "all men are born free and equal, endowed by their Creator with certain inalienable rights, among which are life, LIBERTY, and the pursuit of happiness."

"They do not believe these rights are abrogated, or at all modified by the colour of the skin, but that they extend alike to every individual of the human family.

"As the above-mentioned rights are in their nature inalienable, it is not possible that one man can convert another into a piece of property, thus at once annihilating all his personal rights, without the most flagrant injustice and usurpation . . . (Printed by Reverend Elijah Parish Lovejoy in the Alton, Illinois *Observer*, July 20, 1837).[8]

An angry mob cornered Lovejoy in his newspaper office and dumped his press into the Mississippi River before setting fire to his building.

In 1846, Henry Thoreau, who did not approve of slavery or the Mexican War was jailed for refusing to pay his one-dollar poll tax. Ralph Waldo Emerson paid Thoreau's tax.

Uncle Tom's Cabin

The Power of Storytelling. In June 1851, a powerful 36-part serial story called "Uncle Tom's Cabin" was published by Mrs. Harriet Beecher Stowe. The character of Simon Legree, with his whips and bloodhounds and the martyred Uncle Tom, and Eva's dash for life across the ice as she was chased by bloodhounds made a lasting impression on the Congress and a thousand theater stages. The story personified the Fugitive Slave Act of 1850. To the North, this story was "real" life in the South.

Fugitive Slave Act of 1850. "Runaways could be seized and shackled wherever found, could not have a jury trial, could not testify or summon witnesses, and could be shipped sough to their master no matter how long they had been free. In 1850 therefore 20,000 Negroes in the North had escaped through the abolitionist network: the Underground Railroad.[9]

Lincoln's June 17, 1858 "House Divided" Speech. "A house divided against itself cannot stand. I believe this government cannot endure permanently half slave and half free . . . I do not expect the house to fall; but I do expect it will cease to be divided. It will become all one thing, or all the other.

When Lincoln's "Emancipation Proclamation" went into effect on January 1, 1863, 3,063,392 slaves were freed in ten seceded states, but 441,702 slaves in states that had not seceded were still slaves. The Czar of Russia, however, had freed the serfs in 1861. The Spanish Crown had long ago abandoned slavery as a mode of production, but American slavery persisted longer than most areas of the world. Only in comparison to South Africa could you call the U.S. enlightened. Even after the Civil War, there were Black Laws which required that "all freed Negroes to go to bed early, rise at dawn, speak respectfully to their employers, and perform no skilled labor without a license."[10]

The Manitu Story

To give you a completely different story of control, we will look at control as practiced by the Algonkian Indian tribes.

One Indian tribe, the Fox Algonkians of the Great Lakes Region, in particular, had a very negative attitude towards vertical control. While Europeans subscribed to vertical, hierarchical control where the highest layer delegated authority to each successively lower pyramid-layer, the Fox Indians, subscribed to "manitu." "Mana" is a power in the universe that is given to each individual as a condition of the high quality of their individual performance in a given activity. If you succeed, you possess Manitu, if you fail, you do not have it. There is no hierarchy. Any individual can possess Manitu by demonstrating success. If a Fox Indian wins in combat over another Indian, the winner does not get to control the loser. Since the loser has unlimited access to Manitu, he can win the next encounter.

The Manitu Story "At the onset of adolescence, each Fox male goes out in the forest where he fasts for four days and four nights. During the course of this fast he has a vision of a powerful manitu—an animal, bird, manitu-human, or natural object. The boy is told by the manitu that henceforth he will be under his protection, and that he will control the particular power possessed by the manitu. In the course of the visitation the manitu instructs the boy in acceptable ethical and moral behavior . . . But the grant of manitu power and supernatural guardianship is not outright; the manitu needs the services of the boy as much as the boy needs his. In exchange for supernatural power, the boy agrees to present to the manitu peri-odic gifts of tobacco, which the manitu craves but can get only from humans and to adhere to his guardian's ethical precepts in order to please him. The boy-manitu relationship is couched in terms of mu-tual obligations, not in terms of one-way power flow. If the boy neglects his obligations, the manitu may withdraw his support; if the boy fails in some important undertaking, this evidence that the manitu has not done his part entitles the boy to seek a new protector . . .

"In 1667, Father Allouez, on a mission to the Fox, told them that Jesus Christ, as represented by the cross, was a powerful manitu. He was amazed by the alacrity with which the Fox "accepted Christ," not realizing that the Fox . . . always ready to accommodate any deity, of whatever origin, who can demonstrate the possession of power. In 1671 warriors, undertaking a war expedition against the Sioux, painted the cross on their bodies and shields, put them-selves under the protection of the cross-manitu, and gained a deci-sive victory over their enemies. They returned, proclaiming the white man's manitu. The following year, however, another expedi-tion against the Sioux, under similar manitu protection, was disas-trously defeated. In a rage, the warriors repudiated the white man's manitu, tore down the cross Allouez had erected, and refused to let the priest re-enter the village.[11]

Deconstruction

1. Control is not mediated through a central hierarchy in the Fox tribe, it is equally available to each individual. "The control of power is dangerous; powerful beings are to be feared, not adored or admired" (p. 572).

2. If Europeans worship vertical control, the Fox Indians thinking it immoral for one man to control another man, worship individu-alism. European armies, that typically conscripted Indians into their subordinate ranks, had no such luck with the Fox Indians. They flat out refused to accept orders and would respond: "Why don't you do it yourself?"

3. *How do the Fox Control?* Just as each individual was directly re-lated to the manitu, each Fox Indian directly related himself to the body of tribal rules governing coordinated activities. His access to the rules was not mediated through an officer, priest, master, or boss. All age groups and both genders participated in tribal meet-ings. There were no control positions in their organization.

4. *Rebels.* To the Europeans, the Fox Indians resented and rebelled against all attempts to limit and control their freedom of choice and action.

Guilds

Craftsmen, merchants, and artisans began to migrate to medieval cities, to the protection of the city walls. It is here that the more enlightened pre-industrial pre-modern business organization began to flourish. Guilds represent the earliest division of labor through craft specialization. Guilds became an exclusive association of producers. Each guild was run by master craftsmen. Control was by a system of rules about conduct. While long apprenticeship periods insured journeymen knew how to do quality work, apprenticeship also was a way for masters to control access to their craft (p. 27). To control entry, increase the standards, rigor, and length of the training. The practice is still found today. For example, The American Medical Association controls the availability of Doctors in order to keep doctoring profitable as a profession and maintain high quality standards. In England, guilds and the crown controlled printing by specifying how many print shops could operate in a given city. Restricting the number of producers, allowed prices to be set by the guilds.

Guild Social Control. Initiation, apprenticeship, and solace (fine system) have already been discussed as powerful control mechanisms in the craft system. Deviations from performance and group norms lead to sanctions, including fines and whipping.

The step from slave and serf to craftsman is a small one. The craftsman was controlled by the guild. To be a freeman the craftsman had to stop practicing the trade and get rid of all his tools (p. 29). A serf could be free, if he stayed away from the manor for a year and a day (p. 31). Slaves, on the other hand, had to purchase their freedom or be set free. Freemen could become more skilled and therefore more useful in the pre-industrial economies.

Coming to America: White Indenture. To get to America, people sold their labor for a pre-specified time period (2–3 years, depending on skill level) in exchange for ship passage. This was an indenture contract. Contracts were sold to planters and merchants at the American port of call. Masters had to provide room and board. 50% of white immigrants to the Northern Colonies came as indentured servants (p. 56).

Pre-modern Feudal Japan

Japan exercises strong culture control over its employees. There are strict values about respect for authority and putting the work group and the company and the nation ahead of self-interest. Hard work, long hours, and group consensus are strong Japanese values.[12] In Japanese firms, there is a combination of pre-modern and modern controls. The modern control is the bureaucracy of departments, chain of command, formal offices, and vertical layers of authority.

In the formal bureaucracy, men tell other men what they want to hear. They conform.

The more pre-modern control is the "**dokikai system.**" In dokikai, men go out to a sing-a-long bar and after a few drinks tell each other exactly what they think. The "dokikai system" is like a fraternity. When you are hired you are an "entering class" or "**cohort.**" As with the entering pledge class, the cohorts are socialized and initiated together, bonded together, and build social ties that last throughout their career. After the "entering class" has done its apprenticeship, cohorts are distributed throughout the bureaucracies formal departments, locations, and specialized units. But, the "dokikai system" forms an overlaying, informal network of business relationships, where the real work, decisions, up-front communication gets done. "It is in the **dokikai** that men, lubricated with alcohol, speak to one another with **honto**—expressing their true feelings—rather than with tatemai—saying what is expected" (Toffler, 1990).[13]

Individualism

In the pre-modern organization, the spirit of individualism was a dim light in the darkness of feudal tortures. The individual ethic, as with Columbus, was an exploitative, colonizing, flesh-peddling horror. Individualism was over-shadowed by a strong community of fraternal or slave-society control so that the individual would act out the wishes prescribed by the social order.

Summary

In the pre-modern period, control was physical and with the exception of some Indian tribes, control over others was hierarchical. Control flowed from the top down. The top had property-control rights over the subordinated. Slavery flourished because modes of production were pre-industrial and depended upon large pools of cheap labor. Abolition, contrary to popular belief did not come from Lincoln or some other politician. Abolition was the result of changes in the economy that favored other modes of production in which slave skills were not as crucial. In the next section, modernization does not skill labor much beyond sweat shop conditions. In America, large pools of immigrant labor from Italy, Ireland, Poland and other countries was all that was needed. More recently, immigration from Mexico continues to feed low technology enterprises in agriculture, domestic work, and manufacturing.

The point here is that as the mode of production shifts, the mode of control must also shift. Control is more an instrumental thing than a movement toward freedom.

❑ MODERNIST CONTROL ❑

Modernist control starts with division of labor and central control of financial and technical resources.

Capitalism. Capitalism is defined in Webster as "the economic system in which all or most of the means of production and distribution, land, factories, railroads, etc., are privately owned and operated for profit, originally under fully competitive conditions. It has generally been characterized by a tendency toward concentration of wealth, and in its later phase, by the growth of great corporations, increased governmental control."[14]

Modern Capitalism was supposed to do away with the cruel forms of torture as well as the greed of the pre-modernist period. And for a brief historical moment, craftsmen flourished. However, as modernization progressed, capital got monopolistic control and workers were again de-skilled and dis-enfranchised to fit the mode of production that generated the best cash flow. They were less skilled than in the craft-guild system. De-skilling allowed very routine jobs to be performed efficiently and economically by children in large factories. Long after Indian and African slaves were emancipated, children were a preferred mode of cheap labor.

Child Labor. "In 1900 the industrial edifice of the United States was supported in part by the labor of 1,752,187 children less than 16 years old. In Southern cotton mills . . . one fourth of the "hands" were children, and 20,000 of them were under 12. Girls of six and seven worked 13 hours a day.[15]

Labor Control. Recently, in North Carolina, a chicken-processing plant produced a fire that killed numerous employees. An investigation found that the doors of the plant were locked. The company believed the employees would steal the chickens from the plant if the doors were not kept locked. The security of employer was obviously more important than the security of them employees.

If production efficiency maximized and the human condition is minimalized, business control yields some real horror. As with the story of De Las Casas about Indian torture and the story of Uncle Tom's Cabin, the following story was a stimulus to reforming labor control.

Packing Town Jungle Story

"There were men in the pickle-rooms, for instance . . . scarce a one of these that had not some spot of horror on his person. Let a man so much as scrape his finger pushing a truck in the pickle-rooms, and . . . all the joints in his fingers might be eaten by the acid, one by one. Of the butchers and floorsmen, the beef-boners and trimmers, and all those who used knives, you could scarcely find a person who had the use of his thumb; time and time again the base of it had been slashed, till it was a mere lump of flesh against which the man pressed the knife to hold it . . .

"There were those who worked in the chilling-rooms, and whose special disease was rheumatism; the time-limit that a man could work in the chilling-rooms was said to be five years. There were the wool-pluckers, whose hands went to pieces even sooner than the hands of the pickle-men; for the pelts of the sheep had to be painted with acid . . . and as for the other men, who worked in tank-rooms full of steam . . . their peculiar trouble was that they fell into the vats; and when they were fished out, there was never enough of them left to be worth exhibiting,—sometimes they would be overlooked for days, till all but the bones of them had gone out to the world as Durham's Pure Leaf Lard" (From Upton Sinclair's 1906 novel: *The Jungle*, In Butterfield, 1976: 330).

Tales of Bribery. From the outset of the industrial revolution labor conditions were deplorable, but bribes, corruption, and greed kept the law makers at bay. People read *The Jungle* and screamed for reform in the meat supply industry after reading that "government inspectors in the packing plants were bribed to pass tubercular cattle and hogs dying of cholera; how poisoned rats were shoveled into the meat-grinding machines; and filth scraped from the floor was turned into "potted ham." (p. 331).

Deconstruction.

1. *Food Control.* Sinclair's story was so popular that for a year it out sold all other American books. His story of bribery and corruption, that very year Teddy Roosevelt and Congress implemented a meat inspection law to control food processing. People were more outraged by the possibility of getting tainted food than by labor conditions.

2. *Reluctant Changes In Control.* Reaction against the greed of the robber barons, the exploitation of child labor, and the debauchery of the beef industry—gave rise to tougher interpretations of anti-trust legislation, workmen's compensation legislation, etc. The Department of Labor, Department of Commerce, and Bureau of Mines formed to get control of American business run a muck. As with Abolition, the laws were enforced with much resistance and reluctance.

3. *Socialism.* Some socialists advocated a class warfare of industrial workers against their employers. "It is the purpose to wipe out, root and branch, all capitalistic institutions for present-day society"

Impersonal. People blindly obey the directiveness of anyone who occupies a particular office.

Do you feel that your employees loyalty is towards their supervisor as people or solely towards the positions that they hold?

Normative. Control of the social productive order is by normative rules, procedures, and directives.

Are there specific step-by-step procedures that employees must follow when dealing with particular situations?

Short-Term Goals. Control is toward short term profit.

Would you say that this company is aimed at short-term of long-term profits.

Pyramid of Surveillance. Bureaucratic pyramids are a (supposedly) rational ordering of offices.

Are there numerous levels of management, and if so, is each lower office under the control of a higher one?

Externally Driven. All sorts of controls are legally mandated.

Are there any organization outside the company that exercises some type of control?

Conform to Rigid Standards. Social Science has been used to standardize human beings.

Are employees pressured into compliance with specific guidelines defining one's professional behavior and appearance?

Technical Gaze. Electronic surveillance mechanisms.

Do you employ any type of electronic surveillance mechanisms to monitor employee's actions?

(p. 341). Fight the employers with sabotage and violence to do away with money-privileges.

4. *More Reluctant Reform.* Child Labor laws were implemented; the Women's Suffrage movement took shape; strikes became legal. Change came very gradually.

Woodrow Wilson's Inaugural Address

"We have been proud of our industrial achievements, but we have not hitherto stopped thoughtfully enough to count the human cost, the cost of lives snuffed out, of energies over-taxed and broken, the fearful physical and spiritual cost to the men and women and children upon whom the dead weight and burden of it all has fallen pitilessly . . . Our duty is to cleanse, to reconsider, to restore . . . every process of our common life . . .

To get around the dark side of capitalism, Wilson implemented a workman's compensation act, a political practices act, and a utility act in 1912, his first year in office. He also established the Federal Trade Commission, toughened up the antitrust law, and then there was the Federal Reserve Act of 1913. He sought to de-center the monopolist's control over the free enterprise system of America.

External Control. By 1919, Americans began to stand up to captains of big business and demand fair wages and safe working conditions. U.S. Steel workers, for example, went on strike to stop the 12-hour work day and the 68 hour work week. Big Steel, which had made a ton of money on World War I, broke the strike with the aid of military force. In coal strikes, the police were called in by big money wielders. "In West Virginia police paid by the Weirton Steel Company forced 118 strikers to kneel and kiss the American flag" (p. 375). Big money from big factories filled with big machines controlled labor.

Monopoly Control. When Teddy Roosevelt took the presidency, the industrial revolution was transforming all that was pre-modern into the modern industrial empire. Teddy needed a "big stick" to beat off the evil robber barons, the grafters, and the enemies of the Union. "When he swung it at big business he often missed, and he often failed to follow through with specific action. But his bold example inspired a host of reformers . . . "[16]

Andrew Carnegie knew little about steelmaking, but he was a genius at driving people who did. After he retired he gave away $350 million and supplied the White House with Scotch Whiskey.

John D. Rockefeller made a billion dollars by eliminating competition from the oil industry. "Individualism has gone, never to return," he said.

Andrew Mellon, the Pittsburgh banker . . . bought up another man's process for making aluminum and was converting it into a rich monopoly.

Philip D. Armour and the Chicago "Beef Trust" mechanized the nation's meat. "I like to turn bristles, blood, bones, and the insides and outsides of pigs and bullocks into revenue," he said.

J. Pierpoint Morgan "re-Morganized" railroads, banks, and other major companies, and kept **control** of them all through voting trusts. "I am not in Wall Street for my health," he growled.[17]

A Conversation between Morgan and Bryan

"America is Good enough for me," said J.P. Morgan, and the response which was made by William Jennings Bryan made even the titans of Wall Street smile. "Whenever he doesn't like it," said Bryan, "he can give it back to us."[18]

The modernist strategy with regard to competition was to eliminate it wherever possible. J.P. Morgan, the story goes, bought a mining company from John D. Rockefeller and the entire steel business of Andrew Carnegie, then the world's largest steel producer. Morgan offered Carnegie $157,950,000 in 1899. Carnegie held out for $447 million—and got it.

To the end of his days Carnegie worried for fear he had asked too little. Once, while breakfasting with Morgan on an ocean liner, he remarked lightly, "I find I made a mistake. I should have asked you for another hundred million." Morgan's reply could not have been crueler. "If you had, I should have paid it," he said.[19]

In February 1902, Roosevelt dusted off the Sherman Anti-trust Law and proclaimed that J.P. Morgan's Northern Securities was a monopoly. Morgan's company was about to consolidate control over most of the nation's railroads.

Deconstruction

1. *Central Control.* Monopoly is an extreme form of central control that serves to cancel competition. The modernist style is to always consolidate and centralize control.

2. *Capitalism.* Money talks! The fittest survive and the strong inherit the earth. Man is fitted and controlled to the machine mode of production. The cheaper the labor that can be fitted to the machine, the better.

3. *Massification.* Mass production is not possible without mass distribution, mass finance, mass consumption, and mass education.

Alvin Toffler's (1980, 1990) last two book have asked that we de-massify control in each of these areas. But, for the Modernist epoch, the task was to massify.

Henry Ford and Fordism

Fordism. In 1914, Henry Ford pioneered the five-dollar, eight-hour day, and the automotive factory-system where a worker stayed stationary as the parts flowed to his station. Henry had to control the immigrant workers to make them comply with his new assembly-line system. Beyond this, his grand vision was to make workers prosperous enough in income and leisure time to be mass consumers of the mass produced car.

Ford's Sociological Department

Henry wanted to be sure that workers would use their five dollar a day wages toward righteous ends. From 1914 to 1920, Henry set up his Sociological Department. Department head, John R. Lee and a staff of thirty, and eventually 150, set out to investigate, inspect, counsel, and correct 32,702 employees.

"Each investigator, equipped with a car, a driver, and an interpreter was assigned a district in Detroit . . . each worker was expected to furnish information on his marital status, the number and ages of his dependents, and his nationality, religion, and (if alien) prospects of citizenship . . . . Did he own his home? If so, how large was the mortgage? If he rented a domicile, what did he pay? Was he in debt, and to whom? How much money had he save, and where did he keep it? . . . His social outlook and mode of living also came under scrutiny. His health? His doctor? His recreations? The investigator meanwhile looked about sharply, if unobtrusively, so that he could report on "habits," "home conditions," and "neighborhood." Before he left a given family, he knew whether its diet was adequate; whether it took in boarders—an evil practice which he was to discourage; and whether money was being sent abroad. All this information and more was placed on blue and white forms . . .

" . . . Ford employees were classified into four groups: those fully qualified; those excluded under the basic rules upon age, length of service, and so on; those disqualified by bad personal habits; and those debarred by unsatisfactory home conditions allied with improper habits. Though a moderate resort to liquor was not forbidden, "excessive use" came under the ban. So did gambling. So did "any malicious practice derogatory to good physical manhood or moral character." A household dirty, frowzy, and comfortless; an unwholesome diet; a destruction of family privacy by boarders; an excessive expenditure on foreign relatives—these were among the reasons for condemnation.[20]

Deconstruction.

1. *Penalty.* Ford's use of inspection, interviews, and observation in the private homes of employees was a way to control the quality of worker habits away from work. With this penal system, where a condemned employee could be put on probation for up to six months until the "correction" was assured. Incorrect employees, often went before a committee in the Sociological Department who would judge and decide their case. " . . . when a black sheep returned to the fold with bleats of repentance, he was usually given another chance" (p. 556). Correction might mean moving to better housing, patching up a marriage, kicking out borders, and learning English.

2. *Schooling.* In May, 1914, a mandatory school in English language was established for immigrant workers. Those who did not progress were discharged. The instruction included material on "Ford patriotism" (p. 557). English was needed so immigrants could better take orders, which in turn, improved efficiency. The result was the normalization of the immigrants into "correct" American practices. Schooling was part of the "Americanization Program" at Ford.

3. *Transformation.* The "Americanization Program" and the surveillance work of the Department were part of a transformation mechanism to make higher quality employees. Ford recruited low-skilled, immigrants, paid them more than they could get elsewhere, but in exchange demanded conformity to Ford standards. Besides immigrants, many Ford employees (400 to 600) were former convicts. Ford wanted to rehabilitate them. "Only the head of the sociological department and a special adviser knew the identities of men in this special category" (p. 563).

4. *Discipline.* Workers who were problems were transferred to "bad" jobs for a week, such as the "cylinder shake-out gang." They were indeed happy to get back to their old jobs (p. 564). Absenteeism and tardiness problems were assigned to the Sociological Department for exorcism. "Imperfect cooperation would mean discharge . . . a man found late for the third time in a year was haled before "a fair and impartial court" in his "department" (p. 564). Part of the penal system involved the imposition of fines and pay scale reductions.

5. *Panopticism.* Panoptic control, according to Foucault (1977: 201) induces a state of conscious visibility assuring the automatic functioning of power. The panoptic surveillance and inspection of the Sociological Department is permanent in its control effect, while not needing to be continuously applied. The worker gazes

and corrects his/her own behavior. The spouse, the children, the priest, the supervisor, the co-worker could all be informers to keep the worker in the straight and narrow.

War and Fordism. As the World Wars all but demanded mass production systems, worker resistance to highly fractionated, repetitive, de-skilled, and boring work did not matter much until the Japanese flexible production system came out of the closet in the 1970's to yield a better control-structure for making automobiles.

In the 80's and 90's U.S. auto makers are grudgingly surrendering control over job design, work group norms, and work-pace and work-scheduling over to the workers. In Europe, labor unions resisted Fordism and retained more of the craft tradition, particularly in West Germany. For example, at Porsche, there is a strong tradition of apprenticeship and craftsmanship that dates back to pre-modern rationality. Porsche remains a highly skilled, craft company.

Post-War Fordism. The American economy is a story of the love affair with the automobile. Auto workers, in particular, were privileged players in this love triangle between low-skilled (but high paid) workers, centrally controlled capital, and mass consumption. Post-war unions were controlled by attacking them as communist (e.g. the Hartley Act of 1952, during the McCarthy period).[21]

Unions played the Taylorist production game by bargaining wage gains in exchange for giving up worker control over the work process. People did not control the pace of their own work. Management had to habitualize workers to de-skilled work systems. Bureaucratic corporate rationality was as entrenched as slavery in the American way of life. Women and minority groups had limited access to the higher-wage mass production jobs. When they did get access it was at lower wages and in marginal job categories. The auto union work force was predominantly white and male. In the Civil Rights and feminists movements of the 1960's and 70's, the auto work force became a little more balanced. Fordism dominated until the 1973 recession, the end of the post-war boom.

Control and "The Depression"

The Stock Market Crashed Thursday, October 24, 1929. Herbert Hoover was President. A feeble Federal Reserve Board had not been able to control Wall Street. By Tuesday, the 29th, the bottom had fallen out and the depression had begun. In July of 1932, 10,000 unemployed veterans demonstrated on the White House Steps. Hoover, after a few weeks, sent in the Army with tear gas, bayonets, sabers, and torches to reclaim the capitol. By 1933, 15 million Americans were unemployed. The Hoover administration did not pay unemployment or Veteran benefits. People who were out of work were on the dole, living in cardboard shacks, standing in soup lines, and waiting for something to happen.

The Forgotten Man

Franklin Roosevelt's New Deal . . . These unhappy times, call for . . . plans . . . that build from the bottom up and not from the top down, that put their faith once more in the forgotten man at the bottom of the economic pyramid" (p. 414).

Wilson supporters labeled Roosevelt's ideas "socialistic."

Remember the Social Darwinism notions of pre-modern times (survival of the fittest, God's destiny for rich and poor) required strict non-interference. Roosevelt, on the other hand, felt he was driving the money changers from the temple and putting people back to work.

After World War II. Control permeates the whole organization. Control systems inform management about what, when, where, and how long employees are engaged in work. People are monitored by electronic surveillance, by human surveillance, and by self-monitoring procedures.

Henri Fayol focused on control of people, actions, and thinks to verify everything occurred in conformity to his plans, his instructions, and the principles laid down.[22]

The justification for control is that it leads to greater efficiency and effectiveness; without control bankruptcy will take place. Accounting, finance, MIS, and operations management are control functions.

Does productivity benefit some groups while oppressing others? Should workers want managers to help them be more productive? To use a metaphor from an earlier story, the John Wayne bought into the "should" ideology more than the Dustin Hoffman. Since colonization, the productivity of workers is a powerful "common sense" assumption: "all the more powerful because it is invisible."[23] The pursuit of rational goals like productivity, efficiency, quality at the expense of environment, quality of life, and equality are not questioned in bureaucratic discourse. The legitimacy of short run efficiency over long term quality and environmental gains as a privileged bureaucratic goal is just beginning to be questioned. For decades quality has been marginalized by short run, quarterly profit objectives. The interests of "customers" have been marginalized until the last decade when the ideology of excellence began to take a more dominant role in bureaucratic discourse. In sum, there is an important relationship between power, ideology, and language that comes through in the modernist stories.

When your Story is Profit comes from Cost, then Other Storylines do not get heard. William Deming, for example, preached to Americans in the 1940's a message to which only the Japanese decided to listen. Deming taught that if you aim for absolute quality, costs of production will decrease over time, prices will be lowered, and customers

HE WORKS, SHE WORKS BUT WHAT DIFFERENT IMPRESSIONS THEY MAKE	
Have you ever found yourself up against the old double-standard at work? Then you know how annoying it can be and how alone you can feel. Supervisors and co-workers still judge us by old stereotypes that say women are emotional, disorganized and inefficient. Here are some of the most glaring examples of the typical office double-standard.	
The family picture is on HIS desk: Ah, a solid responsible family man.	**The family picture is on HER desk:** Hmm, her family will come before her career.
HIS desk is cluttered: He's obviously a hard worker and a busy man.	**HER desk is cluttered:** She's obviously a disorganized scatter-brain.
HE's talking with co-workers: He must be discussing the latest deal.	**SHE's talking with co-workers:** She must be gossiping.
HE'S not at his desk: He must be at a meeting.	**SHE's not at her desk:** She must be in the ladies' room.
HE'S not in the office: He's meeting customers.	**SHE's not in the office:** She must be out shopping.
HE'S having lunch with the boss: He's on his way up.	**SHE's having lunch with the boss:** They must be having an affair.
The boss criticized HIM: He'll improve his performance.	**The boss criticized HER:** She'll be very upset.
HE got an unfair deal: Did he get angry?	**SHE got an unfair deal:** Did she cry?
HE'S getting married: He'll get more settled.	**SHE's getting married:** She'll get pregnant and leave.
HE'S having a baby: He'll need a raise.	**SHE's having a baby:** She'll cost the company money in maternity benefits.

Table 6.2. *Gender Impression Management in Modernist Bureaucracy.*

will give you their business and their loyalty. This is what Japanese auto producers did in the 1970's and 1980's. In the 1990's, even though J.D. Powers surveys of quality in cars say the U.S. car made by Ford or GM is every bit as high quality, fuel efficient, and low cost as the Japanese car, American consumers do not believe the survey results. Americans do not believe the US makes quality cars. President Bush went to Japan in January of 1992 with the big three auto executives to break open the Japanese markets. American Presidents and CEO's needed to do this three years ago. A man on the street report on Japanese News coverage elicited: "Hey, why should we in Japan buy American cars that Americans do not want to buy?" Instead of talking to the Japanese heads of state and captains of Japanese industry, they should talk to the Japanese customers. Ask them what kind of car they want to have in Japan. But modernists are not big on asking customers for anything but their money.

Control is manifested through stereotype categories. The categories are contained in the stories people tell.

A Sexist's Story about Forklift Girls

Before computer type set, heavy metal page forms of lead type had to be moved about. It was men's work and men shouted obscenities while they worked. It was a male work culture. Then came affirmative hiring legislation.

I headed up their printing division. We had five unions in there and they had bindery men and bindery women and I didn't know anything about it. The government came in on us one day and lowered the boom. We had no journey**women** anywhere because the unions didn't allow it. Men had all the key jobs. One of the things they came in with was in my materials handling group. We had these stand up trucks. You stand up and turn the wheel to drive them. They said I couldn't have all men and I must put women in there. So we did. And a little girl, she must have been 5 feet tall applied for the job. The government says there is no difference between men and women. Well after about a week on the job the girl came in and applied for a transfer because her breasts had all turned black and blue from turning the wheel. She was kind of big busted. I wanted to get that guy back in and say: "let me show you the difference between men and women" [Boje, 1983, LAC p. 10].

A Story of Sexist Reversal

Like the way we called 'em bindery men and bindery women? It was a bindery woman's job. And we had a lot of Smiths (women) sewing and we tried to put men in there and they refused. The women called them cutoff girls and they were men and they didn't like it anyway. It fact, the government came in and they made many specific rules and regulations that I must comply with (Boje, 1983: 27).

Deconstruction

1. *Stories.* Stories carry the sexist and racist themes and categories.

2. *Dualisms.* Bindery men and Bindery women is a dualism. Pointing out the size of a woman's breasts is a dualism. Instead of modifying the work, the methods, the machines, the systems, it is assumed that the dualism dominates their reality options.

3. *Government.* Government is big brother, making us do things we do not want to do. Big brother is stupid and cannot see the difference between men and women.

4. *Journeywomen.* The language had no category for females. There was journeymen and bindery girl but no journeywomen and bindery boy words in the language of the work culture. The categories control!

Feminist Critique of Modernism

In these two stories, white males are using questions of efficiency and effectiveness to conceal their need to control the division of labor between males and females. The machines could be remade. In the movie Aliens, Sigourney Weaver operated a mighty big fork lift to defeat the Alien. The big myth is that women want and need to do the repetitive jobs and the relationship jobs, leaving men to control the power-jobs. Women are often made the scapegoat as capitalists try to cut labor costs by putting women into traditionally-male job categories at lower rates of pay. Is this the fault of women or is this the fault of capitalist's greed?

Bureaucracy is rule-based and impersonal. Does this chain of command and hiding behind rule books facilitate or hamper efficiency and effectiveness? It is against the rules to be relational or democratic. But, who makes these rules? Do they make sense? Impersonal examples: wholesale firing are rifs ("reduction in force"), people are called "human resources," displacement of poor people by government highway projects is "urban renewal."[25]

Sexual Harassment. The statistics are alarming. Statistics vary, but by all reports every working woman has been sexually harassed verbally. By most accounts over half have been harassed sexually. Males accused of doing the harassment are seldom punished and oftentimes it is the female that is blamed and dismissed. Does sexual harassment have anything to do with control? You bet it does. Does sexual harassment have anything to do with modernism? You bet it does. Most control positions are held by men, and most subordinate positions are held by women. People in lower positions in the pyramid are afraid not to be submissive, even sexually submissive. And if the positions of power are predominantly male, who does a harassed female plead her case to?

In bureaucracy, the female is a marginalized group. Females take more of the fringe jobs, more of the temporary work, and attain fewer central positions. Bureaucracy has routinized and normalized women into a more passive, more powerless, more submissive, and more co-dependent role. Women are co-dependent when they take on the responsibility of taking care of a dominating male.

Voices. In bureaucracy men have a voice that women do not have. And that voice is paternalistic. In bureaucratic-speak, you talk from your position in the pyramid to some other position in the pyramid. It is one-directional, from the top down, and back talk is insubordinate. The pyramid is an authoritarian regime. Bureaucracy is more about domination than it is about meeting customer or public needs. It is more about conformity than about innovation. It is about selling the official story, while suppression the informal story.

Panoptic Control. Lower levels of the pyramid receive more surveillance and gaze than do the higher levels. Women do a lot of clerk-work in open, windowless areas of desks and files.[26] How many of you have looked at old pictures of women seated at accounting tables arranged in row and column while males gaze down at them over horned-rimmed glasses? Secretarial offices are often without much privacy. Phone operators, mostly female, and customer-service operators, mostly female—are tied to electronic surveillance mechanisms that monitor their calls, silences, breaks, and attitude. Calls are sampled by supervisors, usually males, or by a cadre of clerks, usually female, to insure that customer courtesy is being sustained. Dialogue control does not have to be observable in a large room of desks or listened to by electronic monitors to be panoptic. People are recruited for their docileness. People are trained to speak and act in controlled ways. The panoptic gaze gets internalized in the routinization and regulation of the work itself.

Disciplinary Control Mechanisms. The female job categories are more subject to performance evaluations, promotion reviews, and disciplinary procedures. In nursing, for example, a "bad" letter can be put into your file that affects your promotion and salary and assignment options and you are never told it is there. You act in a controlled way because you never know what higher ups and Godly doctors are going to put in your file. In the U.S., nursing reforms over control are being put on the back burner while big medicine recruits and imports third world nurses who will put up with the A, B, C's of management that American nurses are loath to tolerate.

The Weak are the Second Sex. Anyone, male or female, of any color, who is in constant contact with dominant oppressors uses "femininity" skills (p. 92). For Blacks it is the "Uncle Tom" role. For females it is the submissive and victim role. For white managers, it is the subordinate role to a workaholic, domineering, ego-centered, screaming boss like the Q.T. Wiles story from the last chapter.

> "In the political context of a male-dominant society, the expressive role is primarily a support role, one that allows women to negotiate the dangerous terrain to which they are assigned, but that does so at enormous political and psychic costs" (Ferguson, p. 93).

Male Feminization. All people (both genders) in subordinate status act more domestically, more pleasing, and more female. They manage their impressions to seek approval of the dominant boss. They are expected to display loyalty, to be a good little subordinate, and to never show resistance. They are more gentle and polite, more sympathetic and patient, and more forgiving. "Bureaucrats use their "feminine" skills to imitate their superiors, while women use similar skills to please men, but not to imitate them" (p. 95).

Women try to act more male, be "one of the boys" to cope with their secondary status. "Women are not powerless because they are feminine; rather, they are feminine because they are powerless, because it is a way of dealing with the requirements of subordination" (p. 95).

Co-dependents. Co-dependents learn to anticipate demands, moods, preferences of their superiors. They even take responsibility for the Boss, for his bad day, for his temper. Co-dependents clean up after the boss, by hiding their mistakes, covering for their excesses, smoothing the way after an angry episode. "Let's keep it down, the boss has had a tough day."

Self-Disclosure. Women are expected to do more self-sharing and to expose more of their bodies than are men. Women are expected to "linguistically-stroke" males.

Diversity Control. The modernist story is one of white male paternalistic domination. As women, internationals, and minorities make the bureaucracy more diverse, the white male paternalistic pyramid is going to change. Diversity means that more voices will be raised against the single and dominant voice. Sexism and racism will break down. Many voices will enter the bureaucratic conversation. Giving more voice to women and minorities is a political act. The status quo bureaucracy resists the inclusion of other voices. Other voices are systematically marginalized.

As attitudes towards diversity in the work place have run the gambit from tolerance to celebration to diversity as an asset, the bureaucratic discourse has been opening itself up to tolerate, encourage, and now cultivate many voices. Rather than making everyone adopt the white male voice, the female voice, the Asian voice, the Black voice, and the Indian voices are expected to hold their own in the discourse, the team meetings, the agenda setting episodes. To reach an increasingly diverse environment of customers in narrower and narrower niches requires a diverse network of ethnic, racial, and gender communities. Communities are brought together in a network of relationships.

With the coming of the network, white males fear a loss of control over the definition of truth. How can we enable people of diversity to work through and sort out differences in ways that are productive?

Androgynous Control. A balanced persona is part male and part female. In the traditional family and the traditional firm, discourse was

Attitudes toward Diversity by Decade
1940's
How can we eliminate diversity? There were contracts, deeds, and rules against putting women and minorities into certain jobs, positions, and properties.
1950's
How can we tolerate diversity? With increasing participation, management sought ways to be tolerant.
1960's
How can we manage diversity? With legislation favoring diversity, it had to be more managed so as not to interfere with the majority.
1970's
How can we celebrate and affirm diversity? Respect for other people's cultures, values, and customs was the in thing to do. Have a luncheon with ethnic food, a day to celebrate African American heritage. Roots was big.
1980's
How can we build diversity? Companies like Xerox began to balance their regional hiring to reflect the regional availability of qualified minority applicants. If a community had 4% qualified Hispanic engineers in a community, then try to hire 4% qualified Hispanic engineers. Building diversity was seen as a competitive advantage.
1990's
How is diversity a global asset? As we enter the global village, having a diverse team of people makes the firm better able to adapt itself to different values in different countries. Having more diversity is an asset to creativity, innovation, and long term flexibility.

Table 6.3.

sexist and paternalistic. Central control is a manifestation of the traditional family hierarchy. Flat, de-centralized control, with many voices is a more feminine ideal. Being responsive to mother earth is a feminine ideal. The postmodern attitude is diversity and strength. The differences make us stronger. Traditional control and surveillance and panopticism is directed at limiting participation in the bureaucratic discourse in order to perpetuate white male control. Postmodernism seeks to breakdown central control to enable a network of high self-control and high diversity to take its place. The new role of the leader is to establish space for the dialogue among the strong diverse elements of the organization. Control switches from containment to liberation of the oppressed voices. This is not a re-assertion of paternalism where the male helps the females to voice their views. Rather, it is creating space for meaningful discourse.

In short, there are ample bureaucratic controls in place to make females in lower positions more susceptible to power manipulations, including sexual harassment.

Summary Critique of Modernist Control

1. *Prediction.* The future is not as predictable as the planning systems people are asked to conform their actions to. Events in the firm's environment such as recession, competition, changes in customer preferences, etc. will throw a plan off course. Look at how the Gulf War changed people's travel habits.

2. *Monitoring.* People's performances are monitored and compared to pre-set performance norms. But, the organizational situation and environmental turbulence are not that predictable. Performance must deviate from pre-set standards in order to adapt to unforeseen contingencies. Time and space (movement) monitoring are pre-occupations of modernist control systems.

3. *Short Term Results Orientation.* The control time span for American management is short term. What is the quarterly return? The result is that physical plan, human resource, and production systems are gutted to gain short term advantage. The cumulative gutting of the corporation takes it out of effective long term competition. It is possible to juggle figures around in order to make the short term balance sheet look terrific.

4. *Pyramid Dictators.* In the modernist system, management dictates control standards to the rest of the organization. The top of the pyramid dictates performance standards to each level below it. Accounting does the measurement for all levels.

5. *Language.* Language categories control. Control occurs through the words used in people's language that classify people, activities, and things. Words like: correction, deviation, exception, rules, hierarchy, documentation, directives, evaluations, reporting, dictate, monitor are one type of control. Words like black, white, female, Mexican, French are another form of control.

6. *Rigidity.* Bureaucracy promises rigid and conforming behavior. People are evaluated on their conformity instead of their value-added behavior.

7. *Tell them what they want to hear.* Rather than be controlled, just tell the system what it wants to hear. Use the weird category system presented to you and put activities and people in random categories. The reports are not valid, but the bureaucracy is happy. People threatened by control react by sabotaging the numbers. If control is excessive, people react by withholding performance.

❑ TRANSITIONING FROM MODERN
TO POSTMODERN CONTROL ❑

How do individuals survive in a mechanistic and bureaucratic modernist organization? Instead of feminizing subordinancy, one strategy is to rebel and go underground. As modernism gives way to postmodernism, the next decades will see outright co-habitation of the two control rationalities in the same firm. People will have to simultaneously play the modernist and the postmodernist control game.

Rebelling Against Formal Control. To run a flexible network of information contacts throughout the firm, to create new ideas that will add-value to customers, to be an entrepreneur, to introduce ideas that keep up with customer demands, many righteous Americans side-step the formal bureaucratic chain of command. They rebel outwardly, and more often, they just go underground. They use the informal control network to go around, under, and through formal control.

Behind the formality of bureaucratic control is an intelligent network of relationships that adapts to customer demands, that goes around relationships that is controlled by turf-protectors, and modern feudal tyrants. Often it is a battle between the informal and the formal. The formal network controls the channels, the approvals, the chain of command. Their game is to put people into specialized units within functional departments, partition them away from other people, and monopolize their access to information.

Break up bureaucratic Control Monopolies. Alvin Toffler (1990: 173) refers to this as the breakup of the rigid little information monopolies: those overspecialized departments (cubbyholes) that store specialized knowledge, control access, and monopolize the individual in a hierarchy of tight supervision. If you want your computer repaired, you have to get a sign off from several vertical layers. Managers speak horizontally to other managers in computer services, and in a few weeks a repair person comes to your office.

Modern Control is Just Not Very Efficient. In a flexible network, you have a need, you go directly to the person who can solve your problem. Instead of going up three levels of bureaucracy and over two horizontal jumps through managers, then down three levels to some isolated service unit, you go direct. If bureaucracy is not efficient, then why do we continue to teach and practice modern management?

Control is its Own Reward. Once a manager has lost control over the information channels, she has lost control. Once people interpret their own rules, the manager has lost control. Once people are skilled enough in network navigation to get what they need when they need it, the manager is irrelevant. That's right, layers of meaningless bureaucratic machinery are maintained so that managers can control information and thereby control their own jobs.

Since most Americans work inside of production or service bureaucracies they cannot change and since most Americans want to do work that builds a more viable company, they rebel by breaking the control rules and working around the system.

How to Rebel against Bureaucratic Control and Survive long enough to Create Post-Bureaucratic Firms

Evaluation Survival. People are under the gaze every minute of every day. In a web of relationships with other departments, your supervisors, your colleagues, and your customers, evaluation is not about performance or efficiency, it is about the hierarchy sustaining control. The evaluation game is to find out higher up's preferences, and in particular the preferences of each evaluator. People play to the numbers by recasting what they do into the available categories. The more you are a rebel, the more you are an innovator, the more you add your creativity to the enterprise—the more you will be criticized in a modernist evaluation. This is true even when your achievements contribute to the bottom line and add value to your internal and external customers.

Breaking the Mold. The America 2000 vision of the Department of Education is to get a half billion dollars from Congress to set up 500 "break the mold" schools. Communities, helped by education design teams, will take the government resources and the seed money and put together unique programs such as a year round school, a program that focuses on math and science or performing arts. The education machine is so entrenched, that rather than trying to fix it, just step out of it and build an alternative model. Give parents the choice of which school they will send their children to. This will pressure the old, factory model of education to get quality-oriented in order to be competitive. The challenge to the new schools is can they ignore the book of mechanical education.

Think Small Business. Small business provides one half of all jobs in the U.S. Alvin Toffler (1990) predicts that the family business will become a dominant employer and a mainstay in de-massified control. De-massification is the opposite of mass consumption, mass production, and mass distribution. In de-massification, the small, even family business is a node in a flexible, niche-oriented system of custom-consumption, flexible production, and de-controlled distribution.

Right to Privacy. Microprocessor technology has increased opportunities for electronic surveillance of workers by a central staff. According to skeptical postmodernists this is creating a new aristocracy of a core of skilled workers (doing surveillance tasks and getting more privileges) and a growing periphery of de-skilled workers who are of lower status than the central core.[27] There is a new "kidscan" computer chip that is the size of a pin head and can be surgically implanted under a few layers of skin. British Telecom's hand-held videophone with a liquid-crystal-display for face-to-face camera technology will be in full production in just five years. Is this an invasion of privacy? Scan-chips are already being hidden in the bodies of expensive automobiles so police electronic surveillance machines can track down a stolen car. Instead of sending someone to an overcrowded jail, they can be jailed at home by attaching and locking an electronic sensor to the person which will signal a central authority when that person strays too far from home. If this trend continues, the electronic gaze will become a permanent part of our work lives. Decentralizing bureaucracy will not matter much if gaze is everywhere.

Self-discipline. We work in systems that use social science evaluation and engineering surveillance to monitor, classify, normalize, and objectify our organizational participation. The imposition of external control obviates our development of internal control. It is impossible to self-actualize when the system you work in has no degrees of freedom.

It is difficult to self-discipline your spontaneity and creativity when you work in a clockwork, time and motion determined, machine. To be self-disciplined you have to pace yourself, align yourself, order yourself, and structure yourself. Self-discipline within an externally-disciplined system means disciplining your time, and your talk to be able to avoid the teeth of the meshing system gears, finding the spaces between the assembly lines, and most of all, looking busy, the way busy is valued at the treadmill.

Self-Dependent. If you live your life to please someone else, then you grow to be co-dependent, addicted to a life of figuring out what the other needs, wants, and expects. This is a dysfunctional form of self-discipline. To be self-disciplined in a personally healthy way is to get assertive about pleasing yourself, instead of pleasing others. "I do not need more structure, more supervision, more examination, more reportability, or more inspection." Or, "I must do these things for myself." Through healthy self-discipline the individual asserts independence, self-reliance, self-affirmation, and self-sufficiency.

Serving Customers. To survive the Neo-modern organization, the self-disciplined individual does not become selfish, rather he or she becomes the servant of the internal and external customer. Rather than serving a status-oriented, status quo-oriented system, the individual serves the customers. If the individual serves the customers, then there is less need for direct supervision, electronic surveillance, and continuous examination. To avoid control, work directly with your internal and external customers. Serve their needs. Let the customers have power over you, instead of giving power to the modern bureaucratic machine.

Of course adding value to customers, even though it improves the bottom line, does not mean that you will be valued by the system. It can mean just the opposite. To get credibility in the system, without playing the system game, you need to project an image that lets you and your customer orientation survive.

Bob   "I observed the power of customer service at D'Elia Motors in Greenwich, CT. Larry Surman, the assistant service manager, patiently pursued a problem with my car until the problem was identified, diagnosed, and repaired. Larry's tenacity was coupled with a pleasant disposition. I received constant feedback and a successful resolution was equitable.

Telling Your Story. You will have to tell different interpretations of your story of customer service to different people in the system in order to give them a "correct" image of your role in the system. "I am spending time with customers to keep them from taking advantage of our system." "I am spending time with customers to get them to buy into our new product line." "I am spending time with customers to sell them on your way of doing things." "The customer wants me to do it their way this time." "I am going out to be with customers because that was priority one on our new corporate objectives." You might picture yourself as *Terminator II*—the metal monster that faces Arnold Schwarzenegger. It liquifies, then hardens again in a new shape-now a man, now a machine, now a knife. You show similar flexibility in your dealings with customers.

In each case, you are making your story into their story, giving them a fragment of your story, and letting them fill in your many blanks with their own version of reality. It is covert; it is manipulative; it is underground; it is survival. In the end, all the system wants is to tell your story their own way. "Oh Bill, he is doing that a different way because of how the customer reacted and in order to get this result our way the next time around."

Underground. Do not tell them. Form an underground of people who are sympathetic to the cause of the customer and whom you can trust to keep their mouth shut. Then, you and them, do the deed the right way, and avoid the gaze. How many performance reviews do underground managers write on their underground mavericks and underground champions and their underground entrepreneurs that are quite fictitious stories. They report a story of the activities of their people that is acceptable to upper management and at the same time hides the true activities of their people. The modern system is happy and the underground gets to provide quality goods and services to its customers. Upper management often prefers to hear a story instead of reality or they may not be equipped to deal with a reality story. Tell the story in the organizationally acceptable way, using the acceptable and correct language, and reporting the organizationally-relevant categories, classifications, and charts.

Leadership Stories. Your boss says: "we want to bring in the new paradigm, the new way of doing things, a customer-oriented system." "Oh, by the way, you need to get some more approval signatures on this form and you are changing things too fast. Wait a few more months." The leader says he is leading the system to become customer-driven, but demands you stop providing customer-driven actions. There are many companies that preach the vision of customer service, but walk the bureaucratic walk. There is leadership, but its effect is to discipline the bureaucratic machine into an even more ingenious machine.

Instead of playing the Neo-Modern Game, the Final Option is to Move on to Postmodernism. Modernism is so deeply entrenched in American business practice, it is not likely to die a slow and painless death. For example, Rosabeth Moss Kanter found that bureaucratic culture-control mechanisms operated in the firm she called INDESCO. As people served in middle management jobs, they were quickly socialized into the value and behavior patterns of top management. To gain admittance to the top, you had to conform to the values and actions of the top group (inner circle).[28] The more you conform, the more you become a co-conspirator in your own inspection, in your own self-censorship, and in your own loss of self.

❑ POSTMODERN CONTROL ❑

The major issue of postmodern control is *choice.* America 2000 will be an increasingly diverse and heterogeneous society. Organization control must come to grips with and celebrate diversity in the work place, environmentalism, and individualism. This means that there will be many more voices than the predominantly white and male voice of bureaucratic discourse. Postmodern thought is focused on individual freedom. How can the individual be an equal participant in the work enterprise? Control in de-centered networks of small businesses or in de-centralized big businesses has to focus control on value-added issues. How can the individual add value to the customer? Finally, there is room in postmodernism for an expanded definition of efficiency and effectiveness that takes the role of the environment into account. Consumers are beginning to demand that supermarkets recycle, that producers package goods in environmentally sensitive ways, and that consumption that rapes the environment is not "really" very efficient or effective over the long run.

Postmodern Environmentalism. Post-modern control encompasses choices within heterogeneity and individualism, as well as opposition and co-responsibility. The notion of co-responsibility leads us to consider the type of environment in which post-modernism will flourish. How do we re-define efficiency and effectiveness? The environmental audit is one step.

Schools in Japan, Europe, and the U.S. are teaching kids the environmental three R's: Reduce, Reuse, Recycle.

Environmental Audit. Swiss Air spent one million dollars this year on an environmental audit to learn how it could do business in ways that preserves and does not needlessly damage the environment. Ben and Jerry's ice cream do environmental audits each year as part of their accounting. In both cases, they seek to define a broader notion of efficiency and effectiveness.

Recycling. How much of the material that is being put out for trash can be recycled? Companies are beginning to set up recycle containers for paper, plastics, wood, green waste, metal, rags, toner cartridges, pallets, and much more. Recycling depends upon employee involvement in determining the waste items that could be recycled, they are the ones who must make a recycling program work and systems for measuring recycle accumulations and savings.

Customers. Customers are demanding that retailers cut down on wasteful packaging, provide recycled bags, and alternatives to paper and plastic bags such as reusable canvas bags.

Many environmentally-sound alternatives make short-term cost-saving sense. But even if it costs a bit more now, saving mother earth, for many customers, is worth a few pennies more. Non-toxic cleaning supplies, chemical-free cotton, using natural jute twine instead of plastic, etc. are all small steps to a better ecology.

The postmodern customer is a business partner in finding ways to promote environmental awareness and more environmentally-effective practices.

Automotive Industry. If continuous quality improvement has been the industrial battle cry of the Japanese for the past forty years, what will it be for the next forty years? I think the answer is environmentalism. Look at the 1992 Tokyo Motor Show. There is exhibit after exhibit of more environmentally-sensitive automobiles. Japan is building its technical arsenal by massive R & D in solar-powered cars, electric cars, and hydrogen combustion engines. This move is fueled by tougher emission control laws in Japan and especially in the U.S. in States like California. Not only is fuel efficiency being legislated by the U.S. Congress, but in California by the year 2003, 10% of all car sales must be "zero emission" vehicles.

The question is, will the U.S. be a leader in environmental R & D, or will we follow in the footsteps of the Japanese automakers? The U.S. has produced hydrogen-, methanol-, solar, and battery powered prototypes, but does the U.S. have the same sense of urgency as Japan about safe-guarding the Japanese environment and protecting its world wide markets?

> "Japan has the lowest rate of energy use to gross domestic product and the lowest per-capita sulfur dioxide and oxides of nitrogen emissions among the industrial countries of the world."[29]

As Japan produces larger cars, with bigger engines, the smog-producing oxides of nitrogen have increased air pollution in Tokyo, Yokohama, and Osaka. But, the momentum is there. The Ministry of International Trade and Industry (MITI), is in the process of issuing tough auto manufacturing guidelines. MITI wants 200,000 electric vehicles in service by the year 2000. And, they are investing $100 million to develop a new high-performance battery, beginning this year.

While the U.S. it trying to catch up to the Japanese quality lead, the Japanese are investing in the long term to take their next leap forward in the automotive industry: the leap toward environmentally-sensitive automobiles. What is the U.S. going to do this decade? Chrysler is spending $1 billion on a 3.3 million-square foot new-car development center that in two years will house 7,000 employees. They want to reduce the time it takes to get a new car design to market, set up a wind tunnel, design labs, and a small test track (p. 39). Design teams will be located on a single floor, with corridors converging on large meeting spaces. Their project is designed around "simultaneous engineering"— a system of organization to solve manufacturing problems at the same time as the design process is under way (p. 39). It all sounds very postmodern; we will wait and see if they produce more cars like the Viper or if they take up the challenge to get into the "zero emissions" car race.

Control and Third Wave

There are at least two schools of thought on control in the post-cold war, post-hierarchical, and postmodern period. One is Alvin Toffler's Third Wave and the other is the Postmodern. We will state some of the affirmative positions, then move to the skeptical.

Third Wave and Postmodern Both Share These Elements. In both the post-industrial and the postmodern perspectives, the freedom and autonomy of the individual is incompatible with inflexible, rigid, bureaucratic pyramids. In both views, flatter organizations mean less opportunity for vertical promotion, but more lateral movement. Both views stress the declining loyalty of the individual to any one firm. Both reflect a nostalgic appreciation and yearning for a high-skilled, craft-based, more fraternal economy. Peer pressure and control replaces top-down control. Both favor equalizing, democratizing, diversifying, and pluralizing power relationships. Both forecast a post-hierarchical, post-bureaucratic, and post-authoritarian control system. Both openly advocate that people resist central control, protect their autonomy and freedom.

Intelligent Networks. What if we replaced stupid bureaucratic tables of organizations with vertical controls over-specialized cubbyhole departments with an intelligent network among diverse social units? Most managers would be out of work. The few managers that were left would work on network management: combining, recombining channels of information and resource flow, expanding and contracting sectors of the network among many organizations to sustain value added interactions that meet changing customer requirements. The network would be able to reshuffle and reconstitute itself in response to new patterns of customer preference. The boundary between organization, supplier, and customer would fall. An intelligent network is a value added network, where every participant adds-value to each network transaction. An intelligent network is a quick response deployment of suppliers and producers. An intelligent network is lean and mean. It is intelligent because the network adapts the configuration of the network to suit the particulars of customer needs. Instead of being fed products and services, the customer pulls the products and services, controlling the configurations of materials, transformations, suppliers, and people to bring them what they want, when they want it, where they want it.

Self-Aware Networks. Alvin Toffler (1990: 108–109) points out that these intelligent networks are self-aware. They monitor their own value-added performance. The network adapts by constantly redefining its pattern, improving the choice of channels, and redistributing traffic to under-utilized sections of the network in order to sustain quick response and quality performance. An example of a self-aware network is the Toyota flexible manufacturing system. Customers use computer terminals to select custom car features. The information goes directly to the scheduling computers that order-up their particular car. The results of many customer choices are fed to vendors so they can anticipate demand cycles and be ready to feed the right combination of parts Just In Time for producing the customer's car. Information access has been de-controlled. In the bureaucracy, you just did not share that kind of data between producers, dealers, customers, and suppliers.

Bob   "At a flavor and fragrance company, I observed a self aware supervisor. When he was appointed to his position, he notified his manager that he could accomplish the tasks of his department with three workers not the four that he inherited. But in return for a reduced staff he wanted to adjust the compensation of the remaining three. He also wanted flexibility to loan people to the other two departments and to borrow workers from those departments as the work flows changed.

Getting Skeptical About Postindustrial Versions of Postmodern

Skeptical of Post Industrial Control. Alvin Toffler and the post-industrials have it wrong. Here's why. The vision of the post industrial school was that a grand service economy, teaming with high-tech, high-skill jobs would overtake the smokestack industries of steel, textiles, and other manufacturing in the rust belt of America. It is only recently, that people have begun to ask: Hey, just what jobs are we to have in the post-industrial economy? Donald Regan, Ronald Reagan's Chief of Staff, put the question to Alvin Toffler: "So you all think we're going to go around cutting each other's hair and flipping hamburgers!"[30] Toffler and members of the Heritage Foundation were the experts arguing that America was best served by letting the rust belt, smokestack industries die on the vine. After all, we had made the first wave jump from agricultural to the second wave: industrial economy. Now we were jumping from the second wave of industrialization to the third wave of information/service economy.

For some odd reason, which had something to do with the needs of the cold war, America bought into the utopian dream of the high-tech service economy which requires very high skilled people, while at the same time de-investing and trashing the American school system. Teachers are the most underpaid people in American and they are supposed to train the high-teckies for the information age. Well if we are in the information age, how come Johnnie can't read, why is Jill on drugs, and how come the high-tech companies, the computer companies, the electronic industry in general are on the run? If we are moving away from muscle work, then how are illiterate high school graduates going to do all this fine mental work? The soothsayers of the information age blame mass consumption, mass production, mass education economy, that demonic and satanic evil-machine for fabricating people who are unsuited for high-tech employment.

SMOKESTACK CONTROL Second Wave	POST-SMOKESTACK CONTROL Third Wave
1. *Examples:* Rust belt industries: Auto, ships, clocks, steel, rubber, coal, textiles, bauxite, nickel, oil, nitrates, copper, rail; all mass production assembly line firms; Wall Street financiers that centralize money-control (e.g. J.P. Morgan); IBM firms that dominate/centralize standards & practices.	1. *Examples:* Family & small business, work at home, job-sharing, flextime; specialty steels, specialty chemicals, info technologies, CAD/CAM computers, health services, personal security, training & teaching, research scientists, financial analysts, computer programmers, leisure & recreation, tourism, care for the elderly, child care, "hamburger flippers."
2. *Characteristics:* De-skill jobs to simplest components, people work in isolated cubby holes, identical cogs, top-down pyramid control, long cycle time, non-diversity, red tape, strong boundaries between units and firms, monopolization of knowledge.	2. *Characteristics.* De-massification of markets, production, distributions, education, media, finance; global production, capital flows across national borders; focus on value-added behaviors; flexible manufacturing, niche markets, short-run production, tailor made.
3. *Post:* Post-IBM, post-smokestack industries, post-muscle technologies, post-industrialization, post-bureaucratic.	3. *Post Is:* Information technologies, hi-tech, service economy, new knowledge economy.
4. *Control Mechanisms.* Goon squads, strike breakers, information monopolies, monopolies of force, slave masters, feudal lords, money monopoly, top-down command, vertical integration, control over turf (people, budgets), control over information channels, information hoarding, control links between cubbyholes.	4. *Control Mechanisms.* Free flows of information, break up the information monopolies, flexible production control, de-colonize suppressed groups (unleashing informal teams to become market-driven); Junk bonds to decentralize Wall Street control of finance; diversity of forms in one firm.

Table 6.4.

Postmodern Skepticism of Post-Industrial Control. In the post-industrial, third wave society people are knowledge workers. With the information revolution, firms can operate in wide-global regions, lots of small firms can sub-contract with larger firms, individuals have freedom in flexible information networks, managers will not control channels, and info-control is power. Post-modernist critique the post-industrial thesis:

1. Can the economy sustain high standards of living when we no long produce goods (Miles & Gershuny, 1986; Lyon, 1988)?[31]

2. Will information networks and information technology be used to increase surveillance over the periphery by those at the center of

the network? A kind of TRW nightmare. (Hamelink, 1986; Webster & Robins, 1986).[32]

3. Can people who are uneducated and illiterate become hi-tech entrepreneurs? Will the work force continue to be de-skilled as women are given jobs at lower rates of pay than men, part-timers and temporary workers are hired without health plans?

4. Instead of post-industrial, aren't we really locating our bureaucratic production assembly plants in third world countries (Harvey, 1989)?[33]

5. Will most large firms be a few privileged people at the core and a lot of temporary help and sub-contractors without benefits or control at the periphery (no middle class or an alienated underclass)?

Skeptic's Summary. The Third Wave explanation suppresses alternative interpretations. What if people become more dominated under the Third Wave than they were in the first and second? People are still controlled, only now the medium is not physical or muscle-control, it is information control. Jones (1991) critiques three areas of post-industrialism.[34]

1. *Technocentrism.* Humans are defined and viewed in terms of their relationship to information systems: staff who design, develop, and support it, or as users of it. If managerial work is mainly oral communication, computers are not that imperative (Mintzberg, 1990).[35] All solutions are not based in information technology.

    Postmodern Critique. Information technology is one element of a socio-technical-linguistic system. Entrepreneurship, emancipation and individualism are also critical determinants of value-added outcomes for customers, suppliers, and workers. The flexible, network organization changes power and control relationships.

2. *Technological Determinism.* Information technology is the motor of social change and social progress. But, information technology is also political. The Third Wave is optimistic: info technology has no down side, no negative impacts, it is neutral.

    Postmodern Critique. If information networks are a source of power, power-seekers will seek to centralize those networks. Behind a network lies the decisions of how to layout the terminals, who gets what capacity, and the limits of access to various people in the network. Technology is a product of human choice, a social construction, and a social product. Anything social, is also political. The core uses information systems to dominate the periphery. Some groups will define and control it, others will have decidedly more marginal impact. People at the privileged core can threaten people with peripheralization and marginalization. We need, therefore, to examine critically individual rights, responsibilities, and entitlements (Leadbeater, 1989; Wood, 1989). Information systems can control customers and suppliers. Power relationships operate through the information networks and information technologies.

3. *Rationalism*. Power is defined rationally as the control over information, knowledge, information networks. Information is also irrational: full of gossip, exaggeration, error, and distortion. Decisions about information are also irrational. Reports are generated and committees meet, but their role is less as information processors, than it is to symbolically validate decisions. People have too much information. Giving people free access to all information, such as in the Thomas confirmation hearings, may not increase democracy.

Postmodern Critique. The Third Wave exposes people to the controlling gaze. People are more visible to surveillance. Individuals further internalize their self-control (Foucault, 1977).[37] This process is facilitated by the rationalization of knowledge. High-powered and decentralized computer systems allow people to be geographically separated and still subordinated to the gaze of electronic monitoring and surveillance. If people are subjected to more electronic surveillance, this will further erode their freedom. The fact that networks are flexible, global, and diverse, does not obviate the gaze.

Getting Skeptical of Post-Fordism

The (supposed) end of Fordism in America was co-incidental with the Arab Oil embargo in 1973. This was not the only factor. The Euro- and Asian- markets were beginning to boom, and worker productivity in the U.S. had been falling rapidly since the mid-1960's. After 1973, America was ready to try new ways of organizing people, management, regulation, and capital.

Critique of Flexible Production System. Flexible production system involves flexible work processes, but also is part of flexible labor markets, flexible consumption, and flexible financing. In short, *control is made flexible and de-centered.* With flexibility, cycle times get faster and individual control decreases. The cycle time to work a product, the cycle time to change to a new auto-model, the cycle time to move capital, the cycle time to get a service to the customer—all get faster. Kaizen (continuous improvement involving everyone) is part of flexibility and faster cycle times. Flexibility means that work is more temporary, more sub-contracted, more a networking of geographically-dispersed teams. We are not convinced that people are going to have higher standards of living or better quality working lives by being temporary workers.

With de-centering, skills are supposed to accumulate back to the individual. Modernism, however, persists with labor sub-contracting-management avoids medical plans, pension plans, high-wages, and union control.[38] Female, minority, and third world labor pools become more attractive capital investments. The Maquiladora program in the U.S. allows the flexible capital control and ownership to stay in the U.S., north of the Mexico border, while factories are employing cheaper labor located below the border (p. 153). In this way modernist control structures flourish and are able to continue Tayloristic control practices by exploiting third world, cheap labor markets. Increasingly, the modernist form of organization is becoming a global player, using its computers, faxes, and satellite communication to split up its production and capitalization across many countries.

With this flexible accumulation, you get a core of privileged workers who have all the benefits, no more middle management, and an extensive networking to a periphery with few benefits, but lots of autonomy. Corporations, universities, and government bureaus are increasingly sub-contracting any function they can get away with to the peripheral network of smaller teams of people. The core exercises flexibility by outsourcing: changing contracts, stopping contracts, and creating sub-contracts to respond to customer demands. To retain a part of the privileged core and not be cast into the ranks of the temporary workforce, people are willing to be **more** controlled. One of the biggest growth industries in America is temporary employment services. Recent articles in *Time* and *Newsweek* suggest that middle managers are becoming more temporary, contract workers. They are brought in to do some re-structuring, get a project started, and then are terminated.

Small Business

One of the fastest growing majors in business schools is entrepreneurship. Small business accounts for 50% of U.S. employment. With flexible accumulation, we predict even more people will work for small businesses that are part of a sub-contracting network servicing each other and larger businesses. This means a return to family-style business and entrepreneurship. It also means that migrant workers in Los Angeles and other metropolitan cities will work in sweat shops without safety, without environmental controls, and with lots of exploitation.

The rapid growth of 'black,' 'informal,' or 'underground' economies has also been documented throughout the advanced capitalist world, leading some to suggest that there is a growing convergence between 'third world' and advanced capitalist labour systems (Harvey, p. 152).

Why is Small that Beautiful?

Boj   "The last time I was owner and CEO of a small business I was controlled by the bank. I was controlled by payroll. I could not separate home and work life. I worked double the hours I work now, without benefits, and with a lot more stress. Small businesses struggle to survive. They claw and bite and pick each other to death. If you have a downturn, you fire everyone to survive. In the first year 80 to 90% die. Most of the ones that survive, die in the next two years. If you want to see exploitation and primitive working conditions, visit the small businesses of America. It is not the utopia that it is made out to be. Even when people buy into franchises, the franchise, not the person who buys a store, wins out. Franchisers in printing, for example, will keep selling the same franchise to one hope-filled couple who goes bankrupt in a year, to another and another. After enough failures, the location builds a following, gets its equipment working right, and out of the manure of everyone else's failure, one in ten will succeed. In short, small business is not my American Dream.

Los Angeles is home for 104 different language groups, from Vietnamese, to Korean; more Samoans live here than in Samoa. These immigrant communities are spawning thousands of small business ventures every year in Los Angeles and other immigrant centers. Unions are stumped. You can only unionize work forces that are massed together in big government and big business.

What are the control characteristics of small businesses? Small businesses are often family-based, paternalistic, under-financed, and cutthroat competitors. Small businesses pay less wages and benefits than big business. Small businesses, are quicker to exploit female labor and immigrant because they can pay them less.

Getting Skeptical about Japanese Management

Sub-contracting by a large business to a diverse peripheral network of small business is a long-established way of doing business in Japan. A lot of people think all Japanese workers are guaranteed life-time employment. On the contrary, life-time employment goes to core-workers and these are mostly males. Women workers at manufacturing plants, such as Toyota are prohibited by law from working shift work. The women are excluded in this and other subtle ways from so called "life time employment." In the U.S., Americans working for Japanese firms have been duped into thinking they were going to get life-time employment, only to find out that when profits and sales dipped, they were back on the street.

Glass Ceilings In Japanese Firms. A typical story is a white, male, American manager goes to work for a Japanese firm only to find that upward career mobility is blocked by a "glass ceiling." He starts his climb to the top, but finds that he does not know about important resources, cannot get access to important decisions, and in general is left out of the informal information loop. Remember, the Japanese form of organization is very **fraternal.** Japanese new hires bond with other new hires like a fraternity pledge class. In the Japanese firm, the Japanese go out for drinks with their pledge brothers and do business. When they need mentoring and counseling, they go to their pledge brothers. The white male is as much an outsider as if he had gone to a fraternity-sorority exchange and found no one to talk to. With the flexible networking of the Japanese, the white male worker (and other nationalities and gender) do not get past the glass ceiling to the core of privileged, life-time employees, at the top of the Japanese pyramid. The stories circulate that non-Japanese managers in Japanese companies are told what to do, do not get to implement ideas, and experience the Japanese firm as quite bureaucratic. "I gave them ideas, but I was told that the higher-ups in Japan were not interested." The individual is always the **gaijin**—foreigner.

❑ SUMMARY ❑

In today's organizations, control is not pre-modern, modern, or post-modern. Competing control themes abound.

In some organizations we see the carry-over of the brutality inflicted on Damien, the slaves in America, and the Native Americans. We also observe the contrasting pre-modern control of the Manitu and guilds.

Modernist control has its heritage in Upton Sinclair's *The Jungle*, child labor, and the Captains of Industry, especially Henry Ford. We also took a close look at the female perspective in the modern bureaucracy.

Recognizing the resistance to post-modern control, we suggested a number of alternatives to make the transition from modern to post-modern control.

Post-modern control is characterized by choice. This phenomenon exists in the paradoxical situation of heterogeneity/individualism

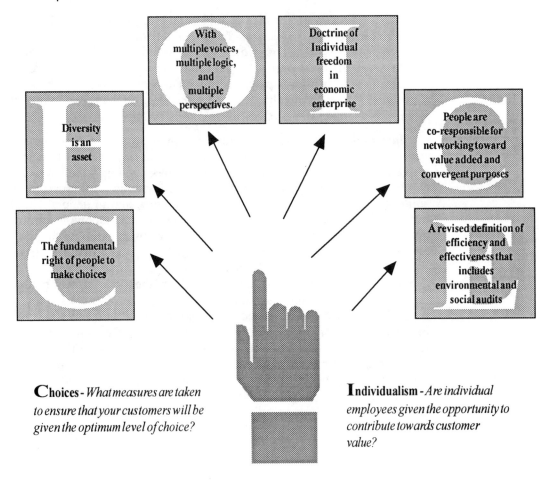

Choices - *What measures are taken to ensure that your customers will be given the optimum level of choice?*

Individualism - *Are individual employees given the opportunity to contribute towards customer value?*

Heterogeneity - *Do you feel that your company possesses cultural diversity? If so, do you see this as an advantage or disadvantage?*

Co-Responsibility - *Are workers provided with an equal feeling of responsibility concerning customer value?*

Oppositional - *Do all your employees have the opportunity to speak their minds without fearing the consequences of views conflicting with those of upper management?*

Environmental Audit - *What steps does your company take to satisfy customers' growing concerns for the environment?*

and opposition/co-responsibility. This central theme flourishes within an environment of re-defined effectiveness and efficiency.

NOTES

1. Sexton, Robert L. and Robert Leroy Miller. *The Economics of American Historical Issues.* Dubuque, Iowa: Kendall/Hunt Publishing Co. 1991: 26–27.
2. Foucault, Michel *Discipline and Punish: The Birth of the Prison.* Translated by Alan Sheridan. New York: Pantheon Books, 1977: 3–6.
3. de las Casas, Bartolomeo. *The Tears of the Indians.* Translated by John Philips Printed in 1656, London: Angel in Cornhill.
4. Lovejoy, Paul E. *The Transformation in Slavery: A History of slavery in Africa.* Cambridge: Cambridge University Press, 1983: 246.
5. Facts and figures come from U.S. News & World Report. Lewis Lord with Sarah Burke. Reprinted in *Reader's Digest,* January, 1992: 98–102.
6. Brodie, Fawn M. *Thomas Jefferson: An Intimate History.* New York: Bantam Books, Inc. 1974: 42.
7. Butterfield, Roger. *The American Past: A History of the United States from Concord to the Great Society.* New York: Simon and Schuster (Fireside Book). 1976: 96.
8. Ibid, Butterfield, p. 97.
9. Ibid. Summary of pp. 136–7.
10. Ibid. p. 188.
11. Miller, Walter B. "Two concepts of authority." American Anthropologists April 1954. Reprinted In Leavitt, H. and L. Pondy (Eds.) *Readings in managerial Psychology,* 1st Edition, Chicago: University of Chicago Press. 1964: 569–573. Reproduced by permission.
12. Jaeger, Alfred M. and B. R. Baliga. "Control systems and strategic adaption: Lessons from the Japanese Experience," *Strategic Management Journal,* Vol. 6(1985): 115–134.
13. Toffler, Alvin. *Powershift: Knowledge, wealth, and violence at the edge of the 21st century.* New York: Bantam Books. p. 169.
14. *Webster's New World Dictionary of the American Language.* Second College Edition, New York: William Collins + World Publishing Co., Inc. 1974: 210.
15. Ibid. Butterfield, 1976: 312.
16. Ibid p. 313.
17. Ibid. p. 314–315.
18. p. 315.
19. p. 315.
20. Nevins, Allan, *Ford: The Times, the Man, the Company.* New York: Charles Scribner's Sons, 1954: 554–6.
21. Ibid. Murphy, p. 133.
22. Fayol, Henry. *General and Industrial Management.* Translated by Constance Storrs, London: Pitman Publishing, 1949: 107.
23. Fletcher, Joyce K. "A poststructuralist perspective on the third dimension of power." To appear in *JOCM,* 1992. Flax, J. (1990) *Thinking fragments.* Berkeley: University of CA Press.; Martin, J. (1988) "Deconstruction organizational taboos: The suppression of gender conflict in organizations." Paper

presented at the Acedemy of Management Annual Meeting, Anaheim, CA.; Lukes, S. (1974) *Power*. London: MacMillan.

24. From: *Paths to Power* Natasha Josefowitz, Ph.D.

25. ibid Ferguson, p. 16.

26. Ibid Ferguson, p. 87.

27. Ibid Clegg 1990: 212; See Shaiken, H. S. Herzenberg and S. Kuhn, "The work process under more flexible production," *Industrial Relations*, 25(2) 1986: 167–83. Marxists see flexible production and electronic surveillance as tools capital will use in its exploitation of labor.

28. Kanter, Rosabeth Moss. *Men and Women of the Corporation* New York: Basic Books, 1977: 47.

29. Brown, Stuart F. "The Tokyo Motor Show: The Theme is Green." *Popular Science*, February, 1992: 51.

30. Toffler, Alvin (1990): 67.

31. Miles, I. and Gershuny, J. (1986) "The social economics of information technology." In *New Communications Technologies and public Policy* (Ferguson, M. Ed), Sage, London; Lyon D. (1988) *The Information Society: Issues and Illusions*. Polity, Cambridge.

32. Hamelink, C. 1986 "Is there life after the information revolution? In *The Myth of the Information Revolution* M. Traber (Ed) London: Sage.; Webster, F. and K. Robins 1986 *The Information Revolution: A Luddite Analysis*. Norwood, New Jersey: Ablex.

33. Harvey, David 1989. The Condition of Postmodernity. Oxford: Blackwell.

34. Jones, M. R. "Post-industrial and post-Fordist perspectives on information systems." *European Journal of Information Systems* Vol. 1, No. 3: 171–182.

35. Mintzberg, Henry. 1990. "Retrospective commentary." *Harvard Business Review* (March–April): 170.

36. Leadbeater, C. 1989 "In search of rationality: the purposes behind the use of formal analysis in organizations." *Administrative Science Quarterly* 34: 598–631; Wood, S. 1989 "The transformation of work?" In *The Transformation of Work?*. pp. 1–43, London: Unwin Hyman.

37. Foucault, Michel 1977 *Discipline and Punish: The Birth of the Prison*. London: Penguin.

38. Badham, R. and J. Matthews "The New Production Systems Debate," *Labour and Industry*, 2(2), 1989: 194–246. See p. 201.

CHAPTER

7

A LOOK BACK/
A LOOK FORWARD

Our story book starts with the differences between affirmative and skeptical postmodernism. Healthy, Happy, Terrific versus Manipulated, Alienated, and Damaged. The skeptical postmodernists see a deepening and a widening of the gap between those who control capital and those who do work in sweat shop conditions.[1] Microprocessing and other electronic technology, for example, can control and oppress even very de-centralized work forces. The core becomes a new form of privileged aristocracy using capital and information-control to exploit the periphery of de-skilled and disenfranchised workers. The affirmative postmodernist (like us) see an opportunity to revitalize the entrepreneurial, small business work ethic in ways that will give people skilled jobs, but in smaller, more networked business enterprises.[2] Options vary as to whether flexible accumulation will be an utopia or a nightmare for human-kind.[3] The skeptics see large capitalist nations deepening their exploitation of third world labor markets. Affirmative postmodernists see opportunities to diversify participation in de-centered, flexible networks. The idea of flexibility, choice, and entrepreneurship is scary to most people. Bureaucracy may be a pain in the ass, but it is a predictable and safe pain in the ass. Because of our deep immersion into the modernist, centralist, forms of control, we have lost out on our intuitive ability to be spontaneous, flexible, and daring. One of the dangers the skeptics point to is the fact that bureaucrats are adopting a postmodern-form of language, using words like empowerment, de-centralization, participation, and enlightened control—but still practicing exploitation, manipulation, and surveillance. As an affirmative postmodernist, we recognize that we are in the midst of a struggle between two paradigms. Right now, if you look at any industry, service or manufacturing, public or private, you see both rationalities competing even within the same company in the case of large firms, and between firms, in the case of specialized players in sub-contracting networks. American big business is still de-valuing and de-skilling workers and trying to capitalize technology and exploit third world labor pools. This as a short sighted form of denial and a way to perpetuate domination.

History has shown that people in control, in core and central positions, will do anything to resist power-sharing with the marginal, peripheral, and disempowered. History has also shown that if the gap between the haves and the have nots gets too wide, you get a repeat of the French and American revolution. You also get the L.A. riots. Sweden and West Germany are doing better than the U.S. at developing control systems, based on participation in both capital and production, which de-differentiate differences between leaders and followers (Clegg, 1990). If we go into more small businesses in the U.S., then people will get more control over business capital and technologies to make products and services. If we go toward employee stock options and democratic enterprise control, then workers also get more control of capital and technology. Both forms of organization are more competitive than dinosaur production and service bureaucracies.

> . . . organizational modernity is giving way to possibilities of organizational postmodernity at the leading edges of the capitalist world; yet, to reiterate: no necessity attaches to the outcomes of these possibilities. National institutional frameworks and specific organizations, whether they go down the more strongly collectivist and solidaristic path outlined in Sweden or develop along the segmented and more exclusivist route of Japan, are capable of constructing diverse frameworks within which these possibilities might be fought (Clegg, 1990: 235).

The Optimistic Postmodern View. We believe in flexible networks; people are freer to put together their own informal networks across formal organizational boundaries and across national global boundaries. We can get away from our obsession with central control and actually increase custom-supplier-entrepreneur linkages and inter-company collaboration. These customer-driven networks can be more competitive than centrally controlled networks with a dominant core of control and influence. Production, consumption, distribution, capitalization, and society becomes internationalized and de-centered. Our optimistic view is that colonized, peripheralized, marginalized, and disenfranchised groups will gain wider participation, and be emancipated to pursue more environmentally-sensitive and customer-focused management. Before this is possible the modernist principles of management must become postmodernist.

Stay Healthy, Happy, and Terrific!

NOTES

1. Piore, M. J. and C. F. Savel *The Second Industrial Divide: Possibilities for Prosperity*. New York: Basic Books.; Sabel, C. F. *Work and Politics*. Cambridge: Cambridge University Press. 1982.; Smith, C. "Flexible Specialization, Automation and Mass Production," *Work, Employment and Society*, 3(2) 1989: 203–20.; Pollert, A. "Dismantling Flexibility," *Capital and Class*, 34(1) 1988: 42–75.
2. ibid Rosenau, 1992; Clegg 1990; Murphy, 1989.
3. Campbell, I. "New Production Concepts?—West German Debates on Restructuring," *Labour and Industry*, 2(2), 1989: 247–80. See, in particular, p. 257.

❑ APPENDIX A ❑

❑ DECONSTRUCTION METHOD FOR STORYTELLING ❑

The one skill that opens the door to the new skills of management 2000 is deconstructing stories. People who do not tell stories well, listen to stories effectively and learn to deconstruct those stories with a skeptical ear will be more apt to be victims of not only pre-mod and mod, but postmodern exploitation and power games. Stories have many interpretations. If one interpretation gets pasted over all the rest and becomes a dominant or the only politically acceptable way to interpret events, we have ideology, domination, and disempowerment. Part of exploitation is to deny an interpretation, point of view, or experience, that differs from the dominant view. Rhetoric about healthy, happy, and terrific harmony and unity can mask just the opposite reality. A simple sounding moral or prescription about consensus or teamwork can mask deeper costs in terms of power and domination.

STORY DECONSTRUCTION!

STORY DECONSTRUCTION METHOD

1. *Duality Search.* Make a list of any bipolar terms, any dichotomies that are used in the story. Include the term even if only one side is mentioned.
2. *Reinterpret.* A story is one interpretation of an event from one point of view. Write out an alternative interpretation using the same story particulars.
3. *Rebel Voices.* Deny the authority of the one voice. What voices are not being expressed in this story? Which voices are subordinate or hierarchical to other voices?
4. *Other side of the story.* Stories always have two sides. What is the side of the story (usually a marginalized, under-represented, or even silent) story character?
5. *Deny the Plot.* Stories have plots, scripts, scenarios, recipes, and morals. Turn these around.
6. *Find the Exception.* What is the exception that breaks the rule, that does not fit the recipe, that escapes the strictures of the principle? State the rule in a way that makes it seem extreme or absurd.
7. *State what is between the lines.* What is not said? What is the writing on the wall? Fill in the blanks. Storytellers frequently use "you know that part of the story." What are you filling in? With what alternate way could you fill it in?

Deconstruction is a method to avoid exploitation. It is also a way to escape the unintentional exploitation of others.

Beware of exploitations. What material practices mitigate alternative discourse and produce and reproduce those practices? How does the status quo impose and reimpose its practices? How can marginalized interests be empowered? Changing the story practices of an organization is a political act, because it changes the categories in use, and can re-privilege marginal groups. There are contradictions between espoused theories and theories in practice, between vision and reality, between stated goals and practices. People's stories are part of the talk, deconstruction looks at how they walk.

Stories can Exploit. The ideology reproduced in stories is a form of domination of some organizational members over other members.[1] This includes gender dominations[2]; the threat of high-risk technology to organizational and community members[3]; interest of union members, miners, and citizens[4]; technical rationality as a form of domination[5]; social science research employed as an ideology of domination[6]; organization change as a way get managers and other organization participants to understand their social situation[7]. Management is just beginning to understand the relation between storytelling and management.[8]

What is story deconstruction? Deconstruction is a method of analysis.[9] The goals to recognize and then *"deconstruct"* the constructions. A construction is a story plot, a story point of view, a story moral or principle. To deconstruct means to tear a story apart to reveal any hidden, marginalized, or subtle exploitations, contradictions, or traps. To apply deconstruction to stories, we look at such constructions as dualities, a story interpretation, the voice or perspective of the teller, the plot, any stated rules, as well as what is implied between the lines. You have heard the expression: "Every story has two sides." We think every story has more than two sides, in fact, many sides. And we want you to get skilled at being able to put many sides, many plots, many voices and other constructions in a story side by side.

How to Deconstruct Stories. Look over the seven tactics of story deconstruction listed above. The tactics do overlap. You can re-interpret a story and discover other voices. Your new interpretation can let you see dualisms you missed, and check one plot against another. The point is to unpack and unravel the story to reveal its many facets.

Bob   Whoever told you that life fits nice and neatly into discrete categories has deceived you all these years. The tactics for deconstruction do overlap. So does life.

Student Examples of Deconstructing Stories. Students are asked to collect a story from a mentor or, in some instances, to write up a story that represented their own experience. After collecting the story, students write up several deconstructions using the list of seven in the above table. They begin by reading from our book (or some other book), quoting the concept they intend to connect to their story in a quote. They interpret how the story connects to the quote they have selected. Finally, they select one of the seven deconstruction tactics (see table) and apply that tactic to the point they are drawing from the story. The following are student examples of this approach:

Dualisms. Make a list of any dualisms. A dualism is an either/or category, like black versus white, us and them, top and bottom, male and female, haves and have nots, insider and outsider. Even if the person speaks of men, they are implicitly using the duality of men and women. Learn to spot how people employ characterizations of one another, and of their work practices. Looking at dualities as one way to expose subtle, assumptions, claims and stereotypes one group makes about another group. Most categorizations are simple dualities: good or bad, black or white, pregnant and not, top or bottom, worker or manager, planner or doer, horizontal or vertical, patriarchal or democratic. Sexism and racism are sustained by dualities. Stories contain the categories of domination. In many stories, only one side of the duality is vocalized, yet even when unstated the other side of the duality is quite powerfully present.

An example: In the Boje and Dennehy book, they say, "Planners put people into their spaces at precisely the right times". In the story the foreman was given orders to carry out tasks and he in turn put the workers in their specific places.

Duality. The duality is the Mexican worker is seen as inferior to the American work ethic. A case of ethnocentrism is apparent.

Another example: The Boje and Dennehy book says, "The goal is to survive as a network by keeping customers happy with their services and products." Renee, after talking with Tom, treated the customers with more respect. In this way the customers were happier. When happier, the customers were more apt to pay on time. This shows that the quality of work has improved, because the customers were more willing to work with Renee, and help him out. The customers opinion should be the company's highest priority. If a customer is not pleased with a company, then they will not be inclined to use them again. To keep their business, the company should fulfill the needs of the customer.

Duality. If you treat a customer with respect they will always treat you with respect and would be more willing to work for you. This may not be true for everyone. You may have to use force or threaten a person to get them to cooperate with you.

Reinterpret. A story is a single interpretation of experience. Experience is always more complex than a simple story. The story has picked out some facts, views, and sequences to report and ignored a whole lot more. Two people given the same elements of experience can put together wildly different accounts. Your task is to reinterpret the elements of a given story and put together another scenario.

An example: In the Boje and Dennehy book, they state, "Workers ideas improve work process, increase quality, and build customer satisfaction." The man suggests that they use two buses or better yet, use larger buses. The whole fleet of National Car Rental buses consists of the fourteen seaters. Jose is obviously fed up with the situation and goes so far as to bring the gentleman to discuss it with the supervisor to see if they can come up with some resolution to the problem.

Reinterpret. The supervisor of National would say that they are not as large as the other rental car companies such as Avis or Budget. The competition is fierce, especially around LAX. Since we are not as large as the competition, we don't have the luxury of purchasing larger buses at this time. We are trying to do the best that we can with what we have.

Another example: Boje and Dennehy state: "Shared fate means what I do affects your outcomes and what you do affects my outcomes, even though we do not directly interact". In the story, beyond the minimum, processing of the purchase requisition, Art was apathetic to the needs of GaAs.

Reinterpret. The modernist bureaucracy has created indifference to the outcomes from one organization to the next. In my opinion, networking at TRW has not been properly induced. By establishing the idea of "shared fate", channels of positive communication, where stories are shared, can help to informalize the bureaucracy and create networks.

Rebel Voices. Rebel is the "other" voice, the one left out or marginalized in the account. If a manager tells a story, are they privileging their own voice and not giving any voice to the customer, to the workers, to other managers? One way women have been suppressed is by not having a voice. One racial group suppresses another by denying voice to another group. Paternalism and bureaucracy are male-privileged voices in many stories. Finding your own voice is why you go to school. It is why writers write. It is why storytellers tell stories. Voices sustain privilege. Look at the stories you hear and read to see whose voice is privileged (gets all the air time and power) and which voices are marginal. To rebel, voice what you think the other, the excluded or marginal voice would say in response to the side of the story you are hearing.

An example: "To be rational and objective is male; to be feeling and subjective is female."—Boje and Dennehy. This applies to the story because Marilyn was sensitive to the customer's needs about having baskets for easier shopping. Norm agreed with the idea but since he really worked with them he was not as sensitive and seemed to look at the idea from a financial point.

Rebel. The authority in this story was Norm since he was Marilyn's supervisor. The problem with Norm is that he is not allowing Marilyn to express her opinion or that of the customer. Eventually Marilyn is able to get her voice across after cutting through all the bureaucratic red tape.

Another example: The Boje and Dennehy book says that postmodern planning is responsiveness of the network to the customer. In the story Mr. Brooks gets complaints from customers because they are dissatisfied with the treatment they are receiving. Mr. Brooks and the company feel it is important to please the customer. Therefore, Mr. Brooks corrected the situation by talking to Tom. Tom, in turn, talked to Renee, who is the problem. They tried to fix the situation to please the customers.

Rebel. The voices heard in this story are the owner's, Mr. Brooks, and collections manager Tom DeHaven. Other voices that are being heard and acted on are the customers. The voice of Renee is being heard, but is not really listened to.

Other Side of The Story

Stories always have two sides. What is the side of the story—usually a marginalized, under-represented, or even silent story character.

Boj   When I was a CEO, I would get a complaint from my employee about a customer. After hearing the complaint, my next action was to call that customer and listen to the other side of the story. I learned early on that stories have two sides, and if I react to just one side of the story, I would end up shooting myself in the foot.

Managers get themselves in a lot of trouble when they get one, often biased side to a story and then run off half-cocked to make corrective actions. Getting the other side is related to hearing the other voices.

An example: Authority and Responsibility (Boje and Dennehy) Patti took her authority and extended it to the other workers in the office. So not to seem like a tyrant the next time something went wrong with the inventory, she gave them all equal power so that if anything were to happen, they would all be equally responsible. Even though it is only a small amount of responsibility, it is hoped that it will give the workers a little more of a positive attitude and feeling of participation.

Other side of the story. If the workers were asked, they probably would have been upset, because it is usually the manager's job to handle the inventory and they were being indirectly blamed by the person who should have been handling the job.

Another example: According to the Boje and Dennehy book 'Postmodern planning is network planning. In a network of small and large producers, suppliers, movers and shakers, there are a lot of internal customers. Talk to the internal and external customers to find out their needs." In the story, communication between the different organizations is not expressed in terms of the internal customer but rather "us against them".

Other side of the story. The resistance from one organization to the next is counter productive and flies in the face of goal oriented network planning. Due to the lack of cross-organizational networking, Art chose to hide behind bureaucratic rules instead of working with Sue to find out what really happened to her order.

Deny the Plot Stories have plots, scripts, scenarios, recipes, and morals. Turn these around. Reverse the rule. If the moral of the story is workers get more control over their work after they have received training in timing and charting their own motions then deny this plot by reversing it. A reversal would be: "when workers are trained to monitor their own time and motions they get *less, not more* control because they are becoming little robots.

An example: Boje and Dennehy say, "The excellence movement have given the bureaucrats a hip language. They now use words like "empowerment". In the story, management at the highest levels wanted this project to be a success and gave GaAs the "green light".

Deny the plot. Upper management gave GaAs all resources required to see the project through but failed to empower the organization to bypass the bureaucracy. Through cross-organizational networking Art could have been temporarily assigned to GaAs to see to their (the internal customer) specific needs.

Find the Exception What is the exception that breaks the rule, that does not fit the recipe, that escapes the strictures of the principle? State the rule in a way that makes it seem extreme or absurd. Overstate the rule. Can I measure every facet of every thing I do? If I do measure everything, will I have time to do anything else? Push the rule to see where it breaks.

An example: "The purpose of business, according to Peter Drucker, is to create and maintain a customer"—Boje and Dennehy. Marilyn was trying to do this when she was passing on the customer suggestion about carts and baskets. If one person suggested it others probably also thought it was a good idea also.

Exception. This story I believe is an exception because Three D found that there was a strong desire for the carts and baskets from the customers. I do not believe that businesses should implement customer suggestions if only one customer is going to benefit especially in industries with a high volume of sales.

Another example: "Customers want their goods and services now."— Boje and Dennehy. Three D took nearly two and half months to implement this idea and it was because there was poor networking in the company.

Find the exception: In this case I believe that the delay was beneficial. The company did not want to jump in feet first and spend a lot of money on carts and baskets that no one would use. So I am sure part of the time was spent researching whether or not the carts and baskets would be a wise investment.

Still another example: In the Boje and Dennehy book, Fayol's 12 principles said; "Retaining personnel, orderly personnel planning, and timely recruitment and selection are critical to success". In this story, Budget handled the rush of MCI convention customers successfully by scheduling more employees to work so the customers would be served more efficiently during that specific period.

Find the exception: "Retaining personnel, systematic personnel planning, and perpetual recruitment and selection are critical to success." This won't help a business be successful because if personnel are strictly limited to what they can say and do, and management is constantly changing employees' schedules and their positions, employees will always be unsure as to what they can and cannot do. Therefore they won't work to their full potential.

State what is between the lines What is not said. What is the writing on the wall. Fill in the blanks. Storytellers frequently use "you know that part of the story." What are you filling in? What alternate could you fill in? If you count the number of "you knows" in people's conversations and stories you will find the number quite high. Even if people do not say the words "you know" they often nod their head or turn their head in a way that let's you know, that you are supposed to be filling in the blanks. Any story is a joint or co-production of the teller and the listener. It is co-production because, as the listener, you are filling in the blanks with your own unique experiences which you assume are the images and knowledge the teller wants you to dump into those pregnant silences and in response to all those "you knows." You can not, therefore, just tape record someone's story, you have to also fill in the parts of the story that are dancing inside your own head as the storyteller spins the yarn.

An example: In Boje and Dennehy book, Peter Drucker states, "The purpose of business is to create and maintain a customer". Jose takes the time to listen to the customer and take him to the supervisor's office in hope of resolving the problem. Jose knows that the customers need him just as much as he needs them.

State what is happening between the lines. Each customer adds to the overall success of the company. Quality planning involves treating the customer as king and making sure that they are happy. In the long run, the company hopes that the customer will return and maybe even bring in new business for the company.

Another example: Boje and Dennehy's book states: "The network must service the needs exceptions, wants, quality definitions, and responsiveness dictates of customers." The customers complained to Mr. Brooks because they knew that he would do something to make the customer happy. He did that by getting Renee to treat the customers with respect. Part of planning is listening to what the customer says. You need to know their needs. But, the only way you will know their needs is if you listen to them.

State what is between the lines. My storyteller told me everything up to the end, where Tom talks to Renee about Renee's improvement. He said that this was happening at the time he told me the story, so it did not have an ending. He told me that I could fill in the ending any way I wanted to. I could have said that Renee is having a harder time getting the customers to cooperate with him, instead of having the customers actually cooperate with him.

Why do Deconstruction?

People in organizations tell stories to one another whenever they interact. Interpreting what you hear is part of surviving organization life. Each story is a composite snapshot of relationships among people, relations between the corporate system and the individual, categorizations of enemies, representations of the past, and presentations for the future. To deconstruct is to not fall victim to avoid as much manipulation, alienation, and damage in corporate life.

A Student Example of Story and Story Deconstruction.

Lisa Humphreys
MGMT 355, Sec. 10 A.M.
Dave Boje
Loyola Marymount University
April 28, 1992

Topic and Theme: Control—Use your voice to be heard!

Who: Tanya Golden, National Car Rental, Los Angeles

Story: Tanya was tired of no one ever listening to her. As a woman, she had confidence in herself and was sure that she knew just as much and even more than any male in the company! Tanya had seen employees in positions below her that where men go farther than she had in much shorter amounts of time. These men knew less than she did about how to operate the company, yet they were the ones being promoted. Upper-level management always told Tanya that it was because there wasn't anyone else in the company that could do as well as she could do at that position. "We are afraid to move you to another department because we don't want this one to fall apart!"

This is was a nice compliment to Tanya, but after three years of hearing the same story, she got very fed up. "If I am doing such a good job here, don't you also think that I could contribute to other areas of the company?"

"Of course we have all the confidence in the world in you, Tanya. We just are so happy with the position that you hold now."

Tanya could see herself going no where. She felt that she was a victim because of her sex. Men were the ones always getting all the breaks. Tanya decided to move on. "Since I am not getting the chance I deserve here, I am going to move on to a place where I will be used to the best of my abilities and appreciated for it!"

Tanya now works at Budget Rent a Car in Los Angeles. She is enjoying her new job and has found that the challenge is well worth her while!

DECONSTRUCTION

1. The fundamental right of people to make choices (Boje & Dennehy book, pg. 228). Tanya made a choice to go somewhere else were she would be appreciated. *Deny the plot*—Tanya realized that because she was a woman, that she should not be given the same opportunity as a man and she decided to stay where she was unhappy.

2. He's leaving for a better job, he recognizes a good opportunity (Boje & Dennehy book, pg. 252). Tanya, a woman, is leaving her job because she sees a good opportunity. *Other side of the story*— She's leaving for a better job, women are so undependable.

3. The big myth is that women want and need to do the repetitive jobs and the relationship jobs, leaving men to control the power jobs (Boje & Dennehy, pg. 253). This is indeed a myth. Tanya was doing better work than any person in the company, male or female. *Other side of the story*—Now, all the women have the top-level management positions and the men are the ones getting coffee and making copies!

Notes

1. Deetz, S. (1992). *Democracy in an age of corporate colonization.* Albany: State University of New York Press; Clegg, S. R. (1990) *Modern Organizations,* Newbury Park: Sage; Mumby (1990), D. "Toward a postmodern/feminist critique of organizational hierarchy." Paper presented at the annual

meeting of the International Communication Association, Dublin, Ireland, (June).

2. Hearn, J., Sheppard, D. C., Tancred-Sherrif, P. & Burrell, G. 1989. *The Sexuality of Organization*. Newbury Park, CA: Sage.

3. Alvession, M. 1987. *Organization theory and technocratic consciousness*. Berlin: de Gruyter; Perrow, C 1984. *Normal accidents* New York: Basic Books.

4. Gaventa, J. 1980. *Power and powerlessness*. Urbana, IL: University of Illinois.

5. Alvesson, M. 1987 *Organization theory and technocratic consciousness*. Berlin: de Gruyter; Fischer, F. 1984. "Ideology and organization theory." In F. Fischer & C. Sirianni (Eds.) *Critical studies in organization & bureaucracy* (pp. 172–190). Philadelphia: Temple; Steffy, B. D. & Grimes, A. J. In Press. "A critical analysis of personnel management and organizational psychology." In M. Alvesson and H. Willmott (Eds.) *Beyond managerialism: Critical perspectives in management and organization studies*. London: Sage.

6. Morgan, G. 1986. *Images of organization*. Beverly Hills: Sage; Beuss, R. 1981. *The idea of a critical theory*. Cambridge: Cambridge University; Fischer, F. 1984, ibid.

7. Grimes, A. J. "Critical theory and organizational sciences: A primer." Forthcoming in *Journal of Organizational Change Management*, Expected 1992.

8. Boje, D. 1991a The storytelling organization: a study of storytelling performance in an office supply firm. *Administrative Science Quarterly*, 36, 106–26; Boje, D. 1991b. Consulting and change in the storytelling organization. *Journal of Organizational Change Management*, 4, 7–17.; Browning, L. 1991. Organizational narratives and organizational structure. *Journal of Organizational Change Management*, 4, 59–676.; Gephart, R. P. 1991. Succession sensemaking and organizational change: a story of a deviant college president. *Journal of Organizational Change Management*, 4, 35–44.; Hawes, L. 1991. Organizing narratives/codes/poetics. *Journal of Organizational Change Management*, 4: 45–51.

9. Derriad, Jacques 1978. *Writing and Difference* London: Routledge and Kegan Paul.; 1985 *The Ear of the Other*. New York: Schocken.; Ellis, John 1989 *Against Deconstruction* Princeton, N.J.: Princeton University Press.; Wellberg, David 1985 "Appendix 1: Postmodernism in Europe: On recent German writing.: In *The Postmodern Movement*, ed. Stanley Trachtenberg. Westport, Conn.: Greenwood Press.